D1195754

DATE			

The Book as World

The Book as World

James Joyce's Ulysses

Marilyn French

Harvard University Press
Cambridge, Massachusetts, and London, England

Copyright © 1976 by the President and Fellows of Harvard College
Second printing 1977
Printed in the United States of America
Publication of this book has been aided by a grant from the Andrew W. Mellon
Foundation

Library of Congress Cataloging in Publication Data

French, Marilyn, 1929-
   The book as world: James Joyce's Ulysses.

   Includes index.
   1. Joyce, James, 1882-1941. Ulysses.
2. Joyce, James, 1882-1941—Style. I. Title.
PR6019.09U643   823'.9'12   75-25929
ISBN 0-674-07853-5

To Isabel and Edward

amor parentium
subjective and objective genitive

Acknowledgments

Caritas, fortunately, is not found only in novels, but finding it in living beings is always wonderful. I thank John Kelleher for his wide measure of this virtue, as well as for the great learning he has shared with me and the continuous interest he has granted me. I thank William Hull, who first made Joyce shine for me, and whose rare gift, as teacher and man, is to combine scholarly knowledge and discipline with poetic genius. I thank Allan Davis for support and faith that transcend not only any call of duty but even time and space.

I am grateful to A. Walton Litz and Hugh Kenner for their sympathetic readings and thoughtful suggestions, to Monroe Engel for his advice, to Jim Mahoney and Salina Martin of the Dinand Library at Holy Cross for their good-humored help, and to Virginia LaPlante of the Harvard University Press for her intelligence and carefulness.

The help of my beloved family and friends, nameless here, must be acknowledged in other ways.

For permission to quote from *Ulysses,* by James Joyce, copyright 1914, 1918 by Margaret Caroline Anderson and renewed 1942, 1946 by Nora Joseph Joyce, acknowledgment is extended to Random House, Inc., New York, and to The Bodley Head, London.

Contents

Table

The Book as World

Introduction

After fifty years of intelligent and dedicated exploration, the huge subcontinent of James Joyce's *Ulysses* still contains unclassified flora and fauna, untraced streams. Careful scholarly research has informed us in large part as to *what* is there, but in many cases we are still puzzled as to *why* it is there. The questions that remain to plague the honest critic range from the smallest—"Who is M'Intosh?"—to the largest—"What kind of statement does the novel make?" The last question may in fact never be answered to the satisfaction of all readers, just as there may never be agreement about the ending of *King Lear.*

The greatest obstacle to a comprehensive view of the novel has been the impenetrability of its style. Although many critics from Edmund Wilson on have struck brilliant sparks from its flint, the style of *Ulysses* remains inexplicable, and its relation to "content" obscurant rather than revelatory. Yet as early as 1938 Stuart Gilbert, who was partly a spokesman for Joyce, stressed the importance of the style: "The meaning of *Ulysses*, for it has a meaning and is not a mere photographic 'slice of life'—far from it—is not to be sought in any analysis of the acts of the protagonists or the mental make-up of the characters; it is, rather, implicit in the technique of the various episodes, in nuances of language, in the thousand and one correspondences and allusions with which the book is studded."[1]

Ulysses has an extraordinarily complex structure: it is possible to trace many different patterns and themes within it. Richard Ellmann, for instance, links the chapters in dialectical triads: "if one chapter is external, the next is internal, and the third a mixture; similarly if one episode centres on land, the second will be watery, and the third amphibious."[2] The Homeric correspondences and continuing allusions to such themes as Hamlet or the Ireland-Israel parallel are also structuring devices. But because there are so many of these, and no one appears to comprehend them all, it seems arbitrary to designate any one as the structuring principle of the novel. Only by focusing on style can the basic structuring principles of *Ulysses* be revealed.

Style, in the narrow sense, refers to the particular linguistic and formal handling of the characters and events in a work. A particular style conveys a particular tone; tone expresses point of view. The relation among these elements may be diagramed:

Style (or technique): the visible linguistic and formal surface.

Tone: the implicit emotional and intellectual content of the surface.

Point of view: the attitudes that underlie the thought and feeling of the tone; the narrational standing place.

Ultimately, all three are one, although for purposes of discussion they may be divided.

But the style of *Ulysses* is not fixed; it changes almost from chapter to chapter. It is possible to define the point of view of one episode and yet to be unable to define that of the next. Beyond or behind the narrational point of view lies the authorial point of view, which must be distinguished before there can be any assurance as to what kind of statement is made in the novel. Critical assertions that the novel is nihilistic or affirmative have been based mainly on the critic's personal sense of it. Support for either position can be drawn from the text: *Ulysses*, like the Bible, lends itself to opposing causes. One's personal sense of the novel may be very good indeed, but it is lamentably open to attack. Interpretations supported by evidence of or hypotheses about outside influences on Joyce may be illuminating but are not definitive. Even Joyce's statements about his own work can be misleading—sometimes intentionally—and are often metaphorical rather than literal, like the descriptions of Technic in the chart Joyce gave to Stuart Gilbert.

What is necessary is a close, chapter-by-chapter reading of the text, with emphasis on discovering the point of view underlying each episode, and on considering the effect of the style in each episode. The relation of each narrational point of view to the "plot" must be examined. Those elements that cohere will point to the authorial point of view.

[1]   The Reader and the Journey

C. J. Jung, in a rhapsody of love-hate, complained that there is no Ulysses in *Ulysses* except the book itself.[1] Most readers have concluded, with some reason, that Bloom is Ulysses. Richard Kain claimed that mankind itself is "the fabulous voyager."[2] This is closer to the truth. In another work on Joyce, published in 1965, Kain and Robert Scholes noted that the readers at whom they were aiming were not the "literate" among the general public, but Joyceans as opposed to non-Joyceans.[3] They implied that the second categorization ensured them the wider audience. Joyce, who aimed at being God, would have been pleased to think that less than twenty-five years after his death mankind was being divided according to whether or not its members had sat at his feet.

For one unit of mankind—the reader—is in fact the Ulysses of the title. The novel is a journey modeled partly on the *Odyssey* and partly on the *Commedia*. Unlike Dante's poem, *Ulysses* concentrates on one realm only, although another is included in the coda, Penelope. The principal realm contains elements of Inferno, Purgatorio, and Paradiso, but by conflating them, Joyce obviates Dante's categories. The realm that Joyce deals with is the real, as opposed to the ideal and the perversion, although it includes all three. In this singular realm, only one guide is provided, but he changes hats—or adds coats—during the journey. The journey itself resembles that of Homer's Odysseus who, in traversing the still unfamiliar territory of the Mediterranean, was moving outward in space, and whose stopping places represent a particular psychological condition or problem. So each discrete episode of *Ulysses*, using a character or event of *The Odyssey* as a reference point, moves the characters outward in space to a new place in Dublin, while the narrational comment moves the reader outward in space to a new distance from the action and simultaneously probes some area of consciousness.

The journey taken in *Ulysses* is the book itself, and only the reader traverses it entirely. Bloom and Stephen are analogous, comically and seriously, to Odysseus and Telemachus, but neither of them makes the long journey through the novel. Their treks are shorter, if through world and time enough; they are unaware of large portions of the novel, unaware of many of the analogies and correspondences or of the commentary that accompanies their actions. The reader is the only person who sees it all, who is aware of all elements inside the novel as well as all things outside to which it alludes. Some of these allusions are essential for a full understanding of the book. For instance, Bloom does not understand the meaning of *parallax*, but the term is one of Joyce's many clues to the method of the novel.

The reader is Ulysses; the novel is the journey; and the journey itself is one of exploration. It simultaneously investigates an outer and an inner space, which symbolize different areas of human concern. The outer space represents the intellectual aspiration to be more than human, to transcend the human condition; the inner space represents the basic elements that make up the human condition. At the same time, the novel is an exploration of a spiritual and moral wilderness as bewildering and deceiving as the landscape of *The Faerie Queene*. Neither Spenser nor Homer, however, but Dante provided the model for the structure of *Ulysses*, which consists of a series of concentric circles in an uneven cone shape, like the upcast reflection of the lamp and shade hanging over Bloom and Molly in the Ithaca episode, casting "an inconstant series of concentric circles of varying gradations of light and shadow" (736). These circles are levels not of states of damnation or salvation, but of perception. Their gradation expresses increases in distance from humanity, and the varying distances are Joyce's equivalent to Dante's moral hierarchy. The world lies at the center; what changes is the distance from which we readers view it and the angle from which we view it. We, not the characters, occupy the various levels: they move only linearly. And for our tour of these ascending levels, Joyce provides a guide, a narrator. The narrator wears a variety of masks. He begins objective, becomes ironic, then openly derisive, and ends indifferent and impersonal. In the Penelope episode, the coda to the action, the narrator is an entirely different voice—resembling a comic Beatrice.

The levels of perception constitute the steps traversed on the voyage out. They are not as ordered as Dante's circles: they are "inconstant." We move out, then back a step; out again, and back. We end at an Archimedean point from which we can no longer distinguish the separate elements on earth. This staircase into space is not a long unbroken ladder. At each level we move around the circle and view the events below us from a slightly different angle. These changes in angle constitute the journey through inner space, for each angle provides us with a hard look at some basic human state. These states share the focus with Stephen, Bloom, and Dublin, and they universalize the subject matter. The Lestrygonians episode, for instance, is a meditation on eating; the items mentioned in the chapter are true everywhere, not just in Dublin.

Each new style announces a new "landing stage" in the space we traverse on this journey. Erich Kahler draws an interesting comparison between Dante and Milton when he describes the difference in their conceptions of space:

Dante's universe had been a well-ordered, finite world held within the infinite will of the Creator. The planets and the stars of the firmament were enclosed and moved by the *primum mobile,* and above in the empyrean sat enthroned the all-embracing ruler of the universe. Man's relation to the universe was identical with his relation to God. Milton adds a further dimension to this realm, splitting it and making it undergo a twofold transposition; beyond the beyond, beyond the Elysian and the infernal regions, true cosmic space opens out for the first time. His questioning involves the relationship of man to God but also the relationship of God himself to the cosmos . . . In Dante, man is at the center . . . but dependent on a divine cosmic order. In Milton, man as such is no longer at the crux of the drama; but in his satanic autonomy he stands in an infinitely expanded, profane universe. Consciousness has conquered new realms.[4]

For Joyce, space is Einsteinian, curving back on itself, and it is a realm through which man may travel. Such travel is aimed not at finding God, but at seeing man better: in Kahler's terms, consciousness has claimed and domesticated the space that so horrified Milton and Pascal. The image closest to a divine one is the narrator, who is omniscient, but who shows the other face of God. Whether the narrator is contemptuous, impersonal, or indifferent, he is always malevolent toward the tiny, foolish, and disgusting creature, man: he is at worst a *dio boia* or hangman god, at best a *deus absconditus*. The movements of the novel as a whole are like the movements of this century, which has been engaged in probing outer space further than ever before at the same time as probing more deeply than ever into inner space, the human psyche. These movements are also simultaneous, like those of a scale played in contrary motion. Both thumbs begin at middle *C:* one hand moves up an octave, the other down. This double journey or movement can be charted throughout the novel (see table).

The Two Journeys in Ulysses

Chapter	Inward			Outward
	Primary focus	Secondary focus	Tertiary focus	Narrational point of view
Telemachus	Plot (Stephen)	Religious and political character of culture	Sonship	Close to the character, no apparent distance
Nestor	Plot (Stephen)	Cultural values embodied in history and literature	Sonship	Close
Proteus	Plot (Stephen)	Philosophical and theological traditions of culture	Movement into adulthood	Close
Calypso	Plot (Bloom)	Home versus Eden and wasteland	Gestation in womb	Slight increase in distance, irony
Lotus-Eaters	Plot (Bloom)	Opiation and pain	Dublin, birth into the world	Same as Calypso
Hades	Plot (Bloom)	Death	City of Dublin	Increase in distance, separation from character
Aeolus	Plot (Stephen, Bloom, Dublin)	Gaps in humanity's self-conception	Rhetoric, language	Much distance and irony: an overview
Lestrygonians	Plot (Bloom)	Food, eating	Violence and cycles of nature	Close view with irony, same as Calypso and Lotus-Eaters but with one separation from character
Scylla and Charybdis	Plot (Stephen)	Creative process	Shakespeare	Immediately close

Chapter	Inward			Outward
	Primary focus	Secondary focus	Tertiary focus	Narrational point of view
Wandering Rocks	Plot (Dublin)	Gaps and inter-sections in human relations	Entrapment of individual with-in culture, esp. church and state	Great distance: an overview
Sirens	Emotion (narcissistic)	Language, style: relation of word to act	Plot	Distant, but closer than Wandering Rocks
Cyclops	Emotion (ag-gressive)	Language, style: relation of word to act	Plot	Same distance as Sirens
Nausikaa	Emotion (sexual)	Language, style: relation of word to act	Plot	Close to characters in each part, distance suggested by difference in tone of two parts
Oxen of the Sun	Language, style: relation of word to act	Coition and con-traception, truth	Plot	Very distant and serious in intention if not tone, irony perceptible only at great distance
Circe	Emotion (secret, hidden)	Identification of act, word, thought, feeling	Plot	Seemingly immediate
Eumaeus	Language, style: relation of word to act	Deception and error	Plot	Distant and blurred, confused
Ithaca	Narrative point of view	Relations of things in universe	Plot	Archimedean
Penelope	Earth, nature, sex, continua-tion	Plot		Immediate

The downward or inward motion of this double journey is an inves-tigation of the foundation of human life, its basic necessities. The inward journey does not become obvious until the fifth episode, Lotus-Eaters, but it actually begins with the first chapters, which deal with intellectual rather than physical needs and constrictions.

The first three chapters center on the character Stephen as a particu-lar being. Implicitly, however, they deal with the donné of any intel-lectual life. There is little intrusiveness on the part of the narrator; the secondary subject matter is inherent in Stephen's thoughts about himself. Telemachus deals with the first fact in any intellectual life: sonship, the condition of being heir to spiritual and political traditions over which one has no control. Nestor and Proteus develop this prob-lem to consider those traditions as they are embodied in history and literature (myth), and in philosophy and theology. Thus, the first three chapters present not only the character of Stephen and his dilemma, but the cultural and intellectual setting of the novel as a whole. Stephen moves out into the world as we all do, already subject to a set of ideas, a world we never made.

The next three chapters present the character and dilemma of Bloom, but their secondary subject matter is emotional and physical necessity. Calypso focuses implicitly on home, the starting place, the rock of Ithaca, and contrasts it with Eden and the wasteland. It sets up the tension, important throughout the novel, of the real as opposed to the ideal and the perversion. But whereas Stephen is consciously considering cultural configurations as they impinge upon him, Bloom is unconscious of any particular theme in his thoughts. The notion of home appears in Calypso as a texture, not as intellectualization of a problem. Explicit commentary begins in Lotus-Eaters with the word game, the many flower names and references to forms of opiation. These clue words only point to the real subject, however. By ranging widely among the various forms of opiation adopted by different people, classes, and cultures, the chapter suggests that humanity in general finds necessary the occasional dulling of the mind and the senses. The apathy and paralysis of Dublin that is usually inferred to be the subject of this chapter is not exclusive to Dublin. Moreover, apathy and paralysis are not roots, but flowers: they are responses to the true subject of this chapter—human pain. Calypso presents home, the omphalos, the womb; Lotus-Eaters shows Bloom moving out into the city, the world. It presents parturition, which entails loss, separation, and pain that can be alleviated only by some form of opiation. Hades presents the next step in this process—death. In Hades, as in Lotus-Eaters, the secondary subject matter is clearly signaled by word games.

Aeolus offers a more complex form of presentation. Both Bloom and Stephen are present in this chapter, and in it the three kinds of necessity are merged. The secondary subject matter is signaled by allusions to wind (even a belch occurs) and "Aeolian" terms, but also by discussion of rhetoric and the presence of numerous rhetorical forms—wind created by humans. These allusions are only signals, however. They do not bear the direct relation to theme that death words do to Hades, or food words to Lestrygonians. The subject of

Aeolus is gaps in human conceptions, the puffed-up vanity that lies at the root of illusion and delusion, ideal and perversion. Since Stephen appears in the episode, it focuses on verbal expression of this condition—the discussions of oratory, or the headlines, for instance. Since Bloom also appears, there is a focus on practical and material manifestations of this condition in elements like MacHugh's and Crawford's physical deterioration, O'Molloy's financial degradation, and the noise of the printing presses.

Lestrygonians returns to a simpler approach. Maturation in the womb (home), birth, and death are universal experiences. At the next level of necessity is food. In this episode, as in Lotus-Eaters and Hades, the secondary subject matter is clearly indicated by the many food terms. As in Lotus-Eaters, however, the surface theme points to a deeper one: implicit in the notion of food is the method of acquiring it. Not only humans but animals as well must eat, must kill for food, and must excrete that which cannot be used. The grim necessity of this process lies under the gloomy texture of Lestrygonians. Scylla and Charybdis returns to Stephen and an indirect, or more abstract relation of style to theme. There are clue words in this episode; there is even a clue theme. The conversation in the library focuses almost entirely on Shakespeare, and Elizabethan terms and allusions are rife throughout it. But the real subject of Scylla and Charybdis is the creative process itself; the biography or myth of Shakespeare operates metaphorically to describe this process.

These nine chapters offer the groundwork for the rest of the novel. They name and meditate on the foundations of human life: the particular world one is born into exists before one is conceived (Telemachus through Proteus) and experiences gestation, parturition, and decease (Calypso through Hades). Blown-up conceptions of what it means to be human are undercut by subjection to the need to find food, and the tension between these poles of experience results in creativity (Aeolus through Scylla and Charybdis), which is seen as a search for order or significance in one's personal life universalized.

Wandering Rocks is a transitional chapter. The narrator is visible in this chapter, but he is less intrusive than in Aeolus. The subject of the chapter, which is gaps between people, is indicated by two devices: juxtaposition and intercalation. Each of these devices works dually, so that at the same time the gaps are demonstrated (inadequacy of communication), larger and less easily perceived patterns of similarity are suggested. Both of these also have dual manifestations: gaps and similarities are sometimes serious, sometimes comic. As befits a transitional chapter, Wandering Rocks adumbrates the greater breadth of the latter half of the novel in which the gaps between elements grow wider at the same time that the similarity of human experience is narrowed and solidified.

The seven chapters, Sirens through Ithaca, are more complex than anything that precedes them, but they use and extend the same devices used earlier. However in the first ten chapters "plot" is primary and theme is secondary; in the next seven theme is primary, linguistic expression or style is secondary, and "plot" is tertiary. Four chapters—Sirens, Cyclops, Nausikaa, and Circe—focus primarily on human emotion; two—Oxen of the Sun and Eumaeus—focus primarily on verbal expressions of experience, and one, Ithaca, focuses on the idea of relationship itself. Each of these chapters provides extended narrator comment rather than clue words, and each focuses firmly on one area of experience.

Sirens is about emotion in stasis, that is, feelings which are contained, not acted upon—loneliness, yearning, sorrow. As the chapter probes inward into the universality and nature of such feelings, the narrator pushes outward with his verbal expression of these feelings. Thus, a subject introduced at least as early as Proteus is picked up and developed: the real is knowable only through a particular mode of perception. Mode of perception dictates mode of expression. In the second half of *Ulysses*, style—mode of expression—is more important than reality itself, which lies, as plot, like the fetus concealed beneath the womb concealed by the belly. The same relationship among elements exists in Cyclops, which deals with human aggressiveness, in Nausikaa, which deals with human sexuality, and in Circe, which deals with the hidden springs of all three emotional poles—the narcissistic or inward turning, the aggressive, and the sexual. In each of these chapters a specific emotion that seems clearly recognizable and universal is muddied by the operations of the narrator, who is capable of turning a seemingly peaceful occurrence into a massacre, and a seemingly violent scene into a ritual dance, or of linguistically manipulating sexuality so that within the bounds of one episode it can appear as *agape, eros,* and romantic sentimentality.

By emphasizing the dependence of an emotion on language, this method undermines the reader's sense of reality. If what happens is almost totally contingent on how it is described, act and word are equally potent. The chapters Sirens through Nausikaa thus prepare us for the full attack on reality launched in Oxen of the Sun, in which a single scene is described in a wide variety of styles.

The theme of Oxen of the Sun is coition and contraception. Sexual intercourse leading to procreation is the central metaphor for what actually occurs stylistically in the chapter. Each style is the result of an act of coition, an honest intelligent effort to know—Biblically—reality. Each intercourse of mind and reality bears fruit—the style itself, which is parent to the succeeding mind, which performs the same task differently. The accumulation of renderings of reality works against its supposed aim. The reader ends not with a sense of reality reinforced by many modes of perception, but confused about where the reality lies, and more than likely, outraged by the chapter. A similar result occurs with Eumaeus, in which dishonest and unintelligent language is used to express reality. Joyce's irony does not spare himself or his art: all coition is impeded by contraception. Reality is obscured by the very power that is attempting to penetrate it.

Circe, which lies between Oxen and Eumaeus like a valley between two mountains, probes into human emotion beneath the surface level. It investigates secret feelings, the hidden springs of sexual, aggressive, and aspiring behavior. In it, all things are identified: act, word, thing, and person not only have equal weight, but are consubstantial with each other. Thus, phrases only spoken or thought earlier in the novel, rise to speak their own lines. So do objects, and characters fictitious within the fiction. Real characters speak fictitious lines, that is, lines they would not speak on the naturalistic level. The intimation is that at the deepest conscious level of feeling, all kinds of experience merge into one experience, and that experience is dominated by guilt. The attacks on human feeling leveled by the narrator from Sirens through Nausikaa are internal in Circe: the human psyche itself attacks itself.

The theme of Ithaca is relationships, but in this episode the "plot," the human story, drops even further from sight. The relationships investigated are not just human relationships: cosmic, natural, artificial, and human elements all have equal weight, are given equal attention. If the opening chapters of *Ulysses* offer a picture of the world or culture into which humans are born, the last episode in the novel proper takes us beyond the circle of human life and into the universe itself, into the eternal. For cultures vary in space and change in time, but the cosmos does not—not effectively, at least, given the short span of human memory, the even shorter span of an individual life, and the coarseness of human perceptual equipment. Each of us is born into a universe in which we are no more important than water, fire, or an embalmed owl.

The final chapter, Penelope, is not so much an investigation as an assertion: it places mankind firmly on earth as part of nature. But if nature is the only place providing comfort for the race, it provides little enough to the individual, who is drowned in its cycles, is just one more member of its dying generations.

The downward journey as a whole, therefore, is a voyage through the burdens of the human condition, the needs and constrictions all people are forced to live with. At the same time, the reader is voyaging upward or outward with the narrator and is forced to look down at the human from an ever-increasing distance. The narrator's role is essential to this journey. He does not, like Dante's Vergil, merely explain significances and comment on the scene lying before the poet-traveler: he creates that scene, provides the level and the angle of vision. We see only what the narrator wants us to see and we see it always through his eyes. In one way, the journey is a voyage through his mind. It makes sense that Joyce, attempting to write the epic of a relativistic era which is also the era of the common man, would force the reader to occupy Dante's role of journeyer, while the author's surrogate, a malicious omniscient narrator, plays the role of guide. The lack of any widely accepted revealed truth (Beatrice) or a usable literary tradition (Vergil) makes necessary a different assignment of roles and a different approach to the reader. The author divides himself in two: his sentiment becomes the "plot," the human reality; his intellect becomes the mode of perception which batters that reality. Our guide through the human material is the contemptuous intellect, but we are seduced by the material itself. The schizoid author merely suggests, intimates his truth; his method forces us, the readers, to affirm it. The journey is made in company with the guide, and the description of the guises of the narrator is also a description of the stages of the journey.

Our outward journey begins in the world, at the "rock of Ithaca," as Joyce called it in a letter to Harriet Weaver.[5] This rock is actually a style, the "initial style," which is stream of consciousness. We are at Stephen's shoulder. The narrator is unobtrusive here: he merely records Stephen's actions and the scene that surrounds him. The first three chapters are largely devoted to Stephen's thoughts, which we automatically attribute to a character, not the narrator. There is little or no distance between character and narrator, and therefore little or no irony in the comment. Irony on the part of the narrator is unnecessary, since Stephen provides enough of his own. Indeed, the narrator's voices are archetypes or conflations of the many smaller ironic voices heard in the novel, in Mulligan's mockery, Lenehan's silliness, Simon Dedalus' sarcasm, Virag's virulence, and Stephen's self-mockery. The irony of the characters is like a set of tributary streams, leading into the river occupied by the narrator, which is the thing itself, unaccommodated contempt.

The first step upward or outward occurs in Calypso. Irony is implicit in the very first sentence of the chapter: "Mr Leopold Bloom ate with relish the inner organs of beasts and fowls" (55). Although a few pages elapse before we are apprised of Bloom's Jewishness, the irony of the first sentence is emphasized by Bloom's musings on the Jewish pork butcher, Dlugacz. Also, the fact that we are within a consciousness other than Stephen's slightly increases our distance from both characters.

Lotus-Eaters adds a new character to the cast: the city itself of Dublin. Although in Calypso Bloom makes a trip to the butcher shop, most of that chapter occurs inside the house on Eccles Street. In Lotus-Eaters we are shown the city proper, the buildings and people that occupy it. At the same time, we are directed to observe one aspect of Dublin (and of civilization as a whole): its habit of turning substances and activities into opiates. That this habit derives from the need to dull pain is made explicit, so that we become aware, beneath the contempt we may feel for those who use religion, work, or chemical substances as opiates, that the pain is there, and general.

Hades uses the same method to meditate on death. In fact, the style in these first six chapters does not seem to change very much. The secondary subject matter is introduced with no ripple, since it appears simply as Bloom's thoughts or as comments about him. But in the middle of Hades there are two breaks in decorum: the conversations among the other men that we are permitted to overhear when Bloom is absent. We realize instantly that the point of view resides not just with Stephen, nor with Stephen and Bloom, but somewhere else.

These breaks in decorum are precursors. In fact, in almost every chapter until Oxen there is something—a strange statement, a strange style—that announces what is to come next or later. And in Oxen and later chapters there are continual references to elements that appear earlier in the novel, the "retrospective arrangement." We do not have long to wait for what these breaks portend: Aeolus announces the presence of a narrator with large type.

An unawareness of the presence of a narrator has caused confusion in critical comment on this episode. Yet it should be clear that we are shown some scenes in which Bloom and Stephen participate and other scenes in which they do not. The perspective is above them, although it includes them. The opening of the chapter requires an aerial view of the city: the headlines not only comment on but interact with the vignettes that follow. The tone of both the headlines and the vignettes is mocking. Ellmann points out that the subtitle for the chapter in the schema given to Carlo Linati is "The Mockery of Victory," but in fact everything and everyone in the chapter is mocked.[6] The matter of the mockery is gaps—the distance between illusion and reality, past and present, potential and actual. This kind of mockery seems familiar to us: we understand it, we are not discomfited by it. It is easy to miss the few hints given in the chapter that the satire will eventually dissolve the space beneath our feet and send us hurtling into the void.

With Lestrygonians and the library scene we take a step backward, one more in our "inconstant series." Again we are placed close to the characters; but again there are suggestions that the narrative point of view lies beyond them. We overhear another conversation about Bloom when he goes to the yard. The formal eccentricities and word play in Scylla and Charybdis also make us question where the point of view resides. Although many hints are given in Scylla and Charybdis as to the method of the novel, the prime clue is never explicitly offered. The narrational method of the novel is composed of two main strands: Stephen's ironic mode of thought, taken to extremes, provides the tone of the narrator's voice; and Bloom's circling mode of thought provides the direction of the movement from chapter to chapter and within each chapter. Together they comprise the narrator's point of view and the narrator's approach.

Wandering Rocks is an entr'acte. The chapter moves high above the city so that we can see the interactions occurring within it. We are shown gaps and correspondences by the narrator's juxtapositions, intercalations, and associations. What we see is evident to no one within the novel. Stephen, who has more awareness of significances than any one else within the book, sees only one thing—deformity. He sees what no one else can see, and his vision is a true one, but it is partial compared to the vision we are offered. The narrator has removed us from the world and is offering us a god's eye view of it. The focus is the city as a whole; the point of view is subtly ironic, emerging mainly from the arrangement of items. There is some explicit ironic description: "Poddle river hung out in fealty a tongue of liquid sewage" (252), for instance. But there is no explicit comment, as there is in Aeolus and later chapters.

The presence of a full-blown narrator is announced with a trumpet flourish, a blazon, by the prelude of Sirens. The new perspective is one from which the narrator mocks everything and everyone, as in Aeolus, and in which he is clearly responsible for selecting the scene or detail we are shown. We have the sense, in reading Aeolus, that we are present in the newspaper office, that the narrator is merely commenting on an "actual" scene. In Sirens and later chapters, the "actual" scene alternately appears and vanishes, giving us the sense that the narrator is showing us only what he wants us to see. This change is in keeping with the progression of the theme. Aeolus posits a reality that may be opposed to illusion and delusion; that reality is summed up or epitomized by Stephen's parable; but in later chapters reality itself is undermined and shown to be merely one mode of perceiving the essentially unknowable.

The point of view of Sirens does not reside with Bloom, nor is he the primary focus of the chapter. Although we are directed to his emotions more than to any others, we see the bar and its occupants both before he arrives and after he leaves, and we see as well as hear the inner room where the singing goes on. Many of the passages usually attributed to Bloom's consciousness are actually the derisive narrator's comment on Bloom and the others. The main focus of the chapter is human emotion in stasis. What is unusual is that the narrator mocks the characters not primarily for their behavior, but for their feelings. Now behavior is fair game for satire, but feelings seem less subject to volition: if one's feelings are ludicrous, what is one to do about them? In this episode Bloom is in the Ormond Bar because he does not want to act on the Molly-Boylan matter. He avoids confronting Boylan, then writes a furtive letter to Martha Clifford. But these actions and passivities are not the objects of the narrator's derision. It is Bloom's sorrow over what is happening that he mocks, Miss Douce's yearning, Si Dedalus' grief, Richie's lostness. Yet everyone at some time feels grief and loss, yearning and loneliness. By mocking these emotions, the narrator includes the reader in his derision. The reader is forced either to side with the narrator and declare such emotions contemptible, thus detaching himself from his own feelings, or to side with the characters, Bloom in particular, and admit his fellowship in a ludicrous and contemptible human company.

The same process occurs in the next two chapters. The subject of Cyclops is aggression and violence by humans against humans, animals, and vegetables. The narrator here splits himself in two (much as the author has done), one voice commenting derisively on what goes on in Kiernan's pub, the other embellishing the scene by a variety of literary transformations of violence. The effect of the complex interactions of the three "voices"—Thersites, the naturalistic dialogue, and the elaborating narrator—is again to force the reader either to side with Bloom's simplistic and ineffectual statements or to side with one of the many proponents of violence who dominate the chapter.

Nausikaa opposes love to war. The narrator describes the church service and the group on the beach in language appropriate to the character Gerty MacDowell. Although he allows us one last time to overhear Bloom's interior monologue, at the end he conflates items from Bloom's consciousness, Gerty's consciousness, and the Canon's cuckoo clock in a final derisive commentary. The subject of the chapter is human sexuality, which is shown from a number of perspectives, but always as a problem, present or potential. In the face of the idealization of sex implicit in the image of the Virgin, the romanticization of sex that Gerty has bought, Bloom's down-to-earth views seem real, honest, and sensible. But if we agree with Bloom's views, we are put in a position of countenancing his act of public masturbation. There is no clearer "solution" to the problem of sexuality than to those of aggressiveness and lonely sorrow.

Oxen of the Sun, as its blazon announces, removes us to a different plane. The narrator posits a scene—men drinking in the hospital refectory—then presents the scene and the characters in styles drawn from the entire span of the English language. The subject of the chapter is dual: coition between people leading to conception parallels coition between mind and reality leading to expression, otherwise called literature. The different styles are honest, intelligent attempts to render the human condition, but they draw the reader into another dead end. Each style is beautifully done; each shows an aspect of the characters that is true to them; but each reveals a scene that is slightly different from the others. What we end with is a sense that we have not really seen what is happening at all. Insisting on the ineffability of reality, the narrator forces us to realize that we do not want a rounded or cubist vision, a compilation of truths which is supposed to present the whole truth but actually shows us only the void; what we really want is a promise of certitude, an exclusive vision stamped with the author's guarantee of authenticity.

Joyce refuses, throughout *Ulysses*, to offer any such thing. Ellmann discusses the addition of an "uncertainty principle" in Wandering Rocks.[7] That uncertainty is in fact built into the entire novel. There is no fixed style, no fixed narrational point of view, and even the structure moves inconstantly. The inconstancy of the characters is a microcosmic analogy to that of the world which is the novel. *Ulysses* is an epic of relativity. The games played with language undermine every apparent certitude. Every act occurs in the void, every person lives there. This is why it is necessary that Molly commit adultery: everyone commits adultery, if only in the mind; certitude can be demanded or expected of no human being and no structure. Yet there is a reality, a world that coexists with the void, the rock kicked by Dr. Johnson, a "matutinal cloud" (667) observed by both Stephen and Bloom. The journey on which we are embarked takes us through the world, the human condition, and the void all at once.

Oxen of the Sun moves us farther up and away from the world than the preceding three chapters. Afterward we are taken down again. Circe, which combines the subject matter of Sirens, Nausikaa, and

Cyclops—human emotions—shows what is concealed beneath them. It deals not with the subconscious, as often supposed, but with the secret terrors and aspirations that are normally concealed from other people. The narrator splits himself into hundreds of different voices; the whole world is infused with his malevolence as "hallucinated" characters and even objects pour out a steady stream of contempt. The narrator's comments also appear as stage directions, some written in the style of earlier avatars of our guide. The chapter mingles elements from the consciousnesses of Bloom and Stephen with outside elements; it provides a "retrospective arrangement" of items from the entire novel. Only the reader is aware of all the items. Circe is an hallucination prepared by the narrator for the reader.

Bloom and Stephen alone are not the focus; in fact, neither is present at the opening of the chapter. Their secret fears and aspirations are hypostatized, and in the process, the secrets of others are revealed. Mrs. Yelverton Barry, for instance, is shown to be as lascivious as Bloom; the appearance of Edy Boardman in Nighttown may reflect her hidden fear or desire, or simply the fate of an alter-ego, a secret Edy Boardman. The advice of Old Gummy Granny and the behavior of the crowds in the political fantasies in which Bloom appears are revelations of the feelings hidden beneath the surface of political manifestations.

These four chapters—Sirens, Cyclops, Nausikaa, and Circe— show us the narrator at his most virulent. He bombards a set of emotions with contempt and mockery. The universality of emotion ensures the reader's participation. The thrust that lies beneath satire is an intellectual one: in general, the mode exhorts man to let reason guide his behavior. Often the plea demands the subjugation of desire, as in sixteenth-century English pastoral satires; often it urges man to make reason the mediator among tumultuous emotions, as in the last book of *Gulliver's Travels.* The satirical voice of the narrator of *Ulysses* is the voice of intellect pointing at the ludicrousness of human emotions, but it urges not the mediation of reason among them, nor even the subjugation of desire, but the suppression, the eradication, of all emotion. Clearly this is not a possibility for most human beings; we regard those who achieve some semblance of it, through religious meditation or drugs, as nonhuman, whether saints or sinners. Joyce permits no modification of the narrator's position: we must choose the total eradication of emotion or we must accept our ludicrousness. If we do the latter, if we affirm the existence and validity of emotions, accepting, however wryly, their comical aspects, we also affirm the right of Stephen and Bloom to be human rather than superhuman. That Joyce intended this to be our response is proven by the last two chapters.

With Eumaeus, the narrator returns us to the level we first visited in Oxen of the Sun. Again we are far from the world; it is difficult to find the characters, impossible to observe them closely. Eumaeus is a companion piece to Oxen. Oxen uses language as revelation; Eumaeus uses it as obscurant. Oxen offers many forms of truth; Eumaeus offers deceits, errors, falsehoods. Not only the language but the events of the chapter are a network of deceits and errors. Consider Bloom's mistaking the nature of the Italian conversation, the false Simon Dedalus, the questions about the identity of Skin-the-Goat and Murphy, the newspaper account of Dignam's funeral. The language itself is deceitful. It seems to be based on Bloom's, the language of the common man. But the narrator's syntax is overblown, clichéd, pretentious. Yet in the end we have about as much sense of what really happens in Eumaeus as we have in Oxen. It would seem that truths and falsehoods are equally dependable vehicles of the real. The concluding paragraphs of the episode conflate a description of Bloom and Stephen with lines from a ballad that seems to bear no relation to them. Through the ballad, however, the narrator is thumbing his nose at the reader. It describes a marriage that the singer desires. Clearly the narrator knows that the reader is involved in the coming together of Stephen and Bloom, and he is mocking him for his interest.

This episode sends the reader reeling into Ithaca, knowing that the moment is at hand. But Ithaca, the most glorious chapter in the book, shows us the narrator in his fullest powers. A new form indicates a new step: we are higher up in space than we have been before, at a time when we long to be close to the characters, to have their thoughts and feelings made palpable to us. We have reached the dominant key, "the utmost ellipse consistent with the ultimate return."

The narrator uses a form and terminology derived from the two disciplines that have most profoundly attempted to explain the universe: religion and science. Predictably, he makes mincemeat of both, not by directly attacking their content, but by educing, through a catechismic form and scientifically termed answers, the most trivial and uninteresting information possible. The subject of the chapter is relationships, which is all, philosophers tell us, that humans can know. Bloom is central, but he is merely mankind in relation to a past, a present that includes another representative of mankind, and a future that includes his adaptation to the act of the person presently occupying the bed. He is seen in relation to earth, which includes water and fire, to the cosmos, and to nature itself. But he is not seen in relation to, or in terms suggestive of, emotion: that has been eradicated. The result is a series of more or less significant facts. The irrelevance to human concerns of the facts we are given incites our rebellion. The narrative form involves a seemingly total eradication of the personal; it represents the triumph of factual objectivity. We are too high in space to perceive facial expression, subtleties of gesture, tone of voice. We only know that Bloom turns on the tap and draws forth an insane treatise on the properties of water. Even actual dialogue is lost to us: utterances are reported in abstract summary.

But the very impersonality of the style is what confers poignancy on the scene: it draws its emotional content from the reader. The miserable factual report of Bloom's few friends and close conversations elicits a more poignant sense of his loneliness and aloneness than all of Stephen's effusive self-pity in *A Portrait of the Artist As a Young Man*. The objective style frees the reader to feel the hyperbolic "cold of inter-stellar space" as a reality, to feel the beauty and distance and longing for order implicit in "the heaventree of stars hung with humid nightblue fruit" (698). Bloom's ludicrousness is never neglected by the unflagging narrator: in this episode Bloom again pimps for Molly, bumps his head, and scratches his body. But from where we stand in space, even as Bloom picks and smells his toenail or dreams of his elaborate, hopeless cottage, he is at once a comic figure and a single vulnerable man alone on the globe, moving through time only toward death, and aware of it.

Such a perspective often engenders cosmic irony; from such a height, humankind with its self-important busyness appears to be merely a deluded ant-heap. But Joyce's brilliant use of the impersonal style, in which the narrator becomes the embodiment of the indifferent universe, forces upon Stephen and Bloom the burden of humanness in an inhuman universe, emphasizes their frailty, their helplessness, their small size and short duration. Their actions and their persons become haloed with a kind of dignity and courage, for both are aware that they travel between birth and death "through the incertitude of the void." It is hard enough to get through the day safely, even harder to get through with decency, with small acts of kindness, but the difficulty is profoundly greater when one is aware that the day is only the light part of the void.

Bloom's position in bed has occasioned some derision—and it is funny—but it is also a serious symbol of the position of each of us in the face of an everchanging neverchanging nature and an indifferent universe. As Bloom falls asleep, the narrator leads us out into the reaches of space: at the end, Bloom is only a dot in an expanse.

The action is complete. Penelope is a coda uttered by a different narrator, who is the antithesis of our brilliant intellectual satirist. Molly is ludicrous in her own right, and her monologue contains many of the elements that are threaded through the rest of the book. But Molly is unaware of her ludicrousness, unaware of contradiction, unbothered by enigma. She represents the certitude so lacking in the rest of the novel, a certitude that is intellectually ridiculous but contents her. As the flesh that accepts, she is the countervoice to the narrator's rejecting intellect. The style of her monologue clearly symbolizes flow and continuation; the items contained in it point to her abrogation of linear thought.

Her monologue is necessary to the novel because it is basically the accepting flesh that keeps us going, that is biologically geared to adapt and survive, and that makes an unhappy life sometimes bearable. Insofar as Molly represents continuation and flow, eternal recurrence, she stands in contrast to Stephen and Bloom, who, as they are unique, are doomed. Her monologue is "the indispensible countersign to Bloom's passport to eternity" because the continuation it promises is the only immortality of the race. Her relation to the rest of the novel may be imaged as the circle in a theta, describing the continuation of the race, and crossed by the linear, horizontal span of the individual. Bloom and Stephen will be immortal as long as people read *Ulysses;* Molly's monologue implies that the humanity they represent will be immortal as long as the race endures.

Thus, the journey leads inward in a consideration of what it means to be human, to feel pain, to have to eat, to die. The journey leads outward into transcendence of the human condition, a transcendence which finds human actuality ludicrous. The double movement accomplishes several things at once: at the same time that we move away from the world with the mocking intellectual narrator, we move more deeply into it with the characters (Telemachus through Wandering Rocks), their emotions (Sirens, Cyclops, Nausikaa, Circe), and our emotions for them (Oxen, Eumaeus, Ithaca). We are drawn into the novel to the point where we are crushed ourselves in the hopeless bind that is human life. Thus, our contempt and our sympathy are elicited simultaneously, and we are torn in half. The conflict can be resolved only with our participation. The impersonality and inhumanness of the styles of Eumaeus and Ithaca are designed to elicit our fullest sympathy for the human concerns that are so notably absent. Frank Budgen comments that it is up to the reader of Ithaca "to assign the human values."[8] What the reader supplies, of course, are his own values, and this is why there is so much contention about precisely what happens in the novel. It is impossible to be immaculate in distinguishing one's own values from those suggested in the text when the two are not identical: any critic is suspect. But particular values are suggested by the text and can be discerned. If we want to hear what Joyce is telling us, it is necessary for a time to suspend our own moral preconceptions.

The guide is never sympathetic to the characters. His lack of sympathy indicates that he is not subject to their necessities: he is a god, whether subhuman or superhuman, the perversion or the ideal. The voyager searches for the real—in the plot, in Stephen, Bloom, and Dublin—but it seems to elude him. The "real," as Joyce presents it, is a combination of plot, of human condition, and of contempt for both, all of it existing as a shaky bridge across a void. So the reader ends with a strong sense that there is an ultimate reality, and that it resides in the humanity of the characters, the sands and stones of Dublin, and the void which contains them all.

[2] *The World as Book*

Joyce sprinkles clues to the import of *Ulysses*, and pointers to his method, throughout the novel. Continuing motives like parallax, metempsychosis, and retrospective arrangement, major themes like tradition and the individual, the necessity for action, certitude and the void, vie with lighter material such as the comment "Only Once More That Soap" (123) in Aeolus, or the reference to "this chaffering allincluding most farraginous chronicle" (423) in Oxen of the Sun. So generous is self-reflective comment in this novel that it is difficult to determine which are the salient details.

One of Stephen's major concerns in *Ulysses* is the process of artistic creation; in its course, he reaches some conclusions about artistic direction and method. These conclusions fit *Ulysses* as it stands and must be seen as Joyce's explanation of his own method. In Aeolus, for instance, Stephen selects from the numerous verbal modes mentioned in the chapter, the scrupulous meanness of his parable, and he fixes on his subject matter: Dublin and Dubliners. In creating his more elaborate fiction on Shakespeare, he thinks, "Local colour. Work in all you know. Make them accomplices" (188). The metempsychosis theme appears first in one of Bloom's chapters, Calypso, but its importance is left to Stephen to explain. "You have spoken of the past and its phantoms, Stephen said. Why think of them? If I call them into life across the waters of Lethe will not the poor ghosts troop to my call? Who supposes it? I, Bous Stephanoumenos, bullockbefriending bard, am lord and giver of their life" (415). Stephen's adaptation of Maeterlinck's lines—"If Socrates leave his house today he will find the sage seated on his doorstep. If Judas go forth tonight it is to Judas his steps will tend" (213)—provides a commentary on what occurs to the reader

in the course of the journey in *Ulysses,* and the journey itself is described in Circe: "the fundamental and the dominant are separated by
the greatest possible interval which is the greatest possible ellipse consistent with the ultimate return" (504). This statement is linked with
the reference to Maeterlinck as Stephen continues: "What went forth
to the ends of the world to traverse not itself. God, the sun, Shakespeare, a commercial traveller, having itself traversed in reality itself,
becomes that self" (505). Stephen is interrupted by "that fellow's noise
in the street," which is God, ultimate reality, the not-self, or on
another level the book insofar as it is independent of the reader's participation in it.

The term *parallax* is a source of confusion to Bloom, but Stephen
relates it to artistic creation: "The rite is the poet's rest. It may be an
old hymn to Demeter or also illustrate *Coela enarrant gloriam
Domini.* It is susceptible of nodes or modes as far apart as hyperphrygian and mixolydian and of texts so divergent as priests haihooping round David's that is Circe's or what am I saying Ceres' altar and
David's tip from the stable to his chief bassoonist about his almightiness" (503-504). *Ulysses* opens with the first line of the Latin Mass;
Circe opens with the rest of the line: *"Introibo ad altare Dei"* (3); *"ad
deam qui laetificat juventutem meam"* (433). Both are uttered in a
mocking spirit, and Stephen distorts the second phrase by making the
Catholic God female. These "nodes" are continued in the black mass
that follows the apocalypse, in which the lines are dedicated to the
devil. That the theme is so treated is less remarkable than that it is
treated at all in a work concerned with an agnostic and relativistic
world. But *ultimate reality* and *void* are terms used in the twentieth
century to describe part of what used to be called God: *Ulysses* is a
hymn to those things, and its method consists in a series of modes of
perception exercised on a coherent scene. It is a black hymn: the void
is terrifying, and ultimate reality is ineffable. What is celebrated in
Ulysses is the glory not of God but of man: Stephen asserts "the
eternal affirmation of the spirit of man in literature" (666).

Nevertheless the aesthetic upon which Stephen builds, the same
aesthetic upon which *Ulysses* is built, has a theological base. Joyce—
and Stephen—adopt the scholastic analogy of the artist with God.
This is explicit in Aeolus when Stephen exhorts himself: "On now.
Dare it. Let there be life" (145). The Shakespeare fiction is based on
the same assumption: the artist creates his own grandfather (as Joyce

creates Bloom's in Circe); he projects from his own experience to build a world from which he cannot learn: "He goes back, weary of the creation he has piled up to hide him from himself, an old dog licking an old sore. But, because loss is his gain, he passes on toward eternity in undiminished personality, untaught by the wisdom he has written or by the laws he has revealed" (197). The artist has the power to call the dead into life, the real metempsychosis, the real raising of Lazarus. And God himself is "the playwright who wrote the folio of this world and wrote it badly (He gave us light first and the sun two days later), the lord of things as they are whom the most Roman of catholics call *dio boia*, hangman god" (213). One reason for the importance of Shakespeare in *Ulysses* may be that it is said that after God, Shakespeare created most.

The importance of certain areas of scholastic thought to Stephen's aesthetic in both *Portrait* and *Ulysses* has been widely recognized.[1] The elements of scholasticism most important to *Ulysses* are the notion of the world as God's book, and the analogy between God and the artist.

The great Catholic structuring of the universe separated the creations of God into two parts: scripture, and nature or the entire universe. Both were books; both had to be read if man were to discover truth. The universe and the world were full of signs, signate matter with substantial form.[2] "Signatures of all things I am here to read" (37), Stephen believes, but he "never could read His handwriting except His criminal thumbprint on the haddock" (562). God manifests himself to Stephen only as *dio boia*, whose malevolence informs the omniscient and superhuman mind that is the narrator of *Ulysses*.

Commenting on Plato, Hugh of St. Victor uses the analogy of the artist with God: "Now there are three works—the work of God, the work of nature, and the work of the artificer, who imitates nature."[3] The artist discovers truth by reading the book of nature and, in his turn, creates. As Erich Auerbach explains it, "The artist, as a kind of figure for God the Creator, realized an archetype that was alive in his spirit."[4] Joyce, steeled in the school of old Aquinas, read God's book, the world, and created his own in that image. *Ulysses* is a symbol of the universe, a microcosm containing micro- and macrocosms of its own, and it offers us a profusion of communications as anonymous as seawrack and seaspawn.

Joyce, who describes himself in *Finnegans Wake* as "middayevil down to his vegetable soul" (423), trained himself to read God's book, to penetrate to the significance of a Ballast Office clock or a run-down boot heel. Aware that, lacking revelation, the significances he expressed in his epiphanies were reflections of his own mind, forms of self-encounter, he struggled to find a structuring principle that would posit a reality which transcended the vagaries of perception. In more practical terms, he sought for a way to proceed after *Portrait*, which is a document to solipsism, a record solely of Stephen's perceptions. What he hit on, in *Ulysses*, was the notion of building this problem right into the book, making the book an expression of the tension between humans' sense that there is a reality, and their hovering terror that in fact they create it. It is Aristotle and the popular image of Berkeley who provide the wide metaphysical antithesis of the book.

This is why small factual details were so essential in the composition of *Ulysses:* the recitation and repetition of place names, names of actual people, the actual geography of Dublin, all provide the reader with a firm concrete base, a sense that there is a reality similar to one's sense of one's own world. Most literature imitates nature only in details; it imposes on those details an order that is not to be found in life. Although Joyce did the same thing, his method was to produce the illusion of chaos, to appear not to select, to include insignificances, enigmas, and incertitude such as exist in life.

Joyce literally set out to create a replica of the world—not a metaphor for it, but a copy of it—reproducing within it all the coincidences, mysteries, and incertitude that pervade actual life. The reader is forced to live through and suffer June 16, 1904, to encounter things he does not know or understand, just as if he were living through a real day in his own life. Like the world, the novel does not lay its truths at our feet; it presents an apparently inscrutable surface on which nothing seems to be labeled right or wrong, significant or insignificant. R. M. Adams, who painstakingly researched many details of the book, concludes that "the complex of contacts and relationships among . . . [the] background figures becomes so choked and enigmatic as to leave the reader hanging in a curious void between hint and shrug . . . Close reading of *Ulysses* . . . reveals that the meaningless is deeply interwoven with the meaningful in the texture of the novel."[5] Ellmann also comments that Joyce "introduces much material which he does not intend to explain, so that his book, like life, gives the impression of having many threads that one cannot follow."[6]

We can theorize about the identity of the man in the mackintosh, or whether Miss Dunne is Martha Clifford, or who sent the postcard to Dennis Breen. But we can never know more about the tens of characters who have walk-on roles in Wandering Rocks, or the subject of the conversation between Corny Kelleher and Constable 57C. The whole purpose of introducing such details is that we shall not know: the artifact *Ulysses* is finite, but it does its best to imitate infinity; it treats incertitude, but creates uncertainties. The reader, of whom much is demanded by this novel, is placed so that he must undergo the same suffering of doubt and ignorance as the characters.[7]

The correspondences and actual details have a similar function. The fact that various characters walk the same streets, see the same shops or the same "matutinal cloud," or meet the same people confers on these streets, shops, cloud, and people a solidity, a reality. One way to test the reality of an object is to compare one's perceptions with those of others: Banquo's ghost does not appear to Lady Macbeth or the guests; hallucinations are private, like the monsters of delirium tremens. Joyce builds into his book the solid substance of things. This is all the more necessary since the modes of perceiving them are so spaced out, so private and eccentric. Beyond this, there are many correspondences in the thought of Bloom and Stephen. I suspect, although I have not had the patience to trace it, that every subject considered by the one is also considered by the other. Both think about Hamlet and Christ; both think in their own ways about modes of perception (with Bloom not understanding parallax); both walk the same beach and think about the same things while doing so. There are correspondences on other levels as well: both are dressed in black, carry talismans, live in omphalos-symbols, are exiles. Since Bloom and Stephen represent opposing halves of the human race—*l'homme moyen sensuel* versus the artist, or the common man versus the uncommon one, or moral versus spiritual man—these correspondences imply that there is a community among men composed of objects, experiences, and ideas, that all men are concerned with the same things.

The correspondences reinforce the reality of the streets and pubs of Dublin, the "matutinal cloud," Myles Crawford, the beach at Sandycove: they all exist, are really out there, are actual, despite Stephen's questions about *esse est percipi*, or Bloom's problems with parallax. The correspondences between Bloom and Stephen suggest an additional, human dimension, an objective experiential reality.

Bloom and Stephen are nevertheless unaware of many of the correspondences between them: they dredge up a few in Ithaca, but these are mostly insignificant or purely ridiculous—Bloom Stoom and Stephen Blephen, for instance. The correspondences are carefully wrought for the reader's eye alone. Just as we can see more of Dublin in the course of our journey than either of the characters can, so we can see the interconnections among things that are invisible to them. The "interrelatedness of everything" may, however, suggest a higher order, an encompassing pattern of divine or diabolic nature.[8] Partly to prevent the reader from making such a leap, and partly to remind him of the uncertainties of life, Joyce implants the mysteries and igno-rances, coincidences and correspondences that are meaningless. The appearance of the HELY's sandwichmen, for instance, has no signifi-cance that I can descry. They are a concrete detail ("Local colour," Stephen says) and so add to our picture of Dublin, but they recur, which suggests they bear larger weight. They get separated in Wandering Rocks so that the word is split, a comic embodiment of gap in a chapter devoted to gap and relationship, but even that does not add much. One could spin a web, as Joyceans love to do, and point to the relation of HELY's to *helios*, to the debasement of light in Dublin and so on, but in fact that does not add much to comprehen-sion of the novel; such spinnings seem weavings of wind, useless if entertaining exercises in ingenuity. There are hundreds of such details, and they are mixed thoroughly with more significant ones. The tests of significance that can be applied to these details are relevance and weight. If an image recurs, if it is related to others, if it fits into the pattern formed by the larger themes of the novel, it is relevant. If what it adds to the pattern of larger themes is new, or if it provides a new level of a larger theme, it has weight, is significant.

Another function of the correspondences and the precursors and backward references is to act as symbols for the intermeshing, in life, of past and future. It is always possible in life to look back and see precursors of and correspondences with some present state; there are always elements in the present that seem mysterious, some of which prove later (or are taken as proving) to have significance. The "retro-spective arrangement" is also a prospective arrangement; there is con-tinuity as well as discontinuity. The suggestion that everything hap-pening has significance if we could only see the larger pattern occurs simultaneously with the suggestion that all patterns mankind selects are arbitrary and personal.

The allusions—correspondences that reach outside the book—have a function, or functions, somewhat different from the correspondences and mysteries. On the lowest level, they serve to fix character: the esoteric nature of Stephen's allusions, the comic errors and misunderstandings that occur in Bloom's, provide a good deal of our knowledge about them. On another level, the allusions represent the past, or civilization. People may not think about the past as much as Bloom and Stephen do, but it is always with us, lying in our institutions and our standards. As Shakespeare implicitly hovers in the back of our minds when we read any piece of English literature, so he hovers in *Ulysses*. The diversity of the allusions, which link history, literature, theology, philosophy, politics, and art with the characters and the plot, contributes to Joyce's pretense that the book is encyclopedic, containing all areas of thought as well as things like bodily organs and colors. On the highest, or widest, level, the allusions serve to compress time, to identify this time with others, and thus to assert the unity and likeness of all times. Particular episodes, such as Cyclops or Oxen of the Sun, emphasize this identification, as do the themes of metempsychosis and retrospective arrangement.

To identify all times is to assert the circular nature of time, eternal recurrence, which underlies *Ulysses* as well as *Finnegans Wake*. The characters are pitted against this circle of time; what changes is the mode of perception only. Zion forgets Kevin Egan, landlords change, buildings crumble, but things remain the same. Only the way we see them changes. Thus, a number of literary renderings of heroism occur in Cyclops, literary renderings of sexual banter occur in Oxen. On this level, Bloom and Stephen merge with their literary prototypes: all heroes are incarnations of the values of the civilizations that create them, and have therefore a kind of kinship within a typological tradition. Bloom shares certain virtues of Christ, Elijah, and Odysseus; Stephen shares certain virtues of Satan, Swift, Hamlet, and Shakespeare. The citizen is a metempsychosed Achilles, Lenehan a modern version of Chaucer's Franklin—both much debased. Molly is Helen, Calypso, and Penelope. But at the same time, all are unique beings, part of their time and culture, and with unmistakable personal attributes. Their individuality is set off against their participation in a world-mind, a collective conscious. It is as though they move in and out of focus: generally they are clear, shot in close-up, but sometimes they blur into a background of figures whose field they share. The difference is not between seeing them better or worse, but between seeing two different configurations.

The city, Dublin, is dichotomized in the same way. Dublin is a character in the novel, as fictional and as real as Bloom and Stephen. It is shown for the most part in its most negative aspects, although the language of its inhabitants is vivid and taking. It seems to contain no healthy institution, to permit no satisfying way of life. It has an aura of despair, poverty, drunkenness, and waste, its physical appearance being symbolized by the filthy rivers. It seems to contain no inhabitants with probing intellects, artistic standards, or personal grace and elegance. Yet the fact is that Joyce's class at the university was a brilliant one, that literature and the theater were undergoing a dynamic revival, and that its citizens included a first-rate dramatist, Synge, and Yeats, the greatest English-language poet of the century. Joyce treats intellectual Dublin as a pretentious and mendacious coterie. Although Stephen sings a song by Yeats, it is not attributed, and the unwary reader could easily place its origin in another time and place. The only mention of Yeats shows the poet in his most unappetizing aspect. Part of Joyce's reason for treating shabbily the literary figures of his time (who had treated him, it seems, with unusual tolerance and respect) was perhaps malice: he seemed to expect from others instant recognition of his genius and his superiority over them. But there were more important reasons as well.

One reason was Joyce was not an aesthete. In other words, he did not find the production of great literature a sufficient reason for human suffering, as Homer did. Since Christian salvation has become a less potent force in literature, the art has devoted itself increasingly to the person of the artist or to the process of artistic creation. The artist has become the savior of mankind, and the processes of his mind have become equivalent to human processes in general. This is the approach that Joyce took also in *Portrait*, notwithstanding its irony. But he went beyond this approach. If salvation could be talked about at all, it had to be the salvation of the common man: the emphasis had to be on everyday life, not on art. As a matter of fact there is one artist in *Ulysses*, Stephen, whose fate and future are important. But the shabby treatment Joyce accorded to the other literary figures emphasizes his feeling that art was for mankind in general a means and not an end. Literature must affirm the spirit of man, not man the spirit of literature.

The second and more important reason for Joyce's downgrading of everything in Dublin was his intention to show the city as a center of paralysis. This was an old notion, which informs both *Dubliners* and *Portrait.*[9] *Dubliners* opens with a story of death associated with the three words *paralysis, gnomon,* and *simony.* The diseases described by these terms dominate the book: every character in it is a victim of one or more of them. Simony, the purchase of something sacred in exchange for something of only momentary value, is essentially a devaluation of the sacred. What simony meant to Joyce is suggested by a passage in *Stephen Hero:* "I like a woman to give herself. I like to receive . . . These people count it a sin to sell holy things for money. But surely what they call the temple of the Holy Ghost should not be bargained for! Isn't that simony?"[10] Such a bargaining of sexual pleasure for marriage is the subject of "The Boarding House," and the reverse bargain, in which a man flatters a girl who cares for him in order to get money from her, is the subject of "Two Gallants." Other stories in the volume, such as "After the Race," deal with a simoniac act unconnected to sexuality. *Gnomon* is a more obscure term. Joyce stipulates "the word *gnomon* in the Euclid," which denotes the parallelogram that remains after an identically shaped parallelogram has been removed from one of its corners. It thus refers to an incomplete form, a form with its own image, or perfection, or soul lacking. The term seems to connote a radical inadequacy or gap. Indeed, many of the characters in *Dubliners* suffer from inadequacy at the root, and their inadequacy combines with their perverted values to create the paralysis and death that pervade the city.

The characterization of Dublin in the earlier volume is retained in *Ulysses.* Dublin is a land of the dead; it is Eliot's wasteland, Pound's Western civilization, and Ford's parade's end. Joyce's prime symbol for completeness in *Ulysses* is coition, which is a change from *Dubliners,* where completeness is not even suggested. However, the subject is handled in *Ulysses* with much ambiguity and comedy, and the implication is that completeness is not possible. Hugh Kenner finds the world of Wandering Rocks a hell, where "faulty relation of the mind with things parallels faulty relation of the man with other social beings."[11] But the truth is that faulty relation is a fact of life. A person does not exist authentically with very many other people. The ugliness, the paralysis and death of Dublin are not exclusive to that city. And in the inward movement of the novel, in which Joyce swings in on the basic facts of life like pain, death, and the ugliness of the whole process of eating, Dublin becomes merely a representation of civilization as a whole. On the one hand, it is a very real place, described in such detail that it feels accurate, as indeed the detail is for the most part accurate. The city is unique and particular; we know its shops and houses, its streets and pubs. On the other hand, it is a representation of the idea of city, and by extension of twentieth century civilization, and by implication and allusion of all cities, all civilizations—or syphilisations. Despair, loneliness, and apathy no doubt exist in every culture, but city living seems to nourish them, to cause them to grow with the rapidity of cancerous cells. Modern, even 1904-version technology increases man's sense of impotence and paralysis. At one level Bloom's impotence with Molly expresses modern man's impotence with nature. An epic dealing with the twentieth century must include not just relativism but the texture of twentieth century civilization.

Critics have discussed *Ulysses* as being primarily an indictment of modern civilization.[12] Although such an indictment occurs, it alone would not require the elaborate technique Joyce developed: the simpler styles of *Dubliners* or Wandering Rocks would quite suffice. Joyce does show modern civilization to be grim and life-destroying, but by merging Dublin with Rome and the glory that was Greece, by describing Paris in no better terms, and by portraying two unpleasant Londoners, Joyce merges Dublin with other places and times, and suggests that all civilizations have been repressive and life-denying, a thesis advanced also by Freud. Like Bloom and Stephen, Dublin has two aspects, the mortal and the immortal, the individual or unique and the kind or archetype. All three characters contain the polarity of the particular and the universal.

Indeed, *Ulysses* is built out of polarities, starting with the split in Joyce's own nature. There was a contradiction between the cold clear eye that saw through surfaces to the deformed skeleton, and the responsive ear that listened with sentimental pleasure to the old songs. The satirist etched with "scrupulous meanness" the characters of "The Boarding House" and "Grace," while the romantic sentimentalist who wept at music took the position of a Manfred in "The Holy Office" and wrote *Stephen Hero* (although no doubt it was the satirist who tried to destroy that novel). A movement toward reconciliation of these impulses or attitudes appears in the best stories in *Dubliners,* such as "Clay" and "The Dead," where the tone is so beautifully handled that the main characters are fully felt to be simultaneously poignant and contemptible. *Stephen Hero* was probably abandoned because Joyce realized it was overly sentimental, romantic, and pretentious. He injected an ironic tone into *Portrait* to try to undercut its egotism and effusion. But the marriage was still an uneasy one for him, and the tone of *Portrait* is frequently unclear. The solution he hit upon in *Ulysses* was to build his self-division right into the novel, to create the work as the God of Genesis created man, in his own image: "His own image to a man with that queer thing genius is the standard of all experience, material and moral" (195). The cold satirist's mind became the sardonic narrator; the warm sentimental heart became the material on which the narrator worked. The author is "all in all"; he is the boy and the mature man; he is "bawd and cuckold. He acts and is acted on. Lover of an ideal or a perversion, like José he kills the real Carmen. His unremitting intellect is the hornmad Iago ceaselessly willing that the moor in him shall suffer" (212). The narrator is pitted against feeling itself in some episodes, and against the sentimental as embodied in the characters. The virtues of the major characters— Bloom's goodness, Molly's beauty, Stephen's artistic nature—could easily be those of characters in a Dickens novel, and drawing further on our pathetic emotions are the characters Dilly, the Breens, Martin Cunningham, even Simon in his grief.

There is a multitude of polarities throughout the novel, on every level. The languages of the Western world are built in polarities: we think in them. Stephen and Bloom, Plato and Aristotle, Christ and Satan, church and state, land and sea, civilization and nature, cyclical and linear time—this is only a handful. In addition, the characters themselves are divided: both Stephen and Bloom are anguished by conflicting emotions and attitudes. And on the highest level, the reader is torn by the opposing pulls of narrator and "plot." Satirical and sentimental attitudes find echoes within the reader; both exist in unstable balance in the fluid of any mind, and most of us are, like Joyce, loathe to allow either to attain permanent preeminence. A writer may list toward one or try to tread a line between them. Joyce chose to include both and to carry each to its ultimate extension. Sirens and Nausikaa present sentiment at its soupiest, Circe at its wildest and most terrifying; but the satire in all these chapters is cruel and virulent. The rebellion of the reader against their narrational stance becomes intense in Oxen, Eumaeus, and Ithaca, where the human is increasingly obliterated. Because the novel allows one "side"—the satirist—to win, we are free to uphold the other, and to affirm the whole.

The Void, Incertitude

Joyce set out to write the epic of his age, a work to stand with the *Odyssey* and the *Commedia*.[13] The twentieth century lacks a body of shared belief but it has a shared perspective, a structure of belief. Relativism is no doubt the intellectual structure that characterizes this century, despite movements counter to and beyond it. It lies beneath our investigation of outer space, inner space (the psyche), and the world. Consider, for instance, the anthropological comparisons of different cultures so popular earlier in this century. Relativism brings with it two major philosophical problems: the difficulty of asserting what is objectively real, and the concomitant difficulty of asserting what has value or significance in a world where nothing is fixed. The literature of this century has tended to merge the two: the significant *is* the real. Relativism posits that reality cannot be known—there are at least thirteen ways of looking at a blackbird—yet we agree that there is a blackbird, and that this fact is significant.

Twentieth century fiction resembles the work of another era in which profound changes were occurring, late medieval and early Renaissance allegory, in which the nature of good and evil had to be discovered even though the protagonists had revelation as a guide. Things are not what they seem, Redcrosse discovers, as did many a dreamer or wayfarer before him. Too late one finds oneself in a garden when one ought to be on the path, or taking the false Una for the true one, or confusing a Radigund with a Britomart. It is essential to make delicate distinctions that are often too subtle to detect unless one has traveled the same territory before. The reader of such works, unless he is forewarned by the poet, or unless he has traveled similar literary territory before, is just as ignorant as the protagonist and does not realize until too late that love for the rose is idolatrous and narcissistic.

Robert Scholes and Robert Kellogg, comparing Renaissance allegory with modern fiction, find a similarity between the allegorist, who "expected his readers to participate strenuously in his work, bringing all their learning and intellect to bear on his polysemous narrative," and the modern novelist, who "often expects just such intense participation, but being empirically rather than metaphysically oriented . . . makes the great question that of what really happened inside and outside the characters he has presented; whereas the allegorist made the question of what these characters and events signified the primary question for their audience."[14] But it is crucial to realize that for artists of the twentieth century, "what really happened" *is* the significance. Revelation has faded, like the giants in the earth: truth is what really is—objective reality—and the nature of this reality, they seem to suggest, is precisely the matter at question. The nature of the real is what Wallace Stevens probes through most of his poetry, and what scientists try to discover. It is the twentieth century that has raised the old term "ultimate reality" into its deity. In the simplest terms, every act has reverberations within a field. If one does not impose dogmatic characterizations on the acts, but still desires to label them "good" and "evil," one must trace all the reverberations of every act to discover its effect. Graham Greene, for instance, is fond of portraying acts of apparent generosity that have disastrous consequences. It is impossible to trace all the reverberations of any given act, but the full manifest is necessary before one can finally stamp a categorization on it. Thus, what is real—the full picture—is also what is significant, what carries moral weight.

Joyce built relativism and its problems into both the "content" and the "form" of *Ulysses*. Stephen is bothered by relativism, and the incertitude that comes with it. He is distressed by his lack of a structural principle—a father—whether as God, as a vital and usable literary, spiritual, and moral tradition into which he may unthinkingly fit, or as a fixed good, a suprahuman principle to which human concerns such as literature must be dedicated. He concludes that both world and church are founded "macro- and microcosm, upon the void. Upon incertitude, upon unlikelihood" (207). Temporarily accepting the void, incertitude, and holding to the here and now, he exhorts himself to act despite his unsureness, and composes his grimly comic parable of the virgins and his brilliant fiction about Shakespeare. The first step is to have intercourse with the real,

Shakespeare's tumble in a cornfield with Ann Hathaway, the errors of a man of genius that provide "portals of discovery" (190). From the "swelling act" grows the creation, which is self-encounter. The stimulus—the sperm entering the egg—comes from outside, from objective reality; the growth is the embroidery of the soul in its own pattern. The theme of the Virgin that pervades the novel harps on this one point. If she was indeed a virgin and conceived without intercourse, through divine infusion, she stands as a metaphor for the hypothesized ability of the artist to create without being torn and bloodied, without suffering life, without submitting to the real.

Bloom too is troubled by incertitude. Although the theme manifests itself in many of his actions and feelings, it is most prominent in his problem with Molly. For Bloom has posited Molly as a fixed star around which he orbits; she is his Moly, and her adultery undermines the foundations of his life. He is unable, through most of the book, to find a way to deal with it. Despite authorial or narrative injunctions to act, he continues to hum *vorrei e non vorrei* (even getting the words wrong at first). He does act, finally, by accepting: what he accepts is doubt, incertitude, and the impossibility of ownership (a form of fixing), and only incidentally, Molly's adultery.

By building incertitude into the method of the novel, Joyce places the reader in the same dilemma as the characters. Like Bloom with Molly, we fix on the characters in the opening chapters. By shifting our angle and level of perception, Joyce undermines our certitude about them and the events touching them, indeed about reality itself as it is manifested in the novel. He insists that the reader experience relativity while reading about it. But form is a value structure: it is impossible to write a sentence, much less a novel, without making value choices. Not just the church and the world but art as well is founded on the void: any ordering structure attempts to conceal or transcend incertitude. Although *Ulysses* reveals the void in all its manifestations, by undermining our certitude about reality on the one hand and our point of view on the other, by undermining even our certitude about language, it simultaneously builds a bridge across or founds a world upon that void.

This bridge is composed in part of the concrete details and the vitality of the characters: these give us a fix on the real. The rest is made of the value structure that informs the novel, a statement made under the author's breath that these things are real and significant and good. The last hundred years have taught us that man can live with relativity, that values can still be asserted and maintained, that there are certainties if not certitude. Values are implicit in any cosmic view, and they eventually manifest themselves as a new morality, a new sensibility.

It is doubtful if Joyce ever repudiated the desire, manifested in his early writings, to forge in the smithy of *his* soul "the uncreated conscience of his race."[15] He wrote similar words to Nora in 1912: "I am one of the writers of this generation who are perhaps creating at last a conscience in the soul of this wretched race."[16] The race is humanity, Western version, twentieth century; the conscience is a new sensibility. The almost religious fervor of many Joyceans stems from this fact: despite lacunae in comprehension of some details of the novel, readers sense that they are encountering a moral vision which is new and different, that they are reading one book of the Bible of the next millennium.

The term *morality* is held in some disrepute these days, at least as it impinges on literary criticism. One reason is that narrow moral judgments of literature have been responsible for many cases of internal and external censorship of authors, including Joyce. But to judge a work according to its adherence to a particular moral code is not the same as to examine the values implicit and explicit in a work of art. Part of the function of criticism is, as Wilbur Sanders expresses it, to translate "embodied dramatic meaning into discursive meaning," to assist "that free transposition of imaginative vision into philosophic or ethical position which, though dangerous and necessarily inaccurate, is still important if the reading of literature is to be part of an integrated wholeness about the business of living."[17]

Art does not exist apart from life: to aver that it does is to take the position of the aesthetes in the library chapter of *Ulysses*, a position Joyce himself did not choose to adopt. A work of art is good or great because of aesthetic considerations difficult to delineate, because of its "felt life" and "vital import" and "significant form." But every creation of the human race also contains a value structure. L. C. Knights defines literature as "the exact expression of realised values" which "are never purely personal: even when they conflict with accepted modes they are conditioned by them, and it is part of the artist's func-

tion (whether he is a 'representative man' or not) to give precise meaning to ideas and sentiments that are only obscurely perceived by his
contemporaries."[18] The greatest works of art share not only aesthetic
excellence but a largeness and generosity of moral vision, a sympathy
with and understanding of the human race that is itself an affirmation
of humanity. Whatever Joyce was in life, as a writer he had this mag-
nanimousness.

Joyce's moral vision is religious in that its central principle is charity, *caritas,* which is central also to Judaism, the teachings of Christ,
and Pauline Christianity, as well as to the scholastics. But it begins
from premises different from those of most religious systems, for it
posits a world without God. Without concerning itself in arguments
about the existence of a deity, the novel suggests that there are patterns of significance in human life, if only man had the distance in
space and time to perceive them. But these patterns have only human
reference; the *dio boia* who is lord of things as they are is simply the
human condition itself. As Helen Gardner writes of *Ulysses:*

> I do not find in *Ulysses* either the Christian sense of sin, or what is
> more important, its corollary: the need for salvation by some
> "mighty act," beyond man's power to accomplish, something as
> stupendous as the original act of creation. Joyce is deeply aware of
> the Christian view of human life. Because he is aware of it he is able
> to give us in *Ulysses* a deliberate demonstraton of what it is like to
> live without God. But it is a genuine demonstration. He does not in
> the end uncover a helpless and terrified being confronted with a
> great darkness. He does not come up against a blank wall . . . Al-
> though much that he tells us is horrifying, the effect of his telling us
> of it is to diminish the horror, not to intensify it. The horror is there
> as a part of life, and when we look at it steadily it is not so horrible
> after all. As we read on there seems nothing we need fear or be
> ashamed of acknowledging in ourselves or in others.[19]

When significance has only human reference, "God" is ultimate
reality. The first act, then, is to see, to clear our eyes of the cobwebs of
what ought to be (the ideal). If, like Stephen, we look at the real
through lenses of the ideal, what we see will look deformed (the perversion). Because we are locked in our own modes of perception, and
because our vision is limited, what we see is not ultimate reality, but
some shadow or fragment of it or of ourselves. Nevertheless we must

learn, like Stephen, to look at "dear, dirty Dublin"; like the novel, we must begin with what is palpable, sensible, and substantial. The mystery within Joyce's morality lies within the reality. Joyce repudiates the Platonic elements of Christianity: he begins and ends with the real. The proper ideal resides within the real and requires not transcendence but acceptance. J. Mitchell Morse suggests that Joyce saw himself as a surrogate god of the type described by Augustine, who was "an artist not a humanitarian," who was concerned with the overall aesthetic pattern of the world, of which evil and suffering were necessary parts.[20] To this deity individual fate is unimportant: whatever is, is right. Joyce doubtless enjoyed playing god in his fictional world, and he also enjoyed (as Shakespeare did) the variety and liveliness of people, language, and experience, finding it all "good" in some sense. But the god he presents in *Ulysses* is *dio boia*, and the way things are is rotten not alone in Denmark. The anatomy of the human condition that appears in *Ulysses* shows it to be a miserable trapped state. One must eat to live but must kill to eat. Food becomes excrement, which is then recycled. Some creatures are not killer enough to get their share of food; some get too much. "Dirty cleans" (68) but also spreads disease. Death is, and we both fear and desire it. Paradoxes and endless inescapable traps enclose us all.

Among the traps implicit in the human condition is emotion, that troublemaker Plato and his followers insisted must be controlled by reason. The Catholic thinking that Joyce was trained in is large enough to permit forgiveness for sin, but the grounds of sin are emotions themselves. The seven deadly sins are essentially failures in feeling: one is guilty of wrath or pride whether it is committed in thought, word, or deed. Sin is wrong feeling, but the catalogue itself of seven sins is constricting. There is very little feeling that is right. And since confession and penance are predicated on a firm intent to reform, the procedure, if not the philosophical theory underlying it, implies that it is possible to live without feeling such things as wrath or pride or lust. Joyce's view of such a notion is explicit in *Portrait:* the "habit of perfection" is indoctrination in repression.

Joyce, basing his morality on the real, starts with feeling. Either all feeling is suspect, or none is. He posits emotion as an absolute and as nonvolitional. Feeling may perhaps be subject to volition in a rare few saintly beings, but not in most of us, and we know from Freud as well as from our own experience about the sneaky tactics of repressed feelings. Joyce points out, in *Dubliners* and *Portrait* as well as in *Ulysses*, the special kind of hypocrisy that results from such repression. It is the ground, for instance, of Stephen's contempt for E. C.'s relationship with priests, and it is the subject of the brilliant Swiftian satire on the papal bull in Oxen of the Sun. Sirens, Nausikaa, and Circe emphasize the basic premise that feelings are real and cannot be helped. When feelings are attacked, one is left with nowhere to go. What can one do with one's feelings? One can hide them, but they eventually are exposed, as they are in Circe. Joyce as well as Shakespeare can reach into one's chest and pull out one's heart. There is no safety and no forgiveness for these ridiculous and troublesome appurtenances.

Joyce's handling of emotion is related to Swift's depiction of it in Book IV of *Gulliver's Travels.* Swift posits, however ironically, an ideal society characterized by the absence of passion and the supremacy of duty over feeling, using as his image for such reasonableness the very creature used by Plato to image irascibility and concupiscence —the horse. Joyce adopts Plato's dichotomy, makes his narrator the incarnation of the intellect scorning and demanding the eradication of passion and feeling, and humbles his characters, especially Bloom, as badly as Swift did his Yahoos. At the same time, as Fritz Senn points out, he works "on our susceptibilities, seducing us," so that our sympathies are largely with the Yahoo side of things, and the Houyhnhnm narrator comes to seem inhuman.[21] Joyce defines humanness largely as feeling. The only possible villains in *Ulysses* are Blazes Boylan, who lives by sensation rather than emotion, and John Henry Menton, who seems to feel nothing at all. We may admire Stephen's mind, or enjoy Bloom as a comic figure, but we love them because they feel deeply.

Whereas feeling is a donné, an absolute, behavior is not. How to act is a problem for both Stephen and Bloom. If one has some recognition of the real, one is necessarily aware of the possible consequences of different actions. Stephen is bothered throughout the library scene by questions of how to act, and even of whether or not to act at all. The historical generals mentioned in Nestor, figures like Kevin Egan, Abbas, and Swift in Proteus, Hamlet, and the reference to Cranly's planned revolution provide ample examples of futile, ridiculous, and horrible consequences of action, while the aesthetes of Scylla and

Charybdis provide absurd and laughable examples of inaction. It is necessary to act, Stephen decides in the library: "But act. Act speech. They mock to try you. Act. Be acted on" (211). He goes through a progression. First he exhorts himself: "See this. Remember" (192). Later he muses: "Do and do. Thing done. In a rosery of Fetter Lane of Gerard, herbalist, he walks, greyedauburn. An azured harebell like her veins. Lids of Juno's eyes, violets. He walks. One life is all. One body. Do. But do. Afar, in a reek of lust and squalor, hands are laid on whiteness" (202). Stephen decides to act, indeed he "acts" speech throughout the chapter, even though his behavior and the reaction of the others to him torments him.

Stephen's thought links the theme of action to Shakespeare and to sexuality. Action was indeed an important theme for the playwright: to act, in *Hamlet* and *Macbeth*, is to risk creating horrors. Consider the witches' "I'll do, I'll do, and I'll do," and Macbeth's echo of the phrase when he decides to destroy the Macduff family.[22] Joyce, writing out of a different world, reverses the playwright's emphasis: his characters are exhorted to act. The importance of this theme to Joyce is reflected in his notesheets and is explicit in the novel in Stephen's thoughts.[23] But it is also hinted by certain clues dangled tantalizingly before the reader. The language of Stephen's thought in the library is intimated in Nestor, during Stephen's meditation on acts that are engraved in history: "Time has branded them and fettered they are lodged in the room of the infinite possibilities they have ousted" (25). Shakespeare lodged with Dowland on Fetter Lane; Gulliver also once lived there. Joyce's language is always careful, if sometimes supersubtle. The passage reappears in Sirens, as Bloom sits in the Ormond Bar: "In Gerard's rosery of Fetter lane he walks, greyed-auburn. One life is all. One body. Do. But do" (280). This cannot come from Bloom's consciousness, for it subsumes knowledge he does not have. It is a comment by the narrator, and a rare one in that it does not mock Bloom but exhorts him. It also links Bloom to Stephen in this, their common problem. To ensure that the reader picks up the reference, Joyce inserts it again near the end of the novel, in Eumaeus: "Stephen, in reply to a politely put query, said he didn't but launched out into praises of Shakespeare's songs, at least of in or about that period, the lutenist Dowland who lived in Fetter Lane near Gerard the herbalist" (661). Thus, one must see the real, and one must act. Joyce is not advocating the repression of behavior any more than he is advocating the repression of emotion. The question is how. And the principle of action dramatized in the novel is *caritas*.

Caritas is a much larger and more profound concept than charity: the shrunken meaning of the second word indicates the difficulty of maintaining the first. The word *caritas* does not appear in *Ulysses*, but Bloom is a walking exemplar of it. *Caritas* is love that is given freely, that is neither a quid pro quo, given in hope of gain, nor a disguise for fear. Man's worst fear is of incertitude, and to avoid the sight of that Gorgon's face, man sets up certitudes, false gods. One of these is a belief in the possibility of possession, of property rights, the attempt to own things and people and to impose one's will upon them.

Joyce's Jesuitical training had taught him that the aim of scripture (and by corollary, art) was to teach *caritas*: "Scripture teaches nothing but charity, nor condemns anything except cupidity, and in this way shapes the minds of men."[24] Augustine adds a definition of this virtue and its opposite: "I call 'charity' the motion of the soul toward the enjoyment of God for His own sake, and the enjoyment of one's self and of one's neighbor for the sake of God; but 'cupidity' is a motion of the soul toward the enjoyment of one's self, one's neighbor, or any corporal thing for the sake of something other than God."[25] Hopkins, another Jesuitically trained poet, locates the godliness of things in their selfhood, their "haecceitas." Charity consists in the enjoyment of things in their selfhood, which presumes the ability to see things in themselves and to love them for the divinity in them. This is exactly what Bloom does. *Caritas* is a rare virtue, and Bloom's possession of it makes him a rare man: in this resides his moral superiority. *Caritas* presumes an ability to live with incertitude or, conversely, to relinquish the demand for certitude from the people and things around one.

This relinquishment is the subject of *Exiles*, although Richard comes across as a moral monster because he tries to force Bertha to deny her own nature in order that he may achieve the doubt he desires. Ellmann records a conversation between Joyce and Arthur Laubenstein, a friend of Joyce's son Giorgio. Joyce asked, "Which would you say was the greater power in holding people together, complete faith or doubt?" Laubenstein answered, "Faith." "No," said Joyce, "doubt is the thing. Life is suspended in doubt like the world in the void. You might find this in some sense treated in *Exiles*."[26]

The betrayal theme so pervasive in Joyce's work is linked to this doubt. If one does not blind oneself to the ambiguities and incertitudes in one's human relationships, one is always aware of the possibility of betrayal. Whether or not Joyce was ever able to accept this in his life, he did so in his work. Bloom, at least, is able to live in the void. He allows other people to be. He recognizes the real, refuses to idealize, sentimentalize, or pervert people. He does make negative judgments about them. Almost unfailingly, however, he immediately modifies his judgment, extending sympathy and understanding to them for the particular constrictions and necessities of their lives. He extends *caritas* not only to Molly but to Milly, Mina Purefoy, Simon Dedalus, the barmaids, and even to the citizen, although they are not aware of it.

There is irony in the fact that Bloom, a Jew, is the bearer of this virtue which centuries of Christians have condemned Jews for lacking. In the tradition of English literature, the word *Jew* is often synonymous with cupidity. Stephen draws on Shakespeare's categories when he speaks thus of him:

—And the sense of property, Stephen said. He drew Shylock out of his own long pocket . . .
—Prove that he was a jew, John Eglinton dared, expectantly . . .
— . . . a man who holds so tightly to what he calls his rights over what he calls his debts will hold tightly also to what he calls his rights over her whom he calls his wife. No sir smile neighbour shall covet his ox or his wife or his manservant or his maidservant or his jackass." (204-206)

The difficulty with *caritas* as a principle of behavior is manifest in the novel in the treatment Bloom receives from the objects of his charity. It is also indicated in the critical response to Bloom's behavior. If Bloom articulated his principles of behavior, he would no doubt be treated as a lesser saint, but he is not intellectual or even especially introspective. Therefore he is often viewed with contempt, by critics and by Dubliners. Even the newsboys mock him—which he knows, and tolerates. The contempt that the men of Dublin feel for him is directed as much at his self-effacing, apologetic manner as at his Jewishness. The two "causes" converge in Cyclops when Bloom complains that Jews are persecuted and is told by John Wyse Nolan that Jews should "Stand up to it then with force like men" (333). Contempt for those who prefer mildness is leveled at Jews as a group and at Bloom the man.

The areas of morality on which Joyce concentrates in his demon-
stration of Bloom's goodness are aggression and sexuality, the same
two areas that Freud distinguished as the underlying principles of
behavior. Although both aggression and sexuality are pervasive
themes in the novel, the theme of aggression is limited mainly to
Cyclops. This is because Bloom is not aggressive; he is mocked and
victimized, but he tolerates it thoughtfully, as a matter of choice. The
sexual theme has several focal points: Scylla and Charybdis,
Nausikaa, Oxen of the Sun, Circe, and Eumaeus.

Pacifism was not, early in this century, the popular cause it has
since become, in the Western world at least. Bloom's pacifism, one
manifestation of his *caritas*, appeared more ridiculous then than now.
But even given a general sympathy for his moral position, intellectually he cuts a silly figure in Cyclops, and is abused for it by the
offstage narrator: "Love loves to love love. Nurse loves the new
chemist. Constable 14A loves Mary Kelly . . . And this person loves
that other person because everybody loves somebody but God loves
everybody" (333). Bloom's exit from the pub could have been shown
as a quick escape, Martin Cunningham pushing from behind. It is the
narrational point of view that apotheosizes Bloom-Elijah. Most
narrator comment during the chapter has been derisive of Bloom as
well as of the others and the scene in general, so the triumphant
apparition seems to come from a different voice. What it does is to
turn Bloom into an "unconquered hero" (264), a pacifist who is neither
saint nor martyr but is able to triumph without resorting to violence.
Joyce's contempt for machismo and human aggression is amply
evidenced in the scene, but so is his recognition of violence as an
intrinsic and ineradicable part of human life. His intention was to
show Bloom as a "good man," not a lesser god or saint. Bloom fights
for *caritas*, but only verbally: intellectual warfare was Blake's suggestion for what to do with human aggressiveness. In his fight, Bloom
is both ridiculous and heroic.

Joyce's approach to sexuality was primarily one of exposure. In the
course of the novel he touches on every major aspect of the subject, on
such "aberrations" as homosexuality, narcissistic onanism, sado-
masochism, pandering, voyeurism, varying degrees of adultery, as
well as such "normalities" as denial of sex, romanticization of sex,
idealization of sex, repression of sex, obscenity, bawdiness, premarital

sex, contraception, and sex as a commercial arrangement. He deals with consequences also: Nausikaa contains two versions of what happens to people, mostly women, after marriage, and Oxen holds up Mina and Theodore Purefoy as exemplars of the married faithful.

The sexual themes touch most of the characters. Stephen is shown to be thinking about homosexuality, tender love, the denial of sex (in Oxen), and lust; and Bloom wonders in Eumaeus if Stephen is a homosexual. Stephen searches for a charm to win a woman's love: "*Amor me solo*" (242). The "solo" is important: Stephen is the character who desires certitude, who would love possessively. Bloom thinks about sex for the most part in others: he hypothesizes about the sexual lives and impulses of nuns, Josie Breen, eunuchs, young girls, the barmaids, Ben Dollard, and many others, not always out of a feeling of desire but from honest curiosity. He feels desire for well-dressed women, for Gerty, and for Molly. He carries on a sadomasochistic correspondence with Martha and breathes rapidly over pornographic books. There are also suggestions of sado-masochism in his feelings toward the fashionable women who accuse him in Circe: whether or not he ever sent obscene postcards to them—a hostile and sadistic act—he has had the impulse to do so. The possible consequences of his masochism rise to terrify him in Circe. He pimps for Molly; he is a fetishist. Further examples of sexuality are Kitty and Lynch in the bushes, Gerty MacDowell, the Nausikaa characters in Nighttown, Nighttown itself, Milly and the Bannon boy, the "616" theme in Eumaeus, the foundation of the Shakespeare "biography," subtle allusions to the onanistic or pederastic sexuality of Eglinton and Best, the figure of Blazes Boylan, and many others. Virag's virulent assessment of the female body as a set of objects on display for sale is no more ugly than the banter of the young men in the refectory. Even Father Conmee centers his daydream on the romanticization of an adultery that was possibly committed not fully. Molly and Gerty both think about masturbation, and Molly remembers her love for a woman and thinks about homosexuality, although not by name.

Joyce saw sexual feelings everywhere in a time when such a vision was unacceptable. These feelings are often presented derisively in the novel, but they are so ubiquitous that the mockery is drowned out. The effect of Joyce's handling of the theme is to force the reader to admit the extent and power of sexual feelings, to recognize their reality and their ambiguity. Bloom thinks, "Eunuch. One way out of it" (82). This appears to be the only way out. It is not only Bella-Bello who is the enemy, but the sex-denying nymph in Circe. Bella-Bello represents war and love in sexuality; that is, sado-masochism is an inevitable concomitant of love seen as a power struggle. This figure is more easily defeated than the nymph, who evokes Bloom's sexual guilt. The nymph represents a way of thinking which pretends or assumes that one can be nonsexual. The hypocrisy and titillating behavior that result emerge in a terrible stench when Bloom finally confronts the nymph in recognition.

Pervasive as the sexual theme is, none of the characters—not even Molly—has a contenting sexual life. Molly's apparently easy and natural attitude toward sex seems to come the closest to a good, but even that is much hedged and undercut. The sexual ideals of the past—celibacy or a faithful, enduring, heterosexual marriage—are shown to be as inadequate, ridiculous, or impossible as any other form of sexual behavior.

Probably the reason there are so many sexual laws is that sexuality is understood so little. If all attractions to people, of whatever sex or age, are basically sexual, then it is impossible completely to define what is admirable and what deplorable in sexual behavior (the obviously deplorable—violent sex, like rape or child molestation, if not child prostitution—is absent from this novel). The sexual themes of *Ulysses* merge into a great incertitude about what is natural and what is good.

Bloom is shown to have an enormous range of sexual impulses and expressions. Set against the backdrop of a world in which such impulses are rife, Bloom becomes representative of the sexuality of mankind. Although some critics are horrified by Bloom's uxoriousness, effeminacy, impotence, and masochism, it was clearly Joyce's intention to present, in Bloom, a profile of actual human sexuality and not a walking aberration.[27] Joyce saw clearly the complexity and ambiguity of this area of existence:

Anyway, my opinion is that if I put down a bucket into my own soul's well, sexual department, I draw up Griffith's and Ibsen's and Skeffington's and Bernard Vaughan's and St. Aloysius' and Shelley's and Renan's water along with my own. And I am going to do that in my novel (inter alia) and plank the bucket down before the shades and substances above mentioned to see how they like it: and if they don't like it I can't help them. I am nauseated by their lying drivel about pure men and pure women and spiritual love and love for ever: blatant lying in the face of truth.[28]

He also said that he intended Bloom as a "good man," adding, "If *Ulysses* isn't fit to read, life isn't fit to live."[29] Although this statement indicates his broad intention to make the reading of his novel a simulation of living itself, it clearly has application to the sexual area as well. Joyce understood profoundly, and demonstrates clearly in *Ulysses*, the void at the core of human sexuality.

But although Bloom carries around the burden of socially unacceptable sexual feelings, his behavior is mild enough. His voyeurism frightens no one. His affairs with Martha Clifford and with Gerty are mutually titillating but not harmful. The person who is hurt by his behavior is Molly, who on the day we meet her has achieved a solution to her problem. And it is to Molly that Bloom offers the greatest degree of *caritas*.

The themes of sexuality and aggression overlap in the events centering on Molly's adultery. In accepting her affair with Boylan, Bloom does "slaughter the suitors." His charity toward Molly reflects his acceptance of the impossibility of ownership of another human being and his understanding of the complexity of, and incertitude about, sexuality. Bloom's attitude permits him to remain the "unconquered hero" right to the end of the novel, and it is one of the few things in *Ulysses* that Joyce clearly labels "right." For in Molly's monologue it is Bloom who wins: she may enjoy and exaggerate Boylan's ability as a lover, but she finds him wanting as a man. It is Bloom to whom she grudgingly grants the laurel; it is Bloom she cares about more than any other man.

Bloom's acceptance of Molly's adultery has been the most shocking part of the novel, as shown by most critical reaction, which ranges from denial of it (although Bloom's acceptance is explicit in the text), to contempt for him because of it, to inventing fictive futures in which Bloom will reassert himself as "master of the house." But that is exactly what Joyce did not intend him to be. He is Leopold Paula Bloom, the "new womanly man." Although hints of androgyny hover about both Stephen and Bloom, it is Bloom who is described as fully active and passive, masculine and feminine.[30] Molly (Marion) is, if not a manly woman, certainly a dominant one.

The earliest censors of Joyce showed perception when they tried to silence him, for Joyce was doing more than challenging linguistic and literary conventions. He was challenging profoundly Western sexual mores, the attitudes of an entire culture. But he is still being silenced. Fritz Senn suggests that the "moralistic" attitude taken by many toward *Ulysses* in the early years has not vanished but has simply changed terms: "nowadays the author is generally enlisted on the right side; he is in fact represented as implicitly adding his voice to those expressing righteous disapprobation of his characters." Senn adds: "there is no intrinsic necessity to restrict one's views to censorious glances from superior vantage points . . . One of the potential moral effects of *Ulysses* is that it can condition us, more than any previous novel, to suspend or, at any rate, postpone the moralizing tendency that consists in dispensing blame and credit, in favor of a series of constant readjustments and a fluctuating awareness of the complexity of motivation."[31]

The elements of the sexual theme of *Ulysses*, which is second in importance only to the major themes of the human condition and incertitude, and is related to both, are relegated by the critics to the other side of the fence that supposedly separates "normality" from "abnormality." Critics like Stanley Sultan and Darcy O'Brien resort to Krafft-Ebing in order to explain Bloom, whose problem they see as a "failure to be unequivocally masculine."[32] Hugh Kenner sees "effeminacy" as the problem not only of Bloom but also of the world he lives in.[33] They all see Bloom's sexuality as a sickness that must be cured. Such judgments reflect the same narrow repressive morality at which Joyce aimed his slingshot—this Goliath being, as Senn suggests, enduring and large enough to absorb its antagonist and claim him as its own.

The sexual theme in *Ulysses* is not linked to Bloom alone; Stephen, Molly, and many secondary characters show a wide spectrum of sexual feeling, attitude, and behavior. Almost all of these traits can be called abnormal by people who are sure what normal is. Masochism, homosexuality, onanism, promiscuity, impotence—all refer to conditions that deviate from the single "normal" sexual condition permitted in Western morality—an enduring, faithful, monogamous love between a male and a female of similar racial, religious, and ethnic backgrounds, of suitable and similar ages, and sanctified by a marriage within which the sexual act is narrowly limited in feeling and form. Yet the only seemingly contented couple in *Ulysses* is the Purefoys, who are handled ironically. Bloom's sexual nature is no different from that of others in the novel; we are simply shown his sexuality with more depth than the others.

Joyce would not have endowed his "good man," his Everyman, with such a host of sexual "deviations" unless he meant to make a statement about humanity in general. Otherwise he would have limited them to Stephen. Joyce's intention was clearly for Bloom's sexuality to represent the sexuality of everyone.[34] The sexuality of Stephen and Bloom is not aberrant; most of the elements involved are as familiar to most people as their own body smell. One critic writes that Stephen rejects Mulligan's homosexual appeal "as he has formerly rejected Cranly" and for the same reasons, thus firmly enlisting Stephen in the ranks of the healthy heterosexual.[35] But there is nothing in either *Portrait* or *Ulysses* to indicate that Mulligan or Cranly is engaged in a campaign of seduction, or that Stephen is not as much drawn to these men as they are to him. Stephen is simply recognizing the sexual element in his love for Buck: "Wilde's love that dare not speak its name. He now will leave me" (49). In the library chapter, both homosexuality and onanism are derided on principle, as unfruitful and narcissistic as well as socially unacceptable; but they are at the same time presented as tendencies in Stephen's temperament and his philosophy. As such, they must be dealt with, but there is no suggestion that they will be cured or even resolved: they must simply be lived with. Homosexuality remains a theme in the novel as late as Eumaeus. It is not that Stephen is a repressed homosexual, but that he is aware of an erotic component in his feelings for men, about which he thinks and even worries. This seems quite natural and not at all aberrant, yet it is a sexual problem.

Bloom's masturbation on the beach is sensationally public; even the sexually inexperienced Gerty is able to recognize what is happening. Doubtless most people would not be guilty of such a loss of control. Nevertheless masturbation, impotence, voyeurism, sexual fantasies, sado-masochism, homosexuality, and fetishism are elements that exist to some degree in all sexuality. Molly's way of seeing the world entirely in sexual terms is more familiar to us than we might admit. Joyce uses these sexual elements openly, delineates the shame and concealment that usually accompanies them, and develops them fully.

In the end he shows sexuality, like every other human concern, to be rooted in the void, in a great unknowingness.

In each chapter of *Ulysses* in which sex is a theme, it is given a different coloration. In Nestor, Mr. Deasy recounts wrongly a historical act of adultery that he holds responsible for the usurpation of Ireland: the sin of sex ending Eden. In Proteus, sex has many forms: the love/hate between Stephen and Buck; the engendering shudder in the loins, seen as an ugly clasping and sundering; incest—Crissie is "papa's little bedpal" (39); hopeless desire, which excludes Stephen from the priesthood; Egan's wife having "two buck lodgers" (43); the gypsies arousing in Stephen feelings of "morose delectation" (47); woman as nature, eternal recurrence, loved by a vampire; the ideal love of romance, which is a transformation of the perverted love of a "pickmeup" (49); and tender, sensual yearning. Sex is protean also in Scylla and Charybdis: the list of sexual "perversities" found in the chapter as compiled by Ralph Jenkins includes miscegenation, rape, four cases of homosexuality, incest, masturbation, sodomy, and androgyny. Jenkins concludes that Stephen may be homosexual and necrophiliac.[36]

In other chapters, sex is colored by the thematic approach. Thus, it is an opiate (Martha Clifford) in Lotus-Eaters. It is related to death (making love among the gravestones) in Hades and to eating in Lestrygonians, where it is tied to food and is a hunger itself. In Wandering Rocks it is an incomplete act, as shown by Conmee's musings on a possibly uncompleted adultery, Lenehan's story about Molly, Miss Dunne's fruitless longings, a poster of Marie Kendall as an object of desire, Boylan's and the shopgirl's game, and both Bloom's and Stephen's approaching sex through books. In Sirens, sex is a losing of self, a submissive abandonment to sensual feeling. It touches almost every character, Bloom pre-eminently, but also the two barmaids as they gaze down with sexual and other kinds of yearning at the vice-regal cavalcade, explode with laughter at the "fogey" in Boyd's, and flirt with the customers. Miss Douce has an unreciprocated yearning for Boylan and walks by the sea with a properly titled "gentleman friend." Simon Dedalus has lust for her, Boylan and Lenehan flirt with her, and the other male drinkers flirt with both barmaids. Boylan's jingle to his destination punctuates the chapter with cock-of-the-walk sexuality; Simon's song is sentimentalized sexuality; and even poor

Ben Dollard is accused of bursting membranes with his "croak of vast manless moonless womoonless marsh" (283). Molly is mentioned in this episode with suggestive remarks and overtones; Bloom wonders with curious sympathy about the sexual experience of the barmaids; Si Dedalus' dead wife is mentioned with sorrow; and even Pat the waiter has perhaps "wife and family waiting" (283).

In Cyclops sex is an aggressive act: adultery, "organise her" (319), "corned beef" (324). In Nausikaa, sex is a romantic dream for Gerty, and Bloom meditates on the meaning of sex for women: its operations (menstruation, magnetism, frustration), manifestations (clothing, flirtatious behavior, allure), consequences (housewivery, children, brutal husbands), and denial (nuns, barbed wire, frustration). In Oxen of the Sun, sex is the keystone of authenticity: coition without impediment (prophylaxis) is the one genuine act. This is undercut by the Purefoys. Oxen is all about sex on one level: sex leading to birth and sex prevented from doing so. Stephen considers the Virgin not as a theological problem but as a metaphor for a technical question: is it possible to create if one's hymen is intact, if one has not been gored by the tusk of the boar? The theme of the Virgin and the Shakespeare theme are thus related to sexuality and also to androgyny, because the metaphor places the male creator in the female position and makes woman (as life, sexuality, nature) the gorer. This becomes explicit in Stephen's version of Shakespeare's experience with Ann Hathaway.

In Circe, the hidden emotions and drives underlying surface sexual behavior are exposed, and the subject is examined in its full explosive power and mysterious ambiguity. In Eumaeus, the sexual references are unclear and perhaps false, like everything else in the chapter, but their major form is homosexuality, as in the 616 and Antonio motives, Bloom's suspicion of Stephen, and the lines from a ballad about marriage applied to two men. In Ithaca, sex is emptied of all sensual content and appears strictly as a relation between husband and wife, man and woman (moon, Molly's window), or mankind and nature (Bloom in bed with "listener"). In Penelope, finally, sex is pervasive. As Molly is nature itself in this episode, nature is sexual. Many forms of sexual behavior crop up in the monologue. Again the list includes promiscuity, sexual play without coition, masturbation, homosexuality, various unnamed acts that are probably oral sex, fetishism, and even coition itself.

In sum, the theme of sexuality is pervasive in the novel. It is linked to each element of the human condition and to the incertitude that afflicts each of those elements. Almost every known form of sexual behavior is brought up, not just once, but again and again. Not only behaviors, but attitudes and feelings about sex are referred to continually. Although there are works of literature in which one area of sexuality is treated with more intensity than in *Ulysses*, no work I know of, including the Bible and the *Commedia*, treats a wider variety of sexual postures, or repeats them so often. And *Ulysses* examines at least a few of these in some depth. The question is, what was Joyce's point?

If Joyce's intention had been to present Bloom as a walking aberration, the "deviant" sexual references would cluster only about him. If it had been to present a fallen world in which sex as well as religion had come apart, there would be a suggestion of a norm, a right way. Neither is the case. Since the theme of the book is the incertitude implicit in the human condition, and since everything in the novel is wound up tightly with this theme, Joyce's point should be clear. Because of our fear of sexuality—a fear greater than any other, even of our aggressiveness, as any glance at the kinds of books we censor will show—we surround it with magical incantations, called rules. By those rules we manage to allow ourselves to be sexual under certain narrowly defined circumstances; all other circumstances are sacrificed, like propitiations to the gods. The permitted circumstance is idealized. As in all cases of idealization, the real comes to seem perverse, so we either block it out or condemn it, and are therefore blinded to the real. And the real about sex is that it is a tremendous variety of drives and responses called sexual, all brilliantly colored by the imagination, none of which is really understood. Our incertitude about sex leads to fear. As a result, we build rules like churches upon the void; we repress, ignore, or guiltily indulge in impulses not appropriate to those rules. That Penelope, the coda, which is intended to put a cap on the void, to suggest the natural base of life that continues despite incertitude, should be the most pervasively sexual chapter in the novel implies that profundity Joyce felt sexuality to have. Joyce shares with Freud the sense that aggressiveness and sexuality are the two basic human drives, but the former occupies him far less than the latter. There is aggressiveness in Penelope, but not much. In fact, there is not much aggressiveness in *Ulysses* as a whole. It is mysterious sexuality that obsesses Joyce, who ends by defining mankind not as a political or even gregarious animal but as a feeling, sexual animal cursed and blessed with intellect, cursed and blessed by outer necessity. Sexual intercourse is a metaphor for the relation of mind and reality; thus all perception is a form of intercourse. Joyce turns Plato's arrangement upside down. Feelings and sexuality are problems, true, but because of the "unremitting" and "hornmad" intellect.

Joyce's method as it applies to this theme is identical to his way of treating incertitude. He forces us, by his continual references and examination, to be immersed in both. By seducing us into liking and admiring Bloom, he nudges us toward accepting him, toward offering him a charity we would not easily confer on ourselves. By making Bloom the most extreme and ridiculous exemplar of human sexuality in the novel—perhaps in any novel—he insists that we accept also that part of Bloom, and consequently that part of ourselves. By presenting Bloom in close-up in the early chapters, Joyce arranges for us to perceive the real Bloom; by pressuring us with an increasingly hostile perspective, and meanwhile showing a decent unassuming man in action, he arranges for us to take sides, to defend Bloom. If, out of affection and respect for Bloom and out of sympathy for his entrapment in the human condition emphasized in the early and middle chapters, we suspend judgment on certain questions and perhaps even accept incertitude about moral absolutes, we may be able to extend *caritas* to Bloom, to allow him and the other characters to breathe and to live in their own space, without judging them. If we, the readers, do this, we are participating, whether or not we are conscious of it, in the morality advanced in the novel. The morality of the novel is thereby created as a fact in the actual world. Quite an accomplishment for someone who was after all only man.

[3] *The Rock of Ithaca*

Joyce called the style in which he introduces Stephen and Bloom the "initial style," and in a letter to Harriet Weaver about Sirens, he implied that this style has a significance beyond itself, that it is, in other words, symbolic: "I understand that you may begin to regard the various episodes with dismay and prefer the initial style much as the wanderer did who longed for the rock of Ithaca."[1] Since the initial style is virtually the only one used in the first six chapters, it sets the decorum of the novel; the reader experiences the advent of any new style as a violation of decorum, a breaking of the ground rules. And since no other style occurs more than once in the novel, no other ground rules supplant the original decorum. The reader is left, as it were, with no footing at all, no comprehension of the space he is in. To assure this dislocation, Joyce returns to the initial style on occasion throughout the novel, thus providing the psychologically potent effect of "intermittent reinforcement."

The initial style, a form of stream-of-consciousness, is employed not only in the first six chapters but also in the eighth, Lestrygonians. It appears in combination with other techniques in Aeolus, Scylla and Charybdis, Sirens, Nausikaa, and in a more extreme form in Penelope, the concluding chapter. It is thus the tonic or fundamental, Socrates' doorstep, home plate: it is the place we begin, the place that forms our expectations, the place we remember when we are away from it, and the place we end.

The decorum this style asserts is a tone and level of narration, a particular attitude toward and distance from the material. As it appears in the first six chapters and Lestrygonians, it has three main strands: interior monologue, third person description of action and exteriors, and naturalistic dialogue. The focus is on the monologuist, and in the first three chapters we are aware of no distance between the narrator and the character Stephen. Descriptions of scene and action appear to be objective; feelings and thoughts seem uncensored and unmediated; the two strands are fused. For example, compare two descriptions of treacherous friends, one from *Portrait*, the other from *Ulysses*:

> He [Buck] looked in Stephen's face as he spoke. A light wind passed his brow, fanning softly his fair uncombed hair and stirring silver points of anxiety in his eyes. (*U*, 8)

> A sudden memory had carried him to another scene called up, as if by magic, at the moment when he had noted the faint cruel dimples at the corners of Heron's smiling lips. (*P*, 78)

The description of Buck is objective, untainted by Stephen's hostility, whereas the description of Heron gives us not so much Heron as Stephen's sense of him. The objectivity of description in *Ulysses* is not absolute: we are told by the narrator that Stephen retorts "with bitterness" (6), or that he shields "gaping wounds" (8), and once, after an emotional moment with Buck, the external is made internal: "Sea and headland now grew dim. Pulses were beating in his eyes, veiling their sight, and he felt the fever of his cheeks" (9). In other words, although the first chapters of *Ulysses* contain interior monologue, and *Portrait* does not, although the narrator of the early chapters of *Ulysses* is objective, whereas the narrator of *Portrait* is subjective, the reader has essentially the same relation to the character in both works. We are closer to the later Stephen because we get inside his mind; but the relation to the character taken by the narrator appears to be the same. Thus, we are led to believe that the narrator and Stephen are essentially the same, that Stephen is the commanding center of the novel, and that the point of view will be his.

There is only one description that suggests otherwise, and this is the last paragraph of the third chapter. Stephen looks out at the bay and sees a ship. The passage is written in ceremonious, portentous rhythms, and the symbolic "crosstrees" strikes us: "He turned his face over a shoulder, rere regardant. Moving through the air high spars of a threemaster, her sails brailed up on the crosstrees, homing, upstream, silently moving, a silent ship" (51). Stephen, who responds to everything else, makes nothing of this: he simply sees it. Since we do not expect gratuitous details after three highly compressed and significant chapters, we assume the ship and its "crosstrees" have reverberations we cannot presently determine. Typically, it is both significant and deceptive: as an emblem of salvation, it points to Stephen's rehabilitation, which to some degree occurs; it also bears bricks and W. B. Murphy, the liar of Eumaeus. If the ship is to mean more to us than Stephen perceives it to mean, a distance exists between the narrator and Stephen: in other words, they do not share an identical point of view.

The immediate move to Bloom informs us that this is the case. If we are to be able to enter Bloom's consciousness as well as Stephen's, the narrational point of view must be wide enough to include both. And there is an irony, a distance between narrator and character, from the very first line. Although Bloom is presented from the inside, and most of the description is objective and unbiased, an ironic note is occasionally struck, when Bloom imagines following the young woman from the butcher shop, for instance, or the description of Bloom at stool, particularly in the two uses he makes of the prize story. However, the irony is occasional and subtle; it seems to emerge out of Bloom's actions rather than from the narrational selection or point of view. So, although there is a slight increase in distance, the decorum remains virtually intact.

The first real shocks—even on a first reading—occur in Hades. The first is a conversation between Martin Cunningham and Mr. Power. It is a brief passage, but there is no question that it is outside Bloom's perception:

> Martin Cunningham whispered:
> —I was in mortal agony with you talking of suicide before Bloom.
> —What? Mr Power whispered. How so?
> —His father poisoned himself, Martin Cunningham whispered. Had the Queen's hotel in Ennis. You heard him say he was going to Clare. Anniversary.
> —O God! Mr Power whispered. First I heard of it. Poisoned himself!
> He glanced behind him to where a face with dark thinking eyes followed towards the cardinal's mausoleum. Speaking. (101)

The infelicitous repetition of "whispered" and the final word,

"Speaking," which refers to Bloom's occupation at the moment, emphasize the narrational position. Shortly thereafter occurs a dialogue between Simon Dedalus and Ned Lambert that also appears to be beyond Bloom's perception; then another longer conversation, part of which is about Bloom, that is outside his audition. It is impossible to tell when Bloom rejoins the group, if in fact he ever does. From the time the group reaches the graveyard, Bloom is apparently isolated. He has a brief conversation with Tom Kernan, an even briefer one with Hynes, and he speaks to Menton as the group leaves. But during most of this section, long passages of interior monologue are broken by patches of dialogue. Bloom is sunk in his own thoughts and barely suffers conversation with politeness, and some of the dialogue is clearly independent of him. Like the paragraphs that conclude Proteus, the shiftings in focus at the end of Hades prepare the reader for a wider perspective, one that goes beyond both Bloom and Stephen.

The Basic Style

I call the technique of these chapters the basic style because it is fundamental and is used elsewhere besides the initial chapters. It is the most important single style in the novel. Joyce himself made a stir about it, attributing its innovation to Dujardin, and going so far as to address the French novelist as *"Maitre."*[2] Wherever he got it, the style was a breakthrough for Joyce. Stream-of-consciousness is a variation of the old omniscient narration, but the areas of divergence from its parent are of utmost importance.

In its most extreme form, stream-of-consciousness is pure interior monologue. This form occurs in *Ulysses* in Penelope. In its "pure" state, the style is difficult and obscure because it requires that action be inferred from the thought alone and yet that the thought seem naturalistic. It probably works as well as it does in Penelope because there is so little action. But the differences among various handlings of stream-of-consciousness are only superficial. It contains the same assumptions about experience, whether it appears in its "pure" form, as in Penelope, in the variation found in Benjy's section of William Faulkner's *The Sound and the Fury*, or in its most common form, interior monologue alternated with third-person description of action, as shown elsewhere in *Ulysses:*

Stephen touched the edges of the book. Futility. (27)

On quietly creaking boots he went up the staircase to the hall,
paused by the bedroom door. She might like something tasty. Thin
bread and butter she likes in the morning. Still perhaps: once in a
way. (56)

The major change that stream-of-consciousness effects on traditional omniscient narration is the removal of the summarizing phrase,
such as "she thought" or "he felt." On the surface this is a small
change, but it symbolizes the removal of a mediator between the
character and the reader, which in turn has various ramifications,
among them the loss of a judge, and the liberation from censorship
over form and content. Stream-of-consciousness differs from the
older, epistolary or confessional first-person because it seems not to
assume the presence of an audience. It therefore permits a relaxation
of linguistic form (grammar) and of moral form (manners). The illusion created is a sense of immediacy, as if the character were simply
being overheard, that what goes on in his mind is the whole truth,
unembroidered and undisguised, not intended for a reader's spying
eye and ear. The overall effect is a sense of immediacy and a heightened intensity, but beneath the effect lie assumptions about the nature
of human experience that are subtly transmitted to the reader. These
assumptions constitute a set—they have integrity with each other and
with the devices that express them.

The primary device is the removal of the mediator. The mediator
stands between the charcters and the reader. He symbolizes the
author, although he must not be identified with him. The absence of a
mediator implies the author's withdrawal: the work seems to be
written without his intervention and to be operating beyond his
control. On a metaphysical plane, the author-mediator stands for God
as witness, the aspect of deity that sees all, understands all, and
remembers all, like the chorus in Greek tragedy. His absence therefore
signifies the absence of a universal, enduring memory that can testify
as to the truth and significance of the events. And the absence of this
figure requires that the reader, who becomes the only witness to the
full action, take his place.

The mediator has another function, to judge the events being
scrutinized and guide the reader's judgment. In this capacity he is a
creature wiser or at least more knowing than the characters, who can
arrange, summarize, and censor their thoughts for us, while at the

same time giving us an indication of what he feels—and therefore of what we ought to feel—about these fictive people he knows so much better than we do.

An author need not be as intrusive as Fielding, Trollope, or Thackeray in order to tell us what to think. He may, in a short work, give us only one or two comments that will suffice to fix character. Joyce does this frequently in *Dubliners*. He tells us, for instance, that Mrs. Mooney "dealt with moral problems as a cleaver dealt with meat."[3] The story is written from the outside, and does not contain much authorial comment, but that one sentence precludes any ambiguity in our reception.

An author may offer less explicit, sidelong comment:

He had a right—thought wonderful Maggie now.
(Henry James, *The Golden Bowl*)

Her cold bath was refreshment enough and she saw that a slight trace of fatigue about the eyes only made her look the more interesting. (George Eliot, *Daniel Deronda*)

Without James's pervasive adjective, one might easily decide that Maggie is not wonderful at all, quite the reverse. The implications about the character of Gwendolyn Harleth made by that slight phrase "she saw that" are enormous.

On a metaphysical plane, this aspect of the mediator stands for God as judge. Since the notion of God as judge comes equipped with a particular set of standards, a dogma, those standards are implicit in the omniscient judge figure. Generally in the fiction of the last two hundred years this figure simultaneously upholds moral tenets and "stretches" them, insists on the validity of the spirit that quickeneth when it is opposed by the letter that killeth. The absence of this figure implies the absence of standards absolute enough to tolerate "stretching."

Yet in fact all authors play God; all have standards, since even a sentence, much more a sonnet, subsumes a value structure. And it is unquestionably easier for an author to provide comment on the characters—easier for him and easier for the reader. The lack of comment accounts for the lessened popularity of good fiction in the twentieth century, and for our sense of relief and simplicity when we pick up a novel from an earlier period.

The figures of witness and judge are not identical, nor Siamese twins: an author may provide the witness figure in a human narrator who does not presume to judge, who judges falsely, or who is himself involved in the action and is therefore incapable of impartial judgment. Techniques that omit these figures are more difficult to write and more susceptible of misunderstanding than those that include them. The question of why authors adopt these different styles cannot be answered by the need for novelty.

The lack of certitude that pervades our century undermines our faith both in the "verities"—traditional moral goods—and in the existence of fixed states. Thus, we no longer admire unyielding chastity, and even have trouble reading *Measure for Measure*, but no longer believe in absolute villainy, and thus have trouble with Iago. Joyce was aware of this early, and in *Stephen Hero* he shows Stephen unable to write a wholehearted love poem:

> The *Vita Nuova* of Dante suggested to him that he should make his scattered love-verses into a perfect wreath and he explained to Cranly at great length the difficulties of the verse-maker. His love-verses gave him pleasure: he wrote them at long intervals and when he wrote it was always a mature and reasoned emotion which urged him. But in his expressions of love he found himself compelled to use what he called the feudal terminology and as he could not use it with the same faith and purpose as animated the feudal poets themselves he was compelled to express his love a little ironically. This suggestion of relativity, he said, mingling itself with so immune a passion is a modern note: we cannot swear or expect eternal fealty because we recognize too accurately the limits of every human energy.[4]

Today we do not believe in absolute and enduring love anymore than we believe in absolute hate; suicide, and even murder may be seen as positive acts. Our insistence on the ambivalence, ambiguity, and temporariness of emotion is reflected in the forms of our literature: we have neither tragedy nor comedy in the old sense, but tragicomedy, black comedy, theater of the absurd. Both tragedy and comedy require a backdrop of a known, comprehended order that is at once moral and cosmic. Lacking faith in such an order and in the permanence of mental and emotional states, the writer turns his interest to tracing process or to celebrating the single moment. Yet there is an existent moral order within every culture. It may be imperfectly supported by assumptions of divine sanction, and it may include wide deviations, but a basic morality could be defined that was assented to, if not lived, by most of Western civilization. In other words, the twentieth century is faced with the paradox of a morality that is based on custom, sometimes rigidified into law, rather than on principle. All societies no doubt follow custom rather than principle in moral and everyday affairs; but a society with integrity can dredge up when necessary the principles that underlie custom. We, as a society, cannot. Internalized morality is the most difficult kind to change precisely for this reason. A writer is confronted with readers who agree easily that what Anna Karenina did was quite all right, and who are therefore insensitive to her foolishness, her courage, and her guilt. Such a society does not understand the cost of morality, and therefore lives an essentially unmoral life, following custom while admitting to only the most flexible and broadest principles.

By omitting the judge figure in a fiction, the writer creates a gap, for in fiction, moral judgments must be made. Again, the reader is drawn into the gap, the abhorred vacuum, becoming himself the judge. He is thereby forced to confront his own moral standards or conveniences and to question them. This is essentially the same position the reader faced in traditional novels, but there it was a question of stretching a law, here it is a question of stretching the self. In traditional narrative, the reader and writer shared a dogma that was shown to need qualification; in unguided narrative, the reader is forced to create a morality from the ground up. He may decide, for instance, that Bloom is evil because he does not abide by Jewish dietary laws. This impression will find sufficient verification in others of Bloom's acts, and the reader will create the novel in his own image. But if the reader is a bit more uncertain, he may be enough drawn to Bloom's charity and emotional depth to question his original standard. All of this is obvious: yet one major problem with *Ulysses* has been the unwillingness of readers to assent to or even to perceive Bloom's acceptance of his wife's adultery, much less to call it good.

Oblique narrative techniques are ways of seducing the reader without overtly threatening the moral ground he stands on. Without the sanction of divine law, moral custom is all that many people have: to give it up is equivalent to accepting chaos, incertitude. That is precisely what Joyce asks, knowing full well that most people would choose guilt over freedom, a life-denying certainty over liberating uncertainty. Joyce uses many devices to attain his end, but other works that utilize a judge-less narrative form strive for the same end.

Another device that characterizes stream-of-consciousness is the relaxation of grammatical form. Unusual and fragmented syntax does not abrogate form. Rather, psychological or associative logic is substituted for traditional logic. Employment of such a technique is based on the assumption that mental processes themselves are interesting and important to the reader. It should be obvious that actual mental processes cannot be duplicated in literature, that interior monologue is only a symbol for them, like the blue line on a map that indicates river. But the heightened intensity of fragmented interior monologue often leads readers to forget that it is only a device, and has sometimes led critics to try to draw parallels between certain syntactical combinations and actual psychological states.[5] Consciousness itself, or the illusion of it, has become increasingly interesting to authors since the eighteenth century. Erich Kahler attributes this to the "increasing moral, social, and political seriousness of the narrative material," adding: "the puritanical surveillance of the psychic life and the widespread revolt against hypocritical class conventions added moral burdens and psychic depths to narrative, imposing inner coherence upon it—or, in brief, internalizing it. In this process satire served either as an expression of revolt or (like the erotic additives) a vehicle of moralistic intention."[6]

But it was left to the twentieth century to define man, as Ernst Cassirer does, as the symbol-making animal. This century lays emphasis on perception as an active, shaping occupation rather than as a passive, reflecting state. Fragmented syntax and associative logic symbolize this shaping nature of perception, its mutability and gropingness. These techniques create a sense of immediacy: the reader is receiving not the fruits, a full, considered, and polished thought, but is participating in the process of formation itself.

The difference can be seen by comparing interior monologue as Joyce uses it with the technique used by James in *The Ambassadors*. Aside from a few brief lapses, *The Ambassadors* is narrated entirely from Strether's point of view; he and his consciousness provide the commanding center. James nevertheless uses the traditional omniscient form of narration, standing just outside his character, summarizing his thoughts and deductions and gropings. Joyce's stance with Bloom is also just outside the character, but because of his use of interior monologue, we move between Bloom and the narrator, alternately absorbed in the character's thoughts and looking from the outside at the character. The poles in James's narrative are both outside Strether: one summarizing his consciousness for us, the other looking outward at the world and creating an ironic distance, not between narrator and character, but between the reader's and Strether's awareness of exterior events. The use of third-person narration places the reader on the same plane with the author and allows him to infer truths the character does not perceive. The combination of interior monologue with ironic third-person description operates on two planes at once: the reader is first placed with the character, then stands back and sees or judges the character. Joyce uses irony primarily to distance the reader from the character; James uses it primarily to hint to the reader about a truth not perceptible to the character.

James's syntax reinforces this intention: it circles about and modifies, reflecting the circling, groping process of Strether's mind, but it is always logical, and moves continually if haltingly toward a truth that lies just beyond. We move with Strether and a little ahead of him in apprehending reality, but the reality is truly out there, whole if complex, waiting for a mind large enough to comprehend it. The circling, fragmented, and associative processes of Bloom's mind, in contrast, are an end in themselves. The fragmentation of syntax and the reader's participation in the mental process that is symbolized by it emphasize the process itself, which has no final goal. There is no great truth outside Bloom that *he* must apprehend. His mental workings are themselves a great truth or a part of one that *we* must apprehend. But to communicate this requires other devices.

In addition, fragmentation and psychologically associative syntax permit a wider field of reference than does grammatical syntax. In the description "Stephen touched the edges of the book. Futility" (27), for instance, the disconnected word "futility" has an ambiguous status. It could mean that Stephen sees Sargent as futile, or that he feels futility in attempting to teach the boy, or that he feels a sense of futility in his own life that is projected outward. As the word stands, it suggests all three; a more grammatical summary would almost inevitably curtail the application. The lines "Bloom askance over liverless saw. Face of the all is lost" (273) bring together many themes: Bloom's half-eaten dinner, his companion Richie Goulding, his feelings about his companion, the music being sung, Bloom's feelings about himself as well as about Molly and Boylan. None of Bloom's feelings is free from ambiguity. Fragmentation and association provide an economical way of suggesting and connecting many motives at once without unduly limiting any of them.

A third characteristic of stream-of-consciousness is the removal of censorship. This is also an illusion, since every author carefully selects what is to be included, but it operates to justify a change in subject matter. Lady Mary Wortley Montagu complained about this sort of change in 1755. Writing about Richardson's *Clarissa*, she insisted that "in this state of mortal imperfection, fig-leaves are as necessary for our minds as our bodies, and 'tis as indecent to show all we think, as all we have."[7] That *Ulysses* also received such criticism is a matter of history. But the result of the acceptance of previously censored subjects in *Ulysses* and other works has been largely restorative of the unity of mind and body that Joyce insisted on in *Ulysses* even to including a bodily organ as a metaphor for each chapter. This reunification of mind and body, which is primarily a legitimization of the body, is far from fulfilled even now, but it is connected to Joyce's moral premise: the body is real, as are its interactions with what we separate and call "mind." It and its functions must therefore be accepted, and both are thrust at us by Joyce. It is a sign of Joyce's value structure that the bodily function which has been not only permitted but exalted in the past—male physical prowess—is precisely the one diminished in *Ulysses*. Even male sexual prowess, as embodied in Blazes Boylan, is shown as callow, a mere game. The body in *Ulysses* is a comical and troublesome reality; it brings pleasure and pain, but it is never exalted or denied.

To sum up, the technique of omniscient narration with extended comment places a character (man) in a fiction (world) in which standards—moral, social, or aesthetic—are larger than he is and come rumbling in to put him in his place. It is therefore essential that there be a place for him—hence, the many found orphans and unexpected legacies in eighteenth and nineteenth century fiction. Man, the lost stranger, is discovered to be part of a context, a moral and social outer world, a community.

A technique that concentrates on the interior of a character or characters, and permits only sidelong or oblique comment, posits the mental life as primary but places its goal in the exterior world. The world outside the character may not be a community and may have no place for him, but it has a truth to confer upon him and requires some degree of acquiescence and understanding.

Stream-of-consciousness, in any of its variations, reflects a world with no deity, no final guiding intelligence directing it, and therefore no set of received values. Standards are internal. Such a world is relativistic; nothing within it is fixed; it shows a landscape of flux, of process. It is an apparent moral wilderness, through which the character must make his way alone: he struggles with the conflicting demands of his interior world, and finds in the exterior world mostly reflections of his inner state.

Internalization has two paradoxical consequences. On the one hand, more of the outer reality is absorbed, subsumed by consciousness. This means a reduction in fear: the outer world is tamed by internalization; there is less of it to be hypostatized into unfriendly forces. A character is not vanquished by fear of beheading, but is forced to live with that vaguer form of fear, anxiety, and with guilt. On the other hand, what is outside seems more distant than ever before. Aware that he is locked in his own mode of perception, man feels alienated; he cannot get in touch with the "real," yet he is not free. He is constricted within the prison he himself has created.

The way out of such a situation is a major concern of contemporary writers. "Mystic" and "mind-expanding" experiences are of a piece with experimental techniques that assume the irrelevancy of distinctions between inner and outer realities. Writers as different as Samuel Beckett, who makes consciousness the only reality, and Alain Robbe-Grillet, who appears to concentrate purely on objective "fact," are doing essentially the same thing, attempting to unify experience. Such unification would obviate the rather rigid categorizations that have dominated Western thinking for two thousand years. These categorizations have led to paralyzing hierarchies of value. To exalt mind over body, the individual over society, thought over emotion, white over black—or the reverse—is to choose a half-life. Moderation in choice does not eliminate the problem, which is to think in such categories in the first place. New literary techniques that have developed from stream-of-consciousness are searching for new formulations to replace a mode of thought that is no longer viable. They are consequently esoteric and appeal to a dwindling audience. But their eventual success will be dependent on—and will foster—a change in the nature of the language itself. The changes in handling language that are manifested in stream-of-consciousness techniques may well be a major step in this process.

The metaphysical implications of stream-of-consciousness apply point by point to the opening chapters of *Ulysses*. The world, or decorum, posited in the opening of the novel is relativistic, haunted by incertitude. The sections of the novel written in this style focus on the inner life of Stephen, Bloom, and Molly. Their mental processes or modes of perception define their characters and, to a large degree, the world they inhabit. All three are alienated, unable to accept membership in a community or in any divine order. Molly claims to believe in God, but her religion is comically her own invention.

During the episodes in which this style is used, we are almost totally unaware of a narrator, of any distance between what we are told and where the characters are. We have, therefore, a great intimacy, immediacy, and empathy for the characters. As a result, the later narrative distance is a more terrible sundering than it would have been if we had initially been placed further from them.

The characters' minds move associationally. An example is Stephen's association of the water of the bay with his mother's bile, which ramifies into his guilt, his fear of drowning, and finally his ambivalence toward water as a symbol of sexuality and eternal recurrence. But the novel as a whole picks up this associative set and develops it. Water is what is lacking in Bloom's nightmare vision, the obverse of his East or Eden vision. It is the filthy Liffey, from which the gulls snatch food and into which they then excrete; into which falls Reuben J's son; and on which floats the Elijah throwaway. It is the rain that does not renew the wasteland, the element in which Buck swims easily and saves a life, the element beside which Stephen renews his life force and Bloom masturbates, and the elaborate subject that flows into Bloom's tap. Molly's urination and menstruation are two ends of one dichotomy of water. It is a major theme or motif in *Ulysses,* chained in association to all the major characters and beyond them.

The basic style asserts an intimate and sympathic relationship between the reader and Stephen and Bloom. As that relationship changes, the style changes. Most of the critical interpretations of "what really happens" in *Ulysses* are based on these two characters as they are perceived through the basic style. In fact, however, Stephen, Bloom, and Dublin comprise only one point of a triangle; the other two are the narrator and the reader. Intimacy with the characters is permitted in only about a third of the novel. "What really happens" in *Ulysses* is the process by which the relationships among the three points change, and the person whose future is significant is neither Stephen nor Bloom, who are only fictive and only vehicles (alive as they are) but the reader. Joyce, that imitation god, had bigger—and more—fish to catch than Stephen, Bloom, and Molly.

So brilliantly and vividly did Joyce depict Stephen and Bloom that the characters have become part of the living experience of many readers. But the unique and personal qualities on which the reader's knowledge and affection are based are provided, like the particulars of Dublin mentioned in *Ulysses*, as foundation for the walls and spire of this cathedral of a novel. Bloom and Stephen are representative of humanity, at least of Joyce's conception of humanity. Their modes of thought, their modes of being or general adjustment to life, are indicative of the larger human states they represent.

Stephen: Telemachus and Nestor

In all areas of life, Stephen suffers from what Mulligan mockingly calls "g.p.i.," general paralysis of the insane, a consequence of venereal infection. It is venereal in that it is congenital: both Stephen and Bloom represent man after the fall. Bloom's comic grappling with "Thirtytwo feet per second," the rate of acceleration of falling bodies, is analogous to Stephen's "disease."

Stephen's mode of thought is a tormented dialectic: he thinks in opposites and cannot choose between them. For example, Mulligan is to him a usurper, but also a hero: "He saved men from drowning and you shake at a cur's yelping . . . Would you do what he did?" Scandinavian invaders of Ireland assailed Stephen's people, but Ireland is a "paradise of pretenders then and now" (45). Stephen is a victim of the usurpers Mulligan and Haines, but is a pretender-usurper himself, as in his thefts from Wilde, the telegram cribbed from Meredith, the Shakespeare lecture, which was taken from numerous sources but credits none and which purposely falsifies some facts, as well as the poem plagiarized from Hyde. Water is the fluid of redemption, but it also drowns; the "white breast of the dim sea" (9) is also a bowl of "green sluggish bile" (5) coughed up by his dying mother. Offended by Mulligan's mockery of the church, Stephen silently condemns him: "The void awaits surely all them that weave the wind: a menace, a disarming and a worsting from those embattled angels of the church." But he himself is a weaver of the wind, and he mocks his own threats: "Hear, hear. Prolonged applause. *Zut! Nom de dieu!*" (21).

Stephen's ambivalence causes paralysis, and in the early chapters of the novel, Stephen cannot act. On a practical level, he cannot find a livelihood that he is able to accept in Ireland, nor has he great hopes for one on the Continent. Socially he wants to be part of the Dublin intellegentsia—he is flattered by the men in the newspaper office, he wants to impress those in the library—but he despises his own desire. He asks himself, "For that are you pining, the bark of their applause?" (45), and catches himself preparing his "act" for an audience: "For Haines's chapbook. No-one here to hear. Tonight deftly amid wild drink and talk, to pierce the polished mail of his mind. What then? A jester at the court of his master, indulged and disesteemed, winning a clement master's praise" (25). His young and natural desire for acceptance is what gives poignancy to his otherwise stiff and priggish behavior toward Mulligan and Haines, and his superciliousness in the library. The party from which he is pointedly excluded, the volume of poems to which he has not been asked to contribute, hurt him as—if truth be told—they would hurt any of us. But it is also clear that he refuses to play the game, to behave in a way that would show that he accepted the society he wants to accept him—as Mulligan's behavior does show, mocking and backbiting as it is. Stephen recalls with self-contempt his desire for status in childhood: "You told the Clongowes gentry you had an uncle a judge and an uncle a general in the army." He tries to reason himself out of this continuing desire: "Come out of them, Stephen. Beauty is not there" (39).

But the Stephen of *Portrait* has matured: no longer does he see his position in romantic and adolescent terms, as that of an artist embattled by a corrupt, philistine society which sets traps for him, nets and nooses that he must fly above to escape, but as a man needing a kind of fulfillment his society does not seem to provide for. He is held in his society by his own desire for position in it, and by his guilt. Stephen's guilt is not because he "killed" his mother: obviously he did not. But his mother represents the claims of motherland, mother church, and family, Dilly, who he fears will drown him with her. If he submits to these claims, he will remain in Ireland and take on the burden of supporting the Dedalus family. If he does so, he will drown, and feel the opposing guilt over the waste of his life and abilities. If he succeeds in untying these bonds, he faces the void in the outer world. He will have to give up colleagues, friends, family; his earlier, abortive attempt to escape, the final absurdity of a Kevin Egan, his own failure to do much more than daydream about himself as a successful poet, are oceans enough to drown in out there, too. It is indeed in his head that he must kill the priest and king, but priest and king are real, substantial problems, not just mental concepts.

Sexuality functions on two levels for Stephen. It is a metaphor for a particular adjustment to reality, and it is a real problem. The two levels are intertwined in his thinking: the horror of the cycles of nature, eternal recurrence, is connected to and overlaps his sense of woman as stranger, bearing "tides, myriadislanded, within her, blood not mine" (47). He yearns for an ideal, amorphous love, disembodied gestures of romance untainted by the flesh, but recognizes the falsity of such a vision. He longs for tender love that is also sensual: "Touch, touch me" (49); but he suffers from sexual disgust, having repugnance for the "coupler's will" (38), the beast with two backs, the "instant of blind rut" (208). He is aware of sexuality in his feelings for Buck: "Wilde's love that dare not speak its name" (49), as well as of his "dislove" for the friend who will abandon him. He is thus paralyzed sexually, unable to choose one course of feeling.

Finally, he is paralyzed on the spiritual level: he can neither accept nor totally reject the theological structure the church has erected (which is another thing from the practical structure of the church, which he has no trouble rejecting). He is awed by the power and age of the Catholic church, by its effectiveness at covering the void: "founded and founded irremovably because founded, like the world, macro- and microcosm, upon the void" (207), and by its ability to swallow without choking all the varied interpretations of its basic doctrines made by the heresiarchs Arius, Sabellius, and Photius.

Stripped of its scholarly embroideries, Stephen's religious predicament is simple, even familiar. He cannot believe in the Christian God, sees neither justice nor purpose in the world, but is afraid of his own arrogance in demanding to know and understand before he will offer his faith—which is acceptance. Simple and familiar it may be, but it is psychologically a tormented state: neither Job nor Milton's Satan can live in harmony until—or unless—he submits to God, to the way things are, the facts of the human condition, the necessity of living under a regime that is apparently capricious, unjust, cruel, inexplicable, unquestionable, and unalterable. What Stephen will not "serve" is the human condition itself: "And would he not accept to die like the rest and pass away? By no means would he and make more shows according as men do with wives which Phenomenon has commanded them to do by the book Law. Then wotted he nought of that other land which is called Believe-on-Me, that is the land of promise which behoves to the king Delightful and shall be for ever where there is no death and no birth neither wiving nor mothering?" (395).

Without a god, an absolute, a key to the kingdom, man slips into the void, into relativity, and its last stop, solipsism, belief only in the "ineluctable modality . . . at least that if no more" (37). But part of Stephen wars against this too, as it wars against the rather different sense of godhood and cosmology provide by the aesthetes' version of Platonism and Hinduism in the library chapter. There *is* something out there: there is matter. Aristotle, he muses, discovered this "by knocking his sconce against" it; the world is "there all the time without you: and ever shall be, world without end" (37). Signatures of an unknown hand are waiting to be read: but Stephen cannot read "His handwriting" (562), cannot discover any principle (father) that would make his inner antinomies cohere.

Stephen's spiritual plight is simply described: by now, late in the twentieth century, it is even trite. But basic problems always are: it is the way in which one conceives of them that makes them complex. And Stephen's mind is not simple. Joyce is at great pains to include allusions to history, religion, and philosophy that are not strictly essential to understanding Stephen. He embroiders Stephen's thoughts until, as a character, Stephen becomes impressively knowledgeable, a rare and valuable mind which, given our own knowledge and our own ignorance, we have to feel is one of the best that could be produced by his—or any—society. Instead of playing Stephen off against an inferior set of "peers," as he does in *Portrait,* Joyce here plays him off against the reader himself, who is likely, despite his intelligence and education, to have to scurry for an encyclopedia to understand at least a few of Stephen's allusions, and who is unlikely, despite even a high degree of erudition, to think about his own personal problems in terms of the ideas of Aristotle, Aquinas, Abbas, and Arius. R. M. Adams and W. T. Noon have each suggested that Joyce's erudition may not have been quite as great as supposed, and textual studies have shown that much of the more esoteric material in *Ulysses* was added later, after the basic line of plot and dialogue.[8] The point is not, as Adams unhappily infers, that Joyce is pretending: Joyce makes Stephen "better" than *Joyce* is. Stephen seems to know an enormous amount because he is familiar with some rather esoteric material. His despair is thus lifted from the ordinary; his quandary is the dilemma of a mind armed with the highest and broadest knowledge. He falters, not because he does not know enough to understand, but precisely because he knows so much and still does not understand. If we have respect for his intellect and knowledge, we must also respect his despair.

At the same time, the allusions bring history, philosophy, and theology into Stephen's difficulty, raising it from a personal problem to the general problem facing those disciplines: Stephen's quandary is the quandary of early twentieth-century thought. All our knowledge has led to this: none of it seems able to offer a way out of twentieth century relativism. "Relativism" may be only a metaphor: it may be the term in which we choose to image our ignorance, as the seventeenth century chose "free will." Nevertheless, as a term covering a field of doubts, relativism lies at the root of the twentieth century problems of paralysis, anxiety, and identity. Thus, the allusions connected with Stephen function to transform him from one paralyzed young man in a state of incertitude into a representative of the twentieth-century intellectual dilemma.

Relativism leads directly to solipsism and hence to nihilism. The art Stephen creates solipsistically, such as his imitation of Hyde's poem, is bad. Nihilism precludes art, which is, among other things, an arrangement of values. One of Stephen's other problems is that as long as he is paralyzed spiritually, emotionally, and practically, he is also paralyzed as an artist. His figure thus becomes representative of the dilemma of twentieth century art as well as thought. He tries to create, like the Swiftian spider, out of his own innards. In this condition he writes the spurious poem: by positing a higher, spiritual plane with which he is supposedly in contact, he can avoid reality, avoid being deflowered by contact with it. But this is a dead end, as he realizes in the library.

Stephen's musings on history are linked to his paralysis. The key to the kingdom of truth offered by history is as flawed as that offered by theology. History, a fixed record of man's deeds, would seem to be an absolute, a reality: the deaths of Pyrrhus and Caesar "are not to be thought away." They are real: "time has branded them and fettered they are lodged in the room of the infinite possibilities they have ousted" (25). Still, they might have happened otherwise; they are "fabled by the daughters of memory," but Blake tells us the daughters of memory are children of a world under a cloud. Nevertheless, "it was in some way if not as memory fabled it" (24); that is, there is and was some objective reality. But as Stephen's mind curls scholastically around the question of determinism—"was that only possible which came to pass?"—he recognizes the futility of his meditation—"Weave, weaver of the wind" (25)—and retreats back into solipsism: "The soul is in a manner all that is" (26).

Joyce's sardonic footnote on the relation between history and truth is the brief recounting of history that Deasy offers. This is one of the obscure ironies in *Ulysses*, one of the many allusions that force us out of the book and into either life or another book for verification. Deasy obviously thinks he is recounting fact about "MacMurrough's wife and her leman" and about Sir John Blackwood. Stephen accepts the story of Sir John as fact, and if we lacked the fruit of Adams' careful investigations, so would we.[9] The story is not true, and Joyce knew it was not true.[10] Yet fettered and lodged in his novel it is, parading as history.

The truth of history, Stephen suspects, may lie in *amor matris*, subjective and objective genitive, the love that nourishes even a Cyril Sargent, the love without which men would be trampled underfoot by the world. History, then, is mere continuation, "a tale like any other too often heard" (25), cycles of "famine, plague and slaughters" (45), of invading usurpers who in the next wave become victims. History is the record of man's timelessness and meaninglessness, just as eternal recurrence describes the timelessness and meaninglessness of nature. Both are nightmares: "Day by day: night by night: lifted, flooded and let fall. Lord, they are weary: and, whispered to, they sigh . . . To no end gathered: vainly then released, forth flowing, wending back" (49-50).

The only escape seems to be God, who ends both time and timelessness, who provides the absolute and static moment that is the end of time. But God is only a shout in the street, a clap of thunder, a sharp stroke man-made or given meaning by man, which seems to divide time into sections, history into purposeful units called ages of reason or faith, of Zeus or anxiety. What is left when history is history, when it is over and no longer called "current events," is symbolized by the collection of objects in Deasy's office, by Deasy's speeches, and by Deasy himself: symbols of empire (the coins, pictures of the horses of royalty); symbols of religion (the spoons—the twelve apostles "snug in their spooncase" [29], the pilgrim's scallop shell); symbols of knowledge (Deasy himself, the schoolmaster whose proudest boast is "I paid my way" [30] and who offers a number of bits of information, all of them false).

The line "time has branded them and fettered they are lodged in the room of the infinite possibilities they have ousted" (25) appears in Nestor, among Stephen's meditations on history. It is a clue, one of Joyce's subtle games. It points toward the solution Stephen reaches gropingly in Aeolus and in Scylla and Charybdis, the practical and moral imperative to act. The theme of action is appropriately linked with history, which is a record of acts, whether or not they really occurred, of behavior adopted in the face of the void. History presumes to tell the story of the "real," and it is in the library that Stephen, speaking of Shakespeare, discerns his own inability to accept reality: "Lover of an ideal or a perversion, like José he kills the real Carmen" (212). Stephen, too, idealizes or perverts, on every level. His extreme intellectualization of his problem impedes his solving it. When the ideal deity fails him, he turns at once to *dio boia;* when ideal love does not appear, he moves to Nighttown, where he continues to live in his mind. He sees only deformity in the place and inhabitants of Dublin, as shown in Wandering Rocks and Circe.

Three steps are necessary for Stephen to overcome his paralysis. He must first accept his participation in the human condition, accept nature, fallibility, and death. Such an acceptance would then make it possible for him to accept his own feelings, to give up idealizing and perverting them. These two actions would finally make it possible for him to act in other ways, which would mean the end of his paralysis. Such an end is not equivalent to reaching some new Jerusalem where everything will become clear; it offers merely survival, the ability to live and grow. Joyce's standards are not very high compared to other noble aspirations recorded by the written word. He suggests that "high" is not where man should aim, that the idealization invariably leads to the perversion.

Stephen is not "saved" in any ultimate sense in the course of *Ulysses*, but he does tentatively take the three necessary steps. He leaves 7 Eccles Street armed with at least the knowledge of what he must do to survive and create. The Proteus episode summarizes all the aspects of Stephen's problem, incertitude. It also shows Stephen making the first hesitant step into adulthood, survival.

Proteus

The episode is carefully structured. It opens with a consideration of external, that is, objective reality. Each change in that reality is attended by a change in Stephen's internal reality. We are aware of the connection between them; Stephen is not. Joyce is insisting on the connectedness of external and internal reality even as Stephen questions it. What we see is that each shift in scene is accompanied by a shift in subject. The metaphor for the chapter is Stephen wrestling with the sea god Proteus, relativism itself, in order to pin down its true shape, objective reality. The disguises of Proteus are various modes of being, potential lives: Stephen is seeking a way to be.[11]

The chapter opens with one pole of the dichotomy: "Ineluctable modality of the visible: at least that if no more, thought through my eyes." From an acceptance of solipsism, Stephen moves to rejection of it and an assertion of the existence of objective reality, the "things" whose signatures he must read. He vacillates between the two poles, shutting out objective reality by closing his eyes, and discovering the "ineluctable modality of the audible," then opening them to discover again the real, "there all the time without you: and ever shall be, world without end" (37).

The two theses of the opening paragraph are not synthesized: their dialectic provides the tension of the chapter. As he opens his eyes, Stephen sees the enduring world and the midwives, symbols of the beginning, birth, the process that makes the world endure.

Birth is what Stephen seeks, birth into a way of life. In the next section he considers his physical birth and adds, "Creation from nothing" (37). This passage sets divine creation (*ex nihilo*) against misbirth: the ideal against the perversion. Stepehn desires the former, desires to conceive his life and his work by divine infusion, like the Virgin. His fear of intercourse producing a monster, a misbirth, is well supported by the chapter, in which every form of life available to him is somehow monstrous. By association, he moves to sex, sin (inextricable for Stephen), and his own grim birth. Stephen's disgust for the clasping and sundering of sex cannot be reconciled with a belief in a *lex eterna* that transcends the accident of physical conception. Again, he moves between perverting sex, seeing it as bestial only, and idealizing it, annulling its physical component.

The scene changes: Stephen feels the breeze and sees the sea, thinking in literary terms. His thoughts move from birth to his father, thence to his uncle. In this long section Stephen considers various modes of life available to him in Ireland. Uncle Richie, the "drunken little costdrawer" (38), represents a way of life common in the Dublin that Joyce presents. Waste, poverty, and emptiness are all that it bleakly holds. "This wind is sweeter" than Richie's tuneful whistle. Ireland holds only "houses of decay." The dedicated life of an Abbas issues only in "fading prophesies" for the "hundred-headed rabble" (39). Stephen reverses Abbas' pious admonition into *"descende"* (40), in a section devoted to the clergy, whose life also Stephen could share. His contempt for the well-fed, gelded priests moves into a comic envisionment of how Occam first came to question the nature of transubstantiation.[12] Stephen then recalls his first departure from the church, caused by his insistent youthful sensuality. His contempt is impartial: he mocks the church; he mocks cruelly his own boyhood fears and sexual desires; and he mocks the female objects of his obsession. He does defend himself, however, making an appeal to nature, the stock answer to sexual guilt: "What about what? What else were they invented for?" (40).

The earlier reference to Swift is picked up by an allusion to Dryden's supposed pronouncement, "Cousin Stephen, you will never be a saint" (40), and leads into the bitterest consideration of all, his literary aspirations. Again he mocks himself, and again it is for his desires that he castigates himself, this time for the hollowness and superficiality of wanting primarily fame and immortality from his writing.

The section sums up his possibilities if he remains in Ireland: he can be a common man like Richie Goulding and end like his uncle; he can join the clergy, whose life is unacceptable to him and whose dedication is only devoured by a rabble whose hatefulness, Stephen believes, drove Swift mad; or he can become a member of Dublin's literary coterie, writing or receiving reviews like Yeats's for Lady Gregory, referred to in the library, or the Pateresque lines on Pico: "When one reads these strange pages of one long gone one feels that one is at one with one who once" (40). He turns away from all of them, partly because they are in themselves inadequate to fulfill him (Richie, priesthood), and partly because he has contempt for his motivations. He is afraid of his desire to impress people like the Clongowes gentry, to possess the prosperity, invulnerability, and power of the priesthood, to achieve an easy acclaim for his literary efforts. It is in the section on his literary daydreams that the "no-one" motif connected with both Stephen and Bloom first appears. The motif occurs frequently when Bloom and Stephen, as well as Gerty MacDowell, are feeling shame but think that they are safe because "No-one saw: tell no-one" (40). This motif is one of Joyce's comic hints, because of course we *are* seeing, Joyce is telling all the world. The intimation is that we stand on a different level from the characters. We have been let in on Stephen's most secret shame.

A new metamorphosis is ushered in by a new scene, the "damp crackling mast, razorshells, squeaking pebbles" (40), and a phrase from *Lear*. There is an accompanying change in the direction in which Stephen is moving: he crosses "the firmer sand towards the Pigeon-house" (41). This firmer foundation supports him as he considers the modes of existence open to him if he leaves Ireland. The first is a deracinated life like that lived by Patrice Egan, who is half-Irish and half-French, but is essentially homeless. Patrice is reminiscent of Gabriel Conroy, who has denied his roots without putting down others, who denies his tradition in an effort to be "Europeanized" (Chekhov dealt with such people also, perhaps more kindly), and who loses, in the process, any character at all. Patrice is precious and affected, pattering on about religion as if he were comparing brands of tea. Stephen sees some of these traits in himself, and remembers with humorous contempt his brief sojourn in Paris: "Just say in the most natural tone: when I was in Paris, *boul' Mich*, I used to . . . Proudly walking. Whom were you trying to walk like? Forget: a dispossessed" (41).

The memory leads into the event that brought him home, his mother's death, but this time pride saves him from guilt, pride in face of the attacks of Mulligan's uncharitable aunt. He gazes at a more heroic landscape, "piled stone mammoth skulls" (42), and reverts to Paris and the hero Kevin Egan, for whom the drama of the Irish struggle is still alive. Egan has given up everything—"loveless, landless, wifeless"—for ideas and actions he thinks significant, but his dedication has been as futile as that of Abbas. He lives in the past without perceiving the futility of both his heroism and his exile, in a delusion, ignorant that he is "unsought by any but me" (43), Stephen thinks, because "they have forgotten Kevin Egan, not he them" (44). The line "Remembering thee, O Sion" (44), in allusion to Psalm 137, and the thought of the betrayed hero mark the lowest point in Stephen's meditations. Betrayal, in fact, is the personal problem that both Stephen and Bloom have to face in this novel. Arnold Goldman relates their feelings about it to Joyce's own pervasive sense of betrayal.[13] As is usual when dealing with Joyce, however, one must be careful to distinguish Joyce's feelings in life from those he depicts in his characters: Bloom handles betrayal in a way that Joyce himself was never capable of doing. As Stephen stands at the edge of the sea meditating, he becomes suddenly aware that he must change direction or drown: "Here, I am not walking out to the Kish lightship, am I? He stood suddenly, his feet beginning to sink slowly in the quaking soil. Turn back" (44).

Turning, he returns to what is, the actual rather than the potential: the situation at the tower, and his renunciation of it. "He lifted his feet up from the suck and turned back . . . Take all, keep all." He returns also to his isolation within his mode of perception: "My soul walks with me, form of forms," and to his inclination, implicit up to this point in his weariness and his Hamlet-like inability to make choices and act, toward suicide: "hearing Elsinore's tempting flood" (44).

The flood follows him, but he climbs up on a rock and surveys a dead dog and wreckage on the beach, which he associates with the wreckage of history, of language, and of building. A live dog appears and terrifies Stephen, who then glimpses two figures he mistakes for the midwives. He is caught here between death and life. Then he imagines the Scandinavian invasions of Ireland in the eighth and ninth centuries, and identifies Mulligan with the usurping invaders: "When Malachi wore the collar of gold" (45).[14] The movements of the live dog are wound into his musings on pretenders-usurpers. These are highly ambivalent because he knows that Mulligan is not just a usurper but also a hero, and he thinks that he himself is neither: he is afraid of the dog and he deems his own timidity about dogs and water to be cowardice. Thoughts of swimming and a drowned man lead him to confront the source of his terror, "waters: bitter death: lost" (46), and his guilt. The poles here are action, with the horrors that are consequent to it (invasions, slaughter), and inaction, with the guilt it brings. The drowning man is an image for his mother and for Dilly, who, he later thinks, will drown him with her. His guilt is legitimate: he is unwilling to come to the aid of his family. This abandonment is seen here as cowardice, the fear of drowning in Ireland.

The appearance of the gypsies recalls sensuality, and sensuality reminds Stephen of his irremediable participation in humanity; this association ties many of these subjects together. The dog moves through protean transformations (a microcosmic analogy to the movement of the chapter and the movements of history that it traces) from dog to hare to gull to buck to bear to wolf to calf. Nature also metamorphosizes, the wavelets becoming "herds of seamorse," serpenting waves. What stops the dog, fixes him firmly in his true shape, is his own image, Socrates finding himself on his doorstep: his fellow dog, dead. He sniffs the body "like a dog." The animal is identified with mankind: "dogskull, dogsniff, eyes on the ground, moves to one great goal. Ah, poor dogsbody" (46). This brief passage has complex associations. It recalls Deasy's "all history moves towards one great goal, the manifestation of God" (34), and thus aligns the dog with history (mankind) and God with death. It also picks up Mulligan's "Ah, poor dogsbody" (6) addressed to Stephen, thus identifying the dog with Stephen as well. The dog is again identified with Stephen when he digs and Stephen thinks "something he buried there, his grandmother" (46), recalling Stephen's riddle.[15]

In short, in this section the dog is turned into an emblem for human-ity, moves through transformations that parallel those of history, and is stabilized by the real, another dog. History and nature move toward one great goal, death, which is God (dog backward, god of the damned in Circe.) But for the first time Stephen accepts an identifica-tion with what is outside him. Despite his fear of the animal, he recog-nizes that he too is a pretender-usurper, he too moves only toward death, he too is a creature of animal impulse. The dog is chastised for smelling the dead dog, urinates on the sand, and changes form again, becoming by implication a fox and panther. Stephen's associations with the panther lead him to thoughts of sensuality and his dream of the night before. This time Stephen's thoughts anticipate the change in scene, and he looks again at the gypsies.[16]

Stephen meditates on the couple with "morose delectation," pleas-urable disgust about their sexuality.[17] He confronts two traditions with each other, a seventeenth-century canting song by Richard Head that uses gypsy terms, and Aquinas' language. Stephen is balancing the two forces that draw him, his perverse sensuality and his sense of sex as sin. He concludes that they are equal, at least as literature: "Language no whit worse than his. Monkwords, marybeads jabber on their girdles: roguewords, tough nuggets patter in their pockets" (47). The gypsies pass, and Stephen looks at himself.

Stephen tries to imagine how he looks to the woman, then moves to a consideration of femaleness itself, the processes of nature as they affect women. Both sexuality and nature move toward death: he writes his *liebestod* and thinks: "Oomb, allwombing tomb."[18] Still self-conscious, he moves back into solipsism and thinks about Berke-ley and the problem of *esse est percipi*, which is here a comic consider-ation of identity, Stephen mocking himself for the exalted terms in which he couches his problem.[19] He mocks his own "high" language and the unreality of his vision, repudiating his old self, the Stephen of *Portrait*, whose aesthetic disconnects art from life, who ignores the reality of "the long dray laden with old iron" (*P* 209), and who com-poses a villanelle that has little connection with real emotion out of a scene with an unnamed "she" on the steps of a tram (*P* 223-224) Using the motions of the soul as his subject matter, this Stephen too com-poses lines, the real intention of which is to seduce:

You find my words dark. Darkness is in our souls, do you not

think? Flutier. Our souls, shame-wounded by our sins, cling to us
yet more, a woman to her lover clinging, the more the more.
    She trusts me, her hand gentle, the long-lashed eyes. (48)

But this Stephen is tougher and wiser than the boy of *Portrait*, and he
mocks his own rootless effusions: "Now where the blue hell am I
bringing her beyond the veil? Into the ineluctable modality of the
ineluctable visuality. She, she, she. What she?" (48). He searches his
mind for an objective correlative to "sheness" and comes up with a
woman he saw earlier in the week. Again, however, he finds himself
idealizing. He corrects himself: "Bet she wears those curse of God
stays suspenders and yellow stockings, darned with lumpy wool" (49).
    The feelings Stephen has been idealizing and perverting are simple
sensual longing. He drops his poeticising, lies back, and allows himself
briefly to feel his emotions, rather than mock them, as he usually
does. For a time, he accepts his own sensuality: "he watched through
peacocktwittering lashes the southing sun. I am caught in this burning
scene. Pan's hour, the faunal noon. Among gumheavy serpentplants,
milkoozing fruits, where on the tawny waters leaves lie wide. Pain is
far." He recalls the line from the Yeats song he sang to his mother, but
in his mood of submission to his body, he does not return to his guilty
feelings, and moves instead to an acceptance even of the situation with
Buck and to its underlying guilt-laden facts. Buck has been a "staunch
friend, a brother soul: Wilde's love that dare not speak its name. He
now will leave me." He decides not to blame Buck or himself, insisting
only that he must be loved as he is, "all or not at all" (49). When
Stephen concludes his thought by urinating in the water, it is as if he
were comically putting a seal on his decision to accept a piece at least
of the human condition.
    The water, the weeds, his own urination evoke a profound sense of
the eternal recurrence of nature. Stephen watches the writhing weeds,
and the tides trapped like him, like the moon, like the femaleness he
has been considering. Eternal recurrence is the only immortality, but it
means individual death. This is a dismaying truth, but it is truth:
"God becomes man becomes fish becomes barnacle goose becomes
featherbed mountain. Dead breaths I living breathe, tread dead dust,
devour a urinous offal from all dead" (50). Like the dog, Stephen sniffs
the air of the dead, like the dog he adds his urinous offal to nature's

store. Stephen is wearing the clothes of a dead man. Like the fox, he lives by rapine, is both murderer and victim, for he feeds on the dead and is fed upon. Standing among the ruins of nature and civilization washed in by the tide, among "human shells," a porter bottle, broken hoops, nets, discarded backdoors and two "crucified shirts" (41), he feels his own rotting shells of teeth. He does not fully perceive his own participation in the erosion of nature: "why is that, I wonder, or does it mean something perhaps?" (50). He leaves behind another bit of his personal ruins, the dry snot, to become one with the sand, the rock, and the sea.

In the course of the chapter Stephen makes some small choices. This does not mean that he is a changed man in later parts of the book. Joyce's realism is uncompromising: life is like that: the small choices we make define us almost without our awareness, so that the large ones are made before we reach them. The mental motions toward acceptance of his own participation in history, in death, in mankind, which Stephen makes in this episode lead to a conclusion that contains the same elements as the opening, but with different emphasis. He is still, at the end of the episode, concerned with certitude versus incertitude, with personal identity and objective reality, but the tension between these poles is diminished. His musings on the dog involve an identification with other animate beings, with history, and therefore with mankind. The rejection of all possible ways of life is an attempt to transcend being human: here he accepts that he must play some role, that he also is a pretender-usurper as well as a victim. Characteristically identifying himself with both Christ and Satan, he admits his participation in history—that nightmare from which, he says earlier, he is trying to awake: "Come. I thirst. Clouding over. No black clouds anywhere, are there? Thunderstorm. Allbright he falls, proud lightning of the intellect, *Lucifer, dico, qui nescit occasum.* No. My cockle hat and staff and his my sandal shoon. Where? To evening lands . . . Evening will find itself in me, without me" (50).

Stephen's tentative acceptance of his own sensuality, which means surrendering himself to eternal recurrence and death, allows him also to accept death. It is necessary to accept death in order to choose life. This motif is a minor one throughout the novel. It is in the Hades chapter, in the midst of death, that Bloom also chooses life. He thinks, "In the midst of death we are in life" (108), and later: "I do not like that other world she wrote. No more do I. Plenty to see and hear and feel yet. Feel live warm beings near you. Let them sleep in their maggoty beds. They are not going to get me this innings" (115). In Cyclops, Thersites says of Bloom: "Didn't I tell you? As true as I'm drinking this porter if he was at his last gasp he'd try to downface you that dying was living" (329), and Stephen returns to the subject in Circe: "Bah! It is because it is. Woman's reason. Jewgreek is greekjew. Extremes meet. Death is the highest form of life. Bah!" (504). But it is after his acceptance of death that Stephen chooses life, although in this episode he has come close to rejecting it. "Where? To evening lands . . . Evening will find itself in me, without me." Aware that he is moving toward death, he can live: death will come in its own time, both within and without.

This chapter is sprinkled with phrases emphasizing Stephen's effort to see himself as part of the larger unit of mankind: "One of her sisterhood lugged me screaming into life" (37); "The cords of all link back"; "My consubstantial father" (38); "Whom were you trying to walk like?" (41); "To yoke me as his yokefellow, our crimes our common cause. You're your father's son" (43); "Their blood is in me, their lusts my waves" (45); "Dead breaths I living breathe, tread dead dust" (50). There are also elements emphasizing his separateness: his rejections of various lifestyles, for instance, and phrases like "There all the time without you" (37) and "Tides, myriadislanded, within her, blood not mine" (47).

Stephen's choice of participation prepares him for his next two crucial scenes: in Aeolus and the library. He takes, in Proteus, the first step out of his paralysis. Since Joyce has been at such pains to make Stephen representative, it is likely he intends his "progress" to be so also. Stephen's change is an indication of Joyce's criticism of all who think themselves more than human, or free from any human "vice" or "virtue."

Bloom: Calypso, Lotus-Eaters, and Hades

Bloom is from the outset a character set in opposition to Stephen. In age, "racial" background, education, physique, interests, religious attitudes, intellect, and temperament, they represent opposing sides of humanity. The most profound difference between them is in their stances, their particular adjustments to outer reality. Bloom is explicitly labeled "Everyman or Noman" (727), and his lack of apparent distinction makes it easy enough to take him for *l'homme moyen sensuel*, whereas Stephen is shown from the beginning to be superior in intellect and knowledge.

Bloom's habit of mind is a circling one, as opposed to Stephen's dialectical mode of thought. Bloom moves around subjects, stopping briefly in different positions but reaching no final conclusions. He simply continues around the circle:

> Mr Bloom glanced from his angry moustache to Mr Power's mild face and Martin Cunningham's eyes and beard, gravely shaking. Noisy selfwilled man. Full of his son. He is right. Something to hand on. If little Rudy had lived. See him grow up. Hear his voice in the house. Walking beside Molly in an Eton suit. My son. Me in his eyes. Strange feeling it would be. From me. Just a chance. Must have been that morning in Raymond terrace she was at the window, watching the two dogs at it by the wall of the cease to do evil. And the sergeant grinning up. She had that cream gown on with the rip she never stitched. Give us a touch, Poldy. God, I'm dying for it. How life begins. (88-89)

Here Bloom begins with a negative judgment on Simon Dedalus and moves to a positive one, thence to thoughts of Rudy, his own longing for a son, to Molly, sex, and "how life begins." The "subject" of the paragraph is fatherhood in a number of its aspects. Bloom's thought, because it circles, is able to contain all these aspects without necessarily giving prominence to any one.

Here is another example of Bloom's circular thought:

> Heavenly weather really. If life was always like that. Cricket weather. Sit around under sunshades. Over after over. Out. They can't play it here. Duck for six wickets. Still Captain Buller broke a window in the Kildare street club with a slog to square leg. Donnybrook fair more in their line. And the skulls we were acracking when M'Carthy took the floor. Heatwave. Won't last. Always passing, the stream of life, which in the stream of life we trace is dearer than them all. (86)

There are two subjects here, connected by association, but both move similarly. "Heavenly weather" leads to the desire for Eden—permanent heavenly weather—to the knowledge that it is a heat wave and will pass, thence to a consideration of transiency and back to the love of life which begins the paragraph. The pleasant weather evokes thoughts of sitting happily under sunshades watching cricket, moves to the game itself, to its inadequate playing in Ireland, to the memory of a good play that seemed to lack polish, to a line from a song reflecting the strong-arm Irish approach to such things, and then returns to the weather.

Bloom has a long meditation on the East in Calypso. Although broken up by other events, it is a good example of the way his mind works. It begins when he leaves the house thinking considerately of Molly and crosses to the sunny "bright" side of the street. The warmth of the sun and the aroma of freshly baked bread arouse sensuous pleasure, which he associates with the East. He thinks about it in concrete images expressing its romance, its beauty, and its terrors, but he ends by deflating his own romantic dream: "Probably not a bit like it really" (57). The subject recurs, however, in the butcher shop when he looks at the advertisement for the model farm at Kinnereth. On his way home, he thinks about it again, mixing romance and one of his business schemes, but as a cloud begins to cover the sun, he decides the East is "no, not like that." He falls into despair, and it is the thought of Molly and the sight of the sunlight that save him from the "grey horror" (61). Warmth, Molly, and sunlight, the sensual beauty of life, is what saves Bloom from despair: they are explicitly equated, for his thought changes as he returns to the house.

Bloom has the ability to entertain contrary or paradoxical notions at the same time without conflict. It is the nonintellectual Bloom rather than Stephen who shares Bruno's notions about the meeting of extremes, and about paradox. He is described in Ithaca as walking "repeatedly in several different directions" (711). "Dirty cleans" (68), he thinks, and "Poisons the only cures" (84). "Pleasure or pain is it?" (157) he wonders about a starving boy smelling the aroma of food. He is able to see things and appreciate them in all their contradictory selfhood. He loves and cares for the cat without sentimentalizing her or denying her nature: she is glossy, clean, intelligent, vindictive, and cruel. He is "aware of their greed and cunning" (153), but he pities the gulls' hunger and spends money to feed them. His ability to accept ambiguity in processes and in animals extends to people, not only to people with whom he is not closely involved, like Simon Dedalus, but to those toward whom it is hardest to feel charitable: his child, his wife, even himself. An acceptance of contradiction is the root of his charity and compassion for others, for when we stop insisting that people be what we think they should be, when we stop idealizing and perverting them, when we see and appreciate them in their selfhood, we automatically relinquish those "rights" Stephen describes Shakespeare as clutching. This relinquishment is at the root of Bloom's realization that "nobody owns" (96, 97). "How can you own water really?" (153). He is able to accept his daughter's growing up without trying to constrain her: "Yes, yes: a woman too. Life. Life" (89); "She mightn't like me to come that way without letting her know. Must be careful about women" (100); "O well: she knows how to mind herself. But if not? No, nothing has happened. Of course it might. Wait in any case till it does. A wild piece of goods. Her slim legs running up the staircase. Destiny. Ripening now. Vain: very. He smiled with troubled affection" (66).

All of this adds up to the ancient and most exalted of Christian virtues, *caritas.* Bloom's possession of this virtue makes him a superior being, as superior in the moral sphere as is Stephen in that of the intellect.

This is not to claim that there is no shabbiness in Bloom's moral coat. The pathetic and ludicrous business with Martha Clifford and his shame and guilt about it (the word "no-one" appears three times in the section where he picks up and reads Martha's letter [72, 77, 78]), his voyeurism, his servile acceptance of Dublin's anti-Semitism, and his distasteful habit of rationalizing the impulse behind his kind acts by imagining that he will derive some practical advantage from them (as when Bloom asks Hynes to put down M'Coy's name and thinks "Leave him under an obligation: costs nothing" [112], and again after he tells Menton about the dent in his hat and thinks "get the pull over him that way" [115]) are small faults, the kind least acceptable in literature, where we like our flaws demonic and our heroes killers. These faults hurt no one else. It cannot even be claimed that Martha Clifford or, later, Gerty are corrupted by Bloom, as both are willing participants in a mutual titillation.

In addition, all of Bloom's faults are representative. Dublin's pervasive sexual difficulties are Catholic and Irish. Sexual problems may even, as Freud suggests, be inherent in and the root of civilization. Bloom clearly accepts sexuality as a given, and as a problem. He thinks "Eunuch. One way out of it" (82). He does not imagine that he can, or ought to, eradicate desire, as Stephen sometimes does. Bloom's solution to the problem of desire may not be admirable, but what solution is? The ideal solution—a marriage that remains satisfying—is reached about as often as any other ideal on earth, and Bloom has tried for it and failed.

Bloom accepts the terms of his society about Jews, up to a point. In his eagerness to be accepted by his fellows, he participates in the mockery of the Jew Reuben J., about whom he thinks, "now he's really what they call a dirty jew" (183), but he also, when confronted in the pub scene with a greater degree of hostility, is able and courageous enough to fight back verbally. It is important to remember that he is completely alone in Barney Kiernan's: there is not one other Jew there to help him. Given that he must, no matter where he goes in 1904, live in a climate of anti-Semitism; given that his choice lies between living in a ghetto of some sort and trying to be a member of society as a whole; and given that he has no attachment to Judaism or any other religion, it is hard to condemn him severely for his tolerance of anti-Semitism.

Finally, Bloom's mercenary interpretation of his own kindness is of a piece with his businessman's culture. We know, from his kindness to creatures who can offer him no repayment—the gulls, the cat, the blind stripling, Mina Purefoy, for instance—that his kindness is natural and spontaneous, not motivated by calculation. It is his interpretation of his own motives that is distressing. His rationalization is typical of a world where kindness is considered ludicrous and sentimental—even as Bloom's compassion for Mrs. Purefoy is viewed by one critic[20]—where good deeds are performed in order to get good customers, where courtesy is good business. It resembles nothing so much as the thinking behind Father Purdon's sermon in "Grace."

My point is not to whitewash Bloom but to show that his moral flaws are flaws inherent in his society. Without those flaws, he would indeed be a saint. It is Bloom's flaws that make us take him for the common man: his moral foibles, his comic errors of fact, his confusions about science, literature, music, and religion. His range of interests is actually far wider than that of any "average" man. His interests in science and social reform make him seem typically twentieth century; his misapprehensions make him seem average. Thus, the real ground of his superiority is often overlooked. And it is Bloom's moral superiority and Stephen's intellectual superiority that isolate them from the community and make them representative not just of mankind, but of the best of mankind.

The much-discussed question of whether the coming together of Bloom and Stephen really changes either of them is irrelevant: the novel happens to us, not to them. It is enough that both exist. Bloom's humanity stands as a *tao* or way: it is the direction in which Stephen must move, although he will never be a Bloom.[21] By the time he meets Bloom, Stephen has already taken his own path: their meeting is comic, in that it represents yin and yang touching without recognition (for them), and serious because it represents momentary integrity (for us). But even their communion is comic: they do not fit together. The excellence and failures of each stand as active principles in the larger world: Stephen's movement toward acceptance and the ability to act represents the way; Bloom's incarnation of a "light to the gentiles" (676), which is comic in the terms in which he thinks of it, represents the goal.

Together, Bloom and Stephen represent Joyce's definition of humanity. Among their attributes are notable absences: neither is athletic, a warrior, a football hero; neither is much given to worldliness or to the more modern heroism of government and business. The kinds of power most respected in the world are missing in Bloom and Stephen. It is an interesting indication of Joyce's intentions in using the *Odyssey* as a frame that the kinds of power Odysseus possessed included both intellectual keenness and emotional depth but also physical strength, prowess as a warrior, if a reluctant one, ability as an administrator, and a sense of personal power that made him able to hold his own diplomatically with gods as well as kings. The few hints in *Ulysses* that Bloom possesses similar powers are comic: he is a warrior in Cyclops, but only on a verbal level; he argues with authority about some soup on a train; and he manages to maintain his equilibrium at Val Dillon's dinner.

Joyce is clearly offering a new hero: mankind itself, possessed of intellectual excellence, artistic standards, moral fineness, and depth of thought and feeling. This hero, who includes both Stephen and Bloom, is within the Christian tradition, for he eschews power in the world. Joyce is true to his realism, however, and does not conveniently reward his unworldly heroes with worldly power, or intimate divine reward. Virtue, they say, is its own: it has to be, echoes Joyce. Worldly power is not only extraneous to Joyce's conception of humanness but also downright destructive of it. This is apparent in his handling of princes of the church and state, as in Wandering Rocks, of politicians and businessmen wherever they appear in *Ulysses* and in *Dubliners*, of athletes like the citizen, and even of the lower orders of worldly institutions, such as the robot-like constables, or Tom Kernan, who is a smaller Bloom without his moral fineness, and the rest of the Dublin crew who fill pub and street. Joyce's definition of mankind is characteristic of one strand of twentieth century religious, political, and moral thought.

It is antihierarchical, even anarchical; it renounces the world but not the body; it is Christian in its repudiation of worldly power and physical might, but it also repudiates the Christian notion of reward, of a heaven that confers ultimate justice on earthly sufferers. Taken as a whole, humanity for Joyce is intelligent, compassionate, sexual, and uncertain. It suffers and it strives. It achieves immortality because it endures, because its patterns recur from millennium to millennium. Bloom and Stephen are incarnations of absolute values, but they are not absolute: they are wanderers. Their configurations will change as the world changes, but their characteristics will endure.

Joyce's ambidextrous manipulations set Stephen and Bloom against each other, as two halves of a human whole (with Molly being the fluid in which both exist), and at the same time place them together, as a unified representative of humanity. It is necessary to consider both movements in defining Joyce's conception of humanity. The characters have as much in common as they have in opposition.

Both live in states of servitude, Stephen to "two masters" (20), (church and state), Bloom to Molly and the cat. Stephen lives in a tower that is an omphalos; Bloom in "Calypso's cave," which was an omphalos. The omphalos is at once womb, femaleness (the principle of nature, for Joyce), and self, the navel into which Vishnu peers. Both Stephen and Bloom are victims of usurpers (Mulligan and Boylan); both have severe sexual problems; both are to some extent exiles from their society. On a lighter plane, both are dressed in black, are keyless, and carry talismans (ashplant, potato). Both have abandoned the religion of their ancestors; both suffer from guilt, in particular existential guilt, the kind of guilt that probably infects all people—guilt about being what one is, not being better, more, or at least different. Both yearn for a kind of paradise, Stephen for certitude, Bloom for an imagined Eden. These are essentially the same thing: one is an intellectual principle that gives order to life, the other is the sensuous incarnation of that order. They both suffer from the same nightmares. Stephen is tormented by the meaningless cycles of nature and history, and by his imprisonment in relativity; Bloom also is anguished by recurrence:

> The oldest people. Wandered far away over all the earth, captivity to captivity, multiplying, dying, being born everywhere. (61)

> Trams passed one another, ingoing, outgoing, clanging. Useless words. Things go on same; day after day: squads of police marching out, back: trams in, out. Those two loonies mooching about. Dignam carted off. Mina Purefoy swollen belly on a bed groaning to have a child tugged out of her. One born every second somewhere. Other dying every second. (164)

Stephen attempts to make sense of the world theologically, Bloom scientifically. Theology and science are the two disciplines that attempt to explain the universe; they are also the focuses brought to bear on Stephen and Bloom in the last chapter where they appear. The inadequacy of these forms of investigation to make the world comprehensible is a source of desolation to both characters. But Stephen is more tormented by his incertitude than Bloom is. The visible symbol of the difference in their adjustments to reality is Molly, Bloom's Moly, the seemingly fixed center about which he has chosen to circle. Like Stephen and Bloom, Molly is representative: she incarnates nature, sexuality, sensuality. Bloom's impotence with Molly can be seen as a paradigm of man's impotence with nature in the twentieth century; her infidelity is both real and symbolic. Finally, she represents Bloom's degree of acceptance of his own body, of his own fallibility, of death, of his participation in a larger, and necessary, process. His offering of Molly to Stephen is at one level pandering, but on another level a suggestion of the way Stephen must go.

Innumerable small details connect Bloom and Stephen: themes, allusions, parallel paths. In Nausikaa Bloom occupies the same space that Stephen occupied earlier in the day, in Proteus, and he echoes many of Stephen's thoughts.[22] Although most of these details are hardly noticeable, Joyce has been faulted for them. But they are not gratuitous: Joyce is suggesting that there is a common experience of humanity, an experiential reality that parallels the objective reality symbolized by physical aspects of the city: the same beach evokes the same thoughts because we are alike and because it is the same beach; it exists as a single real, comprehensible experience.

Joyce once said he had no imagination, and in a sense this is true. He could not imagine complex convolutions of plot: none of his work has much plot in the traditional sense. Nor could he annul himself enough to enter imaginatively into the experience of a character totally different from himself. The character of Bloom is probably the highest parameter of his empathetic imaginative ability. The "plot" of *Ulysses* consists of the peregrinations and encounters of Bloom and Stephen, tracked out against the correspondences. The novel is like a circle built of two-by-four uprights in the shape of a trellis, on which the correspondences, allusions, and analogies are strung like colored yarn to create a solid fabric.[23] The soil in which the uprights are planted is Homeric but contains grains of many other monuments of the past from the Bible to Shakespeare, and the purpose of the structure is Dantean. Whether the correspondences and allusions work seriously or comically, they provide the novel with a substructure, which works like a subplot.[24] A subplot like the Gloucester plot in *Lear* parallels the major plot and suggests that the action is a basic pattern of human experience, a myth, not simply phenomena, like the adventures of Roderick Random. The correspondences and coincidences, the analogies and allusions, strongly imply the existence of an ultimate reality that man cannot comprehend, an ultimate pattern that contains and goes beyond the whole but which is beyond the vision not only of the characters, but even of the reader. The similarities and differences between Stephen and Bloom operate in the same way. Their communal attributes indicate a common human experience; their differences indicate the particular attributes they represent.

From the time that Bloom leaves his house on the morning of June 16, 1904, to voyage through the city of Dublin, that is, from the opening of Lotus-Eaters until Wandering Rocks, the narrator's focus extends beyond the characters of Bloom and Stephen to include the character of Dublin, which becomes the character of the world. This journey is through the human condition.

Characteristically, it begins in a high-handed way, with violations of decorum. We have been placed on a plane with the characters, and are not expecting much narrator intrusion, but suddenly we are offered hundreds of flower names, gratuitously, it would seem. We learn from Stuart Gilbert that the chapter is called Lotus-Eaters, but that fails to explain it. As Bloom moves through the city thinking and feeling, the narrator is commenting and pointing. The camera eye of Lotus-Eaters focuses on the instruments of the city's disease, on innumerable forms of opiates. Religion, smoking, drinking, and sex, which are sometimes opiates, are considered in the very first paragraph of the chapter. But everything that occurs in the chapter is seen in this light. It is here that Bloom first thinks, blunderingly, about the rate of acceleration of falling bodies. This is the world of the fall, and in it soldiers look hypnotized, Bob Doran drinks to forget his domestic miseries, Bloom concentrates lecherously on the stylish woman simply to bide the conversation with M'Coy, horses eat their way into oblivion, and cabmen have no will of their own. Martha Clifford's letter keeps Bloom's mind off Boylan and Molly and his own actual impotence. Almost every item in the chapter is seen as an instrument that "lulls all pain" (81). The church and its services are referred to numerous times in the novel, but it is in this chapter that religion is viewed as the opium of the people. Not just drugs like chloroform and laudanum but even the game of cricket, even a bath, can be used as a soporific or tranquillizer.

But if Bloom is looking and Bloom is thinking, Bloom is not drawing conclusions. If he were, this chapter would be a Brownean or Burtonian consideration of depressants. It is not. Bloom is unaware of the larger implications of his momentary perceptions. He thinks, life is like that, and ambles on. He thinks the same thing about his bowel movement in Calypso. Bloom is not extending his knowing; he is not looking at a drugged city; he is not aware of the flower names (some of them being used to describe his sensuousness); Bloom does not know that the unofficial name of this chapter is Lotus-Eaters. He is only living, looking. The narrator and the reader know all these things: the narrator is pointing them out to us. In the process, what he points to is pain. The chapter so overwhelmingly drowns us in opiates that it sends us to question why they are so necessary, so ubiquitous. To describe human pain is to risk being sentimental: Euripides is hard to take these days. By describing opiation rather than pain, the narrator avoids the realm (human emotion) he so loathes, keeps his perspective (contempt), but manages things so that we will see both.

If Dublin is a center of drugged lethargy in Lotus-Eaters, it is a city of death in Hades. Not only human but animal death—the steers, for instance—and cultural death—the "dead side of the street" (95)—are meditated upon. Again, if this meditation were written from one point of view and lacked the concrete particulars that structure it, it could be a chapter in *Hydriotaphia*. Bloom is gloomy, and everything he sees reminds him of death. But he is not consciously meditating on death. The funeral itself, the other characters and their responses to the graves of Parnell, O'Connell, and May Dedalus, are contained in a focus that goes beyond Bloom. Everything dies, not just animals, people, and plants, but art forms, cultures, and natural phenomena. The narrator, still maintaining his cheerful demeanor, letting Bloom do most of the work, trots us through a wide variety of the ways death can be viewed, and a variety of forms of death.[25] In the process, the absoluteness and ubiquitousness of death are emphasized: pain and death are the basic elements of the human condition, as these two chapters unsentimentally remind us. Everything else happens in this context.

But pain and death are hardly exclusive to Dublin; they are universal. Thus, Joyce manages to suggest simultaneously the character of the city of Dublin and the character of all human experience. The description is not biased: there are pleasant experiences of opiation— sitting out under sunshades on a blue day watching cricket, taking a bath, seeing the botanical gardens. Death is seen as rest or is regarded with humor when Bloom thinks about putting gramophones in coffins or considers people making love among the gravestones. It is viewed satirically: "The Irishman's house is his coffin" (110). But the overwhelming thrust of both chapters is to show human life as painful and constricted and the human creature as unalterably hobbled by burning ropes of pain, loss, and death.

The highly subtle anatomy of the human condition that begins in these chapters lays the groundwork for what will follow. In Lotus-Eaters and Hades, in Lestrygonians, and to some extent in Aeolus, we are primed almost without our awareness toward sympathy with the human race. So when humanness is attacked and finally abandoned, we draw support and sympathy not just from the humanity of Bloom and Stephen, but from the picture of life that is shown in these early chapters.

[4] *The City*

The chapters Aeolus, Lestrygonians, Scylla and Charybdis, and Wandering Rocks comprise a rough unit. Aeolus, providing the first major break in decorum, lifts the reader away from the characters to show him the city as a whole. It begins, as is proper to an anatomy, with the heart of Dublin, its trams and porter, mail and newspapers: reality and verbal expression of it. In the course of the episode we are carried back to Bloom's side and then to Stephen's; the camera eye moves in for close-ups, then pans out again. Lestrygonians and Scylla and Charybdis focus again on the characters, and the library scene provides our last close look at Stephen. With Wandering Rocks we move up and out again over the entire city.

In these chapters, Dublin becomes as important as Bloom and Stephen, and takes its place as the third character in the plot. Although the city figures in Lotus-Eaters and Hades, it is primarily in these episodes that the substance of Dublin—its buildings, streets, sounds, smells, and motions—is asserted. Just as the early chapters, by placing us within the minds of the characters, hypostatize them, present them as dependable actual persons, these chapters hypostatize the city, make it a dependable piece of reality. Although the city and the characters continue to appear in the latter half of the novel, their appearance is undermined by the narrative voices; it is on the former half of the book that we depend for our sense of their reality.

There is some variety of narrative voices in these chapters. One is the objective, impersonal reporter of the first four episodes, who seems to be the same as the narrator of Lotus-Eaters, Hades, and Lestrygonians, but the latter has become a name-dropper, placing clues like string tied to bushes throughout these episodes. This name-dropping occurs also in Aeolus and in Scylla and Charybdis, but in those chapters there is also a shift in narrational point of view. The shift is prepared for by brief scenes in Hades that occur outside the perception of the character, Bloom. The narrator of Aeolus uses the same techniques employed in earlier chapters, but adds derisive comment and ironic juxtaposition to his devices. The character-narrator of the library scene adds derisive word play and play with form to his bag of tricks. Wandering Rocks adds ironic narration and intercalation to the impersonal narration and also uses juxtaposition, but in a different way from Aeolus. In effect, every narrative device that appears in the latter half of the book is introduced in the first half. The latter half elaborates and develops these devices in accordance with Joyce's incremental way of working.

Bloom's episodes concentrate not only on him but on aspects of the basic human condition: pain, death, hunger. Stephen's episodes concentrate not only on him but on ideas and language, expressions of the human condition as well as part of it. As the characters become less important, so does Dublin, but all three elements continue to provide the particulars on which Joyce structures his anatomy of the human condition.

Aeolus

This is a marvelous chapter, one of the many small masterpieces in the book. It opens IN THE HEART OF THE HIBERNIAN METROPOLIS, the center of the city, with machines of all kinds—tramcars, mailcars, printing presses—clanking away. It moves into a vivid evocation of the society, mind and manners, of the newspaper office, then ends where it began, "before Nelson's pillar," but that pillar will never be the same (nor is it in fact).

Aeolus is a complex network of contrasts. On the surface they appear to be typical ironic contrasts between past and present, language and behavior, potential and actual, as well as thematic contrasts, such as that between Roman and Greek, British and Irish. In fact, however, so many items are involved, and so many of them function in more than one polarity, that it is impossible to delineate a clear pattern in the chapter. This complex relationship among elements is also reflected in the point of view, which is made up of a mutal interaction between the invisible narrator of the sections and the commentator visible in the headlines. They are a comedy team, in which neither plays the straight man. What they are regarding goes beyond Stephen and Bloom, beyond the characters in the newspaper office, to include the city of Dublin and, by extension, human civilization as a whole.[1]

Because the contrasts are so intermeshed, this is a difficult chapter to dissect. It is necessary to explore first the contrasts inherent in the "content" of the sections, second the effect of the headlines, and last, the positions of Bloom and Stephen.

Both Crawford, the editor, and Professor MacHugh extol the past at the expense of the present. Crawford laments the lack of great barristers like Whiteside and Butt; J. J. O'Molloy retorts that there are no longer any Grattans and Floods in journalism. MacHugh goes even further and laments the victory of Roman civilization over the Greek. There are multiple ironies here. First, as these three men point out, they comprise "all the talents" (135) of Dublin. If the press and bar are no longer great, it is because they themselves are not great. But they are not great, they believe, because they are victims, oppressed by Britain: they are the "fat in the fire" (131). MacHugh especially feels victimized. Even Stephen, usually so aware of ambiguities, compares the language available to him—"penitent, leadenfooted . . . mouth south: tomb womb" (138)—with the shimmering language Dante found at his hand. The irony of this is left to the reader to infer, although the headline wryly comments RHYMES AND REASONS. MacHugh rationalizes Ireland's condition by insisting it has been "loyal to lost causes," that it represents the "empire of the spirit" (133) and the triumph of the intellect and imagination. This position is not directly attacked within the scene; in fact, it is indirectly supported by the quotation from Taylor's speech. Nevertheless, what these triumphant martyrs are doing is hanging around an office idly talking until they can gather enough momentum to adjourn to the nearest bar, as it is suggested is their custom. Furthermore, when the editor does hold up one "great" figure, it is the Great Gallaher, the shallow braggart of "A Little Cloud," whose feat, according to Crawford, was to use an advertisement as a map, thereby evading censorship laws. However, the editor really has something special: he believes Stephen to be capable of producing a great work, he predicts World War I, and he knows beforehand about the assassination of General Bobrikoff!

These ironies suggest the contrast between actual and potential that exists in the characters. J. J. O'Molloy, once the "cleverest fellow at the junior bar" (125), has drunk and gambled himself into debt and debility. Liquor has caused the deterioration of Crawford's brain as well as his complexion. It is suggested that MacHugh also suffers from Dublin's endemic disease: he is hungry and unshaven, his dirty hair soils his unglazed collar, and his shirt cuffs are stained and frayed. Lenehan quips that "he mostly sees double" (134). At one point Mac-Hugh is described as holding up two quiet claws, at another, a trembling thumb and forefinger. He is an important character because he is so much like Stephen that he becomes an image of what Stephen would become if he remained in Ireland. The professor is intelligent and educated, gracefully articulate and witty. He loathes the culture that underlay the Latin language he teaches and which underlies the English he speaks. He mentions Pyrrhus, echoing Stephen in Nestor; he brings up Antisthenes, an allusion that Stephen will later steal. He is the one whom Stephen respects and the only one who might possibly understand Stephen's parable. He is even perceptive enough to realize that the parable had been suggested to Stephen by their discussion of Moses. All three of these men, however, are ruined: they have accomplished nothing and will accomplish nothing. The other characters, Lenehan and O'Madden Burke, are contemptible hangers-on. The only "successful" characters mentioned in the episode are Doughy Daw, the producer of popular verbal diarrhea who baked his way to wealth, Ned Lambert, who is saved because he is related to wealth, and the tawdry Gallaher. Bushe is supposed to be a great barrister, one of whose graceful speeches is quoted by O'Molloy, but the editor cannot even remember his first name, and some more or less private difficulty has kept him from rising in his country.

The professor, the editor, and the lawyer are not without intellect, knowledge, or grace. Even the erratic, brain-damaged Crawford is interesting. The paranoia of the three may not be entirely unjustified: there is something wrong in a country where only fools attain power and bright people invariably fail. It is at least deducible that these men are victims of a culture which entertains perverted values. But they are part of that culture. Crawford asks Stephen to write a piece for the *Journal:* "—Foot and mouth disease! the editor cried in scornful invective. Great nationalist meeting in Borris-in-Ossory. All balls! Bulldosing the public! Give them something with a bite in it. Put us all into

it, damn its soul. Father Son and Holy Ghost and Jakes M'Carthy"
(135). What Crawford asks for is something real, something that
sounds supiciously like *Ulysses.* He is momentarily great. But we
know that if Stephen wrote such a thing, it would not be published in
the *Journal,* and when the editor holds up his example of a great press-
man, it is Gallaher.

The contrast between Hebrew/Irish and Roman/British cultures
appears to be wholly favorable to the first pair. The connection between Hebrew and Irish cultures is a continuing theme throughout the
book, handled sometimes seriously, as here, and sometimes comically, as in Ithaca. There is a legendary basis for the parallel.[2] The
theme has relevance to the characters of Stephen and Bloom: both are
"losers" in a worldly sense, yet both uphold a particular excellence,
more spiritual than material, and both triumph in spiritual ways over
their culture. The allusion to Pyrrhus found in both this chapter and
Nestor reinforces the subtle assertion that winners lose and losers win,
that the cultures of Israel and Greece actually triumphed over their
conquerors. It is the defeated Moses, who never reached the promised
land, who was the inspiration for Michelangelo, Bushe's speech,
Taylor's speech, and Stephen's parable, and who is exemplary to the
Gaelic movement.

The various pieces of oratory provide another set of contrasts.
Doughy Daw's popular dough ("All very fine to jeer at it . . . but it
goes down like hot cake" [126]) stands at one pole, the pole of power.
His speech shows Dawson to be as vacuous as any of the holders or
maintainers of power in the novel. The pole of power attracts the winners who lose. At another pole are the passage from Bushe and Taylor's graceful and moving evocation of the loser who wins. But even
their argument is undercut, because of course the Jews did not win:
Moses may have come down from Sinai "bearing in his arms the tables
of the law, graven in the language of the outlaw" (143), but that has
not prevented generations of Jews from being persecuted, or Bloom
from being abused by the very people who acclaim the speech. This
realization lies behind Stephen's parable.

Both the speech and the parable are pieces of truth, but the points of
view behind them are utterly different. Taylor idealizes heroically the
story of Moses, while Stephen uses it ironically, euhemerizing the
story. If one reads the story of Moses in the Bible, one can trace the

dedicated single-minded leader and the chosen people moving massively to fulfill God's purpose. Had one been present during the exodus, however, such a pattern would not have been evident. The prospect might have seemed, to an ironic sensibility, bleak and hopeless, with a muttering, fickle, lice-ridden rabble led in circles for forty years by an unsure, bad-tempered, stuttering leader who kept trying to get water out of rocks. Stephen's brilliant parable of the two Irishwomen, losers in their society, climbing to the top of a pillar that commemorates a member of the conqueror nation and conqueror sex, looking out at a wilderness of churches, and spitting dead plumstones down on the sterile promised land is a fable of *dio boia*, a grim and hilarious vision of an Israel led by the other face of God. Taylor's speech affirms what Joyce would like to affirm but could not. In *Stephen Hero*, Joyce made explicit the aim he chose: "He was persuaded that no-one served the generation into which he had been born so well as he who offered it, whether in his art or in his life, the gift of certitude."[3] But certitude is difficult to achieve in a relativistic world. Stephen's parable offers only truth, not certitude. His vision and Taylor's are mutually exclusive. They are not paradoxical, nor do they illuminate each other, as do the terms of an ironic contrast. The parable is written in the voice that dominates the last half of *Ulysses*, the voice of *dio boia*; and one of the differences between it and Taylor's speech is distance from the subject matter. Taylor's speech could not have been written without a wide span of history intervening between it and its subject; Stephen's parable is written from inside Dublin, contemporaneously with the "events" recounted. Taylor's vision is located safely within certitude about the nature of the universe; Stephen's is not, and having no intrinsic force, it achieves its force by parody, by pointing out the holes in a vision that has certitude.

What the contrasts in the content or plot of the sections of Aeolus finally force the reader to see is the void itself. No one position is unambivalently right, no perspective can contain the whole. The wind is an emptiness, and in this chapter we are weaving the wind. The contradictions are so multiple that more than one narrator is required, so that we may be exposed to more than one perspective. The headlines compound the contradictions of the episode, cube them. They function in various ways, and sometimes in several ways at once.

IN THE HEART OF THE HIBERNIAN METROPOLIS, for example, is funny because of its peculiar journalese formality. It is straight in that it indicates without ambiguity the focus of the chapter: the heart of the city of Dublin. It is ironic as a comment on what is in the heart of Dublin: not blood cells but tramcars starting out from Nelson's pillar. This irony is compounded when the tramcars are later becalmed. But each of its effects is a result of the juxtaposition of headline and section: the effects arise as much from the gap between the two as from their connection. This is the case also in the next section, THE WEARER OF THE CROWN: the "wearer" turns out to be a heap of mailsacks. The disparity within the connection mocks imperial presumptions and, by extension, all human illusions or delusions of grandeur. Through the confluence of items like this, animate and inanimate elements are equated, leveled. This is a mechanistic world, its heart is a pillar erected to a conqueror, and its lifeblood is machines, tramcars. Everything—people, things, and animals—are objectified within it. The leveling continues in the next section, which comments satirically GENTLEMEN OF THE PRESS over rolling brewery barrels, Davy Stephens, and Red Murray working with scissors and paste. The description of the brewery barrels levels men and objects: "Grossbooted draymen rolled barrels dullthudding out of Prince's stores and bumped them up on the brewery float. On the brewery float bumped dullthudding barrels rolled by grossbooted draymen out of Prince's stores" (116). The sound patterns and repetitions emphasize an action in which men and barrels are equal participants. This passage is also a preview, being written in the style of Sirens. Davy Stephens, the mad newsboy, is called "a king's courier": his importance derives from the papers he carries. And Red Murray's scissors are given as much attention as he is.

On the whole, the juxtapositions burlesque the subject matter.[4] The gap between the headlines and the sections serves to mock man's grand ideas about himself, his elevated characterization of his trivial being and activities. This is one effect of the formal WILLIAM BRAYDEN, ESQUIRE, OF OAKLANDS, SANDYMOUNT over the fleeting figure of an important man whose "brains are in the nape of his neck" (117). But because the headlines, which are very much like real newspaper headlines of the 1880s to the early twentieth century, move chronologically, the mockery here is directed not only at foolish self-importance, the foolish awe of the common man for the powerful, and the unworthiness of the powerful, but more particularly at Victorian pretensions to gentility and respectability as reflected in the press. The same kind of mockery is implicit in WITH UNFEIGNED REGRET IT IS WE ANNOUNCE THE DISSOLUTION OF A MOST RESPECTED DUBLIN BURGESS. The euphemism and paronomasia of "dissolution," the hypocrisy of "most respected Dublin Burgess" juxtaposed with the thought of the drunken wastrel Paddy Dignam, the clanking of the machines, and Bloom's shuddering memory of the rat mocks Victorian pretensions but also makes a grim joke of death itself. The headlines toward the end of the chapter, from SOME COLUMN!—THAT'S WHAT WADDLER ONE SAID, mock Stephen's seriousness about his parable and, at the same time, the crassness and crude vivacity of contemporary journalism.

Thus, not only human pretensions but attitudes, institutions, and ideas are mocked, all in the same breath. Imperial presumptions are mocked, not only by THE WEARER OF THE CROWN, but elsewhere, for instance, in the placement of THE GRANDEUR THAT WAS ROME over MacHugh's water closet. ERIN, GREEN GEM OF THE SILVER SEA over Dawson's orotund speech is a jab at Irish taste and the Irish ethos. There is an overtone of this in the juxtaposition of MEMORABLE BATTLES RECALLED with Crawford's crazy raving, and O, HARP EOLIAN with his twanging of dental floss between his teeth: the harp is Ireland's instrument. The aeolian harp is played by the wind and Crawford is Aeolus, so there is a comic allusion to the Homeric parallel as well. A slap at religious formulations of experience appears in the connection of AND IT WAS THE FEAST OF THE PASSOVER with Bloom's confused memory of the Haggadah which ends: "Justice it means but it's everybody eating everyone else. That's what life is after all." This is another preview, for in Lestrygonians the subject is "everybody eating everyone else" (122). The title SAD is a comment on Bloom, mocking his compassion for J. J. O'Molloy and, by extension, mocking human compassion itself. But the content of the section—Bloom's musings on the needlessness of the lawyer's failure, Dawson's lifeless and pretentious speech, the explosive comments of the listeners—seems to justify the sarcasm. Thus, in a small way, we are pulled in conflicting directions here, as we will be in whole chapters later in the novel: we want to be compassionate, we want to be on Bloom's side, especially since no one else in the chapter is, but sarcasm seems a more appropriate response to these items than compassion.

The author does not even spare his own novel: ONLY ONCE MORE THAT SOAP mocks the method of the book, its patient accumulation of seemingly insignificant details, and what is more, the headline is a lie —the soap does appear again later. Not only man and objects are leveled, but times are leveled. The chronological changes in the style of the headlines move like a leitmotif for Oxen of the Sun, emphasizing that all times have their delusions and pretensions, their vulgarity and absurdity.

Bloom thinks "Everything speaks in its own way" (121). In this chapter, everything screams at everything else, possibly so as to be heard over the machines. The effect is a motion of leveling—an intention long recognized in other parts of Ulysses, especially Cyclops.[5] All cultures have similarities with other cultures, all men have similarities, and men have likeness to things. At cultures in their actuality (Stephen's parable), their idealized truth (Taylor's speech), their pretensions (Dawson's speech); at men in their actuality, their potentiality, and their pretension; at human emotions, death, and the mocking novel itself—the narrator breezily, sardonically, joyously thumbs his nose.

The last large polarity is between Bloom and Stephen. Bloom is treated badly by the gentlemen in this scene. Compare his reception in the office with that of the wastrel O'Molloy, who has come to borrow. Bloom is at first slighted by Crawford, then laughed at by the professor and "clamndever" Lenehan as they watch him being mocked by the newsboys. At the end of the scene, Crawford treats Bloom with outrageous rudeness and contempt. Yet in contrast to these mere talkers, Bloom has substance: he is a conscientious and responsible man, and he has compassion. Compared to them in worldliness, however, Bloom is ludicrous: he lacks their presence, their urbanity, the education of an O'Molloy or MacHugh, the assurance possessed by even a nonentity like Lenehan. He is meek, apologetic, and simple, and in the light that Aeolus casts, he does not shine.

Stephen, by contrast, is more appealing here than he has been before. His spiritual movement in Proteus, where he tentatively accepts his participation in humanity, and his acceptance by the "talents" of Dublin relax his manner so that his youth and shyness show through. The professor has a respectable intellect and he shares many of Stephen's attitudes; the editor places trust in Stephen: "You can do it. I see it in your face" (135); and O'Molloy is impressive as he repeats

Bushe's speech. These are men whom Stephen can respect despite their failure, and "his blood wooed by grace of language and gesture" (140), he attains a new perception: "It was revealed to me that those things are good which yet are corrupted which neither if they were supremely good nor unless they were good could be corrupted" (142).[6] Stephen's inflexibility bends a bit further. Absolutes are not possible; they cannot be held up to castigate others, nor need Stephen measure himself by them. Hearing in the moving speech of Taylor finally only the record of a dead world-view, Stephen has a moment of self-pity: "Gone with the wind. Hosts at Mullaghmast and Tara of the kings. Miles of ears of porches. The tribune's words howled and scattered to the four winds. A people sheltered within his voice. Dead noise. Akasic records of all that ever anywhere was. Love and laud him: me no more" (143). He recovers, aware as the men move out toward the street of "Dublin. I have much, much to learn" (144). The thought becomes an inspiration. He thinks: "Dubliners," and begins to compose his parable. He has to exhort himself to act: "On now. Dare it. Let there be life" (145); but the completed parable stands in sharp contrast to the adolescent, morbid, pseudo-erotic poem quoted earlier in the chapter, and to the passage he composes while O'Molloy lights his cigarette: "I have often thought since on looking back over that strange time that it was that small act" (140), a passage that resembles the phrasing of Beaufoy's story read by Bloom in the outhouse. Both the poem and the opening of the "story" stand as examples of Irish art: the decadent airiness of much of its poetry (the poem is taken from Douglas Hyde, who became president of Ireland), and the cheap sentiment of popular fiction. Stephen's parable is good; it is better even than some of the stories in *Dubliners.* It is more concise, sharper, and larger in reference. Like his later Shakespeare story, it is built out of small real details: it picks up the conversation about Moses, the midwives of Proteus, and the pillar that stands at the heart of the city. It is important because it shows Stephen able to act, and also the particular direction he must move in as a writer.

This contrast between what happens to Stephen and what happens to Bloom in the chapter has a strange effect. Bloom is, in the earlier chapters of the novel, far more likable than Stephen, and we are dismayed to see him treated so shabbily. At the same time, we recognize his ludicrousness. The treatment of Bloom makes us resentful of Stephen's warm reception in the newspaper office, yet we are pleased to see Stephen able to act and interact. The derision of Bloom has begun, and at the same time that we laugh with the narrator at the character, we begin to have qualms about mocking a good man, and part of our mind begins to build up a defense of him. That defense will grow as the novel progresses and the derision increases.

While the chapter appears to be made up of easy contrasts, in fact it undercuts every possible position. Nothing in it is held up as unqualifiedly good or bad. The episode points out the gaps between different perceptions, different aspects of the same things, and different characters. Laughing, it pulls out the carpet from under our feet and points downward—to the void. Aeolus weaves the wind into a porous bag.

Lestrygonians

"This is the very worst hour of the day" (164) for Bloom, his lowest daytime point: he is even more depressed here than in the cemetery. This depression occurs partly because he is hungry, his thoughts after lunch being more cheerful than those before. Joyce insists on the integrity of body and mind.

The subject of the chapter is eating, as much a basic necessity as are pain (Lotus-Eaters) and death (Hades). Eating is examined from what seems every imaginable angle, but in its largest and most important reference, it is tied to the theme of eternal recurrence. Eternal recurrence is the nightmare that torments Stephen (history being one form of it) and oppresses Bloom; it is the subject of Bloom's thoughts at his lowest point here, as it is in Calypso. No doubt recurrence was Joyce's nightmare too: *Finnegans Wake* is his last attempt to deal with it, to turn the nightmare into a hymn.

The chapter opens with a list of foods: "Pineapple rock, lemon platt, butter scotch. A sugarsticky girl shovelling scoopfuls of creams for a christian brother. Some school treat. Bad for their tummies. Lozenge and comfit manufacturer to His Majesty the King. God. Save. Our. Sitting on his throne, sucking red jujubes white." From these indigestible placebos, we move to the blood of the lamb and "birth, hymen, martyr, war, foundation of a building, sacrifice" (151), all forms of bloodletting in which man "eats" man. Just as in the earlier chapters all creatures and their activities are regarded as being in pain and trying to dull pain, or are viewed in relation to death, everything in this episode is seen in some relation to food. Religion and state, love, birth, death, literature, reform—all activities and institutions are considered in this light.

For instance, religion and its representatives are discussed in these ways: priests want women to have many children, but large families "eat you out of house and home" while the priests themselves have no families and live "on the fat of the land" (151). Bloom remembers a nun he once met who came from a convent with a name like candy (Carmel) and claimed poverty but "fried everything in the best butter all the same" (155). Religious organizations offer food as a bribe to conversion in time of famine. Even the luminous crucifix reminds Bloom of the phosphorescent codfish and Molly's craving during her pregnancy.

Empire and its symbols are shown in the same light. Bloom considers the royally appointed confectioner, the jujube-sucking king, the aristocratic Lady Mountcashel hunting "uneatable fox" (160), the constables being fed and marched out like a herd of mindless cattle, the revolutionaries against British rule who do more talking and eating than acting, J. H. Parnell "eating orangepeels in the park" (165), Sir Frederick Falkiner and his fellows on the bench conversing after a good lunch, and the exotic fare of the aristocracy.

In this episode even literature is subject to the law of "you are what you eat." The intellectual woman is dowdy because she has "no time to do her hair drinking sloppy tea with a book of poetry" (160), and literary people like Lizzie Twigg and Russell are "etherial" because they are vegetarians: "Dreamy, cloudy, symbolistic. Esthetes they are. I wouldn't be surprised if it was that kind of food you see produces the like waves of the brain the poetical. For example one of those policemen sweating Irish stew into their shirts; you couldn't squeeze a line of poetry out of him" (166). Blindness too arouses thoughts of food. After Bloom helps the blind stripling, he thinks, "They say you can't taste wines with your eyes shut or a cold in the head" (181-182).

Joyce plays the same game here as in Lotus-Eaters and Aeolus, larding the chapter with clue words. He uses food names idiomatically, as in "egging raw youths on," "drop him like a hot potato," "decoy duck" (163), or the brilliant description of J. H. Parnell, "eaten a bad egg. Poached eyes on ghost" (165). There is justification for the accusation, directed against Aeolus in particular with its wind imagery and rhetorical devices, that such word play makes the novel a *tour de force*. But so is a piano concerto for the left hand. There is no inherent weakness in such game playing unless it distracts the reader from the core of the work, which is the charge leveled at Joyce. In fact, however, the word play directs the reader to the core of the work: it points to the thematic line, reminds the reader of the presence of a narrator, and points to the hypothetical core of language itself—a theme to be taken up slightly in the library and fully in Sirens.

The food names in Lestrygonians point to its subject, and Bloom's circling mind reveals eating in all its essential ambiguity. The starving, tattered Dilly Dedalus is juxtaposed with rats drinking, puking, and dying in barrels of porter intended for human consumption. Reuben J. Dodd's son swallows sewage-laden Liffey water. The gulls wheeling hungrily over the river pounce greedily on Bloom's offering. He pities them, "aware of their greed and cunning," and aware that "they spread foot and mouth disease" (153). Oysters are "unsightly like a clot of phlegm. Filthy shells . . . Garbage, sewage they feed on" (174-175).

Yet food is good. Bloom remembers "frying up those pieces of lap of mutton . . . with the Chutney sauce she liked. And the mulled rum . . . Sitting there after till near two . . . Happy. Happy" (156). He enjoys his "strips of sandwich, fresh clean bread . . . Sips of wine soothed his palate" (173); "Glowing wine on his palate lingered swallowed. Crushing in the winepress grapes of Burgundy . . . Seems to a secret touch telling me memory" (175). Most of Bloom's pleasant memories in this episode are related to food, for instance, his memories of Molly. And hunger is unquestionably an evil. Consider the "barefoot arab" (157), poor starving Dilly, and Bloom himself, who is far more depressed before he eats than after: "Must eat . . . Feel better then" (168); "Feel better. Burgundy. Good pick me up" (179).

And yet, and yet, all ends as it began, in filth. Bloom urinates after lunch; the pigeons have a "little frolic after meals. Who will we do it on?" (162); and the cycle begins again. A dog laps up its own vomit; a loafer gnaws his own crusted knuckle; a Hapsburg eats "the scruff off his own head" (175).

Curled at the center of this chapter lie the two themes, relativity and recurrence. The word *parallax*, a motif running through the novel, occurs first here. Parallax refers to the apparent change in the position of an object resulting from a change in the direction or position from which it is viewed. In astronomy the word denotes the apparent difference in the position of a heavenly body with reference to some point on the surface of the earth or some hypothetical point, such as the center of the earth or a point on the sun. The term could have served as a title for this novel.[7] It is analogous to Stephen's modalities of perception, although the emphasis is reversed. Stephen is obsessed with the mode of seeing, the point of view and his imprisonment within it: "Ineluctable modality of the visible: at least that if no more, thought through my eyes" (37). Bloom, in contrast, is concerned about the position of the "fixed" object. Although Bloom constantly changes his position about any center, his interest is not in finding a final position but in understanding the center, whatever it may be. His frustration at not understanding the meaning of the word *parallax* is a comic analogue to his depression at not being able to ascertain anything that remains fixed:

> Ah.
> His hand fell again to his side.
> Never know anything about it. Waste of time. Gasballs spinning about, crossing each other, passing. Same old dingdong always. Gas, then solid, then world, then cold, then dead shell drifting around, frozen rock like that pineapple rock. (167)

Even here a food image—pineapple rock—appears. This paragraph provides another correspondence with Stephen: it is analogous to Stephen's meditations at the end of Proteus about cycles of recurrence ("god becomes man becomes fish"[50]). Later, Bloom thinks "never know whose thoughts you're chewing" (171), which is analogous to Stephen's "dead breaths I living breathe" (50). Bloom's interest is predominantly in objective reality; Stephen's in the mode through which that reality is perceived. The whole process of Bloom's thought could be characterized as parallactic drift. This chapter exemplifies that mode of thought as it glides from subject to subject, always tied (without Bloom's awareness) to the subject of food.

It is the notion of recurrence that oppresses Bloom at the "very worst hour of the day":

His smile faded as he walked, a heavy cloud hiding the sun slowly, shadowing Trinity's surly front. Trams passed one another, in-going, outgoing, clanging. Useless words. Things go on same; day after day: squads of police marching out, back: trams in, out. Those two loonies mooching about. Dignam carted off. Mina Pure-foy swollen belly on a bed groaning to have a child tugged out of her. One born every second somewhere. Other dying every second. Since I fed the birds five minutes. Three hundred kicked the bucket. Other three hundred born, washing the blood off, all are washed in the blood of the lamb, bawling maaaaaa.

Cityful passing away, other cityful coming, passing away too: other coming on, passing on. Houses, lines of houses, streets, miles of pavements, piledup bricks, stones. Changing hands. This owner, that. Landlord never dies they say. Other steps into his shoes when he gets his notice to quit. They buy the place up with gold and still they have all the gold. Swindle in it somewhere. Piled up in cities, worn away age after age. Pyramids in sand. Built on bread and onions. Slaves. Chinese wall. Babylon. Big stones left. Round tow-ers. Rest rubble, sprawling suburbs, jerrybuilt, Kerwan's mushroom houses, built of breeze. Shelter for the night.

No one is anything.

This is the very worst hour of the day . . . Feel as if I had been eaten and spewed. (164)

Nothing is fixed, nothing endures. Not man, nor the edifices he builds, the concrete evidence of history. Even the universe moves through its cycles and ends as frozen rock. We hunger, we eat, we digest, we ex-crete, and we hunger again, yet the process leads nowhere but to death.

In addition, our hunger makes aggressors, killers of us. We must kill to eat:

Stink gripped his trembling breath: pungent meatjuice, slop of greens. See the animals feed.

Men, men, men.

Perched on high stools by the bar, hats shoved back, at the tables calling for more bread no charge, swilling, wolfing gobfuls of sloppy food, their eyes bulging, wiping wetted moustaches. A pal-lid suetfaced young man polished his tumbler knife fork and spoon with his napkin. New set of microbes. A man with an infant's sauce-stained napkin tucked round him shovelled gurgling soup down his gullet. A man spitting back on his plate: halfmasticated gristle: no teeth to chewchewchew it. Chump chop from the grill. Bolting to get it over. Sad booser's eyes. Bitten off more than he can chew. (169)

The scene at the Burton has only one moral for Bloom: "Eat or be eaten. Kill! Kill!" Yet he handles it so delicately, raising "two fingers doubtfully to his lips" (170), pretending to be looking for someone in the restaurant in order to "explain" his departure, rather than offending someone by looking as if he did not like the place or its occupants; this is a typical example of Bloom's sensitivity and grace. Hunger, however, reduces man to an animal as subject to his needs as are the rats, the gulls, the pigeons, the dog, the flies: worse, the predator man preys even on his own kind.

Most of the people Bloom sees in this chapter are pathetic—the starving Dilly, mad Breen and his anguished wife, the blind stripling, Bob Doran, the insane Farrell, the starving boy standing over the grating. Some are simply animals—the goose-stepping constables, the men in the Burton, "no brains" (173) Nosey Flynn with his dewdrop and the lice eating him (it is a typical irony of the novel that the information passed on by this "no brains" is all accurate).[8] The thrust of the chapter as a whole is to plunge the entire human race into its most basic condition—hunger—and to show humanity to be as pathetic and helpless, as cruel and predatory, as the gulls. You are what you eat: but we eat garbage. And in the largest circle, that of recurrence, we too are chewed, swallowed, and excreted.

In this chapter the rather gooey quality of Bloom's sexuality is first made explicit. After watching the two flies stuck together, he has a vivid recollection of making love to Molly on Howth Hill, a memory that is also tied to food and hunger and eating. Sexuality, in this chapter, is another form of hunger: it too can cause great joy, as on Howth, or great anguish ("Me now" [176]), or great humiliation, as in Bloom's ignominious retreat from an encounter with Boylan at the end of the chapter. Of course, Boylan will have to be met—dealt with—eventually. Nothing, no part of the human condition is simple, or unambiguous, and no part is avoidable.

This chapter is written almost entirely in the basic style of the novel. But there is an intrusion: "Dribbling a quiet message from his bladder came to go to do not to do there to do. A man and ready he drained his glass to the lees and walked, to men too they gave themselves, manly conscious, lay with men lovers, a youth enjoyed her, to the yard" (176). This is not Bloom's voice nor that of the impersonal narrator. The tone is derisive: the passage implies that Bloom, needing to urinate, is thinking of himself as a great phallus, capable of lying with a goddess. The phrasing deflates his supposed self-image. The style previews Sirens and Cyclops, reminds us that there are other points of view in the novel, and leads into a section that takes place outside Bloom's consciousness, in which, for once, he is praised. Also the style heralds a general deflation of Bloom in the chapter. In the preceding portion of the chapter Bloom mostly thinks and acts with dignity; in his own way he is profound. Just before this passage he has his most poignant recollection of Molly and experiences anguished thoughts about what he has become. After this passage, with its mockery, he is praised as a "decent quiet man" who "has been known to put his hand down . . . to help a fellow" (178). After he leaves Davy Byrne's, he helps the blind stripling cross the street and receives no more thanks than he got from the gulls. But then while walking on a public street, he slides his hand inside his clothes to feel his belly. The word "no-one" appears here, as it did earlier in the middle of Bloom's memory of making love to Molly on Howth. Also, this experiment corresponds to Stephen's experiment with blindness in the Proteus episode. Next he runs into the museum to avoid meeting Boylan. Bloom must be deflated. Joyce insists he is a man, with the illusions, delusions, and absurdities of a man. Whatever Bloom is, he is not the beautiful boy or heroic man beloved by the goddesses of myth. For a moment he imagines he is. No matter. He is, as he must be, pitiable, ridiculous, admirable, and contemptible, all in the space of a few pages.

Scylla and Charybdis

The point of view in this chapter is very strange. It is less distinguishable than any other in the novel. Although it seems to follow the form of the basic style with a few exceptions—the mock blank verse and the mock drama—it is an extremely derisive style, like the narrator's voice in Sirens. In Sirens, however, the derisive voice mocks every character who appears, whereas in the library scene, everyone is mocked except Stephen. Indeed, Stephen is so self-conscious in this scene that it is impossible to determine whether the following passage is narrated about him or by him in a drama he is composing mentally: "Here he ponders things that were not: what Caesar would have lived to do had he believed the soothsayer: what might have been: possibilities of the possible as possible: things not known: what name Achilles bore when he lived among women" (193).

The mock verse drama, the mock prose drama, the word *Entr'Acte* when Mulligan appears, and above all the word play—"He came a step a sinkapace forward on neatsleather creaking and a step backward a sinkapace on the solemn floor" (184)—inform us unmistakably that there is an arranging hand. But in this chapter Stephen is so busy composing, watching, and manipulating that it is possible to imagine him composing the chapter itself in which he appears, making himself his own grandfather or at least creator. The anguish and sense of failure he feels at the end of the chapter—"Are you condemned to do this?" (207); "Life is many days. This will end" (214)—puts him back in perspective as a character, but at the height of this intense and eloquent chapter Stephen is as much author and stage director as character.

The narrator has donned Stephen's clothes, just as Stephen has donned Buck's, and attributes such an act to Shakespeare: "A player comes on under the shadow, made up in the castoff mail of a court buck" (188). The narrator is permitting Stephen to create *him* so that this chapter has its own form of circles within circles, "wheels within wheels." In Eumaeus, which has generally been taken as written from Bloom's point of view, although it clearly is not, the narrator adopts Bloom's language and point of view and parodies them; here he adopts Stephen's language and point of view and allows those to write the chapter. As a result, the chapter is full of mockery and derision, but not of Stephen. And Stephen appears here under the name of "Mocker" (203).

The mockery is couched in the form in which it will appear in Sirens, lyrical word play. Such word play occurs earlier in the novel: "A corpse rising saltwhite from the undertow, bobbing landward, a pace a pace a porpoise" (50), and "Grossbooted draymen rolled barrels dullthudding out of Prince's stores and bumped them up on the brewery float. On the brewery float bumped dullthudding barrels rolled by grossbooted draymen out of Prince's stores" (116). This technique involves the use of onomatopoeia, repetition, and pun to render the sense, sound, and sight of experience. But it also violates traditional logic—grammar—and traditional meaning: "corantoe" is not a verb, nor is "twicreakingly" a word that appears elsewhere in English: "Twicreakingly analysis he corantoed off" (184). Out of context the sentence would be meaningless; in context it is funny, picking up all at once the creaking shoes of the librarian who is trying hard to be quiet, the echo of his well-intentioned but fatuous utterance, and his effeminate way of moving. In this chapter there is not a single word of direct disparagement of AE, Best, Eglinton, or Lyster, yet we end with a strong impression of their facile ways of thinking, their superciliousness, fatuousness, and that special brand of disconnection found often among intellectuals which is a kind of deracination from their human roots. Part of this impression is caused by the tone of their dialogue: "—Interesting only to the parish clerk. I mean, we have the plays. I mean when we read the poetry of *King Lear* what is it to us how the poet lived? As for living, our servants can do that for us, Villiers de l'Isle has said. Peeping and prying into greenroom gossip of the day, the poet's drinking, the poet's debts. We have *King Lear:* and it is immortal" (189). But part of our impression also derives from the way the characters are described: "said beautifulinsadness Best to ugling Eglinton" (204); " 'History shows that to be true,' *inquit Eglintonus Chronolologos*" (206); "Judge Eglinton summed up" (212); "Mr Secondbest Best" (203); " 'What?' asked Besteglinton" (204). Many of these characterizations emphasize the sycophancy of the group, each of whom seems to be a step in a hierarchy presided over by Russell. "Quakerlyster" (209), who tries so hard to please, gets pinned to the butterfly board nevertheless. He is "softcreakfooted, bald, eared and assiduous" (190). "Brisk in a galliard he was off and out. In the daylit corridor he talked with voluble pains of zeal, in duty bound, most fair, most kind, most honest broadbrim" (200). Mulligan is at various times "Monk Mulligan" (205), "Sonmulligan" (208), "Cuck Mulligan" (212), clucking, "Puck Mulligan" (216). The word play sometimes turns into nonsense:

Peter Piper pecked a peck of pick of peck of pickled pepper. (191)

Leftherhis
Secondbest
Bestabed
Secabest
Leftabed. (203)

Such a technique does more than stiletto the characters: it turns language upside down. Northrop Frye relates word play to lyric, which he says is "the genre in which the poet, like the ironic writer, turns his back on his audience. It is also the genre which most clearly shows the hypothetical core of literature, narrative and meaning in their literal aspects as word order and word pattern."⁹ Words and word order are arbitrary, generally agreed-to symbols for experience; literature is a group of words in a certain order composed in a certain form, also arbitrary and generally agreed to. This chapter uses lyrical word play, expressive of the hypothetical core of language, to enunciate a hypothesis about the roots and nature of artistic creation, which is based on a metaphysic that in turn is based on the void. Wheels among wheels indeed. Fatherhood is a symbol, among other things, for what is passed down by tradition and history in a body of learning, or as Stephen says, "battling against hopelessness," it is "a mystical estate, an apostolic succession, from only begetter to only begotten. On that mystery and not on the madonna which the cunning Italian intellect flung to the mob of Europe the church is founded and founded irremovably because founded, like the world, macro- and microcosm, upon the void. Upon incertitude, upon unlikelihood" (207). The church, literature, and language are all founded upon the void, and this chapter exposes that fact sharply.

Stephen's theory about Shakespeare, filched piece by piece from a number of sources, using and falsifying fact and legend, is a fascinating fiction, but its importance in the novel has little to do with Shakespeare. It is a prime symbol, like the "shrine" cantos of *The Faerie Queene*. First, it is an incarnation of Stephen's metaphysically based aesthetic theory: the artist is a god who creates reality. It also incorporates Stephen's personal problems, identifying them with Shakespeare's, which elevates Stephen and his problems to archetypal stature. Third, it presents a working out of these problems, a course of possible action. The fiction also is patently the solution to the problem: it is Stephen's personal creation of Shakespeare in his (Stephen's) own image. Finally, it provides another statement of the central problem (incertitude, relativity) of the novel. The method and point of Stephen's argument indicate some of the method of the novel *Ulysses;* the derisive narrator and the character Stephen are identical in this episode only; and the Shakespeare fiction is a gloss on the chapter, which is itself a gloss on the novel as a whole.

As usual with Joyce, when stripped of its highly decorated apparel, the argument is simple: "With me the thought is always simple."¹⁰ At the center is the void, incertitude. It is covered by a lid, called reality.

Around it moves the self, able to see only through its own eyes. Anything the self creates is necessarily bounded by its own limits. Not only church and world are erected on this void, but institutions like property rights, which are attempts to impose certitude on things and people. Stephen sees Shakespeare in his own image, that is, as guilt-ridden and frightened about sex, and as believing firmly in his rights of possession of things and people. This image finds some verification in what we know of Shakespeare, but much more in what we know of Stephen. "Amor me *solo*" is the charm Stephen wants, and he contributes to Buck's betrayal by insisting on being loved totally—something no human can offer or demand. The betrayal theme, as mentioned earlier, is linked to incertitude: the only way to avoid being betrayed in life is to be blind to it. Shakespeare is wounded by life (seduction), then betrayed: in the face of this he is driven to act, and does so by using his experience as matter for song. He creates literature from his own mode of perception, in his own image. This theory of creation is largely solipsistic: "He found in the world without as actual what was in his world within as possible. Maeterlinck says: *If Socrates leave his house today he will find the sage seated on his doorstep. If Judas go forth tonight it is to Judas his steps will tend.* Every life is many days, day after day. We walk through ourselves, meeting robbers, ghosts, giants, old men, young men, wives, widows, brothers-in-love. But always meeting ourselves" (213). The artist is "all in all," just as the soul is "in a manner all that is" (26). "His own image to a man with that queer thing genius is the standard of all experience, material and moral" (195).

Solipsism is here related to homosexuality ("brothers-in-love"). But Stephen avoids the pitfall of solipsism by making the first step in artistic creation an encounter with reality, seen here as elsewhere in *Ulysses* as sexual intercourse. The first encounter in the Shakespeare fiction is the seduction, as Stephen sees it, of Shakespeare by Ann Hathaway, the "prologue to the swelling act" both hers and his, and hopefully one day Stephen's: "And my turn? When?" (191). The defloration is the wound in the thigh, the violation of self that becomes a goad driving the artist "into a new passion" (196). The encounter connects with the image of Mary as adulteress rather than virgin; it is sex as sin but also the "portal of discovery." The theme of sexuality is thus linked to the larger theme of relationship between self and not-

self, soul and objective reality. In this chapter sexual encounter becomes a metaphor for encounter with the real (not-self), and one's
particular sexual adaptation becomes an emblem for one's adaptation
to the real. The aesthetes in the library are despised as onanistic or
pederastic, although such proclivities are not condemned elsewhere in
the book:

> He laughed, unmarried, at Eglinton Johannes, of arts a bachelor.
>   Unwed, unfancied, ware of wiles, they fingerponder nightly each
> his variorum edition of *The Taming of the Shrew.* (213)

> The dour recluse still there (he has his cake) and the douce young-
> ling, minion of pleasure, Phedo's toyable fair hair. (215)

> His glance [Best's] touched their faces lightly as he smiled, a blond
> ephebe. Tame essence of Wilde. (198)

There is keenness in Stephen's choice of *The Taming of the Shrew,*
that play of Shakespeare in which the notion of woman as property is
most explicit and most erotic. Stephen's contempt is directed at the
aesthetes mainly because of the asexuality and inversion in their ideal-
ism, their Axel-like willingness to let other coarser spirits do the
living, their romanticization of actual life:

> —People do not know how dangerous lovesongs can be, the auric
> egg of Russel warned occultly. The movements which work revolu-
> tions in the world are born out of the dreams and visions in a peas-
> ant's heart on the hillside. For them the earth is not an exploitable
> ground but the living mother. The rarefied air of the academy and
> the arena produce the sixshilling novel, the musichall song, France
> produces the finest flower of corruption in Mallarmé but the de-
> sirable life is revealed only to the poor of heart, the life of Homer's
> Phaeacians. (186-187)

Joyce's use in *Ulysses* of the "sixshilling novel" and the "musichall
song" provide one comment on this statement.

Onanism and pederasty are picked up later in Buck's song and play.
His bawdiness and mockery of sex are rooted in a repudiation of the
real as extreme as that of the aesthetes. They idealize; he perverts.
Stephen's torment about his own sexual dichotomy is taken up again

in Oxen of the Sun, where it becomes a strand in a larger consideration of one aspect of sexuality.

The polarities usually described as governing this chapter are Plato
and Aristotle, or variations of their emblematic meanings, such as the
"beautiful ineffectual dreamer" and "hard facts." But this is Stephen's
chapter, and his choice is made from the outset. He says, early on,
"Hold to the now, the here, through which all future plunges to the
past" (186). Stephen takes a step toward acceptance in Proteus, and
finds his direction, the real Dublin, in Aeolus. The end of paralysis,
however, requires action, and it is action he considers in this episode.
Action can result in a "sumptuous and stagnant exaggeration of murder," Stephen thinks, and says "The bloodboltered shambles in act
five [of *Hamlet*] is a forecast of the concentration camp sung by Mr.
Swinburne" (187). In this episode Stephen appropriately remembers
Cranly, for there is always, in Stephen's thoughts about this friend, a
strong suggestion of homosexual attraction, and he thinks about the
folly of Cranly's planned "revolution" at the same moment that he
thinks of his own folly in confiding in his friend: "He holds my follies
hostage" (184). Stephen is again engaged in folly and thinks, with
Blake, "Persist" (185).

He makes his problem Shakespeare's as well: "Do and do. Thing
done. In a rosery of Fetter Lane of Gerard, herbalist, he walks, greyed-
auburn. An azured harebell like her veins. Lids of Juno's eyes, violets. He walks. One life is all. One body. Do. But do. Afar, in a reek of
lust and squalor, hands are laid on whiteness" (202). These words are
not spoken aloud: Stephen keeps his real problem private. Again he
silently exhorts himself: "But act. Act speech. They mock to try you.
Act. Be acted on" (211). He finally works it out and speaks, not of
himself, but of Shakespeare: "The boy of act one is the mature man of
act five. All in all. In *Cymbeline*, in *Othello* he is bawd and cuckold.
He acts and is acted on. Lover of an ideal or a perversion, like José he
kills the real Carmen. His unremitting intellect is the hornmad Iago
ceaselessly willing that the moor in him shall suffer" (212).

Stephen's thoughts, a strumming background to his words, summarize the sets of polarities considered in Proteus. These sets are mentioned in a kind of shorthand, alluded to rather than meditated upon.
Items like his desire for sexual encounter set against his sense of sex as
sin, his abortive flight from Ireland set against his exclusion by Ire-

land's literati, above all his still unsure sense of the relation between self and reality—all show that he is still involved in tormenting ambivalence: "I believe, O Lord, help my unbelief. That is, help me to believe or help me to unbelieve? Who helps to believe? *Egomen.* Who to unbelieve? Other chap" (214).

But in fact, some progress is made. Stephen tries, in his own stiff way, to make contact with these men, "begging with a swift glance their hearing." His willingness to open up and tell his story, his concealed desire for their approval (notice for instance how every interruption silences him; he has to be led back to the subject) and his desire for their participation—"Local colour. Work in all you know. Make them accomplices" (188)—make him vulnerable to them. And they wound him twice, once when they pointedly exclude him from a party to which even Buck is invited, and once when they pointedly exclude him from a newly planned volume of verse by younger poets. He watches "in the cone of lamplight" (192), exhorting himself to see, to remember, to listen. He is doing what he describes Shakespeare as doing: opening himself to the real, allowing himself to be wounded, then watching, remembering, piling up details to be used when he creates a world in his image. And at the end he is both anguished and satisfied: "Both satisfied. I too" (210) follows "Are you condemned to do this?" (207). As he leaves the library, he wonders: "What have I learned? Of them? Of me?" (215). Yet all the while, even amid his self-exhortations to action, he is acting: he is creating a fiction about Shakespeare, and an elegant and eloquent one at that, and creating it in his own image.

Stephen in fact takes the three necessary steps out of paralysis in the first half of the novel. Afterward, Joyce said, "he has a shape that can't be changed."[11] Because each of these steps occurs in the void, none signifies salvation, which is certitude. Stephen's acceptance of the human condition is tentative and continues to be an unhappy acceptance; his discovery of his subject matter—reality—is horrifyingly vague, considering the difficulty of determining the nature of that state; and his ability to act in the library makes no easier the other decisions he must make if he is to be able to move into a future. Not only is Stephen not saved, he is not fully aware of what he is doing. Like most of us, he will one day wake up to discover that his character has been formed, has seemingly shaped itself. But again, at the end of this chapter, as at the end of Proteus, he makes a motion of relaxation, a step toward acceptance, toward patience: "Part. The moment is now. Where then? If Socrates leave his house today, if Judas go forth tonight. Why? That lies in space which I in time must come to, ineluctably" (217). At that moment, Bloom passes between Mulligan and Stephen. This analogue to *The Odyssey* is both serious and comic. Stephen and Bloom will meet not-themselves in the course of this day. They will look at each other "in both mirrors of the reciprocal flesh of theirhisnothis fellowfaces" (702). But any final significance of this meeting is moot, for each will then return to self, to the same figure on the doorstep. As an adumbration of a salvational communion, the passage is comic and mocks the reader's expectations. But Bloom is also a paradigm of the direction in which Stephen must move: Bloom accepts his own humanity, accepts reality, and even in the course of the day manages to act with charity. Thus, Bloom incarnates what Stephen "in time must come to."

Accepting ambivalence, accepting even Mulligan, Stephen thinks "Offend me still." He tells himself "Cease to strive" (218). The chapter ends with his memory of the concluding passage of *Cymbeline:*

Laud we the gods
And let our crooked smokes climb to their nostrils
From our bless'd altars.

In the play, the passage continues:

Publish we this peace
To all our subjects. Set we forward: let
A Roman and a British ensign wave
Friendly together; so through Lud's town march.
(5.5.479-482)

The suggestion not made in the novel is that the warring elements in Stephen's heart will ever "wave friendly together"; the prediction made is that as they are what they are, they will be celebrated, as *Ulysses* itself celebrates both sides of every dichotomy, secure in the Brunonian notion that "extremes meet" and form a single, unified circle.

Wandering Rocks

Wandering Rocks is a series of epiphanies of Dublin. Its form is a group of short scenes, seemingly united only by "the pavements on which they occur."[12] The chapter is highly ironical, the irony being achieved by three methods: tone, in the first and last or framing sections; intercalation; and juxtaposition. The intercalations place a passage from one scene in another seemingly unrelated scene. The method is thus contrapuntal, or rather allusive, since each scene is a "theme": themes are played together, or alluded to, within the context of different themes. The form creates great distance alternating with close-up vision: we are far above the city, able to see its interrelationships, but we also swing down close to the characters so that we can hear their conversation and see their physical reality. The intercalations allow us to perceive spatial and temporal relationships not visible to the characters themselves, but above all they assert moral relationships. In other words, we, the readers, can see the interconnections of bits of the city and can observe correspondences among the characters of which they are not aware. And because we are gods, able to see the city whole, we are also able to draw significances from seemingly insignificant details. Each small event, each character is a grain of sand on a bleak, grim shore, although each grain has its own sparkle.[13] The episode is a black mass: the god is hypostatized in many places that are one place (to the eye of a god, presumably, Dublin would be a speck) and at many moments that are one moment (an hour would be a moment to the ear of a god).[14] This is Joyce's answer to Occam's question about how the body of Christ could be present on many altars at once, but the god who is manifested is *dio boia*, "lord of things as they are" (213). Dublin is a land of the dead and dying: every scene, every character in Wandering Rocks manifests disease. This chapter develops the theme touched on in the library scene, because the disease under examination here is the lack of contact with the real, the lack of genuine encounter. Since the latter half of the book clamorously reminds us how difficult it is to be sure of what is real, the episode has ironic overtones that go beyond its borders.

Each short scene is exemplary—just as exemplary as the adventures in a medieval morality drama—if not schematized. There is, however, no hint of a "true" path: this is the world led by a pillar of fire by day and a pillar of cloud at night, the world governed by *dio boia*, "our father who art not in heaven" (227). Lack of genuine encounter has a number of causes: it may be a result of perverse values or radical inadequacy or both. Some characters are incomplete or inadequate because they are young or powerless, or because there is no one for them to make contact with. In some scenes, the reason for the disease is concealed, and what we are given is a portrait of the syndrome. In others, such as the scene in which Martin Cunningham appears, the disease takes on larger proportions, is shown to be part of the institutions that surround the characters. The framing scenes, containing representatives of the two main institutions of Dublin, church and state, show not just disease but total corruption.

Conmee, calculating and worldly, is an aesthetic snob. He prefers, out of aesthetic sensibility, not to see or absorb what is ugly, awkward, or difficult: poverty, discord, and sin. He protests too much that Father Vaughan is a "wonderful man really" despite his "droll eyes and cockney voice" (219). It is incredible that Mrs. M'Guinness could be a pawnbroker: she has such a "queenly mien" (220). The Christian Brothers' boys with their "untidy caps" receive perfunctory notice in contrast to the Jesuitical students.[15]

Because he chooses to disregard the painful, Conmee finds it easy to accept and dismiss the suffering of others: "He thought, but not for long, of soldiers and sailors, whose legs had been shot off by cannonballs" (219) is his thought just after passing the onelegged sailor, to whom he gives a blessing rather than alms. Such thoughts lead the divine to remember complacently Wolsey's famous words about God and King. The steamboat explosion evokes this much sympathy in Conmee: "In America those things were continually happening. Unfortunate people to die like that, unprepared. *Still, an act of perfect contrition*" (221, italics mine).

Don John Conmee manages at once to have contempt for the poor and to remain unaware of it: "Father Conmee reflected on the providence of the Creator who had made turf to be in bogs where men might dig it out and bring it to town and hamlet to make fires in the houses of poor people" (221); "Father Conmee thought that . . . she was one of those good souls who had always to be told twice *bless you, my child*, that they have been absolved, *pray for me*" (222). Neither will he have any truck with sin: "One should be charitable" to the Protestants in their "invincible ignorance" (220); the "tyrannous incontinence" of men is "needed however for men's race on earth" (223). On seeing Kitty and Lynch start guiltily from the bushes, the good man gravely blesses them.

Conmee's tolerance is not rooted in humaneness or compassion or even understanding, but in an aversion to unpleasantness. He likes "cheerful decorum"; he dislikes "to travel on foot the dingy way past Mud Island" (222). The intercalations in the scene are another divine, Nicholas Dudley; the billboard poster of Eugene Stratton; and the dancing master, Maginni, with his foppish clothes and "grave deportment" (220). Conmee is related to the narrator of the first half of Nausikaa: he sentimentalizes existence just as Gerty MacDowell does, and just as Maria does in "Clay." He longs for a past time from which, in his imagination, all grossness has been refined, in which there is only gaiety, courtesy, honor, nobility, and graciousness, and even sin takes on a cast of glamor. The one sin he permits himself to think about is that of Mary, Countess of Belvedere in the eighteenth century, and the sin, comically in this chapter on incompleteness, is an adultery possibly not fully committed, which "she would half confess if she had not all sinned" (223). Honored in the imaginary past as he can never be in this inferior and fleshed world, he sees the cabbages, under a fleeced sky, curtsey to him.

Conmee's sentimentalization of existence is a serious flaw because it affects many others. He is a priest and a rector; his function and that of his institution is partly at least to deal with the sufferings of others. His refusal to look at suffering is a refusal to act in accordance with the beliefs he supposedly holds. His comfortable circumstances, which permit his aestheticism, permit him to ride beyond the "end of the penny fare" (222), are provided by the very people he fails. He is flabby-souled. With the real world, Conmee has no contact: he walks, reading; reigns mildly; and is impotent.

Whatever Corny Kelleher and Constable 57C are discussing is either illegal or immoral. The figure intercalated after the description of Corny and the coffin lid is Conmee, associating the church with death and Corny's slippery calculation. The scene intercalated in the conversation between Corny and the policeman is the unnamed Molly's white arm, flinging a coin. Here the act and person are less important than the object, the coin.

The sailor who has traded his leg for the privilege of begging is understandably sour at his bad bargain, but his phrase "home and beauty" (225), uttered as he moves past the Dedalus sisters, has particular irony, as does the intercalation of O'Molloy, who is doing another sort of begging.

Juxtaposed with the onelegged sailor, one victim, are the Dedalus sisters. The intercalation in this bitter scene ("Our father who art not in heaven" [227]) is the throwaway announcing Elijah's imminent approach. The combination of items emphasizes the nature of God in this world: if there is an Elijah and he does arrive, he will not be able to help the Dedalus girls.

The next scene shows a supposedly sexual encounter between Blazes Boylan and a shopgirl. But there is nothing genuine in it: it describes a series of ritual moves played by a man-about-town and a bosomy "young pullet" who stick to their given roles. The intercalation is Bloom, unnamed.

The next section, in which Stephen appears, is followed by Miss Dunne, possibly the real Martha Clifford. But there is little that is real about Miss Dunne. She lives in a world circumscribed by a typewriter, clothes, cheap novels, and "fellows." She stares out at a poster of Marie Kendall, sex goddess of 1904. She is reading a book in which, she suspects, the hero is in love with a woman named Marion, and she is Boylan's secretary: one suspects a Joycean game. The intercalations in this scene are Rochford's vaudeville machine and the HELY's sandwichmen, as mechanical and artificial as the rest of her world.

The remaining sections have a similar nature. The scene with Lambert, Love, and O'Molloy is a grim comment on the present state of Ireland, and contains intercalations of the face of J. H. Parnell and Kitty detaching a twig from her skirt: Joyce is clearly linking Ireland's economic problems with politics and sexual mores, as well as with Britain (Love). Tom Rochford, the hero, spends his time demonstrating his invention, a machine with slots for announcing vaudeville acts. Lenehan's story about being sexually aroused by Molly is an epiphany of epiphanies of incompleteness. The relation between Dilly and Simon is a hellish parable of father and child, and if the father needs drink, the child too cannot live by bread alone—what little she gets—and, heartbreakingly, buys an old French primer with a penny of the money Simon gives her. Mr. Kernan is often called a small Bloom, but Bloom does not preen himself in his clothes, is not awed by money and power, is not a snob. Simon Dedalus and company have a hail-fellow-well-met camaraderie; united by idleness, love of drinking and conversation, they are witty and jocular, while underneath their badinage runs the anxiety of poverty, the knowledge of waste. Cunningham and the group of castle workers converse with Jimmy Henry in the foreground, damning the inadequacy of the Irish council, while in the background the procession of the lord lieutenant passes nearly unnoticed. Near the end of this pair of sections about Dublin's "respected burgesses" there is a conversation about Paddy Dignam, whom Long John Fanning cannot remember: perhaps a prophecy of the fates of many of these "friends." All of these scenes contain intercalations that provide ironic comment on them. The scene between Dilly and her father has the most disconnected allusions: one to the bicycle racers, the other to Tom Kernan. The bicycle race and the HELY'S sandwichmen are items that thread through Dublin but have no real relation to it. Tom Kernan, the small Bloom manqué, is at least a conscientious worker, and is compared to Simon in both this section and the next, where Simon is intercalated in a section devoted to Kernan. The viceregal cavalcade makes its first appearance in the ninth section, approximately midway in this chapter, and threads through many of the following scenes. In the second half of the chapter, the boundaries of the city begin to tighten as the same people and objects recur in new relations. Mulligan and Haines converse condescendingly about Stephen and "real Irish cream" (249), while the sailor, wounded in an English war, cries out "England expects" (248), the beginning of Nelson's words at Trafalgar, and the Liffey bears out the throwaway announcing Elijah and bears in the Rosevean with its cargo of English bricks.

Mad Farrell and the blind stripling have a genuine encounter: it is physical, it ends with a hurled curse, and tellingly, it contains no intercalation. Patsy Dignam plans to lie to his mother in order to go to a fight that he finally realizes has already occurred. His disappointment parallels the disappointment of the boy in "Araby." Patsy does not understand his father's death; he "couldn't hear the other things" (251) his father said when he was dying. The boy has two things to look up to: the fighter Keogh and the "toff" Boylan. In such a world, Martin Cunningham is complacent to assure his companions that the "youngster will be all right" (246).

Stephen appears twice, in scenes neatly framing Bloom's—three sections before and three after. The first scene, with Artifoni, is an instance of genuine contact. Again there is no intercalation. The intercalations thus function not only as ironic comment on the scenes, but as symbols of the shadow that falls between people, the gap in human relations. The music teacher really cares about Stephen and wants to help him. Stephen is locked in self-pity. He gazes around at the tourists' pale faces, the "men's arms frankly round" the "stunted forms" (228) of their wives. Locked in on deformity, he is unable to do much more than thank the maestro, but even this much contact, Joyce implies, is enough. In the second scene, Stephen sees hell in time: dust faintly covers images of deformity and evil, of grotesque sexuality, and literature that is poison poured in ears. Framed between two intercalations—the midwives and Conmee, emblems of blood-stained mortality and an impotent promise of incorruptible immortality (perversion and ideal)—Stephen strains against himself and the universe, Newton's machine and his own throbbing heart: "Throb always without you and the throb always within. Your heart you sing of. I between them. Where? Between two roaring worlds where they swirl, I. Shatter them, one and both. But stun myself too in the blow. Shatter me you who can. Bawd and butcher, were the words. I say! Not yet awhile. A look around" (242). Patience and curiosity—"A look around"—keep him afloat. He gets caught up in a book of charms and is guiltily perusing one that tells how to win a woman's love when he sees Dilly, and his guilt returns. Stephen's way of seeing in this chapter is related to the point of view in Circe: everything is stunted, deformed, brutal, and grotesque. This chapter, in fact, is closely related to Circe: it adumbrates the Circean Bloom and Stephen; it contains characters who do not appear elsewhere in the novel except in Circe; and it is the day-mare Dublin, complement to the nightmare city seen in Circe. The narrator of Wandering Rocks is showing us moral deformity here, among other things, but Stephen sees it incarnate, in and outside him. Stephen is the only person in the chapter who has any idea of the significance of Dublin's scene.

At the very center of the nineteen scenes stands our hero, Bloom, "mastering his troubled breath" (237) as he leafs through a pornograhic—or at least aphrodisiac—novel. In this scene, he is the equal, no better, no worse, of the onion-breathed, rheumy-eyed, coughing, spitting shopkeeper. The intercalations are the foppish Maginni in "grave deportment and gay apparel" (235) and the "elderly female, no more young" (236) who trips through this chapter. The scene adumbrates the side of Bloom's nature which is "feminine," that is, the masochistic side. His vulnerability is great, and he makes a ridiculous, even contemptible figure, which is especially comic because his scene closely follows Lenehan's "There's a touch of the artist about old Bloom" (235).

The viceregal cavalcade that rounds off this parade is a gem of irony, and another parable of incompleteness. The tone in which it is written is that of the society reporter of a local newspaper: it gushes praise and diminishes anything unfavorable. The reporter assures us that the supreme representative of the British Empire in Ireland is "most cordially greeted on his way through the metropolis" (252). However, the disease of incompleteness that pervades other relationships in Dublin reaches epidemic proportions here.

Gerty's view of the procession is blocked; Dilly sees sunshades and spokes; Farrell looks right through the procession. Some greetings do not reach their object: Tom Kernan salutes the party "vainly from afar," the Reverend Love makes "obeisance unperceived" (252), and Mulligan and Haines, Kennedy and Douce, watch from windows. Some of those who are a bit closer are just not ready for the honor: Richie Goulding and his surprise, the old woman and her incredulity, and Dennis Breen, whose wife plucks him out from just under the horses' hooves. Rochford and Boylan salute a sexual symbol rather than an imperial one. Menton, Nolan, Lenehan, and M'Coy watch with coldness or indifference.

The only close contacts are with watches and mannequins, which are seen to stand at attention, and the HELY's sandwichmen, not quite connected and so incomplete in their way. Marie Kendall and Eugene Stratton smile from their posters. The Poddle river hangs out "in fealty a tongue of liquid sewage" (252). Hornblower, the midwives, some people in the suburbs, Patsy Dignam as well as his collar, offer salutes. Simon Dedalus alone, in a grand gesture, salutes and is saluted in return, in the most damaging comment on Simon in the novel. The last salute is given by the rear view of a pair of trousers.

The episode is given to us to judge, and judge we do. We see a bleak world, grim, contemptible, cruel, constricting, pathetic, and helpless. The nature of the scenes themselves, the associations of each with its surrounding material, and the intercalated material provide many levels of irony and point out the void in human relationships and the moral meaning beneath it. But our response is ambivalent, because we cannot simply condemn. There is an undercurrent of pity in us for poor Bloom and Stephen, for O'Molloy in his haunted mission, for the Dedalus girls. Also we feel affection and respect for kind Martin Cunningham, who functions and tries to do good and whose domestic life is a hell, for Dilly in her indefatigability, and for the two main characters. Because we know more than is shown in this chapter about the characters who appear in it, we know that the chapter does not contain the whole truth. Even from this god's-eye view, we can not see everything.

Thus, the narrator is both omniscient and not omniscient. He knows everything about some things, but disregards others. This limited omniscience will inform the narrational level in the remaining chapters of the novel proper. Reader response is accordingly complicated: we believe and above all enjoy what the narrator tells us, but at the same time we remember other things we know about the characters and the city. The reader is thus required to perform a juggling act just to keep up with the master juggler of all time.

[5] *The World*

Although the structure of *Ulysses* can be described in numerous ways, basically the novel is made up of two large halves and a coda. Joyce felt the division to occur after Scylla and Charybdis, and considered writing an entr'acte to appear in "the middle of the book."[1] Actually, Wandering Rocks is a sort of entr'acte: it is a transitional chapter linking the two halves of the novel. The episode can be included with the first half because its primary objects of attention are still the characters and the city. But it looks forward as well, because Stephen and Bloom are no more important in it than are some other characters, and because the point of view is from above both characters and city.

In the second half of the novel, the styles are more complex, and the characters, the city, and the "plot" diminish in importance. In addition, in the chapters from Sirens through Circe, the point of view resides above the globe, looking downward, in all senses, at human life. The course of our journey can be seen as similar to the structure delineated by the schoolboy Stephen Dedalus when he was at Clongowes (*P*, 16). In the course of the journey that is this novel, we have come far enough to have lost sight of the rock of home; we are in strange waters, or rather atmospheres, in unmapped space. The clamor of critical complaint evoked by the second half of the novel testifies to the voyager's uncertainty concerning his whereabouts and his outrage at being so abandoned by the "author."

Up until now it could be believed, with the minor exception of Aeolus, that the novel does not have a narrator, that the author himself is directly reporting to us the actions of his characters. If Aeolus is viewed as a sort of aberration, it would be easy enough to miss the clues. But the author of *Ulysses* is still securely invisible, and the narrator is still with us and still, in his limited omniscience, scandalously unreliable. Not only that, but he has no respect for the reader and announces his presence by mocking him. The prelude to Sirens announces our arrival at a new landing stage, but it also informs us that the void pointed to in the first half of the book is right beneath our feet.

Sirens

Sirens is frequently censured for its "overture" and because it does not conform to Joyce's description of it as a *fuga per canonem*.[2] But all of Joyce's descriptions of technique on the Gilbert chart are metaphors. For example, "tumescence-detumescence," "labyrinth," and "dialectic" as descriptions of Nausikaa, Wandering Rocks, and Scylla and Charybdis are all figurative representatives of the styles of the actual episodes. There is no reason that *fuga per canonem* should be more literal a description of Sirens than "enthymemic" is of Aeolus, nor any reason to judge the chapter a failure because it is impossible to delineate precisely the eight regular parts that would make it fit Joyce's pretentious description. Sirens *is* a kind of fugue, as are many other chapters in *Ulysses*: its themes are the emotions of the characters in the bar as presented and commented on by the narrator, the actual dialogue, Bloom's interior monologue, and the phrases alluding to characters outside the bar. As these are placed in alternating passages and are juxtaposed with each other, this chapter, like Wandering Rocks and Aeolus, is contrapuntal.

The overture, or prelude, is unusual. Discursively, it is nonsense. In the theory advanced by Northrop Frye that the lyrical mode exposes the hypothetical core of language, he distinguishes two elements in the "subconscious association" that forms the basis of the lyrical mode: Frye calls them "babble" and "doodle."[3] Doodle is essentially visual; babble arises out of sound association; but both can appear as nonsense if they are insufficiently civilized, that is, made subject to the laws of language. By listing phrases, most of which make sense out of context ("A husky fifenote blew"; "Gold pinnacled hair"; "Listen!") but none of which contribute to sense within the context, Joyce reverses the basis of word play that is presented in the library scene, where phrases that cannot stand alone make perfect sense within the chapter. By using language that is for the most part recognizable

English and recognizable syntactic units, yet arranging those units so that they make no sense at all, Joyce is again thrusting in the reader's face the arbitrariness of language, the void at its core. In addition, by selecting and listing phrases that are in fact part of the chapter proper, and then calling them "themes" in a fugue, Joyce presupposes and insists on the existence of a narrator, a selecting, arranging, and self-proclaiming figure. Because it makes no sense, the prelude topples order; it is an outrageous violation of decorum because it breaks the old but, as nonsense, does not offer a new decorum. The reader begins to feel that he is being treated high-handedly by a malicious ringmaster.

There are three styles in this chapter: the style of the dialogue, of Bloom's interior monologue, and of the narrational comment, which at least in some places could be called collective interior monologue. The three styles are easily distinguished. The dialogue is brilliant: naturalistic, slangy, easy, and graceful.

> —O greasy eyes! Imagine being married to a man like that, she cried. With his bit of beard! (260)

> —Not to mention another membrane, Father Cowley added. Half time, Ben. *Amoroso ma non troppo*. Let me there. (270)

Bloom's interior monologue is familiar even when it is merged with the narrational style (slash marks represent the move from one to another):

> Down the edge of his *Freeman* baton ranged Bloom's your other eye, scanning for/where did I see that. Callan, Coleman, Dignam Patrick. Heigho! Heigho! Fawcett. Aha! Just I was looking. (279)
> In liver gravy Bloom mashed mashed potatoes./Love and war someone is. Ben Dollard's famous. Night he ran round to us to borrow a dress suit for that concert. (270)

Bloom's style is distinguishable even when it takes on coloring from the lyrical narrational style:

> Ugh, that rat's tail wriggling! Five bob I gave. *Corpus paradisum*. Corncake croaker: belly like a poisoned pup. Gone. They sing. Forgotten. I too. And one day she with. Leave her: get tired. Suffer

then. Snivel. Big Spanishy eyes goggling at nothing. Her wavyavyeavyheavyeavyevyevy hair un comb: 'd.
   Yet too much happy bores. /He stretched more, more./ Are you
not happy in your?/ Twang. It snapped. (277)

The narrational style is dominant in the chapter. It is used to
describe action and feeling, and to report indirect discourse:

   —O wept! Aren't men frightful idiots?
   With sadness.
   Miss Kennedy sauntered sadly from bright light, twining a loose
   hair behind an ear. Sauntering sadly, gold no more, she twisted
   twined a hair. Sadly she twined in sauntering gold hair behind a
   curving ear.
   —It's them has the fine times, sadly then she said. (258)

   Tank one believed: Miss Kenn when she: that doll he was: she
   doll: the tank. (287)

The merging of styles works complexly: "In came Lenehan. Round
him peered Lenehan. Mr Bloom reached Essex bridge. Yes, Mr Bloom
crossed bridge of Yessex. To Martha I must write. Buy paper. Daly's.
Girl there civil. Bloom. Old Bloom. Blue Bloom is on the rye" (261-
262). The narrator first describes Lenehan's entrace into the Ormond
Bar and his search for Boylan, then Bloom's crossing the bridge.
Snatches of interior monologue follow, then a series of epithets that
both mock Bloom and characterize his mood at the moment, which is
understandably low. Lenehan's peering around is described in a rapid
series of monosyllables, suggestive of quick movement and of a
certain lightness suitable to the lightweight character he is. It also
suggests Boylan, the cause for Bloom's depression. The description of
Bloom's crossing the bridge mocks him for his acceptance of the
situation ("Yes, Mr Bloom crossed bridge of Yessex"). Thus, much is
accomplished with concision: in one short paragraph, the actions of
two people are described, Bloom's thoughts are given (and the reason
for the correspondence with Martha is suggested by its association
with Bloom's depression about four o'clock), the reasons for his mood
are intimated, and he is mocked—for his feelings not his actions.
   Awareness of the presence of the narrator can prevent the errors of
interpretation frequently made about this chapter, even by the usually

perceptive Ezra Pound, who wrote Joyce: "Even I cd. do with indication of whose jag—possibly Blooms it is."[4] For instance, the phrase "Married to Bloom, to greaseaseabloom" (260) is not a thought or speech of the barmaids but of the narrator, who is satirizing both Bloom and them. They are not laughing at Bloom but at a druggist in Boyd's, with whom the narrator identifies Bloom. The lines "Under the sandwichbell lay on a bier of bread one last, one lonely, last sardine of summer. Bloom alone" (289) are not Simon Dedalus' thoughts about Bloom. Simon is talking and presumably thinking about Molly, and the feeling around his words is suggestive: he is thinking about her body as well as her voice. Simon could not be expected to know that Bloom is feeling sad and lonely, nor is there any indication that Simon would be sympathetic if he did know: he has no compassion even for his starving children. In addition, there is almost no interior monologue offered from any character except Bloom.

Most critics focus on Bloom as central in this chapter; that is, they consider the chapter to be "about" him. It is not. He is important, and is central insofar as his is the only mind we enter directly, but the focus of the chapter is emotion itself, of a certain kind. The narrator shows us the bar before Bloom enters it and after he leaves it. The narrator also threads in themes to remind us of the seemingly irrelevant blind stripling ("God's curse on bitch's bastard" [263], echoing his curse on Farrell from Wandering Rocks, is the first reference; later the word "Tap," in a number of variations, tracks the blind boy's approach to the bar) and of the progress of Blazes Boylan from the bar to Eccles Street ("Jingle" and variations). There also are islands within the Ormond Bar, all of which receive narrational attention: the saloon, where Simon and Ben Dollard sing; the bar itself, with the barmaids and drinkers (there is easy intercourse between these two rooms); and the dining room, holding the men who are cut off from the rest—Richie Goulding, Bloom, and deaf Pat, the waiter. Pat, who moves between bar and dining room, is cut off by his deafness. The music unites all of them except Boylan, the blind boy, and Pat, although none of the characters is really aware of the extent of the unity. Simon, for instance, has no idea that Bloom and Richie are in the dining room. While the music unites the characters in the Ormond Bar, the narrator's music unites all the elements of the chapter, weaving the motives clustered around Boylan, the blind boy, and the deaf waiter into the rest. At the same time, the narrator's lyrical language satirizes all the characters. If we have missed the announcement of his presence in the prelude, he reminds us of it often enough in the course of the chapter:

> Upholding the lid he (who?) gazed in the coffin (coffin?) at the oblique triple (piano!) wires. He pressed (the same who pressed indulgently her hand), soft pedalling a triple of keys to see the thicknesses of felt advancing, to hear the muffled hammerfall in action. (263)

> First gentleman told Mina that was so. She asked him was that so. And second tankard told her so. That that was so.
> Miss Douce, Miss Lydia, did not believe: Miss Kennedy, Mina, did not believe: George Lidwell, no: Miss Dou did not: the first, the first: gent with the tank: believe, no, no: did not, Miss Kenn: Lidlydiawell: the tank. (277-278)

This technique is a lyrical style that utilizes word play and many verse techniques such as repetition, alliteration, onomatopoeia, rhyme, inverted word order (anastrophe), anthimeria, and synechdoche and metonomy. It works in a number of ways. By playing with language, it diminishes the importance of what is described. By playing with what is described, it mocks it. In the passage about Bloom—"Bloom. Old Bloom. Blue Bloom is on the rye"—the expression and the mockery of Bloom's feelings occur simultaneously. The mockery attaches itself to feeling and diminishes it just as if we were to say to someone in a tone of highly exaggerated sympathy, "Poor you!"

Everyone in the scene is touched by the narrator's derision. The barmaids are the targets of much of his scorn. They are vain, self-conscious, snobbish "genteel," and totally unaware of their ordinariness and vulgarity. Both their language and their gestures are tissues of clichés:

> —Most aggravating that young brat is. If he doesn't conduct himself I'll wring his ear for him a yard long.
> Ladylike in exquisite contrast.
> —Take no notice, Miss Kennedy rejoined. (258)

After Lydia Douce has smacked her garter against her thigh to an appreciative audience:

> She smilesmirked supercilious (wept! aren't men?), but, lightward
> gliding, mild she smiled on Boylan.
> —You're the essence of vulgarity, she in gliding said. (266)

Poor Miss Douce is infatuated with Boylan. She watches him leave:
"Miss Douce's brave eyes, unregarded, turned from the crossblind,
smitten by sunlight. Gone. Pensive (who knows?), smitten (the
smiting light), she lowered the dropblind with a sliding cord" (268).
Even her sadness has self-consciousness in it, as Bloom notices:
"Bronze, listening by the beerpull, gazed far away. Soulfully./Doesn't
half know I'm. Molly great dab at seeing anyone looking" (284).

The barmaids are presented largely in terms of clichés, and we
recognize that, could they articulate their own feelings, this is the only
language they would know to use:

> From the forsaken shell Miss Mina glided to her tankard waiting.
> No, she was not so lonely archly Miss Douce's head let Mr Lidwell
> know. Walks in the moonlight by the sea. No, not alone. With
> whom? She nobly answered: with a gentleman friend. (281-282)

> Yes, her lips said more loudly, Mr Dollard. He sang that song
> lovely, murmured Mina. And *The last rose of summer* was a lovely
> song. Mina loved that song. Tankard loved the song that Mina.
> (288)

The men in the bar understand the terms in which the barmaids
present themselves, and play their male counterpart roles in similar
terms:

> —That was exceedingly naughty of you, Mr Dedalus told her and
> pressed her hand indulgently. Tempting poor simple males. (261)

The barmaids, as they are presented by the narrator, can be seen in
all the ludicrousness of their illusions, their pretensions, their ignorance, and their vulgar minds and manners. Nevertheless, they are
human beings caught in a constricting social and economic environment. They are lonely, and Miss Douce feels an unreciprocated
yearning. Only Bloom is enough aware of them as persons to show
them human sympathy:

> Got up to kill: on eighteen bob a week . . . Blank face. Virgin should

say: or fingered only. Write something on it: page. If not what becomes of them? Decline, despair. (285)

Thrill now. Pity they feel. To wipe away a tear for martyrs. For all things dying, want to, dying to, die. For that all things born. Poor Mrs Purefoy. Hope she's over. Because their wombs. (286)

Simon Dedalus' manners are more delicately handled, his emotions more gently satirized. His nervousness is indicated by the motif "Chips, picking chips off one of his rocky thumbnails" (261). He flirts with Miss Douce, but his desire is only intimated: "He fingered shreds of hair, her maidenhair, her mermaid's, into the bowl. Chips. Shreds. Musing. Mute" (261); ("Maidenhair" is the name of a pipe tobacco). However, he is martyred and bitter when Lenehan speaks to him about Stephen:

—Greetings from the famous son of a famous father.
—Who may he be? Mr Dedalus asked . . .
—I see, he said. I didn't recognize him for the moment. (262)

He see. He drank. With faraway mourning mountain eye. Set down his glass. (263)

Yet even as Simon is mocked, we feel his grief to be real:

It was the only language Mr Dedalus said to Ben. He heard them as a boy in Ringabella, Crosshaven, Ringabella, singing their barcaroles. Queenstown harbour full of Italian ships. Walking, you know, Ben, in the moonlight with those earthquake hats. Blending their voices. God, such music, Ben. Heard as a boy. Cross Ringabella haven mooncarole.
    Sour pipe removed he held a shield of hand beside his lips that cooed a moonlight nightcall, clear from anear, a call from afar, replying. (278-279)

Again it is Bloom who shows Simon human sympathy. He has no great respect for Simon, but he refuses to judge him: "Silly man! Could have made oceans of money. Singing wrong words. Wore out his wife: now sings. But hard to tell. Only the two themselves" (274).

    Poor Ben Dollard is the jester in this paltry court. He is an object of amusement to his friends and even to himself: "They laughed all three. He had no wed. All trio laughed. No wedding garment" (268). The narrator mocks his gait and his appearance, but the derision penetrates the physical surface to mock the person Dollard is, the croppy boy, and finds him ridiculous rather than pathetic: "He ambled Dollard, bulky slops, before them (hold that fellow with the: hold him now) into the saloon. He plumped him Dollard on the stool. His gouty paws plumped chords. Plumped stopped abrupt" (267). Only Bloom considers his anguish: "Ben Dollard's voice barreltone. Doing his level best to say it. Croak of vast manless moonless womoonless marsh" (283).

Boylan is pitilessly satirized. His greed and selfishness are pointedly drawn when he offers Lenehan the cheapest drink in the bar, and when he drinks: "Boylan, eyed, eyed. Tossed to fat lips his chalice, drankoff his tiny chalice, sucking the last fat violet syrupy drops. He spellbound eyes went after her gliding head as it went down the bar by mirrors, gilded arch for ginger ale, hock and claret glasses shimmering, a spiky shell, where it concerted, mirrored, bronze with sunnier bronze" (267). Boylan's cheap and clichéed self-image—"Come on to blazes" (267)—his ardor—"Boylan with impatience" (267)—and his lechery are all mocked in the brief scene in which he appears. But his complacent self-assurance and cocky callowness are the subjects of a satire that pervades the chapter in a series of verbal motives: "Jingle," "Haw haw horn," and "cock carracarracarra" emphasize his kinship to a cock at the barnyard door. These verbal motives work doubly: they satirize Boylan and they suggest Bloom's torment. They symbolize Bloom's sense of Boylan, which carries with it a sense of his own inadequacy, his lack of Boylan's sort of virility. They reverberate similarly for the reader, who likely feels a grudging envy for Boylan's smug assurance and cocksure ease in the world, and a tinge of contempt for Bloom's inability or unwillingness to encounter his wife's lover. Nevertheless, the reader is forced, in any contest between the two, to choose Bloom with his inadequacies over Boylan with his. Since the reader must choose Bloom as a human being over Boylan, he is somewhat committed to choosing Bloom's way of operating over Boylan's.

It is Bloom who rakes Richie Goulding—the narrator does so only indirectly—but Bloom pities him at the same time:

Tenderly Bloom over liverless bacon saw the tightened features strain. Backache he. Bright's bright eye. Next item on the programme. Paying the piper. Pills, pounded bread, worth a guinea a

box. Stave it off awhile. Sings too: *Down among the dead men.*
Appropriate . . .
　　Never would Richie forget that night. As long as he lived, never.
In the gods of the old Royal with little Peake. And when the first
note.
　　Speech paused on Richie's lips.
　　Coming out with a whopper now. Rhapsodies about damn all.
Believes his own lies. Does really. Wonderful liar. But want a good
memory. (272)

The character who comes in for the most derision is, of course,
Bloom himself. He is mocked in every connection and identified with
others who are mocked. When Bloom is on the street approaching the
Ormond, his name is used as a motif like "Jingle" or "Tap." After he
leaves, the motif "Rrr" (287 ff) suggests the state of his digestion. This
repeated allusion to people who are on the street outside the bar and
who become essentially emblems in the chapter, incarnations of different emotional states, seems to function in two ways. One the one
hand, it reminds us that there is a world outside, a space that is not
steamy and melting with swooning emotions. On the other hand,
since Boylan is moving away from the bar full of triumphant sexual
feelings, and the blind stripling is moving toward the bar full of lonely
sorrow, the existence of inward-turning emotions and sensuality in all
people is emphasized. Even those outside are caught in this sensual
music: the danger lies not in listening to the Sirens but in drowning.
　　Bloom is called Bloowho, greaseaseabloom, Blue Bloom, Bloo-
whoinwhom, ryebloom, Pat Bloom, Bored Bloom, Bloom mur, Sea-
bloom, "Bloom, soft Bloom, I feel so lonely Bloom" (287). During the
scene in the bar, the narrator's derision of Bloom builds slowly,
reaching its climax during Simon's song: "Bloom. Flood of warm
jimjam lickitup secretness flowed to flow in music out, in desire, dark
to lick flow, invading. Tipping her tepping her tapping her topping
her. Tup. Pores to dilate dilating. Tup. The joy the feel the warm the.
Tup. To pour o'er sluices pouring gushes. Flood, gush, flow, joygush,
tupthrop. Now! Language of love" (274). Again the language
expresses Bloom's sensuality and mocks it at the same time: we would
not enjoy having such language used to describe our feelings. The
mockery arises out of a word play that diminishes the content, making
it comic, ludicrous. Always it is the narrator who mocks him, and

because it is invariably Bloom who has compassion for the people in his world, the derision extends beyond Bloom's grief, loneliness, and sensual longing to mock human compassion as well. This attitude is foreshadowed in Aeolus when the derisive SAD heads another instance of Bloom's compassion.

Not only are the characters mocked separately, but as the scene progresses, the emotions of all the characters are aroused by the music, and the narrator's derision reaches lyrical heights:

> Through the hush of air a voice sang to them, low, not rain, not leaves in murmur, like no voice of strings of reeds or whatdoyou-callthem dulcimers, touching their still ears with words, still hearts of their each his remembered lives. Good, good to hear: sorrow from them each seemed to from both depart when first they heard. When first they saw, lost Richie, Poldy, mercy of beauty, heard from a person wouldn't expect it in the least, her first merciful love-soft oftloved word. (273-274)

> The voice of Lionel returned, weaker but unwearied. It sang again to Richie Poldy Lydia Lidwell also sang to Pat open mouth ear waiting, to wait. How first he saw that form endearing, how sorrow seemed to part, how look, form, word charmed him Gould Lidwell, won Pat Bloom's heart. (275)

> Come. Well sung. All clapped. She ought to. Come. To me, to him, to her, you too, me, us.
> —Bravo! Clapclap. Goodman Simon. Clappyclapclap. Encore! Clapclipclap. Sound as a bell. Bravo, Simon! Clapclopclap. Encore!, enclap, said, cried, clapped all, Ben Dollard, Lydia Douce, George Lidwell, Pat, Mina, two gentlemen with two tankards, Cowley, first gent with tank and bronze Miss Douce and gold Miss Mina. (276)

After the singing and after Bloom has left, the crowd gathers at the bar, together in true, if sentimental, unison: "Near bronze from anear near gold from afar they chinked their clinking glasses all, brighteyed and gallant, before bronze Lydia's tempting last rose of summer, rose of Castille. First Lid, De, Cow, Kern, Doll, a fifth: Lidwell, Si Dedalus, Bob Cowley, Kernan and Big Ben Dollard" (290).

Even those who are cut off from the musical orgy are not spared: the sin is feeling itself. I cannot think of anything in literature except "Salmasius'" political attack on Milton that glories in the impairment of another and uses it as a weapon against him, but that is precisely what this narrator does to deaf Pat and the blind stripling:

Bald deaf Pat brought quite flat pad ink. Pat set with ink pen quite flat pad. Pat took plate dish knife fork. Pat went (278).

Bald Pat who is bothered mitred the napkins. Pat is a waiter hard of his hearing. Pat is a waiter who waits while you wait. Hee hee hee hee. He waits while you wait . . . While you wait if you wait he will wait while you wait. Hee hee hee hee. Hoh. Wait while you wait (280).

The "Tap" theme that begins shortly afterward builds gradually into: "Tap. Tap. A stripling, blind, with a tapping cane, came taptaptapping by Daly's window where a mermaid, hair all streaming (but he couldn't see), blew whiffs of a mermaid (blind couldn't), mermaid coolest whiff of all" (289).

After Bloom leaves, we see the group at the bar. Two of the "islands" in the Ormond Hotel have merged and stand together at the bar drinking convivially. Their camaraderie, the closeness they feel as a result of the music, emphasizes the isolation of Bloom standing alone before Lionel Marks's window, of Richie sitting alone "rift in the lute alone sat: Goulding, Collis, Ward. Uncertainly he waited. Unpaid Pat too" (287), of Pat standing alone and unhearing in the dining room, the boots scared and eavesdropping in the Ormond hallway, and the even greater isolation of the youth entering a "lonely Ormond hall": "Tip. An unseeing stripling stood in the door. He saw not bronze. He saw not gold. Nor Ben nor Bob nor Tom nor Si nor George nor tanks nor Richie nor Pat. Hee hee hee hee. He did not see" (290-291). But the Ormond hall is not lonely; it is in the middle of a metropolis and is full of people. It is the blind boy who is lonely and isolated. He has not been shown to have a pleasant disposition: he curses Farrell. But the boy is not mocked here for his surliness: he is mocked for feeling loneliness and sorrow.

Doubtless most people are guilty of occasional amusement at or even derision of someone's emotions: surely we laugh with Mercutio at Romeo. But the narrator's position is so extreme that the reader is forced to rebel against it. By word play and artifice, the narrator diminishes what can be called static emotions—those that do not move outward toward an object, as sex and aggression do, but must be kept contained, emotions like sorrow, loneliness, self-pity, fruitless yearning, and general undirected sensuality. The narrator implies that these feelings are ludicrous, are not deep or painful, that their objects are meretricious. If we consider the Odyssean model for Sirens, we might deduce that the characters who "drown" in their emotions are deserving of contempt, and that those who, like Odysseus, survive the sirens' song are to be praised. But this is patently not the case. Deaf Pat and the blind stripling, who do not even hear the song, are mocked along with Bloom, who clearly survives it (he leaves before the climax of the musical orgy), and Richie, who remains isolated from those who "drown" together. The possession of these emotions alone is ground for attack, makes one a member of a ridiculous circus being viewed from Parnassus. Zeus laughs, but the reader murmurs silently, "Wait a minute! You're being cruel. Everyone feels that way sometime!" But the narrator does not: the degree and impartiality of his contempt for the emotions of sorrow, loneliness, self-pity, longing, and sensuality prove that he is not subject to such states. Thus, he becomes either inhuman or superhuman. Our realization of his inhumanness leads to a corollary awareness: humanness is defined by such emotions. To the set of human necessities suggested in earlier chapters—pain, death, and hunger—we must add the subjection to emotions connected with aloneness. The chapter is comic, the tone is crowing, gaily derisive, but under the surface stand the characters, each alone, separate—the dying Richie, deaf Pat, the blind boy, Bloom, mourning Simon, the yearning barmaids—all of them locked in the aloneness that haunts us all our days.

Cyclops

The nameless narrator who opens Cyclops is unique in *Ulysses* because he is a character in the scene. The vigorous rhythms and vivid diction of his language obscure the fact that he is a walking handbook of clichés, Dublin saloon argot. Like the narrator of Sirens, who also possesses a great store of what Hugh Kenner calls "all the banalities of a hundred tenth-rate operas," he is quite impartial: he despises everyone.[5] During the course of the chapter, he castigates or slanders Garryowen, the citizen, Bob Doran, Boylan, J. J. O'Molloy, the Breens, Queen Victoria, Molly, and Bloom's father, as well as Bloom, his favorite target. In a sense he is omniscient: just as the narrator of Sirens is aware of the private emotions of all the characters in the Ormond Bar, the nameless one knows the dirt about everyone in Dublin. It will not do to ask how he comes to know so much, although some explanation is offered for certain pieces of his knowledge. He is not a realistic character, despite the naturalism of his language. Close observation reveals that he is far too bright, far too absolute in his cynicism, and far too alive in his language—despite all its clichés—to be what he is supposed to be.

The tone of the chapter is set by the nameless one, who hovers on the fringes of the scene, commenting with a scurrility befitting Thersites, and the citizen, who sits hugely in its center, hurling out curses and prophecies. This episode is Joyce's *Iliad*.[6] Between these two aggressive forces flows the spirited if almost ritualistic patter of the pub, of Dublin's drinkers, of any strictly male bar. This world is as male as the world of Nausikaa is female, and as hackneyed in its interests and attitudes. Although the pub at large lacks the animus of the citizen, it does share his basic aggressiveness. Whatever the private emotions of its occupants, the atmosphere of Kiernan's precludes any expression of sympathy, compassion, tenderness, or love; such feelings would be—and are—ridiculed here.[7] Cyclops is about war, aggression.

It is in Sirens, which concerns itself with inward or static emotions, the emotions clustered about aloneness, that the songs are sung which adumbrate the themes of the next two chapters. Cyclops is about war, and Nausikaa about love. Sirens seems to have a full cast of characters of both genders, even though only two females are actually present in the scene, partly because so much attention is given by the narrator to those two, and partly because females like Molly, "Martha" (Clifford and the aria), and the dead May Dedalus are central to male thinking and feeling. Females are almost totally absent from Cyclops, however, and males are almost totally absent from Nausikaa. In both chapters, Bloom represents the absent balancing principle, which is another expression of his androgyny. These three chapters are linked with Circe, which brings to light secret or hidden emotions, and which not only includes many characters of both genders, but makes Bloom's androgyny explicit. The four chapters together constitute the unit of the novel that deals with emotion.

Lestrygonians, in a spin-off from its main theme, touches on the violence implicit in the maintaining of biological life; Cyclops deals specifically with human violence and aggression—to other humans, to vegetation, and to animal life. Included in the larger topic are various kinds of legal aggression (or contest) and transgression (crime), sports, moral transgression, violence against nature and animals, and the violence of the state against transgressors (hangmen, hanging, discipline in the navy), as well as the more familiarly recognized forms of aggression, such as anger, physical violence, and war.

As in Sirens, it is Bloom who gets most of the attention, Bloom whom the citizen most berates, the cynical narrator most derides, the interpolations most mock, and of course it is Bloom who, in this chapter on aggression, is attacked with violence. Wayne Booth describes the narrator of Cyclops as "so obviously hostile to Bloom as to stir up sympathy for him."[8] Certainly the pervasive hostility to Bloom has this effect, but it should not be overlooked that even Bloom is aggressive in this chapter: he argues, even finally taunts.

The chapter has two main lines. One reveals the pervasiveness of aggressive tendencies, fixes them firmly within the human condition, as necessary and basic as is the need to eat. Although some forms of aggression are ludicrous, some hideous, some unnecessary, the thing itself is inevitable. Some forms of eating too are ludicrous, hideous, and unnecessary. The second main line of the chapter is a running commentary on the first: it concentrates on language as action, as creator of the event. Thus, some violent events are ceremonialized by language and appear nonviolent or ritualistic; some nonviolent events are turned by language into violent ones.

At the center of the chapter is the actual scene with its actual dialogue. The discussion in Barney Kiernan's is concerned throughout with aggression, but in fact, until the end of the episode, there is no aggressive physical action beyond that required to raise a glass. To an insensitive observer, such a scene might appear peaceful, a typical afternoon at a pub. The difficulty in differentiating that which can be called aggression from that which cannot is built right into the actual scene. The citizen's speeches, for instance, are ineffectual in context: no one listens to him. If, however, he were standing on a podium with a cheering crowd beneath him, they would have to be termed action. The connection of word and act that is suggested in the library chapter is here linked with human aggression, and the difficulty in separating word and act is linked to the difficulty in determining what is aggressive.

The actual scene as it appears in dialogue carries the first line or purpose of the episode, presenting a variety of attitudes and behaviors which are common in everyday life but which in the context of the entire chapter take on a strongly aggressive coloration. The linguistic theme is carried by the two narrators. The in-scene narrator, Thersites, is responsible for turning apparently nonviolent events into violent ones; the off-scene narrator, who is responsible for the interpolations, transforms the actual scene in a variety of ways. He may turn it into myth, travel guide, nursery rhyme, or journalism; in any case he refutes the naturalism of the scene and, when he deals with violence, invariably ceremonializes it, transforms it into some form of ritual.

The vivid language of Thersites opens the episode *in medias res*, with an accidental and unconsummated act of violence: the sweep almost driving his broomstick into the narrator's eye. Although this act can be seen, like Bloom's "knockmedown cigar" (305), as merely a comic reference to the Homeric material, it has a serious implication. There is a relation between an accidental gesture or a mere cigar and the intentional gesture and the weapon involved in the violence of Odysseus in Polyphemus' cave. The in-scene narrator then moves to the ironic situation of a "fallen" sponger acting as a collector of bad debts for a Jewish merchant against a "bloody big foxy thief," Geraghty. The merchant's Jewishness makes him an object of contempt to Thersites: "Jesus, I had to laugh at the little jewy getting his shirt out" (292). The in-scene narrator's language makes the situation of a bad debt sound far more physically active and vivid than it would likely be.

His bias is opposed by the antithetical bias of the off-scene narrator. Thersites' account of the conflict between Herzog and Geraghty is interrupted by the appearance of a legal contract. This document signals the appearance of the second narrator, who drains the event of all life by presenting it in a ritualized form, a legal contract. Contracts imply aggression, since their purpose is to provide legal recourse against default; they are based on man's distrust of his fellow, which in this case is fully merited. But the juxtaposition of the two descriptions—that of Thersites and that of the contract—of the same event, indicates the subject matter and the method of this chapter. Nonpayment of a debt is an act of aggression against property. The in-scene narrator makes it sound like physical and emotional assault; the off-scene narrator makes it sound like dry, dusty, and formal procedure. Cyclops thus adumbrates the method and a theme of Oxen of the Sun, by pointing to the void between word and act. Most readers are inclined to take the nameless one's description of the scene in Kiernan's as accurate, as bearing the stamp of certitude. But it is no less biased and no more accurate than that of the off-scene narrator. It is the second, after all, who offers us Bloom's apotheosis.

The scene continues with a brief discussion of politics with reference to the citizen as a robber—the "rapparee," "Rory of the hill" (295), the near-throttling of Garryowen, and the interpolated description of the citizen, followed by the first mention of Bloom. The citizen reads out with disgust from the births and deaths columns in a workingman's newspaper the non-Irish names, obscenely mispronouncing the English Coburn as Cockburn. Both birth and death are violent acts, no matter how they occur, and apparently the non-Irish have no business performing them on Irish soil.[9] Bergan pops in with the story of the postcard. Whoever sent it (possibly Bergan himself) was committing an aggressive act against poor mad Breen—a fact that Breen is aware of even in his lunacy. Although the story is funny, we are also aware—probably because of the pity we feel for Josie Breen when Bloom meets her earlier in the day—of the unkind aspects of the action. But the comedy is stronger: we laugh, we do not clack our tongues. And that is like giving a toenail to the devil: he is bound to claim more; we have admitted an alliance with him. Our laughter includes us as participants in the general human aggressiveness. This is part of the way in which the chapter operates to capture the reader. Every time we laugh at violent language or a violent scene, we are countenancing some form of aggression. If we laugh at the execution scene, for instance, we are to some degree laughing at execution. This knowledge operates within us almost subliminally, and we end by projecting our contempt for our own aggressive tendencies onto the characters within the scene.

Death appears with Paddy Dignam's ghost, in an interpolation by the off-scene narrator, and again we find ourselves laughing, this time at death itself, or at least at the dead man's mock-Sanskrit assurances of the presence in the next world of all the comforts of home, "such as tālāfānā, ālāvātār, hātākāldā, wātāklāsāt" (301), and his unheavenly concern about that other boot under the commode. Immediately afterward, Bob Doran names *dio boia*: "Who said Christ is good? . . . He's a bloody ruffian" (302). The in-scene narrator digs at Bob Doran by revealing—to the reader, not to his companions—another sordid side of poor Doran's life. Yet Doran, drunk "and mournful and with a heavy heart . . . bewept the extinction of that beam of heaven" (303).

At Bloom's entrance, Garryowen growls, and the subject matter of the conversation turns even more violent. Rumbold the hangman —who disgusts even the citizen, probably not because he kills but because he works for the wrong Establishment—is described in the style of late medieval translations of the Bible. The subject of hanging leads into the first satire on Bloom. He is mocked for his talkativeness and his pseudoscientific knowledge, but basically he is scorned for his ignorance of how to behave at a pub—or cocktail party—that is, how to repeat clichés and trivialities, pretend to *machismo*, be one of the boys. It is Bloom's great fault, whether the boys are the men in the local pub, Blazes Boylan, or the students in the refectory, that he never learns to act like one of the club, the locker-room gang. He remains insistently "the new womanly man" (493).

Paddy Dignam's insurance—another swindle, this one accidental and reminiscent of Cowley's situation—recalls Bloom's "criminal" past. Bob Doran's drunken farewell is rendered in polite eighteenth century dialogue and becomes something quite different from what precedes it. Bob Doran really seems to care about Dignam's death: he may, like Homer's maidens, be weeping for himself, but he expresses gentle feeling. No one else does. A naturalistic rendering of his behavior could never express that side of him. However, the eighteenth century might well have transformed a drunkard's weepiness into polite conversation. And the whole is undercut by the in-scene narrator's account of Doran drunk in a brothel.

Both narrators take turns getting Bloom, the one by a scurrilous invasion of Bloom's privacy and an attack on him for being a know-it-all, the other by praising Bloom in nonsense and child's primer prose: "Ga Ga Gara. Klook Klook Klook. Black Liz is our hen. She lays eggs for us. When she lays her egg she is so glad. Gara. Klook

Klook Klook. Then comes good uncle Leo. He puts his hand under black Liz and takes her fresh egg. Ga ga ga ga Gara. Klook Klook Klook" (315). The conversation about Nanetti introduces an interpolation, comprising a parliamentary debate concerning the slaughter of animals which moves to the slaughter of humans. There has to be argument even about sport, which is supposed to provide sublimation for human aggressive impulses. The citizen immediately places a standard on sport, opposing "Irish sport," the heavy shot put, to "shoneen games the like of the lawn tennis." It is a pleasant irony that tennis uses the word "love" in its scoring. J. V. Kelleher also tells me that tennis was banned as a foreign game by the Gaelic Athletic Association, which Michael Cusack, the model for the citizen, helped to found.

The citizen's pugnacious approach to the question of games and the in-scene narrator's rage at Bloom's talkativeness provide an amusing juxtaposition with the subsequent interpolation, a journalese account of "a most interesting discussion" (316). The first mention of the boxing match brings up Boylan's name, and from this moment the tension in the pub begins to rise. Bloom naturally supports tennis and maneuvers the conversation away from Blazes. The interpolator presents us with a journalese account of a fairly bloody fight that sounds, because of its language, like a ritual dance in which all blood spilled came from a ketchup bottle. The dislike for Bloom of the citizen and the in-scene narrator exists even before he enters the pub, but there is no sign up until this point that it will issue in open conflict. However, from the mention of Boylan, the conversation moves to the tour, and the on-stage narrator, with his unerring nose for scandal, leaps to an image of Boylan as swindler and adulterer, and Bloom as cuckold. Adultery fits into the category of aggression, for it is legally a crime in some places and is generally regarded as a defiance of moral law. The off-stage narrator then describes Molly in epic terms as fulfilling the Homeric requirements for *arete* in a human woman: beauty and chastity. The interpolation is not parodic; rather, it expresses a way of seeing Molly that is both true to part of her and characteristic of the methods of describing women in certain eras.

After another interpolation, the conversation returns to Breen and the possibility of a lawsuit, legal contention being controlled aggression, and the citizen begins his driving, persistent assault on Bloom.

His Jewishness is under attack, and this brings in the Canada swindle case, in discussion of which there is tacit anti-Semitism. Our Thersites provides nastiness about the Breens and about the swindle, but the conversation moves to the one act of compassion described in the chapter, which may in fact be disguised anti-Semitism: the judge's remission of a poor man's debt. The interpolator immediately jumps into the gap, however, and describes, in the style of Malorian romance, an opposite example of Falconer as a punishing judge in a case where punishment seems uncalled for and irrelevant.

The citizen drives on obsessively. All elements are in place: Boylan, Molly, anti-Semitism. Bloom intelligently, with self-control, ignores his remarks. The citizen does not stop. Echoing Deasy, he gives vent to what is essentially misogyny, which in Joyce's work is the equivalent of life denial, and the conversation moves on to sex. Typically, it is sex as attached to violence that is considered.

Nolan's entrance diverts the conversation to politics; the citizen's hatred drives forward, overwhelming Nolan's and Bloom's moderate views. The citizen's speeches give way to a discussion of the persecution of blacks, of discipline in the name of law, and of "legitimate" violence, leading into the core statement of the chapter: "They believe in rod, the scourger almighty, creator of hell upon earth and in Jacky Tar, the son of a gun, who was conceived of unholy boast, born of the fighting navy, suffered under rump and dozen, was scarified, flayed and curried, yelled like bloody hell, the third day he arose again from the bed, steered into haven, sitteth on his beamend till further orders whence he shall come to drudge for a living and be paid" (329). This is not only a brilliant parody of the Apostles' Creed but a true prayer to *dio boia*, lord of things as they are. It also emphasizes the connection between violence and man's deepest impulses, even his spiritual ones.

With this climax, Bloom speaks out: "—But, says Bloom, isn't discipline the same everywhere? I mean wouldn't it be the same here if you put force against force?" (329). In response to this question, the narrator has a paroxysm of frustration, the irony of his own statement eluding him, the citizen attacks, and the whole company joins in an orgy of hatred, similar to the musical orgy in Sirens and the orgasm in Nausikaa, not just against England but against Irish priests, France, and finally all of Europe. The narrator chuckles to himself over a slanderous story about Victoria, but in the face of all this group hate,

Bloom will not shut his mouth: "—Persecution, says he, all the history of the world is full of it. Perpetuating national hatred among nations" (331). Bloom has literally taken the cross upon himself. He may not have the intellect, knowledge, or eloquence necessary to argue his case, and it unquestionably is a difficult case to support pragmatically. But any man who tries to stand up for such a moral position in such a situation has to have courage and conviction, not to say foolhardiness. Bloom gets the contemptuous response he might have expected, as the citizen spits a "Red bank oyster" (331). The off-stage narrator, describing the handkerchief used to wipe off the citizen's spit, gives us a list of Irish beauties, which comically undercuts the earlier speeches of the citizen by including such things as "a bogoak sceptre," the workhouse, "Tullamore jail," "the Henry Street Warehouse," and "*St. Patrick's Purgatory*" (332).

Bloom pushes on indefatigably, then suddenly collapses as John Wyse Nolan prods him: "Right . . . Stand up to it then with force like men" (333). Critics like Stanley Sultan and Darcy O'Brien, who insist that Bloom's salvation resides in his regaining of manliness, overlook this crucial scene in their interpretation of Joyce's intentions.[10] Bloom collapses in the face of Nolan's statement, but not out of fear, defeat, or cowardice. He, a nonpugnacious Jew in a den of bigoted Christians, has just singlehandedly taken on the entire pub. His collapse is one of conviction. Injustice exists, but forceful methods of attempting to eliminate it only exacerbate it:

> —But it's no use, says he. Force, hatred, history, all that. That's not life for men and women, insult and hatred. And everybody knows that it's the very opposite of that that is really life:
> —What? says Alf.
> —Love, says Bloom. I mean the opposite of hatred. (333)

After this statement Bloom leaves briefly, but he does not do so in order to run away; he is not cowed by the opposition to him; he is not ashamed of what he has said. He leaves in the same way he leaves the newspaper office in the morning, just as brisk and apologetic as ever. Except at the very end, his behavior throughout this scene is marked by restraint, courage, and dignity as well as by his usual moral fineness.

Yet the whole pub has turned against him. The in-scene narrator mocks, "Who's hindering you?" and the citizen scornfully announces "A new apostle to the gentiles." Nolan alone gives Bloom any support. The off-stage narrator prances Buck Mulligan style: "Love loves to love love" (333). The citizen then attacks Bloom's argument by citing abuses of it, which is a familiar way of defeating an essentially irrefutable moral position. Aggression, in the form of imperial exploitation, continues to be the subject. The Gold Cup comes up, and Bloom's fate is sealed. The discussion that follows makes clear that Bloom is held in contempt for no explicit reason. The drinkers suspect that he won on the race, yet he does not treat for drinks nor drink himself, a profound insult to drinkers. He is accused, on no grounds, of all kinds of swindles, of spying or drawing up plans for Griffith, of defrauding orphans and widows. Almost in one breath he is accused of being unduly lecherous (ironically, just after our scurrilous narrator has departed to urinate and along the way given us the secret scandal about himself—he has the clap): "I wonder did he ever put it out of sight," and of being impotent: "And who does he suspect?" (338). His difference, his Jewishness, is held against him far more than Crofton's Protestantism is held against him. The essential difference between Bloom and other men is rooted in his different sense of what is human and, in particular, what is masculine. The two qualities of "manliness" that Bloom most obviously lacks are a pride in physical prowess, with the concomitant willingness to engage in physical violence, and an assumption of superiority over women, or at least over one's wife. In this episode Joyce clearly contrasts him with other males, who find him not fully male. But if Bloom were willing to give lip service to the same standards of aggressive behavior that the others in the pub claim to hold, he would be accepted, Jew or not, drinker or not, cuckold or not. Nolan, a fully licensed member of the club, is cautious and moderate in his defense of Bloom. The in-scene narrator makes explicit that Bloom's sin is insufficient maleness:

> —Well, there were two children born anyhow, says Jack Power.
> —And who does he suspect? says the citizen.
> Gob, there's many a true word spoken in jest. One of those mixed middlings he is. Lying up in the hotel Pisser was telling me once a month with headache like a totty with her courses. Do you know what I'm telling you? It'd be an act of God to take a hold of a fellow the like of that and throw him in the bloody sea. (338)

The ironies here are numerous, for Bloom is currently impotent with Molly at least, although he did father their children, and it is his guilt over Rudy's defectiveness that has caused his present condition.

Martin Cunningham tries to deflect the hostility, and the godly company is duly and ceremoniously blessed in preparation for their campaign. Bloom returns, and the scene races to its exuberant close. The off-stage narrator relates the event as a triumphant departure and as an earthquake; the in-scene narrator relates it in his usual violent language, full of contempt for the citizen, for Garryowen, and for Bloom. The off-state narrator chimes in at the conclusion with a description of a Biblical apotheosis but ends with more mundane details: "And they beheld Him even Him, ben Bloom Elijah, amid clouds of angels ascend to the glory of the brightness at an angle of fortyfive degrees over Donohoe's in Little Green Street like a shot off a shovel" (345).

The analogy between Bloom and Elijah is comic burlesque and serious truth: while Bloom lacks the force of the Biblical Elijah, he lacks also his prototype's hatred. The analogy confers Elijah's glory on a man who has no claims to superhumanness, and is an affirmation less of Bloom than of a way of thinking, a way of being. Bloom is ridiculous; compared to the citizen, he is "the new womanly man," but he is also an unconquered hero.

The antithetical movement of the chapter is developed by the interpolations, which work to transform whatever the reality of the scene may be into a recognized linguistic form. Many of the interpolations are written in a twentieth-century reportorial style; in fact, the chapter contains a newspaper in miniature, with a sports column (the boxing match); reports of a debate, a hanging, an earthquake, and a religious ceremony; special features on a famous handkerchief, ancient Gaelic sports, and physical culture; a literary column on canine verse; a society page devoted to a wedding and a farewell ceremony; and a science page devoted to the findings of Bloom alias Herr Professor Luitpold Blumenduft. The legal contract could appear in the legal announcements column of a newspaper. To complete this journal, the citizen reads out, in the scene, the births and deaths listed in *The Irish Independent*.

The other styles parodied range from nonsense baby-talk and children's books to eighteenth-century polite conversation, Malorian romance, Elizabethan dialogue, the Apostles' Creed, and the Bible, to parodies of Homeric, Roman, and Irish epic. The interpolations thus adumbrate the technique of Oxen of the Sun, although in Cyclops the various styles are for the most part parodies rather than imitations, and are not chronologically ordered.

The second narrator has the most interesting role in the chapter because his comments have such a variety of effects. One effect is the leveling of all times and cultures. For instance, the second interpolation is a parody of Irish literature that uses Irish myth as its base.[11] Its first lines could easily be taken not as parody but as imitation of myth/legend/romance: "In Inisfail the fair there lies a land, the land of holy Michan. There rises a watchtower beheld of men afar. There sleep the mighty dead as in life they slept, warriors and princes of high renown. A pleasant land it is in sooth of murmuring waters" (293). Unless one is alert enough to find amusing the image of warriors sleeping through life, "fishful streams" is the first hint that comedy is to follow. The comedy begins when the list of fish passes three or four, and it is heightened by the changed diction of "the *mixed coarse fish generally* and other *denizens* of the *aquaeous kingdom* too *numerous to be enumerated*" (italics mine throughout this section); which sounds more like the language of a bad reportage, a tourist guide, a poor encyclopedia, or a special feature in a newspaper than like the language of literature: "In the mild breezes (of the west and of the east) the lofty trees wave (in different directions) their first class *foliage*" (294; parentheses mine). The technique here is a mixture of incongruity and pedantry. The phrase "first class" is incongruous with the opening style and, when used adjectivally, is very declassé. The parenthetical elements are pedantic additions, attempts to confer precision to the "picture" drawn by a narrator so dense he does not know that images are not helped by this kind of precision. "Foliage" is also indecorous in the mythic style.

There follows a list of trees that are not endemic to Ireland at all, then a series of words and phrases that could come from a guidebook or encyclopedia but never from a myth: "wafty," "eugenic," "ornaments of the arboreal world with which that region is thoroughly well supplied" (294). The repetition of the word "lovely" in the next sentence parodies not only romance epic techniques (*lovely* is a frequent word in Spenser) but guidebook style as well; the repetition leads directly into another overfilled catalogue.

This is a complicated technique. The comic principle is mainly

Rabelaisian inflation: superfluity of detail coupled with various kinds of incongruity. Superfluity of detail and enjambment of incongruous styles or items, as well as repetition, are characteristics both of the novel as a whole and of this chapter in particular. The interpolations are incongruous when juxtaposed with the "naturalistic" scene. The linking of the high style (myth), the epic (catalogues), and the common written language of the twentieth century press and commerce (journalese) provides a series of undercuttings: the mythic passages are lovely until they are undercut by the catalogues; catalogues are serious things in Homer but mechanical here, and funny as they slide into travel-guide journalese; the journalese passages are funny in their use of Latinate words and declassé phrases, but their artificiality, their attempt to sound "intellectual" or educated, in the manner of a freshman theme, is underscored when they are followed by racy, naturalistic dialogue. The dialogue is funny by itself, but funnier when it is followed by the simple archaic language of the "mythic" style—and we go round the circle again. There is nothing good that cannot be corrupted, and likely there has never existed on earth a good that has not been corrupted. David Daiches points out that the effect of the interpolations in the Cyclops scene is to level all times and cultures.[12] The reason is that each style or technique slides into a corruption of itself. The actual scene gains in liveliness by the contrast in styles, and older forms lose their sanctity. At the same time, the liveliness of the actual scene confers an aura of truth on it, while the older forms fade into the realm of wishful thinking and seem to come from the pen of someone who never saw clearly.

The description of the citizen is written essentially in journalese, but the diction is greatly varied. "Girdle," as it is used here, "graven," "trews," "rushes," "ells," and "cudgel" all come from the literature of fairy tale and romance; words and phrases like "canine tribe," "lofty," and "summit," have an eighteenth century cast; "tawny . . . hue," and "uneasy slumber" have a nineteenth century sound. Some words and the sentence structure are distinctly modern: "his rocklike mountainous knees were covered, *as was likewise the rest of his body wherever visible,* with a strong growth of tawny prickly hair *in hue and toughness similar to the mountain gorse*" (296). Words like "acuminated," "supposition," "paleolithic," and a phrase like *"Ulex Europeus"* are found more often in modern technical writing than in literary descriptions of a hero. The citizen, in other words, is an accumulation of details from all periods of modern English, but the later the period from which the phrase is drawn, the funnier and more incongruous it seems. "Girdle" and "trews" suit a hero; "canine tribe" suits such a description less well, and "acuminated" not at all. The piling up of details, analogous to the exaggeration of the figure itself, reaches a climax in the catalogue of "Irish heroes and heroines of antiquity" (296), which includes Sidney Parade, the rose of Castille, and Captain Nemo. Here it is the content rather than the style that parodies epic or myth: Homer and the epic writers after him describe at length the great size and strength of heroes, and enjoy listing long series of figures carved or engraved on shields, gates, and walls.

So the style builds up the size and prominence of the citizen, reminding the reader of how times past would have seen this hero. At the same time it suggests the ludicrousness of such traits within our world. The corrupt, technical, or sentimental nature of the modern terms used in the description implies that our mode of seeing inevitably casts a light of absurdity upon the assumptions of heroic worlds. It does not take much imagination to see how ridiculous Achilles or Ajax would be if they were to spring through the doorway of a New York apartment: like King Kong or Godzilla, they incarnate virtues that are no longer of use to mankind. The description builds the citizen up with heroic language, then exaggerates it to the point of bursting: this is a familiar technique in satire.

Some of the epic interpolations, however, are not parodic. Those like the one describing Alf Bergen as a "godlike messenger" (298), for instance, operate much as do the various styles of Oxen in presenting the scene before us as it would have been presented in another age. The scene takes on a dignity and shine from another era. The effect, however, is still one of leveling. The juxtaposition of the scene presented "naturalistically" and "mythically" implies that what Homer and Vergil looked at might have been just as crude and mindless as what we see today.

The second major effect of the interpolations is the ceremonialization of violence. This technique operates by using elevated or highly "civilized" language to mask the aggression implicit in a scene. Consider the scene that describes a hanging, which includes interestingly named guests, orphan children, and violence in the stands consequent to an argument about the date of St. Patrick's birth: "In the course of the argument cannonballs, scimitars, boomerangs, blunderbusses, stinkpots, meatchoppers, umbrellas, catapults, knuckledusters, sandbags, lumps of pig iron were resorted to and blows were freely exchanged. The baby policeman, Constable MacFadden, summoned by special courier from Booterstown, quickly restored order and with lightning promptitude proposed the seventeenth of the month as a solution equally honorable for both contending parties" (307-308). The arrival of the headsman, Rumbold, is treated with utter gentility, as is the description of the operations of the Italian pickpocket:

> Commendatore Beninobenone having been extricated from underneath the presidential armchair, it was explained by his legal adviser Avvocato Pagamimi that the various articles secreted in his thirty-two pockets had been abstracted by him during the affray from the pockets of his junior colleagues in the hope of bringing them to their senses. The objects (which included several hundred ladies' and gentlemen's gold and silver watches) were promptly restored to their rightful owners and general harmony reigned supreme. (308)

The conclusion to be drawn from all this is that society uses language to mask or ceremonialize aggression. The hanging never seems real, certainly never seems a bloody and violent act. Joyce emphasizes his point by presenting rather peaceful scenes in violent language. Consider the very end of the passage, where the fiancée of the man about to be hanged appears before the crowd to say farewell to her beloved. A young gentleman steps up and offers her his hand as a substitute. Tears are shed among the crowd, souvenirs are handed out, and "provostmarshal lieutenantcolonel Tomkin-Maxwell ffrenchmullan Tomlinson" says: "—God blimey if she aint a clinker, that there bleeding tart. Blimey it makes me kind of bleeding cry, straight, it does, when I sees her cause I thinks of my old mashtub what's waiting for me down Limehouse way" (310). The point is pursued as the nameless one picks up the narrative line and describes a temperance dance that bored him. It must have been a quiet occasion, but this is how he describes it:

> And one night I went in with a fellow into one of their musical evenings, song and dance about she could get up on a truss of hay she could my Maureen Lay, and there was a fellow with a Ballyhooly

blue ribbon badge spiffing out of him in Irish and a lot of colleen bawns going about with temperance beverages and selling medals and oranges and lemonade and a few old dry buns, gob, flahoolagh entertainment, don't be talking. Ireland sober is Ireland free. And then an old fellow starts blowing into his bagpipes and all the gougers shuffling their feet to the tune the old cow died of. And one or two sky pilots having an eye around that there was no goings on with the females, hitting below the belt. (311)

The nameless one frequently has this task, to render violent a scene which is not. Garryowen sounds like an unpleasant dog, but the nameless one turns him into a killer:

Mangy ravenous brute sniffling and sneezing all round the place and scratching his scabs and round he goes to Bob Doran that was standing Alf a half one sucking up for what he could get. So of course Bob Doran starts doing the bloody fool with him . . .
Arrah! bloody end to the paw he'd paw and Alf trying to keep him from tumbling off the bloody stool atop of the bloody old dog . . . give you the bloody pip . . . Gob, he golloped it down like old boots and his tongue hanging out of him a yard long for more. Near ate the tin and all, hungry bloody mongrel. (305)

This is a massacre *in* language, not of it. The off-stage narrator generally has the opposite role: consider what he does to the same dog. This is his account of Garryowen's curse: "The metrical system of the canine original, which recalls the intricate alliterative and isosyllabic rules of the Welsh englyn, is infinitely more complicated but we believe our readers will agree that the spirit has been well caught. Perhaps it should be added that the effect is greatly increased if Owen's verse be spoken somewhat slowly and indistinctly in a tone suggestive of suppressed rancour" (312).[13] From this one can not only not deduce a truculent dog, one can hardly deduce an animal at all. To complete our uncertainty about the "real" Garryowen, there is Gerty's description of him in Nausikaa as a "lovely dog" (352) who almost speaks.

In addition to pointing to the ways in which language can mask or create violence, this technique points at the void underlying aggression. In a time when revolutionary rhetoric is often held to be equivalent to revolutionary action, this question continues to plague us: in what does violence consist? When mass murder can be covered over by a few euphemisms, and violent language treated as criminal action, the world appears to be judging not acts but language alone.

Whereas the narrator of Sirens diminishes feeling by playing with language, the on-stage narrator of Cyclops augments feeling by aggressive, forceful, and slangy language. The off-stage narrator generally uses language to make violence palatable, to turn a bloody prizefight into a ballet, a hanging into the finale of a musical comedy. There is, however, no question about where Joyce himself stands in all of this. He is pointing to the void beneath human aggression; he levels times and cultures. Beyond this leveling for its own sake—that is, in order to assert the identity of all times and cultures—the technique holds up ideals of the past for our scrutiny. We call the *Iliad* and the Bible great books, and we still consider that they manifest human ideals. Certain of the interpolations do not parody their models but imitate them. Consider this fine "Biblical" passage: "In the dark land they bide, the vengeful knights of the razor. Their deadly coil they grasp: yea, and therein they lead to Erebus whatsoever wight hath done a deed of blood for I will on nowise suffer it even so saith the Lord" (304). The reader is forced to perceive the violence, revengefulness, and hatred that have been admired and maintained as ideals in the course of human history. The scene itself, the events in Kiernan's, proves that these ideals still live.

The speeches of the citizen also have the exaltation, the lyric flow of the best prophetic writing. Their language is alive and stirring:

—And with the help of the holy mother of God we will again, says the citizen, clapping his thigh. Our harbours that are empty will be full again, Queenstown, Kinsale, Galway, Blacksod Bay, Ventry in the kingdom of Kerry, Killybegs, the third largest harbour in the wide world with a fleet of masts of the Galway Lynches and the Cavan O'Reillys and the O'Kennedys of Dublin when the earl of Desmond could make a treaty with the emperor Charles the Fifth himself. And will again, says he, when the first Irish battleship is seen breasting the waves with our own flag to the fore, none of your Henry Tudor's harps, no, the oldest flag afloat, the flag of the province of Desmond and Thomond, three crowns on a blue field, the three sons of Milesius. (327-328)

—We'll put force against force, says the citizen. We have our greater Ireland beyond the sea. They were driven out of house and home in the black 47. Their mudcabins and their shielings by the roadside were laid low by the batteringram and the *Times* rubbed its hands and told the whitelivered Saxons there would soon be as few Irish in Ireland as redskins in America. Even the grand Turk sent us his piastres. But the Sassenach tried to starve the nation at home while the land was full of crops that the British hyenas bought and sold in Rio de Janeiro. Ay, they drove out the peasants in hordes. Twenty thousand of them died in the coffinships. But those that came to the land of the free remember the land of bondage. And they will come again and with a vengeance, no cravens, the sons of Granuaile, the champions of Kathleen ni Houlihan. (329-330)

That the citizen is eloquent, that he is describing in the somewhat simplistic manner of the great Biblical prophets, that he uses rhythms and attitudes drawn from the seventeenth century translation of the writing prophets, are among the ironies of this chapter. He is a chauvinist; he is furiously intolerant; but he is right about Ireland's situation, if not her future. In another age, he would have been a hero, the kind of hero described in epic terms, although not without a punning irony, as one of the "rulers of the waves, who sit on thrones of alabaster silent as the deathless gods" (325). He has the force, the eloquence, and the justice of cause that Amos had, or Jeremiah. On the surface, the reader is given to choose: there is the citizen, and there is Bloom. In fact, the author has assured, through his use of the two narrators, as well as the events of the chapter, that we have no choice. The citizen's massive figure, his truculence, his pervasive hatred, his snarling dog make us fear him and take all his words as dangerous. His eloquence is undercut even within the scene by the fact that no one listens to him, and by the on-stage narrator's report on his seamy side: "All wind and piss like a tanyard cat" (328).

It appears at first that Joyce has come out of the closet in this chapter, that he has openly labeled something as good, another thing as evil. It seems that the choice presented to the reader is between a belief in *dio boia*, as not only the lord of things as they are but a governing principle of behavior, and a belief in love, which is treated with a contempt that does not even bother to be serious: "Love loves to love love." It is true that the reader is forced to choose between a real hero in the old sense—the citizen—and Bloom, that he cannot escape through linguistic manipulations (the two narrators cover that territory). In the process, as we side with silly Bloom against all the noisy forces of common sense and knowledge of the world, we also give support to a new notion of heroism, a new notion of masculinity, a new notion of what it means to be human.

At the same time, however, a countermovement occurs. For aggression is as built in to humanity as are other emotions. Birth and death are violent acts; contention is not only necessary, it is fun. A large number of the violent acts mentioned in this episode are committed by "legitimate" authorities—nations, police, courts. We clack our tongues and shake our heads about violence even as we laugh at the postcard sent to Dennis Breen, bring legal suit against our neighbor, commit adultery, chop down trees, or watch football games. Even Bloom is aggressive in this episode. Aggressiveness is as inherent in the human being as sexuality. Most religions condemn overt aggressiveness and sexuality under most circumstances (war and marriage being notable exceptions), and insist that they be eradicated. Joyce insists they are both part of the human condition, that they must be recognized as part of the real. Once they are so accepted, they can be dealt with on the level of action. That aggressiveness can be fun, that there is something real and satisfying about hate, is testified to by this chapter as well as by the narrative voices that dominate this book.

Nausikaa

From a world entirely male in its occupants and concerns, we move in Nausikaa to one exclusively female. Barney Kiernan's contains a world that is not only male but crudely so, pervaded by the worst stereotypes of maleness: violent language, bravado, aggressive attitudes toward everything, interest only in aggressive activities, in short, what has come to be called *machismo*. There is no compassion or love in such a world; sex is not love but crime (adultery) or an aggressive, self-proving act ("organise her," "corned beef"). Even moderate statements, like those of Nolan and Cunningham, get drowned in the storm of hostility. The two expressions of gentler feeling—Doran's and Bloom's—are seen as ridiculous and somewhat shameful aberrations from proper masculinity. The world shown in Cyclops is essentially antilife.

Nausikaa presents the feminine complement to that environment. It contains a world in which every action and emotion is coated in a frilly, concealing cloak of seeming gentleness, gentility, and love. It is pervaded by the worst stereotypes of femaleness: euphemistic language, coyness, romantically idealizing attitudes toward everything, and interest only in self-image. It too is essentially antilife, because it disguises and denies reality. While it is possible to say that Cyclops perverts reality and Nausikaa idealizes it, both constrict: one can be choked to death as well by a lace scarf as by a pair of brutal hands.

There is no question of Joyce's accuracy: the world of Gerty Mac-Dowell is as true and recognizable as that of Barney Kiernan's pub. Things have not changed much in the fifty years since *Ulysses* was completed. Both scenes reflect still living ideals. Many people, if forced to articulate their standards for male and female behavior, would uphold the modes of behavior and points of view that are examined—and satirized—in Cyclops and Nausikaa. In fact, both scenes slander actual men and women: "That's not life for men and women" (333) could as truthfully be said of the first half of Nausikaa as of Cyclops. It is Bloom, "the most inadequate Messiah imaginable," as Kenner calls him, who challenges and defies both these constricting and falsifying ideals.[14]

The subject of Nausikaa is love, sexuality, but primarily female sexuality and the concerns clustered around it: clothes, children, housewifery, marriage, spinsterhood. Bloom and Gerty think about the same topics, but in very different ways. The narrator is detached from and above all three centers: Gerty, the church service, and Bloom. The style in which Gerty is presented is parodic, satirizing commercial language, particularly in advertisements aimed at women and in "women's" novels and magazines.

The technique in the first part of Nausikaa parodies by imitation, that is, the prose imitates faithfully, reproduces accurately, the style of what used to be called "women's" literature. The comedy and ludicrousness arise from the Rabelaisian technique of accumulation. So many details are heaped on details that the whole becomes ludicrous. Gerty's consideration of "eyebrowleine" (349), for instance, is not a parody but direct imitation of the language of the advertisement of cosmetics. The exaggeration, repetition, and incongruity that characterize Joyce's parodies in Cyclops do not exist here. The parody occurs as a result of the simple accumulation of details. By accumulating many such items and by slanting his presentation of them to emphasize the goal of concealment and disguise that is implicit in such advertisements, Joyce satirizes not only the commercial language but the assumptions and attitudes that underlie it. Again the technique has a multiple effect: it builds a kind of language into a way of life, exposes it, and in the process explodes it.

Gerty is pitiful because the attitudes she holds are those her society has told her are good: she tries to be the "sterling good daughter," the "minstering angel" (355) she believes she ought to be. It is difficult to decipher, through the concealing style, what sort of person Gerty "actually" is: she is a Maria, a Conmee, shrouding certain areas of reality from her own awareness. Among these hidden gulfs are her own anger and impatience, her sexual desires, and her envy of other girls not impaired as she is.

Concealment is the essential quality of the technique in the first part of the chapter. The style works to conceal, and it points to concealment as the basic moral stance of the literature and ways of thinking it satirizes. During her musings, Gerty considers the subjects of physical violence, alcoholism, defecation, menstruation, and masturbation by both men and women, but the language in which she approaches these subjects makes close reading necessary if one is to realize what she is thinking about. Analogous to Joyce's use of language to disguise or transform violence in Cyclops is his use of it here to conceal the force of profound areas of experience on Gerty's consciousness, and consequently on ours. The significance of Gerty's experience of life is snarled and hidden in a knot of petticoat strings.

Her feelings toward her father—surely a profound area of our experience of life—never emerge from the shroud of clichés and devoirs in which they are wrapped:

> Had her father only avoided the clutches of the demon drink, by taking the pledge or those powders the drink habit cured in Pearson's Weekly, she might now be rolling in her carriage. (354)

> Nay, she had even witnessed in the home circle deeds of violence caused by intemperance and had seen her own father, a prey to the fumes of intoxication, forget himself completely for if there was one thing of all things that Gerty knew it was the man who lifts his hand to a woman save in the way of kindness deserves to be branded as the lowest of the low. (354)

> Poor father! With all his faults she loved him still when he sang . . . and they had stewed cockles and lettuce . . . for supper. (354)

Dignam's death is held up as a cautionary example: "her mother said to him to let that be a warning to him for the rest of his days and he couldn't even go to the funeral on account of the gout" (355). All of this sounds suspiciously like a less than peaceful domestic life. It suggests that Gerty might have some rather strong feelings about her father. But she is so busy saying what she ought to say and feeling what she ought to feel that she is able to conceal from herself truths that might be unpleasant.

The outhouse is "that place where she never forgot every fortnight the chlorate of lime" and to which she repairs "for a certain purpose." She never thinks of it by name, and disguises it by hanging in it "the grocer's christmas almanac the picture of halcyon days." Her ways of thinking about the outhouse bring into larger perspective Joyce's reason for including in such detail the scene of Bloom in the outhouse in Calypso. That scene, matter-of-factly described even to the extent of Bloom wiping himself with part of the prize story (which is funny in its own right and a wry comment on the story, as Beaufoy indignantly points out in Circe), symbolizes Bloom's mental acceptance of body and bodily functions. Gerty manages not to have to think directly about defecation even when she is performing it: she sits looking "dreamily . . . and felt her own arms that were white and soft just like hers with the sleeves back and thought about those times" (355).

For Gerty, menstruation is "that" or "that thing":

> He told her that time when she told him about that in confession crimsoning up to the roots of her hair for fear he could see, not to be troubled because that was only the voice of nature and we were all subject to nature's laws, he said, in this life and that that was no sin because that came from the nature of woman instituted by God, he said, and that Our Blessed Lady herself said to the archangel Gabriel be it done unto me according to Thy Word. (358)

> She felt a kind of sensation rushing all over her and she knew by the feel of her scalp and that irritation against her stays that that thing must be coming on because the last time too was when she clipped her hair on account of the moon. (361)

Beyond the self-deception involved in her thoughts about blushing and her mistaking sexual excitement for premenstrual sensation, beyond the fear, ignorance, guilt, and superstition implicit in these thoughts, lies the appalling fact that Gerty must *confess* the onset of menstruation, that no one else has ever discussed it with her. That she cannot think of it by name is characteristic of her way of dealing with reality.

Although she is a virgin and ignorant of sex, she knows perfectly well what Bloom is about. There are frequent references to his hands in his pockets; it is one realistic detail that she sees, selects:

> His hands and face were working and a tremor went over her . . . there was no one to see only him and her [the word "no-one" occurs frequently in this section, on pp. 365, 366, and in a different context, 363]. (365)

> She seemed to hear the panting of his heart, his hoarse breathing, because she knew about the passion of men like that, hot-blooded, because Bertha Supple told her once in dead secret and made her swear she'd never about the gentleman lodger that was staying with them out of the Congested Districts Board that had pictures cut out of papers of those skirtdancers and highkickers and she said he used to do something not very nice that you could imagine sometimes in the bed. (365-366)

But if one were in fact as ignorant about sex as Gerty pretends to be, how could one imagine masturbation at all? Gerty knows what happens in the sexual act and has masturbated herself: "Besides there was absolution so long as you didn't do the other thing before being married and there ought to be women priests that would understand without your telling out and Cissy Caffrey too sometimes had that dreamy kind of dreamy look in her eyes so that she too, my dear, and Winny Rippingham so mad about actor's photographs and besides it was on account of that other thing coming on the way it did" (366). Some place in her head, Gerty has firm ideas of the meanings of "that," "that thing," "the other thing," and something even more amorphous.

In the same way that these subjects are obscured and their nature concealed, large blocks of experience are sugared over and romanticized. Joyce underlines the unreality of Gerty's notions by having Bloom muse on the same subjects. Contrast the two on the nature of marriage and housewifery:

> She would care for him with creature comforts too for Gerty was womanly wise and knew that a mere man liked that feeling of homi-

ness. Her griddlecakes done to a golden-brown hue and queen
Ann's pudding of delightful creaminess had won golden opinions
from all because she had a lucky hand also for lighting a fire . . .
and they would have a beautifully appointed drawingroom with
pictures and engravings and the photograph of grandpapa Giltrap's
lovely dog Garryowen that almost talked, it was so human, and
chintz covers for the chairs and that silver toastrack in Clery's summer jumble sales like they have in rich houses . . . They would go on
the continent for their honeymoon . . . and then, when they settled
down in a nice snug and cosy little homely house, every morning
they would both have brekky, simple but perfectly served, for their
own two selves and before he went out to business he would give his
dear little wifey a good hearty hug and gaze for a moment deep
down into her eyes. (352)

Sad however because it lasts only a few years till they settle down to
potwalloping and papa's pants will soon fit Willy and fullers' earth
for the baby when they hold him out to do ah ah. No soft job. Saves
them. Keeps them out of harm's way. Nature. Washing child, washing corpse. Dignam. Children's hands always round them. Cocoanut skulls, monkeys, not even closed at first, sour milk in their
swaddles and tainted curds . . . Worst of all at night . . . Husband
rolling in drunk, stink of pub off him like a polecat. Have that in
your nose in the dark, whiff of stale boose. Then ask in the morning: was I drunk last night? Bad policy however to fault the husband. Chickens come home to roost. They stick by one another like
glue. Maybe the women's fault also. (373)

Gerty's main interest after herself, however, is romance, romance as
a scented, sweatless, rickless version of sex. She gazes at Bloom, ro-
manticizing:

Till then they had only exchanged glances of the most casual but
now under the brim of her new hat she ventured a look at him and
the face that met her gaze there in the twilight, wan and strangely
drawn, seemed to her the saddest she had ever seen. (356)

Here was that of which she had so often dreamed. It was he who
mattered and there was joy on her face because she wanted him
because she felt instinctively that he was like no-one else. (358)

Joyce allows no subject to pass without irony, and here, despite her
deceitful ways of thinking and seeing, Gerty is seeing a true thing that

no one else in *Ulysses* sees: Bloom *is* sad. And her musings on his foreignness are a parallel to Molly's answer when Bloom asks her why she chose him: "Because you were so foreign from the others" (380). If one seeks for the "whole" truth, one must include even a Gerty MacDowell. Gerty's picture of Bloom nevertheless provides an amusing contrast to his own self-image:

> No prince charming is her beau ideal to lay a rare and wondrous love at her feet but rather a manly man with a strong quiet face who had not found his ideal, perhaps his hair slightly flecked with grey. (351)

> She could see at once by his dark eyes and his pale intellectual face that he was a foreigner, the image of the photo she had of Martin Harvey, the matinée idol . . . but she could not see whether he had an aquiline nose or a slightly *retroussé* from where he was sitting. (357)

> Saw something in me. Wonder what. Sooner have me as I am than some poet chap with bearsgrease, plastery hair lovelock over his dexter optic . . . Ought to attend to my appearance my age. Didn't let her see me in profile. Still, you never know. Pretty girls and ugly men marrying. Beauty and the beast. Besides I can't be so if Molly. (369)

Gerty's musings on sex are funniest of all (italics mine):

> If she saw that magic lure in his eyes there would be no holding back for her. Love laughs at locksmiths. She would make the great sacrifice. *Her every effort would be to share his thoughts.* Dearer than the whole world would she be to him and gild his days with happiness . . . But even if—what then? Would it make a very great difference? From everything in the least indelicate her finebred nature instinctively recoiled. She loathed that sort of person, the fallen women off the accommodation walk beside the Dodder . . . *degrading the sex and being taken up to the police station.* No, no: not that. They would be just good friends like a big brother and sister without all that other *in spite of the conventions of Society with a big ess* . . . Heart of mine! She would follow her dream of love, the dictates of her heart that told her he was her all in all, the only man in all the world for her for love was the master guide. Nothing else mattered. Come what might she would be wild, untrammelled, free. (364-365)

Free, wild, defiant toward the conventions of society, she will fight her way through to be just good friends. Again, however, Gerty is putting her finger on a bit of truth: such a friendship does defy the conventions of some segments of society.

Gerty really believes masturbation to be preferable to intercourse: "besides there was absolution so long as you didn't do the other thing before being married." Such an attitude is probably inevitable in a society that regards sex as sinful. In earlier chapters, the theme of onanism is tied to solipsism; here it is tied to narcissism. The root of both is likely the same: sexual guilt. For Gerty's sense of values about sex is not a result of her narcissism; both her narcissism and her sexual values are symptoms of the constricted world in which she breathes. Vain, stupid, dishonest, and mean though she is, that she is also poignant and pathetic is a result of our sense of her as a victim, like Dilly, of the thin, unnourishing air she lives in. The most crucial and indicative of Gerty's thoughts is her brief allusion to her lameness: "The years were slipping by for her, one by one, and but for that one shortcoming she knew she need fear no competition and that was an accident coming down Dalkey hill and she always tried to conceal it" (364). But what kind of mind would imagine such a thing possible? How can one conceal a limp? Gerty's handling of a real misfortune reveals an ingrained habit of concealment and exposes the underlying attitudes of the society that has taught her what she is supposed to be, for Gerty has not mind enough to penetrate that pale.

Henry James once discussed realism in fiction by using the metaphor of a balloon that rises with imagination but must always be somehow anchored to earth.[15] Bloom's prose hits us like the fresh air we encounter as our very tenuously anchored balloon descends safely to earth. Yet the subjects he thinks about are the same as those Gerty considers.

It is not possible to distinguish whether the subject of this episode is sexuality or women, because the two are completely bound up. The focus is on women, but in all areas—clothing, body, relationships with other women, women as children, virgins, nuns, married, mothers, widows—women are seen in their sexual aspect. Even Lizzie Twigg, who was actually a poet of sorts, is glanced at only with regard to her attractiveness to men. I suspect that for Joyce women had identity only as sexual beings, that is, they were defined exclusively by the sexual roles they occupied. Certainly that is the approach in this chapter and also in the rest of the novel.

Throughout this episode, Bloom riffles through a host of theories and old wives' tales about women's sexuality, menstruation, virginity, but even when his information is false or shaky, he looks directly at his subject. Gerty's thoughts about clothing are amusingly different from Bloom's, yet they are based on the same premise—of which Gerty is unconscious—that its use is for illusion in sexual attraction. Bloom's thoughts about women's relationships with each other are verified by Gerty's feelings about her friends and her perception of their feelings about her. She is probably accurate in her estimate of their feelings; Bloom thinks "the others inclined to give her an odd dig" (369). Bloom wonders about her motivation in flirting with him in a humorous contrast to her "literary" romanticization and shows himself to be almost uniquely without vanity: "She must have been thinking of someone else all the time. What harm?" (371).

Beneath all his thoughts lies Bloom's sense of sexuality as ordained in nature, as an inevitable, undeniable, and natural, if troublesome, part of every experience. The crux of his section is the passage on magnetism:

> Very strange about my watch. Wristwatches are always going wrong. Wonder is there any magnetic influence between the person because that was about the time he. Yes, I suppose at once . . . I remember looking in Pill lane. Also that now is magnetism. Back of everything magnetism. Earth for instance pulling this and being pulled. That causes movement. And time? Well that's the time the movement takes. Then if one thing stopped the whole ghesabo would stop bit by bit. Because it's arranged. Magnetic needle tells you what's going on in the sun, the stars. Little piece of steel iron. When you hold out the fork. Come. Come. Tip. Woman and man that is. Fork and steel. Molly, he. Dress up and look and suggest and let you see and see more and defy you if you're a man to see that and, like a sneeze coming, legs, look, look and if you have any guts in you. Tip. Have to let fly. (373-374)

He sees both sexes as pulled by this force: "Yours for the asking. Because they want it themselves. Their natural craving. Shoals of them every evening poured out of offices" (368).

Bloom's sense of sexual magnetism is connected with his thoughts about Molly and Boylan, which is the one subject he can not specify in words. The thought of the two of them together is still very painful for him:

Was that just when he, she?
O, he did. Into her. She did. Done.
Ah! (370)

Although Bloom sees sexual attraction and its fulfillment as natural and inevitable, he suffers the whole range of emotions responsive to Molly's infidelity. He is angry with Molly, as in the passage from Sirens: "Leave her: get tired. Suffer then. Snivel. Big Spanishy eyes goggling at nothing. Her wavyavyeavyheavyeavyevyevy hair un comb: 'd" (277). He feels resignation when he remembers with anguish his love-making with Molly sixteen years before and considers its irretrievability: "My youth. Never again. Only once it comes. Or hers" (377), and ponders searching for a renewal of passion in a new love: "No. Returning not the same . . . The new I want" (377). But he decides that a new love is not possible: "Nothing new under the sun . . . So it returns. Think you're escaping and run into yourself. Longest way round is the shortest way home. And just when he and she. Circus horse walking in a ring" (377).

Bloom understands the meaning of his relinquishment: "All quiet on Howth now. The distant hills seem. Where we. The rhododendrons. I am a fool perhaps. He gets the plums and I the plumstones" (377). But finally, although still vacillating, he renounces possessiveness: "Liverpool boat long gone. Not even the smoke. And she can do the other. Did too. And Belfast. I won't go. Race there, race back to Ennis. Let him" (382). The end of his half-dream implies a hope to return to full intercourse. The context merges Molly, Martha, and Gerty—"next in her next her next" (382)—but the passage is extremely ambiguous.

Bloom's section of the chapter shows us again his great decency, not only in thoughts about sexuality but in his thoughts about people, even the citizen: "that bawler in Barney Kiernan's. Got my own back there. Drunken ranters. What I said about his God made him wince. Mistake to hit back. Or? No. Ought to go home and laugh at themselves. Always want to be swilling in company. Afraid to be alone like a child of two. Suppose he hit me. Look at it other way round. Not so bad then. Perhaps not to hurt he meant" (380). Bloom extends the same charity to Molly, remembering an occasion when she was cruel to Milly: "What do they love? Another themselves? But the morning she chased her with the umbrella. Perhaps so as not to hurt. I felt her pulse. Ticking" (379-380). His decency appears in his quiet acceptance of a humiliating event of the morning: "Walk after him now make him awkward like those newsboys me today" (375-376), and in the acceptance that lies beneath his comic misrecollection: "That brought us out of the land of Egypt and into the house of bondage" (378).

Bloom's decency and honesty provide a norm, a standard, in a chapter on sexuality that points to the hypocrisy, craven deceit, and artificiality in society's approach to, or rather retreat from, the subject. Fritz Senn offers some humane and judicious conclusions about the chapter: "In the imperfect world of Dublin, 1904, the imperfect solution that the two characters allow themselves to be driven to, passively reactive rather than passionately active, does have some advantages . . . Bloom knows one has to be 'Thankful for small mercies' . . . Substitute satisfactions are better than no satisfactions at all . . . Something approaching love does, after all, take place, and a kind of rapport is established . . . The lack of communication in Ulysses is perhaps less surprising than the occasional occurrence of some imperfect communication."[16]

Still, it is an outrageous and highly comic idea to have the very character who provides the standard, who upholds a saner view of sexuality, perform so flagrant a violation of sexual mores as to masturbate in public. Bloom is never permitted to become an ideal figure: the closer he approaches moral perfection in any given episode, the harder he is pulled down to the level of the messy, smelly, ridiculously human. Joyce is adamant in his refusal to offer the reader the ideal: he insists we see and know, as far as possible, the real.

The narrator stands above the whole chapter. There are portions of Bloom's section that take place outside his consciousness, although they are here, as in Sirens, woven into his monologue. The paragraph beginning "A monkey puzzle" (372) starts outside Bloom's consciousness; the paragraph beginning "A long lost candle" (379) is written entirely outside of Bloom's consciousness, as is the conclusion of the chapter, from "A bat flew" (382). The comment "Cuckoo" is the narrator's. Although Gerty can and does imagine what is going on in the church, we are told about events inside the church that she could not possibly be aware of, such as the accident of the candle flame about to reach the flowers. Some of the satire in the episode is accomplished by the juxtaposition of events within the church with events occurring outside it. At other times, one of Gerty's thoughts is juxtaposed with a contrary thought or act, a technique used for comedy in Molly's soliloquy also. The largest juxtaposition of the chapter is that between Gerty and Bloom. The same is true of the satire: some of it is aimed at Gerty, and by extension at a way of thinking and feeling; some mocks Bloom for his sensuality and senti- ment: "Howth settled for slumber tired of long days, of yumyum rhododendrons (he was old) and felt gladly the night breeze lift, ruffle his fell of ferns . . . Far on Kish bank the anchored lightship twinkled, winked at Mr Bloom" (379). During Gerty's section the satire also glances at both figures: she knew he was "a man of inflexible honour to his fingertips" (365). The satire that arises from the juxtaposition of the church service with the events on the beach is also a double- headed arrow, mocking some notions of Catholicism along with the characters. The service is a benediction, a ritual in which, according to Kenner, the sacrament, like Gerty, "is exhibited but not eaten."[17] The counterpoint parallels the worship of the Virgin and Bloom's "worship" of Gerty: "His dark eyes fixed themselves on her again drinking in her every contour, literally worshipping at her shrine" (361). Gerty is and remains a virgin; the shrine Bloom worships is her genitals. The analogy is funny, but it also points seriously to religion as the root of Dublin's sexual sickness. The canon hands the thurible back to Father Conroy and kneels down "looking up at the Blessed Sacrament" (360) at the same time, the narrator informs us, that Bloom is looking fixedly at Gerty. The problem of the candle —"Canon O'Hanlon . . . told Father Conroy that one of the candles was just going to set fire to the flowers and Father Conroy got up and settled it all right" (361)—occurs just as Bloom is returning his hands to his pockets and inflaming Gerty with that "sensation rushing all over her." The canon has the "Blessed Sacrament in his hands" (363), and Bloom has *his* chalice in his. As Gerty decides she will not be sexual but will remain like brother and sister in her "dream of love," Canon O'Hanlon "put the Blessed Sacrament back into the tabernacle and . . . then he locked the tabernacle door" (365).

There is a circle of ironies here: the idealization of sex in the benediction of the Virgin is related to but also contrasted with Gerty's sentimentalization of sex; the idealization of sex in the benediction of the Virgin parallels and contrasts with Bloom's sexual idealization of Gerty while he is masturbating; and Gerty's romantic sentimentality parallels and contrasts with Bloom's realistic sensuality during the masturbation. Gerty's sentimental and romantic notions are an ironic comment on the bleak life she lives and her actual inadequacy, her moral and physical lameness. Bloom, ambivalently circling, as always, provides contrasts within his own monologue; and his public masturbation—his form of worship—during a service celebrating the Virgin (what better way to celebrate virginity?) has its own sensational irony.

We are presented with three basic standing places: the position of the church on sex, the position of Irish womanhood on sex (a similar view on the sexuality of Irish womanhood is presented in the Swiftian satire in Oxen of the Sun), and the position of Bloom. Because of Bloom's decency and honesty and his approach to sex as natural and human (if a problem), we find ourselves standing with him rather than with either of the others. We also therefore find ourselves defending or at least countenancing his outrageous act. We are voyaging across the abyss of incertitude in the fragile bark of human decency with a fellow passenger who is:

> Cuckoo
> Cuckoo
> Cuckoo. (382)

Oxen of the Sun

This is the most censured chapter in *Ulysses*.[18] As usual, the problem lies in the difficulty of ascertaining the relation of its technique to the actual scene. Anthony Burgess laments, "it is a pity that Stephen and Bloom have to get lost in the process of glorifying an art [literature] that is supposed to be their servant."[19] However, Bloom and Stephen are not the major focus in the second half of the novel. Since Sirens, the focus has been human emotion, and the novel will return to that in Circe. But to ensure that we develop no sense of order as fixed and predictable as that of the *Commedia*, Joyce does again here what he did in Aeolus, removes us to a further circle from which we will return to an earlier one. Like Aeolus and Scylla and Charybdis, episodes in which Stephen is important, Oxen of the Sun has a multiple, interwoven focus. Like Lestrygonians and Hades, it deals with a basic fact of life: coitus leading to conception and birth. This is the backbone; the rest of the skeleton is made up of a series of considerations of contraception (coitus prevented from leading to conception), the Virgin (conception without coitus), fertilization (coitus without love), and other forms of sex or denial of sex. Every person or event examined in the chapter is viewed in this light. For instance, Nurse Callan, who is not an important character, is described as unhappy in her childlessness (as Bloom sees it) and as having a love affair, perhaps with Dr. Dixon (as the young men see it), and is actually assisting at a birth. Thus, the episode is a meditation on sex just as Hades is a meditation on death; the theme of sex is so important to Joyce that he has broken it up into three parts: Nausikaa deals with sex as romantic or sensual love; Circe with its secret and hidden level, erotic fantasy; and Oxen with its serious function of procreation. The flesh upon this body is provided by still another level: coition leading to birth is a metaphor for perception of reality leading to its expression in language. Thus the chapter is also about literature. Ironies attend each level. If coition leading to conception and birth is seen ambivalently, literary expression is shown to be inadequate to confer certitude, incapable of rendering ultimate reality. In the end, reality itself is undercut.

The goddess of the episode, according to the notesheets, is Postverta, a surname of Carmenta, who possesses the power of prophecy and over childbirth.[20] This goddess is able to look backward at the past, which she reveals to poets; appropriately, Oxen contains innumerable references to earlier portions of the novel. The goddess appears in the novel as Partula: *"Per deam Partulam et Pertundam nunc est bibendum!"* (424). She is a convenient image to link the two themes, but in fact the relation between them is not totally arbitrary. Language also arises from parental merging: consider the Latin and mock Old English that open this chapter. A language, like a single human life, has periods of growth and change, full flower and decline. And any single language, like a "race" of people, endures over a span of time, through which it manifests both continuity and difference.

The actual events of the chapter are far from dramatic and seem a comedown from the high activity and vivid language of the preceding three chapters and the one to follow. But the contrast is necessary, for those chapters deal with human emotion itself, this one with the expression of it, the consequences of it. Birth is a dramatic act only to the one giving birth and the one given birth to, and perhaps those intimately involved. But mother and child receive little attention in this chapter. What we see is a group of young men drinking in a refectory. Bloom joins them. There are several interruptions, arrivals and departures. The men are asked to be quieter; upstairs a baby is born. Eventually they leave to go to a pub, Burke's, where the raucous conversation continues. Mulligan runs out on Stephen. That is all.

Interpretations of the chapter that attempt to set up the "embryonic" structure Joyce pointed out only confirm S. L. Goldberg's suspicion that the "generally admitted failure" of the episode is due to Joyce's imposition on the material of "an intellectually conceived view of reality."[21] The cues to embryonic development provide a subsidiary theme and play an intricate game that ties in amusingly with the larger theme of coition, but offer no help in understanding the overall statement of the chapter. They are no more important as a pattern than would be the food and eating allusions in Lestrygonians if traced as a pattern. They simply indicate the theme. Tracing the development of the "fetus" may furnish the puzzle-lover with some evening entertainment.[22] The analogies between Stephen and the fetus, or between the birth of the fetus and the birth of the Word ("Burke's" [423]), are certainly comic and satiric. These are surface elements, however, adding sharpness to the chapter if one is aware of them, but not necessary to one's understanding of the chapter.

What is essential to such an understanding is to see the relation between the themes of coition-birth and language. The chapter offers a Brownean meditation on coition, but an empirical study of the relation between reality and literature. Language provides the physiognomy of all the narrators of *Ulysses*. We do not see the narrators of Aeolus, Sirens, Nausikaa: they are not physical characters. We do not know their names, genders, heights, or ages. Even the narrator of Cyclops, who does take part in the scene, is an opaque figure: we know that he is male, a sponger, a bill collector, and a cynic, but that is all we know. Joyce points this out explicitly in his description of this narrator in Circe: "the featureless face of a Nameless One" (470).

Language is not only the medium of the narrators, it is their entire visible existence. Language creates them for us, as their attitudes create their language. Each narrator is endowed with an aspect of omniscience; that is, each one knows everything about one area of life. The narrator of Sirens knows all about the secret griefs and loneliness of the characters, but nothing of their fortitude and resilience; the narrator of Cyclops knows everything scandalous and scabrous about the characters, but nothing of their generosity or nobility; the narrator of Wandering Rocks can see all of Dublin from the outside, but little about the characters' inner worlds. Even Father Conmee, presented as though from the inside, is not shown as operating under the full pressure of his burden of humanity. Because of these limitations, the narrators are finally deceitful, unreliable. We would not be willing to accept any single narrative voice in *Ulysses* as the bearer of the final truth about the characters, although each of them offers us a piece of truth. The method of Oxen of the Sun is a microcosmic analogue to the method of the novel. In the language of some of the finest periods and authors in English literature, the narrator of Oxen describes one inconsequential scene. Each style shows us a piece of truth, but none bears the final truth, certitude.

Every change in style devolves upon a change in stance. As James pointed out, what one sees from the house of fiction depends on what window one is looking from.[23] Each change of style in Oxen of the Sun is determined by a change of stance; each change of stance results in a different scene and not just a different angle of perception. Bloom as the hatholding seeker is a somewhat different character from Mr. Canvasser Bloom: he has a different posture, a different smile. The callow young men "elegantly" parrying genteel eighteenth-century conversation in the refectory are dressed differently in our imaginations from the group at Burke's: their accents, their laughter, even their bodily configurations seem different. Beneath the changes of name, costume, posture, attitude, in short, of language, the flesh is one. The same group of people occupies our attention throughout the chapter, and throughout the chapter the conversation is composed of male ribaldry, sexual banter. The essence then remains: "I, entelechy, form of forms, am I by memory because under everchanging forms" (189). This is the truth in the conception of metempsychosis.

Bloom is all in all: the hatholding seeker, the traveler Leopold,

childe Leopold, the "passing grave" (390) sir Leopold, Mr. Cautious
Calmer, Mr. Canvasser Bloom, "Mr L. Bloom (Pubb. Canv.)" (418),
"avuncular" (425), "sheeny" (426), "Pold veg" (427). None of these
characterizations is totally false to Bloom; he could believably exist in
each of these historical contexts. But neither is any one of these descriptions completely true to Bloom in the depths to which we know
him.[24] Just as each of the narrators in *Ulysses* presents a developed
truth that is not the whole truth, none of the styles in Oxen of the Sun
presents a falsehood and none presents a whole truth. Like the pieces
of oratory in Aeolus, every style is at once true and limited. Bloom in
his various avatars is consubstantial with himself; he lives in all times
and places; he is never everywhere the same. Relativity and con-
tinuance—all molecules change, yet essence remains—coexist with the
void, with incertitude, with inadequacy, with incompleteness.
Although Bloom's flesh and form remain constant beneath changes,
the fact sharply impinges upon us that no single mode of apprehension
is capable of containing the final truth about man, the ultimate reality
of Bloom, Stephen, or the scene as a whole. Joyce is here doing more
than showing us the hypothetical core of language; he is showing us
the void as it resides in perception itself. This is another link between
the main theme of the chapter and its secondary theme: just as prophylaxis sterilizes coition, any style to some extent sterilizes the
coition of the act and the word. The Father who is act and consubstantial with the Word-Son is of the same essence, is an absolute end,
and is thus absolute reality. This is what Stephen seeks, and what we
seek as we read, but it cannot, within the terms of *Ulysses*, be found,
either inside its covers or, it is implied, in the world itself. In the fallen
world which is the only one man knows, all acts suffer from incompleteness, inadequacy, perversion, or limitation. The paralysis and
disease that Dublin suffers are the paralysis and disease of the world.
Analogously, all words used as acts or to describe acts are incomplete,
inadequate, perverted, or limited. The limitations of language are not
confined to the twentieth century: they exist for primitive man as well
as for civilized man, in village and city cultures; they existed for the
seventeenth century and they exist now. The limitations of any style
are basic human limitations: the great metaphor for these limitations
is original sin, but unfortunately, no baptism can ever wash them
away.

Oxen of the Sun is integrally connected with Circe, and together these episodes carry to a climax the consideration of the subjects dealt with in the three preceding chapters: human emotion and the ineffability of reality. Like Cyclops, Oxen demonstrates the dependence of what we take as real upon its linguistic rendering. And the standing place of Oxen adumbrates that of Ithaca. The perspective from which we view this chapter is further out in space than we have been before: we are far enough from the world to be able to see over a thousand years of time in one glance. The next two chapters return us to a point closer to the world: Ithaca removes us to an Archimedean point, from which the world becomes merely a dot. In addition, Oxen is related to Eumaeus, in that both chapters use language to obscure rather than reveal truth.

The introductory section has four parts: an invitation to the reader to go to a new place—"Deshil Holles Eamus" (383) or let us go right-handwise to Holles Street; an invocation of a new birth; a celebration of birth; and a long statement of exhortation to procreation and of praise for Dublin's obstetric facilities. The introduction informs us of the two main subjects of the chapter, procreation and language. The use of Latin, Gaelic, and Anglo-Saxon (Holles) as well as of Latinate English in the introduction indicates that the subject matter is language considered over a span of time. The content of the passages concerns birth.

Procreation is considered largely in its relation to coition and prophylaxis. The introduction pronounces offensive the consignment of "that evangel simultaneously command and promise" to "oblivious neglect" (383). The "command and promise" is the divine injunction to increase and multiply. Religious groups have been maintaining for some years that if God ordered increase, contraception is sin, and that is the premise of this chapter. However, this premise is handled ironically and comically as well as seriously.[25] That such a handling is in store for us is indicated by the fact that the styles in the introduction are parodies, whereas the styles in the body of the episode are imitations. The strangeness of these parodies may be a metaphor for the strangeness to us in the twentieth century of a positive attitude toward prolificacy. For roughly the last hundred years, birth in general has been seen as a threat rather than a good, and even birth for individuals is considered a qualified good. Birth costs less risk of life and less pain than it once did, but children have increasingly become economic and emotional burdens. If one considers the approach to large poor families taken by Bloom in Lestrygonians, or the handling of the Dedalus family in Wandering Rocks, one realizes that Joyce's feelings about "increase and multiply" were not altogether positive.

The long "Sallustian-Tacitean prelude" presents in highly garbled form the divine injunction to increase and multiply. To present a divine injunction in nearly incomprehensible pedantries—unfertilized Latinate English—is irony enough, but the second part of the prelude, describing the reverence for motherhood and the excellent medical facilities of the Celts, has an additional grim humor in light of the poverty and starvation seen by Joyce nearly two centuries after Swift.

The introduction includes the main elements of language from which English developed. This linkage ties the two themes together in another way. Although the Word that is born is "Burke's," the English language itself is born at the very beginning of the chapter: the whole episode, after all, is written in it. Joyce wrote a description of Oxen as "nine circles of development enclosed between the headpiece and tail-piece of opposite chaos."[26] The opaque fragments that follow at a little distance the new-born Word do not represent the language of the twentieth century, the vulgarity and crudity of which bring to an end all the greatness of the past; rather, they are the chaotic and vivid elements that will contribute to the formation of the next major style or language to be born.

The beginning of the narrative creates through style rather than description the stark world that lay behind Christian Anglo-Saxon epic. Bloom is a wayfarer, filled with "stark ruth of man" (385), a seeker, hat-holding. The section shows an aspect of Bloom that we know to be true and at the same time comically false. Bloom does sympathize with Mina Purefoy and is concerned for her delivery, but he is at the hospital partly because he does not want to go home and encounter Molly. The topics of the section are birth and death, and they are described in the austere, forceful style of a period when birth and death were stark daily realities unmediated by modern conveniences like the Holles Street Hospital and Corny Kelleher's mortuary.

Bloom as the traveler "sore wounded in his breast by a spear wherewith a horrible and dreadful dragon was smitten him" (386) is comic, but the application of such terms to a bee sting contains an implicit mockery of romances where dragons seem to be so large a part of the population that one might suspect they grew in hives. The board containing "full fair cheer . . . that no wight could devise a fuller ne richer" (387) holds, we know, some porter, some bread, and a tin of sardines. Again the joke is as much on romance descriptions as on the actual scene. Lenehan as the "franklin" (388), Chaucer's generous host, is an ironic figure, but the implication hovers that Chaucer's Franklin could have been modeled on a version of Lenehan.

The traveler Leopold, weary "after many marches . . . and sometimes venery" (387), is transformed into a different man, sir Leopold, "the goodliest guest that ever sat in scholar's hall" and "the meekest man and the kindest that ever laid husbandly hand under hen" (388). Again we are seeing a picture of Bloom that is true to what we know of him and yet is in a different perspective from what we are used to. The "husbandly hand under hen" is a mockery when Thersites thinks of it in Cyclops; so is it in Circe, when Black Liz herself rises to accuse Bloom. The very meekness for which he is praised here is what makes him an object of contempt in twentieth century Dublin. But this picture of Bloom is one we would accept as the whole truth of a character if we encountered it in a fourteenth century romance.

In short, in each style we are offered a scene set by a particular mode of perception. When we read the originals, the authors and periods Joyce is imitating, we accept the vision contained in them as the whole and absolute truth. We believe Malory, Addison, Bunyan, Dickens, or at least we suspend our disbelief. In the same way we can believe the narrative styles of Oxen, but because there are many of them and because each one qualifies or alters our perception of its predecessors, we are forced to confront the final inadequacy of any one and to see that ultimate reality is ineffable. There used to be a painter, Eleanor Rice-Pereira, who painted glass sheets, then placed one atop the other, layering a whole group in a kind of vertical cubism. Joyce is doing something similar here, but since literature exists in time rather than space, we are shown each sheet separately and must imagine the vision of the layered whole. In this chapter on language and literature, it is through time, rather than space, that we move. Beneath the changes wrought by parallax, relativity, and modes of perception lies the single scene, consubstantial with itself.

The approach to language taken in this chapter, as opposed to

Eumaeus, assumes it to be a vehicle of truth. The terrible fact that truth is not Truth, or that many bits of truth add up not to a final great knowledge but to a final great confusion and incertitude, need not be underlined. Joyce's use of imitation rather than parody, and his choice of models—the great periods of English prose—indicate his intention to show language as an accurate reflector of attitudes. His inclusion of many periods of linguistic excellence and the chaos with which he concludes the presentation indicate his intention of undercutting our belief in linguistic truths. His approach to the secondary subject matter of the episode is similar. In Oxen, language = truth and sex = authenticity. Sexual intercourse without impediment (prophylaxis) is the genuine encounter with the real, the not-self. The sin against the light is any of numerous acts whereby this intercourse and fruition is impeded or prevented. All of the men in the refectory are shown to be sinners in this kind; yet Bloom, as imperfect as the rest, is also shown to be superior to the rest. The Purefoys, the one example of purity in this area, are ridiculous.

The discussion among the young men begins with the question of precedence in birth, the problematic Catholic rule that the child, rather than the mother, shall be saved in a difficult birth. Stephen immediately moves into a discussion of contraception and masturbation as sins. After this, the major topics that have been mentioned earlier are tossed around randomly, as they would actually be in such a conversation. This is not to say the conversation is naturalistic: in life, no long conversation remains so adhesively attached to one subject. As in other chapters of *Ulysses*, here there is one major subject of consideration; the naturalism is an illusion. The episode has no dramatic line, and no one strand of the theme is designated as more important than another by its place in a careful structure. The structure is chronological. Themes are chosen by their appropriateness to a particular style in the chronological table, not according to dramatic progression. And the major themes of procreation and contraception are handled both comically and seriously.

The comedy of the sexual banter may cause us to ignore a serious undercurrent of the chapter: sex is sacred, procreation is a holy act. By this I mean that true encounter engages the whole self at its deepest levels, involves the greatest risk possible to the self and permits real growth to occur. Procreation exemplifies the physical side of this moral or spiritual experience: it engages the whole self as body, both parents having responsibility for nourishing and protecting the fetus, involves the risk of death for the female and of loss for the male, and permits the growth of a new person.

The bawdiness of the students' references to sex reflects an attitude toward it that has nothing to do with sacredness: the students treat sex as something distant from themselves, something performed by a disconnected body, which requires no personal concern. This is one form of sin against the light, as Bloom realizes. The conversation centers on other forms: contraception, the great shield Killchild; impotence; prostitution, or rather male resort to prostitutes, which has no special name; and comic means of contraception—the handkerchief used to shield Mulligan's hat from the rain, God's sperm renewing the wasteland; an umbrella; a cloak. Stephen is described as a virgin. This is emotionally if not physically true: his fornications have been loveless and irresponsible. Bloom is accused of wasting his seed, whether through onanism, impotence with Molly, or intercourse with prostitutes. Compared with them, Mulligan, the willing "fertiliser and incubator" (402), is a hero. Like the other victors in this novel, however, Mulligan is hollow: his mockery emphasizes his sense of sex not as the encounter Stephen so dreads and desires, nor as the engendering act Bloom is inhibited about, but as an impersonal act, a purely physical feat. It seems that even in its most serious function, procreation, sex is easy only for those who are facile and uncaring.

The lustfulness of the group, and its dependence on impediments to intercourse that assure less risk of both responsibility and consequences, are asserted in a Bunyanesque passage (italics mine):

> for that foul plague Allpox and the monsters they cared not for them, for Preservative had given them a stout shield of *oxengut* and, third, that they might take no hurt neither from Offspring that was that wicked devil by virtue of this same shield which was named Killchild. So were they all in their blind fancy, Mr Cavil and Mr Sometimes Godly, Mr Ape Swillale, Mr False Franklin, Mr Dainty Dixon, Young Boasthard and Mr Cautious Calmer. Wherein, O wretched company, were ye all deceived for that was the voice of the god that was in a very grievous rage that he would presently lift his arm and spill their souls for their abuses and their spillings done by them contrariwise to his word which forth to bring brenningly biddeth. (396)

Onanism and pederasty are included in this list of sins against the light by numerous passages spread through the chapter. Thus, the approach to these subjects taken in the library scene is picked up and developed. That all of these sexual "deviations" are condemned by Biblical injunction and Christian doctrine gives a real base to Joyce's essentially metaphorical handling of them. If sexual intercourse is a metaphor for encounter with the real, then anything short of "full" heterosexual intercourse is a denial, falsification, perversion, or idealization of the real. By the standards set up in this chapter, every male who appears in it is a doomed sinner. However, there is, as usual in *Ulysses*, an antithetical position.

Because the position taken early in the chapter is that appropriate to the era of the styles imitated, that is, strictly interpreted Christian doctrine, and because Joyce's imitations are so strong and passionate even with their comedy, it is possible to conclude that Joyce's position (or at least, that of the chapter) on sex is that it is permissible only within marriage and acceptable there only when it risks conception. But just as the ideal of the hero is undercut in Cyclops, and the ideal of romantic love in Nausikaa, the Christian ideal of sex is undercut here. No one in the refectory, with the possible exception of Nurse Callan, has been able to achieve it. And there is a strong suggestion that if Nurse Callan has maintained her chastity, she is wasting herself (this is reminiscent of Bloom's thoughts about the barmaids in Sirens). Bloom's sonlessness has little to do with his not impregnating Bridie Kelly. A passage containing the familiar Biblical condemnation of exogamy and adultery is undercut partly by its own language and partly by what follows it: "Remember, Erin, thy generations and thy days of old, how thou settedst little by me and by my word and broughtest in a stranger to my gates to commit fornication in my sight and to wax fat and kick like Jeshurum." The passage goes on to urge the people to look forth to "a land flowing with milk and money" (393). The twist in the last word is comic, but it also points out the materialism actually implicit in the Biblical texts. The paragraph picks up Deasy's references to a woman (Devorgilla, wife of Tiernan O'Rourke, although Deasy has the facts mixed up) as being responsible for the downfall of Ireland just as Eve was responsible for the downfall of the world. It picks up as well the citizen's chauvinistic notions about racial "purity." In other words, the exhortation to apartheid and endogamy that was in fact the message of the deuteron-omists is echoed in this novel by two blatant bigots; when repeated in this chapter, it has, perforce, ironic overtones.

Furthermore, despite the guilt of these "sinners," despite the warn-ings given them in the chapter, the thunder, when it comes, does not strike them down but brings rain to the wasteland—although there is no suggestion that the rain means final salvation. The climax of this undercutting of the Christian position on sex is the eulogy to Theodore Purefoy, who is the only man in the novel explicitly to abide by it. A crowing Carlylian voice hails Purefoy as "the remark-ablest progenitor" in "this chaffering allincluding most farraginous chronicle." It then describes the Purefoys' financial difficulties, Theo-dore's exhaustion, Mina's many and unaesthetic physical ills, and mentions the problem of overpopulation: "Malthusiasts go hang" (423). Mina Purefoy's later appearance in Circe as the goddess of unreason contains the same ambivalence. The Purefoy's stupid, blind persistence in reproducing is disastrous for them and not representa-tive to us of high endeavor. At the same time, their behavior does express pure faith; their relation is a genuine at-onement. If relation-ships thrived without defenses, without safeguards, they would neces-sarily be more serious, more meaningful, holy. If every intercourse risked fruition, if every word or act between people ran the risk of total response, of engendering new and unpredictable reactions, all intercourse, physical and verbal, would be sacred.

Joyce's point is complex. The ideal of genuine encounter stands, but like other ideals, it cannot be totally adhered to in the real world with-out turning into a distortion of itself. It is impossible always to live authentically. To live authentically in even one area, sex, is ridiculous and destructive, as the Purefoys show. It is difficult and painful to live this way even partially, as Bloom and Stephen show. But those who make no attempt to live authentically are corrupt and doomed to half-life, like the young men in the refectory. The ideal is too high for those who live in the void. What is necessary, and the best that humans can do, is to have some sense of the sacredness of genuine encounter, which both Bloom and Stephen have.

Not only is Bloom guilty of carnal concupiscence and of using the great shield Killchild, but he is also "his own and only enjoyer," guilty of that sin against the light which is "a habit reprehensible at puberty" but "second nature and an opprobrium in middle life" (409). The phrase "only enjoyer" echoes the wording of the dedication to Shakespeare's sonnets, thus tying this theme to that of Scylla and Charybdis, and reminding us of the onanistic or pederastic aesthetes, and Shakespeare's goring by the boar of sexuality. Mulligan's gay discussion of sterility from both "inhibitory" and "prohibitory" (402) causes has application to Bloom, as does the suggestion "Greater love than this . . . no man hath that a man lay down his wife for his friend" (393). But Bloom's most serious sin is seen to be his encounter with the prostitute Bridie Kelly:

> They are entwined in nethermost darkness, the willer with the willed, and in an instant (*fiat!*) light shall flood the world. Did heart leap to heart? Nay, fair reader. In a breath 'twas done but—hold! Back! It must not be! In terror the poor girl flees away through the murk. She is the bride of darkness, a daughter of night. She dare not bear the sunnygolden babe of day. No, Leopold! Name and memory solace thee not. That youthful illusion of thy strength was taken from thee and in vain. No son of thy loins is by thee. There is none now to be for Leopold, what Leopold was for Rudolph. (413-414)

However ludicrous or comic the attacks on Bloom, there is no question that he understands the cost of his sexual behavior. He shows his usual delicacy in his dismay at the young men's "impudent mocks . . . at the cost of feminine delicacy" (407) and in his real pleasure at learning that Mina Purefoy's ordeal is nearly over; his anguish at his "impotence" and sonlessness is felt to be real even as it is mocked. He lives in reality; there is little he can do to change his state; so he transfers the love he would have for a son to Stephen. He observes him kindly, is concerned for him. Bloom is probably the only one in the company who is thinking about anyone but himself, or of anything but how to boost his own ego through some witticism. Indeed, it is just after the passage describing his observation of Stephen, thinking about him, that the Word is born. These are small acts, like all Bloom's acts, but they reinforce our sense of his somewhat comic decency and reinforce the author's insistence that the great things are the small things, that decency and charity should be mankind's standards. At the same time, these attitudes and actions show Bloom's awareness of the importance of genuineness in human encounter: if he cannot always achieve it, he reveres it.

Stephen's problem is fully developed in this episode. He recognizes his avoidance of genuine sexual encounter to be "sinful." He knows that it prevents him from growing both as man and as poet; he longs for some Ann Hathaway, some Venus, some "boldfaced Stratford wench who tumbles in a cornfield a lover younger than herself" (191). Left to himself, he remains "the eternal son and ever virgin" (392) because of his terror of eternal recurrence. He still cannot accept his participation in the human condition: "And would he not accept to die like the rest and pass away? By no means would he and make more shows according as men do with wives which Phenomenon has commanded them to do by the book Law. Then wotted he nought of that other land which is called Believe-on-Me, that is the land of promise which behoves to the king Delightful and shall be for ever where there is no death and no birth neither wiving nor mothering?" (395). Longing on the one hand for the ideal, which eradicates sex, he on the other hand is drawn away from it by the whore Bird-in-the-Hand into carnal concupiscence. Yet he understands the holy nature of sexuality: "In woman's womb word is made flesh but in the spirit of the maker all flesh that passes becomes the word that shall not pass away" (391).

The theme of the Virgin and the tags from Taxil that are threaded through the book (ideal and perversion) are connected and essentially laid to rest in this chapter. They are one pair of terms explaining Stephen's dilemma. "But here is the matter now. Or she knew him . . . and was but creature of her creature, *vergine madre figlia di tuo figlio* or she knew him not and then stands she in the one denial or ignorancy with Peter Piscator who lives in the house that Jack built and with Joseph the Joiner patron of the happy demise of all unhappy marriages" (391). The choices are limited. A surrender to physicality, to the desires of the body and the cycles of nature, makes one mere creature; procreation through divine infusion, without the bloody breaking of the hymen, without encounter with another, leaves one in a state of "denial or ignorancy" living in a nursery rhyme world, in the pallor and tears of Blake's Thel.

Stephen knows that masturbation or intercourse with impediment, as his with prostitutes, leads to physical barrenness; he sees as sinful such killing of the oxen of the sun. The waste of "those Godpossibled souls that we nightly impossibilise" is "the sin against the Holy Ghost, Very God, Lord and Giver of Life" (389). He also understands that encounter requires action, which frightens him, as does the thunder, punishment for waste of potential. His potential is psychical as well as physical. He boasts that he is a master of metempsychosis, that he can raise the dead: "If I call them into life across the waters of Lethe will not the poor ghosts troop to my call? . . . I, Bous Stephanoumenos, bullockbefriending bard, am lord and giver of their life" (415). But Vincent, in language reminiscent of the religious side of the sexual discussion, reminds him that he must first have intercourse with the real (italics mine): "That answer . . . will adorn you more fitly when something more, and greatly more, than a capful of light odes can call your genius *father*. All who wish you well hope this for you. All desire to see you *bring forth* the work you meditate" (415).

Thus, the equation made in the chapter that language is to truth as sexual intercourse is to authenticity stands in the void. There is no right way, no moral certitude. No course of action in sexual life can lead to salvation, just as none of the many styles leads to certitude about reality. The many styles leave us feeling that we have somehow not seen the real scene at all. The nightmare *muflisme* that follows the passage on Bloom's sonlessness conflates Bloom's Eden vision with the wasteland: "Agendath is a waste land, a home of screechowls and the sandblind upupa. Netaim, the golden, is no more." All things become beasts because of parallax: "Parallax stalks behind." But eternal recurrence is also metempsychosis, as Martha and Milly merge and arise "among the Pleiades" (414).

Stephen's passage on metempsychosis indicates that such a phenomenon was attained, in Joyce's mind, through art, which immortalizes human characters and eternalizes human states of being. It is a piece of comic realism that Joyce sets his seal on this notion by immortalizing many of Dublin's citizens in *Ulysses*. Stephen's thoughts about the signatures of things, related to Bloom's notion that everything speaks in its own way, is mockingly mentioned as Mulligan regards Bloom regarding a bottle: "Any object, intensely regarded, may be a gate of access to the incorruptible eon of the gods" (416). Like the theosophists in the library, who believe that through spiritual apprehension they can reach the "formless spiritual essences" (185) of things, like Stephen trying to read signatures in the wreckage on the beach, like Joyce himself writing his epiphanies, mankind believes it can and keeps trying to penetrate through surfaces to underlying meaning. *Ulysses*, and especially this episode, suggest that although there is an ultimate reality, mankind can reach it only through the prophylaxis of the individual mode of perception.

In a final burst of praise for Theodore Purefoy, the narrator exclaims: "With thee it was not as with many that will and would and wait and never do. Thou sawest thy America, thy lifetask, and didst charge to cover like the transpontine bison" (424). Thus, Purefoy is held up as having the answer to the problems that plague Stephen, who is afraid to act, and Bloom, who does not know what action to take and who hums, all day, the phrase from *La ci darem*, "*vorrei e non vorrei*" (93), I would and would not. Since Mina Purefoy appears fettered in Circe, the "act" theme, the Fetter Lane passages, Bloom's references to the aria, and the beast theme of Oxen are all linked to the Purefoys and their ludicrous act of faith.

The concluding paragraphs of this episode are written in a chaotic and fragmented style, adumbrating the technique of *Finnegans Wake*. This technique, coming after the rounded periods of late nineteenth-century authors, seems to represent the present, 1904. For although we perceive the past through the lens of the styles of great writers, we perceive the present, whatever that present may be, as disjointed and chaotic. Yet there is unity even within this confusion. As the group leaves Burke's at closing time, snatches of dialogue are reported by the narrator. One question could apply to either Stephen or Bloom, both of whom are wearing black: "who the sooty hell's the johnny in the black duds? Hush! Sinned against the light and even now that day is at hand when he shall come to judge the world by fire" (428). This passage identifies Stephen and Bloom and, by extension, all men; it identifies sinner and god, the "he" being ambivalent; and it foreshadows the apocaplyse in Circe. The final paragraph in the chapter reminds us just whose world we are living in. The great sermon is the authentic voice of *dio boia*, disguised as Alexander Dowie:

Come on, you winefizzling ginsizzling booseguzzling existences! Come on, you dog-gone, bullnecked, beetlebrowed, hogjowled, peanutbrained, weaseleyed fourflushers, false alarms and excess baggage! Come on, you triple extract of infamy! Alexander J. Christ Dowie, that's yanked to glory most half this planet from 'Frisco

Beach to Vladivostok. The Deity ain't no nickel dime bumshow. I put it to you that he's on the square and a corking fine business proposition. He's the grandest thing yet and don't you forget it. Shout salvation in king Jesus. You'll need to rise precious early, you sinner there, if you want to diddle the Almighty God. Pflaaaap! Not half. He's got a coughmixture with a punch in it for you, my friend, in his backpocket. Just you try it on. (428)

The narrator of Oxen of the Sun intrudes on the "plot" in a very different way from the narrators of Sirens and Cyclops. There is, in this episode, no stratum of dialogue or of internal monologue. There will be no internal monologue again in the book proper (though there is in the coda). Although Circe contains some dialogue, and Eumaeus a little, after that, reportage of actual speech will also disappear. We are losing the earth, the substantial, the real. The narrator flips through his deck of styles tauntingly: he knows we want, not truth, but certitude. He, or the author behind him, also knows that such is not a gift he can honestly confer on us. Any certitude we feel in life must come from within us, and it can be certitude only about human values, not about divine order.

The structure of this episode is also uncertain. There is a climax of sorts about three-quarters of the way through, when Haines appears in a Gothic scene. Another climax occurs just two pages later, in the evocation of the *muflisme*. The highest point of energy and exuberance is reached shortly before the end, beginning with the word "Burke's" (423). But there is little logical structure in the arrangement of sections: their content is determined by style rather than by dramatic requirements of the material. In Cyclops, where the movement is not chronological, Joyce can adjust the style to the dramatic or satiric requirements of the scene; here the style, the lens through which we look, determines what we shall see. The only guideposts to structure in the chapter are the stages in embryonic development, which serve the same purpose as the physical details about the city of Dublin in other chapters.

No doubt this random structure is a further reason for critical disfavor toward this chapter. Embryonic development used as a structuring principle does seem gratuitous, unrelated organically to the material. But Joyce is writing an anatomy of the human condition: the material is essentially formless, or at least circular. Nothing much does happen in the chapter. Beyond that, Joyce does not see life as a tragedy or even as a comedy. He does not present us with a dramatic unit in which man discovers his significance through misfortune, nor one in which man triumphs over fortune. *Ulysses* is comitragic, or comic-pathetic-tragic, or some combination that we need to call on Polonius to name. Human life is endless, repetitive, eternal, shot through with patterns of coincidence; it is painful, constricting, but it flashes with vivid emotion. Such a vision cannot be prescinded by a five- or three-act structure. Aside from its thin plot and rich characters, *Ulysses* is a series of meditations on human life.

This chapter is a meditation on reality. The metaphor for reality is sexual intercourse; the expression of reality is language. Since the changes in language are the subject matter, those changes dictate the "content." The narrator always speaks directly to the reader. There is no way we can talk about Stephen or Bloom as being aware of what happens in this episode: they are involved in the action only; the chapter takes place far above their heads. But even as the chapter meditates on reality, it insists that reality is ineffable. Man is placed in the intolerable bind of feeling the necessity of coition with a reality that one cannot define much beyond one's perception of it. We must act, but act in the void. What we know about these necessities, Stephen knows too. His knowledge is crucial to one who wishes to create literature. This episode places literature, along with other human expressions, firmly in the void. How can Stephen handle such a problem? Well, he could write a book like *Ulysses*.

Circe

This brilliant chapter has received much worthy critical comment, but certain questions remain to haunt the reader. Most of them arise from uncertainty as to the point of view. Interpretation of the episode is made difficult because critics are confused as to why items from outside the consciousness of a character appear in "his" hallucination, or suffer from a misapprehension that the dramatic form of the chapter guarantees objectivity, or draw unwarranted conclusions about the prophetic significance of the characters' actions.[27] Such difficulties arise because readers try to make sense of the chapter on naturalistic grounds. Like Oxen and Eumaeus, Circe confounds the reader who approaches it seeking naturalism.

Some actual events do seem to occur. Bloom follows Stephen to Mrs. Cohen's and stands outside for a time talking to Zoe. Stephen plays the piano, talks essentially to himself, dances, and breaks a chandelier. There is an argument about money. Bloom takes care of the finances and follows Stephen outside, where he is having an altercation with two soldiers. A crowd gathers. Again Bloom rescues Stephen, probably with some help from Corny Kelleher. There is little beyond these bare bones that can be attributed with assurance to the naturalistic level: even the speeches assigned to Lynch and the prostitutes are often improbable. If we regard the chapter as operating on the naturalistic level with the intrusion of the surreal in the form of "hallucinations" that occur to the characters (thus finding the technique similar to but even more naturalistic than that of Cyclops), we face a problem with the appearance in one consciousness of items from another, and with what Clive Hart calls "the author's expressionistic commentary."[28] If we accept the chapter totally on the surreal level, we face a problem with the few actual events that do seem to occur and are verified in Eumaeus and Ithaca. So although Circe is written in the most objective of literary modes, drama, it is in this episode that the objectively real is most difficult to discern.

In Circe, all the narrative voices that dominate earlier chapters gather together and split themselves fissionally into seemingly endless multiplicity. In place of the exuberant mockers of Sirens and Cyclops, the prancing transvestite of Nausikaa, the solemn-faced pedant of Oxen of the Sun, there are hundreds of derisive voices, including those of a fan, a cap, a horse, a pianola, a bracelet, and a hue and cry. "Everything speaks in its own way" (121).[29] The signatures of things that Stephen is so eager to read in the morning here require no interrogation. Things announce themselves, although Stephen is not listening. The speech of objects has a validity equal to that of actual characters. Imagined characters, fictions within the fiction (like Philip Beaufoy or Rumbold), have an equal claim on our credulity. Even states, conditions, aspirations, fears, "sins or . . . evil memories which are hidden away by man in the darkest places of the heart" (421; a foreshadowing in Oxen of the theme of Circe) are hypostatized. The chapter is like a medieval last judgment, in which everything in the hierarchical universe, from the pebbles and sand at its bottom to the souls and angels near its top, arises to accuse man. Everything joins forces to hound our heroes. Circe is a paradise of paranoia.

It has been assumed that the "hallucinations," surreal as they are, also occupy the naturalistic level, in other words, that they occur inside the mind of a character much as hallucinations sometimes occur inside the minds of actual people. But in actual life, hallucinations are rare, even among people in mental hospitals. Bloom and Stephen are not hallucinating. The hallucinations are hypostatizations of their hidden feelings; on the naturalistic level, the characters are simply feeling. The hallucinations are production numbers staged by the author for the audience; they are a running commentary, much like the comment by the two narrators in Cyclops or the single narrator of Sirens. Circe is a nightmare sent by god-Joyce to the reader.

Neither Bloom nor Stephen is present when the chapter opens, yet the opening scene is as grotesque as anything else in the episode. Not only the speeches of the actors but their actions and appearance, as described by the not-so-objective scenarist, are surrealistic, robot-like, jerky, and above all symbolic. The opening scene has the character of a hallucination or nightmare, although the supposedly invisible narrator is presenting it directly to the reader without referring it to either of the major characters. The figures of Cissy Caffrey, Edy Boardman, and the twins appear, and under their own names, but they are known by name to neither of the major characters. It is questionable if Bloom even sees them in Nighttown. Only we know them, and only we can perceive the significance of placing the babies and baby sitters of Nausikaa in this environment. At the end of the chapter, Stephen calls Ireland "the old sow that eats her farrow" (595), but the disease devouring Irish society is demonstrated all through the chapter. It is not necessary to determine whether the figure of Cissy Caffrey in Circe is identical with that in Nausikaa, or whether the later one represents the real or possible future, or the hidden desires of the earlier one, or whether the figure in Circe is a metaphor for many poor young women in Ireland. The character Cissy Caffrey in Nausikaa will probably become either the potwalloper of that chapter or the prostitute of this one: there are few other alternatives for her. All of these possibilities exist in the image as it stands; each carries its own ironic vibration.

Recurrent motives in the episode and references to motives of which only the reader can be aware thread the novel. For instance, the transformations of the dog that follows Bloom in Circe correspond to the transformations of the dog in Proteus, and they carry a similar meaning, but Bloom cannot draw any significance from them. Indeed, it is the narrator who informs us that these are transformations and not just a series of different animals: the dog appears first as a spaniel before Bloom's entrance into the scene, then is manifested as a retriever, and thereafter is metamorphosized at least ten times, possibly thirteen if one includes the metamorphoses into beagle, dachshund, and Paddy Dignam; like Bloom, he begins and ends as a retriever. The fox is paralleled with the dark horse, but only the reader is aware that these animals are emblems for the two major characters. The figure or name of Elijah is alluded to frequently throughout the novel: a little cloud "no bigger than a woman's hand" (667); "Get down, bald poll" (40);[30] the name on the handbill; the analogy in Bloom's apotheosis. The name Elijah comes to the attention of both characters, but their perception of its significance in their world is not as complete as ours. Elijah appears physically in Circe to point to another of the novel's continuing analogies. He identifies all the characters in the scene with the Christ: "Florry Christ, Stephen Christ, Zoe Christ, Bloom Christ, Kitty Christ, Lynch Christ, it's up to you to sense that cosmic force" (507). Stephen occasionally identifies himself with the Christ, but Bloom does not, consciously at least.[31] The figures of Elijah and his words have symbolic significance mainly for the reader. When Elijah appears in Circe, he speaks in the style of Alexander Dowie; Dowie himself speaks in one of "Bloom's" hallucinations. But neither Stephen nor Bloom hears the preacher's voice at the end of Oxen; they simply see his name on a sign. It is to us the voice in Oxen speaks, and only we know its style.

Another category of violation of physical and psychological realism is the injection into what are supposed to be one character's hallucinations of material from the narrational level of the novel, statements made by narrator to reader that exist on another plane from the characters. For example, the nameless one speaks the comment he only thinks in Cyclops, "Gob, he organised her" and refers to Bloom's profit on the Gold Cup Race; these statements occur in one of "Bloom's" hallucinations, but Bloom cannot possibly remember what he has not heard. Again, when Zoe reads Bloom's palm, Black Liz appears and utters a line from an interpolation in Cyclops. The scene in which Tom Rochford's heroism is discussed occurs in Wandering Rocks, and Bloom is not present, yet Rochford appears in the character of a hero in one of "Bloom's" visions. Lenehan's riddle is a contin-

uing motif—occurring several times after Aeolus, in Sirens for instance—but as far as we know, Bloom does not know it, for he is not
present in the newspaper office when it is told. Yet he repeats it. The
scene of Kitty and Lynch in the thicket also occurs in Wandering
Rocks; Bloom could have only the vaguest notion of it from the conversation in Oxen, yet it is relived in one of "his" hallucinations.

There are also innumerable violations of character autonomy.
Molly utters to Bloom a phrase read by Stephen in Wandering Rocks:
"Nebrakada Femininum" (440). Levin points out: "it was Bloom who
noted at the funeral that Martin Cunningham's sympathetic face was
like Shakespeare's . . . yet it is now to Stephen that Shakespeare appears in the guise of Cunningham."[32] It is highly unlikely that Bloom
could know the story of Shakespeare's will and the secondbest bed,
yet Bello says to him, "You have made your secondbest bed and
others must lie in it" (543). Edward VII appears in a hallucination
supposedly occurring to Stephen, but he is sucking red jujubes—an
image in Bloom's mind in Lestrygonians. The king carries a plasterer's
bucket bearing the legend *"defense d'uriner"*; this refers to Gaffer's
story told when Stephen is not present (the same bucket is involved in
one of "Bloom's" hallucinations, and apparently symbolizes the long-
standing childhood guilt and terror about staining oneself). In the
Edward VII dramatization—for it is time to stop calling the insets
hallucinations—figures appear from Stephen's consciousness—Kevin
and Patrice Egan, the Bawd—as well as from Bloom's consciousness—
the croppy boy, the citizen, and Rumbold. In several places items
from the two consciousnesses and items from outside both are so
thoroughly merged that any attribution is impossible. Consider the
vision that follows Stephen's "Dance of Death":

Bang fresh barang bang of lacquey's bell, horse, nag, steer, piglings,
Conmee on Christass lame crutch and leg sailor in cockboat arm-
folded ropepulling hitching stamp hornpipe through and through,
Baraabum! On nags, hogs, bellhorses, Gadarene swine, Corny in
coffin. Steel shark stone onehandled Nelson, two trickies Frauenzimmer plumstained from pram falling bawling. Gum, he's a cham-
pion. Fuseblue peer from barrel rev. evensong Love on hackney
jaunt Blazes blind coddoubled bicyclers Dilly with snowcake no
fancy clothes. Then in last wiswitchback lumbering up and down
bump mashtub sort of viceroy and reine relish for tublumber bump-
shire rose. Baraabum! (579)

This is a medieval procession like the famous one in *Piers Plowman*. It is announced by the ring of the laquey's bell, the same ring that reverberates through Wandering Rocks. Many of its images derive from that chapter, which is closely related to this one. Neither Stephen nor Bloom sees Conmee or the lame sailor in that chapter. The ironic analogy of Christ with Conmee (riding, naturally) and the picture of the sailor in movement, presumably before he was disabled, are paraded for the benefit of the reader. In Wandering Rocks we are given a series of epiphanies of daytime Dublin; in Circe, a series of epiphanies of its secret side. Corny Kelleher, out of a coffin, is part of Bloom's experience of the day, but he also appears in Wandering Rocks. Nelson's Pillar, "Frauenzimmer," and the plums are part of Stephen's morning hours. The pram is from Nausikaa; the "fuseblue peer from barrel" seems to refer to Kevin Egan; "evensong" possibly refers to the evening service at the beach. Neither Bloom nor Stephen is acquainted with the Reverend Love; Blazes and the snowcake are part of Bloom's experience this day, and Dilly in tatters ("no fancy clothes" is from the song *A Yorkshire Girl*, which is being played) appears to both characters, although "tatters" is Bloom's word. The bicyclers ride all through the town; "mashtub" is a word from an interpolation in Cyclops; the viceregal procession that rounds off this procession, as it does Wandering Rocks, is not seen, early in the day, by either main character. Not only are the experiences of the two characters merged together and blended with things from outside them (Conmee, Love, "mashtub," the viceregal procession), but the separate items are merged with each other by the punctuation. Conmee is joined with the lame sailor; the "two trickies Frauenzimmer" are joined with the characters for which they provided the inspiration, the two women in Stephen's parable, and also with the baby sitters at the beach; Egan, Love, Blazes, the blind boy, the bicyclers and, oddly, Dilly are joined. The grounds of association may sometimes be opaque, but one thing is clear: the entire world of Dublin is moving on a tumbling rhythmic journey toward death.

The apocalypse near the end of the chapter merges figures in the same way. It contains references to Tom Rochford and the Rev. Love, neither of whom is explicitly known by Stephen or Bloom. The Society Ladies lifting their skirts is a Bloomesque vision, although there is also a reference to such an act in the library chapter, when

Mulligan taunts Stephen with having fallen down drunk in the doorway of the Camden Hall. Quakerlyster is a Dedalian phrase. Mina
Purefoy as goddess of unreason, fettered (as is Molly in her appearance, implying that both are linked and bound to the world of substance and action), and the open umbrella have meaning only in the
context given these symbols in Oxen of the Sun, which is a direct
narration to the reader, outside the characters' consciousnesses.

The appearance of Shakespeare's face in the mirror to both Stephen
and Bloom indicates a convergence between them, but *not on the
naturalistic level.* The "subject" of the section of Circe surrounding
this image is marriage and family. Just as every subject discussed or
mentioned in earlier chapters is seen in the coloration of the theme of
the chapter, so marriage in Circe is grotesque, ugly, deformed, or
"deviant." So we see the athletic adultery of Molly with Boylan, the
ugly picture of the widowed Mrs. Dignam and her family, a variety of
distorted matings or issues—in Pasiphae, Grissel Steevens, the
Lamberts—and Noah's exposure to Ham. Given Stephen's interpretation of Shakespeare's life in the library scene, it is appropriate that
Shakespeare should appear here. He is "beardless," "rigid in facial
paralysis" (567), horned with antlers. His beardlessness suggests feminacy, which by this point in the novel is really androgyny, and links
him to Stephen and Bloom. The antlers suggest Shakespeare's and
Bloom's cuckoldry, but the image can be extended to Stephen, who
has just been "cuckolded" by Mulligan with Haines. Adultery in this
novel is a metaphor for the incertitude lying beneath even the closest
human bonds: in this sense all people are betrayed, both in love and in
friendship. The paralysis of Shakespeare is another form of the
paralysis that causes Bloom to be impotent (sexually paralyzed) with
Molly, and Stephen to be unable to love (emotionally paralyzed). The
paralysis endemic to Dublin (from *Dubliners* on) can be overcome
only by action, which is connected with separation (departure or
hate). But Bloom already knows he is a cuckold, and Stephen already
knows he must act: the image in the mirror therefore tells neither
character anything about themselves of which they are unaware. The
image operates to enable us, not the characters, to discover further
planes of identity in the seemingly random world.

Shakespeare speaks in ventriloquy (through Joyce, as Joyce speaks
through his narrator). Shakespeare says, " 'Tis the loud laugh

bespeaks the vacant mind," an immediate reference to the world (Bella, Zoe, Florry, Kitty, and Lynch) that laughs at Bloom and the Molly/Boylan image, and by extension, a warning to readers who may be thoughtlessly laughing with the narrator at the characters. To Bloom he says, "Thou thoughtest as how thou wastest invisible" (error is perhaps forgivable given the difficulties of translating from one sphere to another). This picks up the "no-one" theme that runs through the book and is mentioned a bit earlier in the chapter when Bloom, after admitting various sexual "sins," concludes, "Besides, who saw?" and is mocked by an answer given by "staggering bob": "Me. Me see" (549). Stephen has also felt shame this day. The line connects many threads, including the song "I am the boy/That can enjoy/Invisibility" (10), the note "Tarnkappe" to Hades where the man in the mackintosh is first mentioned, as well as Stephen's remark in *Portrait* that in the "dramatic" mode the author is invisible:[33] "The personality of the artist, at first a cry or a cadence . . . finally refines itself out of existence, impersonalises itself, so to speak. The esthetic image in the dramatic form is life purified and reprojected from the human imagination. The mystery of esthetic like that of material creation is accomplished. The artist, like the God of the creation, remains · within or behind or beyond or above his handiwork, invisible, refined out of existence, indifferent, paring his fingernails" (*P*, 215).

The narrative method of *Ulysses* takes off from this passage in both a serious and a comic way: Joyce uses and mocks his serious notions at the same time. The Circe chapter, written in the mode of drama, adheres even more closely to the passage in *Portrait*. The invisible observer who appears disguised as the thirteenth mourner at a funeral, who sees what "no-one" else does, is Joyce/Shakepeare, or any other author gifted enough to see through surfaces to the hidden feelings that underlie behavior.

Shakespeare crows with a capon's laugh, another reference to his lack of full manliness, and speaks these strange lines: "Iagogo! How my Oldfellow chokit his Thursdaymomun. Iagogogo!" (567). I cannot claim completely to elucidate these lines, but only point to some associations. "Thursday-mom-un" could refer to Stephen, who was born on a Thursday (and born "Today"), who is haunted by guilt about his mother, and whose riddle brings together the theme of guilt and the Shakespeare theme, in that the fox is associated with both Shakespeare and Jesus. The verb makes Oldfellow seem unlikely as a reference to Bloom. It may refer to Hamlet père, who in his symbolic aspect as father is haunting or choking Stephen. However, the line could also be Shakespeare's reference to Joyce, who is creating him (Shakespeare) as his own literary grandfather, and who, in his guise as narrator, is "choking" both characters on this Thursday. The reference to Iago seems less opaque. Iago, Stephen says in the library, is the "unremitting intellect . . . ceaselessly willing that the moor in him shall suffer." Iago is "hornmad" (212). If we take the adjective to mean obsessed with sex, especially with sexual betrayal, it can be applied to the Shakespeare in Stephen's fiction, to this chapter, and to Joyce and the whole of *Ulysses*. Iago as the unremitting intellect describes the mocking narrator of *Ulysses,* and the moor (the "dark" side of experience, emotion) represents the emotions so ceaselessly battered throughout the novel. Joyce adopts Shakespeare's division of experience into Iago/Othello categories, but his Iago is the narrator, his Othello the humanity described by that narrator. Thus, Joyce again identifies himself with Shakespeare. The dichotomy that is the method of the novel is also Stephen's dilemma, the way out of which is to act. A notesheet reference to Oxen associates the Latin *ago* with *itus,* "act" with a "going away."[34] "I ago go go" therefore can be read as a short-hand version of the exhortations to act sprinkled through the novel. The associations with Iago are hate, action, going away, and intellect, a set reminiscent of the earlier Stephen's "silence, exile, and cunning" (*P,*247). Shakespeare's second speech, uttered in "paralytic rage," (568) suggests a view of remarriage as adultery, murder, incest (a view taken by some religious systems also), and ties the Hamlet theme to this section of Circe (marriage as grotesque and deformed), just as it is tied to the themes of other chapters.

Overall, then, the image is an emblem for many themes, of which only the reader is aware and which only he can connect. Stephen does not know Bloom is a cuckold; Bloom does not know that Stephen describes Shakespeare thus. The act theme is part of Stephen's consciousness, but it also reverberates above and beyond him. No one inside the novel could make the connections of "invisible" with the no-one theme, the song of invisibility, the man in the mackintosh, and the description of dramatic form in *Portrait*. It is therefore impossible to make any deductions at all about the effect of this "vision" on the characters on a naturalistic level; it is impossible even to determine how much of this vision occurs on the naturalistic level. On the symbolic level, it can be called a moment of convergence between Stephen and Bloom, but it is a convergence of which they themselves are unconscious. Only we can see it, as only we can see the intermeshing and hidden relations of many characters in Wandering Rocks. As gods, we see a symbolic convergence between Stephen and Bloom: and even on that level, it is ludicrous.

The significance of all this should be clear. None of the dramatizations, nothing that happens in this chapter, happens with the full awareness or comprehension of the characters. Events, characters, and objects drawn from different levels and from the entire novel are merged into a single experience; the only people with knowledge enough to comprehend that experience are author and reader. Perception of this has led Arnold Goldman to suspect that Circe is merely Joyce's "fantasia on his own novel," an in-joke written self-indulgently for Joyce's own pleasure.[35] True, Joyce uses the names of Carr and Bennett, but he does such things all through the novel. Circe merges items from the entire world of *Ulysses:* it merges the consciousnesses of its characters; it offers one unified human nightmare.[36] This is the nightmare of *anima mundi* and symbolizes the submerged oneness of all men. In a way it is a parody of the oneness and truth that lie hidden beneath the veil of Māyā: beneath the individuated forms of the surface lies unity, but it is grotesque, terrifying, and guilty. The question continues to be asked whether or not Bloom and Stephen reach a genuine at-onement. The fact is that they do, in both Circe and Ithaca, but only in the eyes of the beholder, not in their own. The events in Circe symbolize the relatedness of not just Stephen and Bloom but of all people. The episode is the dramatic climax of the book because in it, and only in it, act, word, thought, and feeling are identical. That is why the chapter is so laden with correspondences and coincidences, and why it is impossible to isolate any event within the consciousness of any character. Joyce's method of engaging the reader in the creation of the work here reaches its height: Circe is a nightmare that happens to the reader.

The episode is strewn with correspondences. Consider, for example, the play with the numbers sixteen and twenty-two (sixteen will be picked up again in Eumaeus, in the number six-sixteen, symbolic of homosexual consolidarity) and their relation to the problems of Stephen and Bloom. Bloom has been doing "black slave labor" (554) for sixteen years; Stephen has been "blind" since he broke his glasses sixteen years earlier: "Yesterday. Sixteen years ago" (560). He is still blind, for he cannot read signatures of things: "I never could read His handwriting except His criminal thumbprint on the haddock" (562). Bloom "fell" twenty-two years ago when he was sixteen; Stephen fell sixteen years ago and is now twenty-two. Stephen finds significance in these coincidences, saying, "See? Moves to one great goal" (563). That goal, as enunciated earlier, is the manifestation of God. Bloom has fallen "thirtytwo head over heels per second" (550), and the number associated with gravity is thus linked with the fall of man through sexuality. The coincidences and correspondences in this chapter, like those throughout the novel, suggest the existence of a larger pattern in which all small lives are contained. But the larger pattern has no metaphysical significance, indicates no transcendent purpose; it is earthbound, pointing to the ubiquity and similarity of human needs, constrictions, shame, guilt, and secrecy.[37]

Analogy is employed less in this episode than in some that precede it; the allusions in the chapter are mainly to items within the novel. But there are links with the Homeric trellis-work in the many animal figures and in phrases like "travels beyond the sea" (562) in Zoe's reading of Bloom's palm. Paralleling the allusion to items that appear earlier in the novel is a reversion to the narrational styles of other chapters, generally found in the "stage directions." A long descriptive paragraph ends in a Sirens-like style: "The car jingles tooraloom round the corner of the tooraloom lane. Corny Kelleher again reassuralooms with his hand. Bloom with his hand assuralooms Corny Kelleher that he is reassuraloomtay. The tinkling hoofs and jingling harness grow fainter with their tooraloolooloolooloo lay" (608). There are overtones of Nausikaa: "Kitty unpins her hat and sets it down calmly, patting her henna hair. And a prettier, a daintier head of winsome curls was never seen on a whore's shoulders" (521); and of Cyclops: "Ben Jumbo Dollard, rubicund, musclebound, hairynostrilled, hugebearded, cabbageeared, shaggychested, shockmaned, fatpapped, stands forth" (521).

The dramatic form of the chapter is appropriate to a technique in which details of the imagination are projected as realities. The form not only permits the hypostatization of thoughts and feelings but gives the illusion of objectivity. Narrator comment seems lacking. However, a glance at any of the "stage directions" should dispel that illusion. They make explicit the selection, arrangement, and production of the items in this chapter.

The point of view of Circe, like that of its predecessors, is from far above the scene. What is being examined is the irrational world, which is defined as the world of feelings, and the subject matter is thus connected with that of Sirens, Cyclops, and Nausikaa. The particular feelings being examined are secret and hidden ones, primarily sexual. The two major "clues" offered to the reader are the setting, a brothel district, and the many beast images, which connect the Homeric analogy with sexuality, the beast with two backs. As in Wandering Rocks, the reader is given a surface picture of disconnection and disease, and an underlying intimation of connection, the unity of human experience, whatever its nature. Any significance attending the events of this chapter exists largely for the reader alone. For the characters, significance is obscured. For both reader and characters, significance is ambivalent. Sultan says that Circe "contains the critical action in the novel and that crisis is the battle between Good and Evil which prepares the way for the Kingdom of God. Bloom and Stephen have fought the battle; and although one of them went there to commit Carnal Concupiscence and the other has recovered his ability to do so, they turn their backs on nighttown and proceed to the next chapter: 'atonement.' "[38] This description is difficult to accept for a work that insists on the identification of "good" and "evil." Circe deals with what is secret, hidden *beneath* the naturalistic level: ambitions and desires as well as fears and guilts. The significance of its events must also therefore be derived from the hidden level. On the surreal plane, the ambitions, desires, fears, and guilts of the entire race are played out. The chapter reveals these, just as Sirens reveals "static" emotions or Cyclops reveals human aggressiveness. What Bloom does in those chapters matters, but less so than this revelation of feeling. What Bloom does in Circe is in character: he acts with concern and kindliness. What Stephen does is in character: he talks, has difficulty acting, seems largely unaware of his surroundings, is drunk. What is out of character is Bloom's going to Nighttown in the first place, but his behavior is understandably a bit unusual this day. It is the emotions exposed in the chapter, especially Bloom's (as in other chapters), that are the major subject matter. And emotions are not easily changed. Bloom's guilt about going to the brothel district, his guilt at not having status and respect in his community, at being somehow unmanly because he is compassionate and nutritive, his desire for political reform and political power—all these have been with him for many years and will continue to be part of him. In the dim and frightening light of Nighttown, all rise to mock and accuse him (as well as any of us who have similar secret feelings) in much the same way he is mocked and accused in Sirens and Cyclops. But it is wishful thinking to conclude that because he momentarily fights down these feelings and carries on in spite of them (the vanishing of a "hallucination"), he has eradicated the feelings. Because the major area of secret feeling in most human beings is the sexual one, the major area examined in the chapter is sexuality, not just Bloom's but that of many characters. And Bloom's sexuality is a problem to him just as sexuality is a problem to most people. It has been a problem—this is explicit in the chapter—ever since he entered puberty. Things of this sort simply do not vanish overnight. At Bloom's age, one can hardly be unaware that one is masochistically tuned, and recognition of that or of any other sexual attunement does not cause the attunement to disappear. It is not the unconscious but merely the secret we are intruding upon.

Although Bloom's sexuality is an element in earlier dramatizations, it is most explicit in the famous masochistic "hallucination." Virag brings the subject of sex into full focus: "I am Virag who disclosed the sex secrets of monks and maidens" (519). He approaches the subject in a number of ways. He discusses sex as the purchase of a body as an object for sale.[39] He offers a comically factual, cant-like consideration of venereal diseases and cures. He excites himself with a greedy description of sex as domination: "Woman, undoing with sweet pudor her belt of rushrope, offers her allmoist yoni to man's lingam. Short time after man presents woman with pieces of jungle meat. Woman shows joy and covers herself with featherskins. Man loves her yoni fiercely with big lingam, the stiff one. (*He cries.*) *Coactus volui.* Then giddy woman will run about. Strong man grasps woman's wrist. Woman squeals, bites, spucks. Man, now fierce angry, strikes woman's fat yadgana. (*He chases his tail.*) Piffpaff! Popo!" (519-520). Virag mocks the legend of the Virgin, picking up references from throughout the novel. He laughs in a "rich feminine key" (516) and raises the specter of effeminacy.

Bloom responds to Virag's first approach factually and humanely: "She is rather lean," "She seems sad," "The stye I dislike" (512-513). Typically he gets involved and interested in cures, but finds Virag's intensity intolerable: "I am going to scream" (516). But the fear of effeminacy and the vision of sex as domination reach him; thus they are developed in the Henry Flower and Bella-Bello sequences. Bloom is accused, throughout this section, of a great variety of "sins," including fetishism involving shoes, women's soiled undergarments, and feces; pandering; obscene messages to women "telephoned mentally" (537); sitting on a toilet instead of standing at it; voyeurism; transvestism and female impersonation. At the same time, he "acts out" a masochistic transsexual fantasy. He has a desire to be a woman: "What you longed for has come to pass." But what does that mean to him? It means being a possession, "mine in earnest, a thing under the yoke." It means he will be turned into an object intended for sexual titillation, placed inside of tormenting clothing (clothing is the prime method of arousing desire in Nausikaa[40]), and put up for sale: "As they are now, so will you be, wigged, singed, perfumesprayed, ricepowdered, with smoothshaven armpits. Tape measurements will be taken next your skin. You will be laced with cruel force into vicelike [sic] corsets of soft dove coutille, with whalebone busk, to the diamond trimmed pelvis, the absolute outside edge, while your figure, plumper than when at large, will be restrained in nettight frocks, pretty two ounce petticoats and fringes and things stamped, of course, with my houseflag" (535). For Bloom, being female means experiencing sex as surrender and violation, being treated as maidservant, slave, mere body—a nonperson like the whores—and beast, layer of eggs and giver of milk.

Apart from an understandable curiosity about the experience of the other gender—"To compare the various joys we each enjoy" (537)—Bloom is feeling what Virag (and earlier Farrell) utters: *coactus volui.* The opposite of the will to act, is the desire to be forced, desire to be body only, freed of the will, a slave, released from responsibility. Bloom, like most pornographers, associates such a state with femaleness. But this psychological set called masochism is, in Joyce's eyes, a result, not a root. Bloom begins to protest against these masochistic feelings when the surrender they require (or permit) is extended beyond fantasy into life. When his impotence is thrown up at him, when he is reminded of Molly and Boylan, when he thinks of how he would appear to Milly, he draws back into shame and grief. But when it is suggested that his possessions will be treated with the same contempt as his body, he comically, ludicrously, realistically, rebels:

> BELLO: They will spit in your ten shilling brass fender from Hampton Leedon's
> BLOOM: Ten and six. The act of low scoundrels. Let me go. (543)

Bloom dies symbolically; in other words, that part of his emotional nature gives way to another, symbolized by the nymph. Then, although he has "vanquished" Bello, the litany of his sexual sins is gone through all over again, as it was earlier in the chapter, in the trial scene, for instance. Nothing is changed. The nymph (ideal sexual love, contrasted with Bella-Bello, perverted sexual love, each implying and containing the other) accuses him of reading smutty literature and of a variety of sins while sleeping (snoring, farting, talking in his sleep), and blames him for the exposure of "soiled personal linen, wrong side up with care" (547), for the use of the commode, and finally for sexuality itself, traced all the way back to Bloom's puberty.

The nymph's significance is gradually expanded. At first she represents simply ideal female beauty, but her speech increasingly identifies her with an approach to sexuality opposed to Bloom's: a socially acceptable repressiveness, at once shocked and prurient. That the nymph vision is dramatized implies that these ideas have also (naturally) infected Bloom. But eventually the nymph becomes a nun. Her attitudes are thereby associated with Roman Catholicism, just as Gerty's are in Nausikaa. Finally she denigrates Bloom for feeling any desire at all:

> THE NYMPH: (*Loftily.*) We immortals, as you saw today, have not such a place and no hair there either. We are stonecold and pure. We eat electric light. (*She arches her body in lascivious crispation, placing her forefinger in her mouth.*) . . . How then could you? (551)

> THE NYMPH: (*Eyeless, in nun's white habit, coif and huge winged wimple, softly, with remote eyes.*) Tranquilla convent. Sister

Agatha. Mount Carmel, the apparitions of Knock and Lourdes. No
more desire . . . Only the ethereal. (552)

The snapping of Bloom's trouser button, a small realistic detail, reminds him of the actual human state. He says coldly, "You have
broken the spell. The last straw. If there were only ethereal where
would you all be, postulants and novices?" (553). When he fends her
off, her plaster cracks, and a stench emerges. Sexual guilt is thus the
real threat, the real cause of Bloom's sexual difficulties, as is emphasized by the singularity of the attack. This is the only instance of
aggressive physical action by Bloom in the novel, just as the argument
in Cyclops is the only instance of aggressive verbal action on his part.
The association of the nymph with societal attitudes and with the
church surely suggests that it is his society and not Bloom that is
mainly responsible for his problem. The dominant image for Irish
sexuality in the chapter is the scene itself, the neighborhood with its
brothels, its bawds, its stunted children, and its language used to sell
human beings as if they were meat: "Ten shillings a maidenhead. Fresh
thing was never touched. Fifteen. There's no-one in it only her old
father that's dead drunk" (441). One inescapable conclusion is that
Joyce also believed that brothels are built with the stones of religion.[41]

In this section of Circe, Bloom confronts his sexual guilt and pulls
out of his mood. His destruction of the plaster nymph could be taken
as an indication that Bloom has had some traumatic illumination
which will change his behavior. But in fact a bit later he has to go
through a fantasy in which he is aroused by watching Molly and Boylan perform sexual gymnastics. Bloom's sexual feelings pervade the
chapter and are not laid to rest until he gets outdoors, back into contact with the surface world. We are not shown these dramatizations of
his feelings in order to trace his progress in defeating them. Circe, like
Oxen and Eumaeus, is remarkably without "progress," without dramatic structure. Bloom does not defeat his feelings; he simply outlasts,
endures them. The dramatizations function to reveal what is hidden.
The chapter contains a host of such revelations. Even Stephen manifests desire when he looks at Cissy Caffrey. The appearance of all
Bloom's "loves"—Molly, Bridie Kelly, Martha Clifford, Gerty Mac-
Dowell, Mrs. Breen—functions to reveal his hidden feelings, but it
also reveals the secret feelings of the other characters. Gerty sobs, "I

love you for doing that to me" (442), and Mrs. Breen rubs lasciviously against Bloom's side, flirts, and fades away saying, "Yes, yes, yes" (449). The women who testify against Bloom during his trial recall with precision and delight each detail of his outrageous "acts": Mrs. Mervyn Talboys still possesses the obscene postcard Bloom supposedly sent her.

Like other emotions, human sexuality exists; and like them, it is not easily changed, not possible to eradicate. Bloom feels the network of emotions tied to sexuality while he is in the brothel district; we look at the hidden and "perverse" part of human sexuality in the course of this chapter; but nothing changes. Bloom can momentarily beat down his sexual guilt as personified by the nymph, much as Stephen momentarily beats down his guilt in Proteus—and with a similar argument: "What about what? What else were they invented for?" (40). Interpretations of *Ulysses* that insist on startling changes occurring in the characters during the course of this day seem to evade Joyce's vehement insistence that we recognize and accept the realities of human existence in all their ludicrousness, contrariness, and pain.

The same kind of exposure of hidden feelings is demonstrated in areas other than sexual. Bloom is arrested for feeding the dog, presumably because compassion for animals is not masculine enough. His defense is a pretense to status: he claims to be Bloom, the dentist; John Henry Menton, the solicitor; the "daughter" of Major General Tweedy and a supporter of the police and army; and an "author-journalist" (459). Beaufoy's attack on him for his lack of education is phrased like Greene's attack on Shakespeare. We may be amused at and contemptuous of Bloom's evasions and lies in this section, but we must also be aware that he is trying to conform to the standards of a society even more snobbish about such things than Greene was. The attitudes of the subjects of Bloom in the dramatizations showing him as Lord Mayor of Dublin and Leopold the First are satirical expressions of public attitudes toward authority and are comic footnotes to the aggressive attitudes delineated in Cyclops. They are so superficial and self-seeking, so mechanical, as to undercut the absurdity of some of Bloom's postures and utterances—which are satirical handlings of actual postures and utterances of public figures. Bloom's desire for reform is benevolent and praiseworthy, silly though some of its expressions are, so Father Farley's accusation of agnosticism, which leads to the first attack on Bloom, satirizes the reactionary position of the church on social reform and reminds the reader of actual situations, like the position of the church on Parnell. Bloom retrieves the day by singing an old song and playing comedian, in another satirical comment on political success that is sharpened by the fact that this approach is very successful.

Circe satirizes the hidden feelings, assumptions, and guilts of Cissy Caffrey, Mrs. Breen, Philip Beaufoy, and all the rest of the Irish populace. The scene in the street in which Stephen and the soldiers confront each other to the chorus of the Irish populace satirizes popular Irish attitudes, the attitudes of soldiers and of those who support authority, and of Stephen himself, in his dazed self-involvement and inability to deal with reality. Although in Aeolus and the library chapter Stephen realizes he must force himself to see the real and to act, in Circe he forgets this insight and is wounded as a result. What is being examined in Circe is the hidden side of all men and women, the dark side of the earth. Joyce was at some pains to include in Circe characters and hypostatized ideas from all through the novel.[42] It is the world he is exposing here, not just Bloom.

But while the hidden desires and attitudes of humankind are exposed in this episode, so are its essential fears. The armageddon that is the climax of the chapter expresses the deepest and most pervasive fear of humankind. Beyond individual death stands always the possibility of the extinction of the world, of time and space. It is time and space that entrap man, which he spends his life trying to deny or transcend. He runs races in an effort to defeat time; he builds edifices and writes novels that will extend him beyond his natural temporal limitation. Man wants to go beyond, to annihilate time and space, but their actual destruction subsumes his own. Armageddon is the end of time and, for the prophets, the beginning of the timeless. When the corruption of the world seems too overwhelming to be corrected, poets and prophets have repeatedly turned to the hope for an apocalypse. The purifying fires, they believe, will give birth to a purer phoenix.

Joyce plays with the apocalypse the way he plays with everything else. It is serious and terrifying; it is absurd and comic. Apocalypse is simply leaping "into the void" (598). With the seriousness of a prophet, Joyce shows pure faith maintained in the face of the void and sacrificed to it. Out of the sacrifice comes new life, for the world is not destroyed at all. Pure faith acts, leaping over the hurdle into the void itself, and its acts are fettered in history, from which emerges a new legend announcing the reason for life. Pure faith is unreason, and as Swift knew, and Nietzsche, only unreason can make us go on living in this painful world.

But at the same time, the apocalypse is a comic vision, a black mass celebrated by the damned characters of *Ulysses*, those who are armed against the painfulness of life, who do not find it difficult to accept: Mulligan merged with Father O'Flynn, the irreverent priest in the song, and Haines merged with Love. Characters rush into the void with orgiastic abandon and joy, as the mockers celebrate. If Malachi O'Flynn's two left feet seem symbolic of the anti-Christ, however, they also reproduce the image of Christ as it appears in the Book of Kells.

The dual nature of this climactic scene is emphasized by the speeches of the damned and the blessed that follow annihilation. The damned chant: "Htengier Tnetopinmo Dog Drol eht rof, Aiulella!" (599). The blessed chant: "Alleluia, for the Lord God Omnipotent reigneth!" (600). Adonai, the lord, answers "Dooooooooooog!" and then "Goooooooooood!" (600).

The reversal connects this scene with the opening of the chapter. When Stephen first enters Nighttown, he incants: "to *la belle dame sans merci,* Georgina Johnson, *ad deam qui laetificat juventutem meam*" (433), a carnal version of the Introibo. The Reverend Haines Love (an incarnation of duality in himself) recites in English: "To the devil which hath made glad my young days" (599). Mulligan opens *Ulysses* with: *"Introibo ad altare Dei"* (3); here, Malachi O'Flynn says: *"Introibo ad altare diaboli"* (599).

These speeches dramatize the ambiguous truth. In fact, all living beings are in a dance toward death; an "apocalypse" happens somewhere every day, yet the world goes on; each of us exercises pure faith simply to get through the days, and each of us knows it is irrational; we are all damned and all blessed. The curse and the rite are identical things said in different ways. The matter mankind has to work with is the ugly, pathetic, but inescapable body of the "celebrant": a "grey hairy buttocks between which a carrot is stuck" (599). The spirit mankind has to deal with is the ambivalent, dual, ironic, and insatiable mind and feeling of man experiencing. Stephen explains it all. Pure faith, irrationality, is "woman's reason": "Bah! It is because it is. Woman's reason. Jewgreek is greekjew. Extremes meet. Death is the highest form of life. Bah!" (504). And the poem celebrates the circle, both extremes: "The rite is the poet's rest. It may be an old hymn to Demeter or also illustrate *Coela enarrant gloriam Domini*. It is susceptible of nodes or modes as far apart as hyperphrygian and mixolydian and of texts so divergent as priests haihooping round David's that is Circe's or what am I saying Ceres' altar and David's tip from the stable to his chief bassoonist about his almightiness" (503-504).

The character of Lipoti Virag is essential to this episode. His name suggests *Leopold, virile,* and *virulent.* He appears as Bloom gazes in desire at Zoe: "Lipoti Virag, basilicogrammate, chutes rapidly down through the chimneyflue and struts two steps to the left on gawky pink stilts. He is sausaged into several overcoats and wears a brown mackintosh under which he holds a roll of parchment. In his left eye flashes the monocle of Cashel Boyle O'Connor Fitzmaurice Tisdall Farrell. On his head is perched an Egyptian pshent. Two quills project over his ears" (511). Scurrilous, virulent, intensely alive, Virag discusses the whores as if they were insentient, and discusses sex as if it were a disgusting disease. He is a mass of malice, disgust, unusual words, and odd facts: he is the incarnation of the narrator of *Ulysses.* He is "basilicogrammate," lord of language. He walks on stilts that make him higher than the characters. They are pink stilts, appropriate in a novel whose hero is the "new womanly man," and he speaks in "a rich feminine key." He wears several overcoats, presumably one for each narrational style, and on top of them, the brown mackintosh, cloak of invisibility or at least anonymity.[43] With quills over his ears and a roll of parchment—tools of the writer's trade—and wearing a pshent, associating him with Thoth, Egyptian god of writers, he tears into everything before him with a splendid energetic savagery. He cries "*Coactus volui,*" like the mad Farrell: like Bloom and Stephen and perhaps the novel's creator, he desires to be acted upon rather than to act. He speaks nonsense at times. He brings to haunt Bloom the specter of homosexuality or perhaps just effeminacy, and elicits the figure of Henry Flower, lutenist. He attacks Bloom verbally, like the narrators of the various chapters. And he is Bloom's grandfather.

I suspect another comic game. To the extent that Bloom is Joyce, Joyce has created his own grandfather. If Shakespeare is his grandfather on one side of his lineage, Virag is his grandfather on the other. To the extent that the underside of Bloom's temperament is like Joyce's, sensual and masochistic, the character Virag is the other side of Joyce, the alter ego who flays not only these characteristics but those related to them, compassion and charity. The specter of Henry Flower bears more than a passing resemblance to the lyrical, sensitive side of Joyce, the Joyce of *Chamber Music*, and Joyce himself once gave, as a specification for a drawing of him, that he have in his hat a ticket bearing the number 13.[44] Virag is mad and half-blind, wears a monocle, and can unscrew his head. He spatters every subject he approaches with hate, contempt, disgust, and his difficult but familiar style. He is the visible manifestation of the *dio boia* who narrates the great central section of *Ulysses*.

Like the other chapters in this part of *Ulysses*, Circe satirizes and affirms at the same time. This episode more than any other shows Bloom to be ridiculous and contemptible. His illusions and aspirations are made to appear ludicrous; his sexual nature is shown in such a light that critics go scurrying for Krafft-Ebing to explain it. Stephen's morbidity and self-involvement are carried to self-destructive extremes. The dramatizations of what on the naturalistic level the characters are simply feeling give the feelings immense power. We are led to see that to live through such a night is to survive a terrific battering. Yet in fact human beings do such things all the time. To some extent both characters give up their defenses enough to feel these emotions: Bloom voluntarily gives up his potato to Zoe (but undergoes another fantastic sequence even after he recovers it); Stephen in terror abandons his ashplant and allows life, in the form of Private Carr's fist, to touch him. Both are bruised by their confrontation of their hidden feelings, but both survive. It is that survival which is the great triumph. To survive the emotional battering symbolized by the dramatizations of emotional states offered in this chapter, and to remain sane and decent, is as heroic an act as any of Alexander's.

Norman Silverstein remarks that in this chapter, the characters all suffer from locomotor ataxia, and "men fail to complete satisfactorily all kinds of gestures."[45] Man's failure to communicate fully with his own body and his own feelings is a pathetic microcosmic parallel to his inability to communicate fully with other persons and to the larger fact of the expulsion from Eden, man's inability to communicate with the process or order of which he is a part and by which he is controlled. This chapter, more than any other in *Ulysses*, occurs in the void. Reason, the area of experience that dominates Oxen of the Sun, abdicates to unreason, the nighttime secret world all of us live with, no matter how solid or unimpugnable our surface lives. We cannot do away with this nightmare world, with our guilts, our fears, our boundless aspirations, our egotisms, and our sexual inclinations. Even to face them is terrifying. Yet face them we do, and endure. The final effect of Circe is to expose this underside of things and to assert the essential dignity of man, who must live always with this Nighttown in his soul, yet who, stronger than Ulysses, gives up his defenses and faces the void within himself. The human race, like Leopold Bloom, is psychologically a bundle of conflicts and guilts and ignorances, but it goes on asking moral questions, seeking the good. Bloom's moral stature grows in this episode at the same time that it dwindles, grows as he reasserts his dignity and humaneness in the face of the pressures within him. But it dwindles and grows for us, not for him, changes as we see a part of him we have previously only suspected. Stephen too changes in our eyes: he comments that he was born "Today," and he has this day taken the first steps into maturity and survival. Yet the same problems dog him throughout the novel: life, after all, is "many days."

In the whole of the novel, there is only one other character besides Bloom—Martin Cunningham—who is shown to be caring about or even thinking about other people than himself. Bloom's following Stephen and remaining with him are small acts. But not many people would do what Bloom does: even Lynch leaves. Bloom's small actions are the sorts of action by which most of us, living ordinary lives, are able to show concern and love—*caritas*.

But lest we permit ourselves the luxury of sentimentalization or idealization of Bloom or the human race, beleaguered as both are, Joyce presents us with one of his great visions. The dénouement, Bloom's vision of Rudy as a cross among Cinderella, Little Lord Fauntleroy, and Bo-Peep, is ironic in Joyce's special way. For noble Leopold Bloom can find a purpose to his life only in a fairy-tale/nursery rhyme symbol—a fact that is at once ludicrous, pathetic, outrageous, comic, and true to human experience.

[6]   *The Universe*

We are near the end of our journey, approaching the "greatest possible ellipse consistent with the ultimate return" (504). The return occurs in Penelope; we are moving presently to the point at greatest distance from it, a fifth away, outer space.

In the first ten chapters, the focus is human beings—two in particular. In the next five, the focus is more abstract—human feelings and expression. Then in Eumaeus and Ithaca, what is human is buried or neglected by the dehumanizing voices. The styles of the first ten chapters are on the whole impersonal, but they are naturalistic, and since the focus is personal, we are given a strong sense of human life as we know it. The styles of the next three chapters and of Circe are intensely personal, presented by vivid, malicious voices. The narrative voice of Circe is contained in the stage directions and objectified in the speaking objects and phantoms. The emotion of the narrative voices and the emotion on which they focus combine to create an intense personal experience, even if the actual subject matter can be summed up by an abstract rubric. But in Eumaeus and Ithaca, as in Oxen, impersonal narrative voices take over completely, and the human subject matter gets lost at precisely the point of greatest tension in the "action," and in us. We are avid to know if Bloom and Stephen will really get together, if their meeting will change the life of either. We follow like panting dogs the sausage on the stick, but Joyce is inexorable. We move further and further away from the characters, until our last view of Bloom, from our Archimedian point, is as a dot in space.

It is the dehumanization imposed by the styles of these chapters about which critics complain and indeed this is frustrating.[1] We are awaiting the final truth, the author's statement of ultimate reality, and he stubbornly refuses to give it to us. We have waded knee-deep for six hundred pages through his opacities and games, and now he denies us our reward. Nevertheless, Joyce has complete artistic integrity: the statement he makes at the end of the book is of a piece with the statement made at the beginning, and all through it. We are living in the void and can never wholly know anything. "What really happened" is a reality too complex to be contained in the limited mind of man, much less to be expressed through language, as Joyce proves in Oxen of the Sun. "What really happened" reverberates out into space, and only actual gods could see the last ripple, the final significance. Final significance is identical with final, complete configuration, the whole parallelogram, for to describe what really happened would necessitate including the effect of any action on every atom in the universe, and the interpretation of every action by every being in its field.

In fact, Joyce tried to achieve just such a goal as closely as possible. But he saw reality as ambiguous. His cubist technique is designed to present a number of facets of reality; his satirical approach is designed to goad the reader into producing the affirming response. The de-humanizing techniques of Eumaeus and Ithaca force the reader to reject those techniques and to assert with increasing intensity the humanity that is being so battered and choked.

Eumaeus

The style of Eumaeus is frequently identified with that of Bloom's monologues, and the point of view is thought to reside with him, although the point of view resides with neither Stephen nor Bloom. Long sections describe what Stephen is thinking; there is a lengthy conversation between Stephen and Corley that takes place outside Bloom's earshot; one passage describes Gumley moving sleepily in his sentry box while Stephen and Bloom are in the cabman's shelter; and the last paragraph describes something of what is going on in the mind of a jarvey. Most of the episode does concentrate on Bloom, and the style of the chapter is enough like Bloom's to be sincerely equated with it; but the style of Eumaeus lacks Bloom's acuteness and honesty. The narrative voice is deceptive, using circumlocutions and euphemisms to deal with basic things much as the narrator of Nausikaa does. Like that narrator, this one has star-gazing pretensions to elegance that lead him to fall into pits of clichés. These pretensions are the "elegance" of a half-educated person trying to appear well educated, and they closely resemble the many passages of journalese "erudition" that pervade the novel. Since no doubt Bloom is trying to impress or at least interest Stephen, the style symbolizes the tone of the actual scene. Nevertheless, the style does not do justice to Bloom. Bloom would never be guilty of the pseudo-elegance and clichés of the following (italics mine):

> *For the nonce* he was rather *nonplussed* but inasmuch as the *duty* plainly *devolved* upon him to *take some measures* on the subject he *pondered* suitable *ways and means* during which Stephen repeatedly yawned . . . This was a *quandary* but, bringing commonsense *to bear on it*, evidently there was nothing for it but *put a good face on the matter* and *foot it* which they accordingly did. So, *bevelling* around by Mullet's and the Signal House, which they shortly reached, they *proceeded perforce* in the direction of Amiens street railway *terminus*, Mr Bloom being handicapped by the *circumstance* that one of the back buttons of his trousers had, *to vary the timehonoured adage, gone the way of all buttons.* (613-614)

The technique is also analogous to the first part of Nausikaa in its dependence on the accumulation of such items; a few sprinkled clichés might not be noticed and would likely not be comic. The massive number that appear in this chapter, as in Nausikaa, make comedy inevitable.

Gerty too is fond of "elegant" phrases, but this narrator, somewhat better educated than Gerty, has more at his disposal and is extremely fond of foreign tags. He even uses words and phrases that have long since been assimilated into English as if they were still strangers to the language. Almost every page of Eumaeus contains a number of italicized words or phrases. This is an uncommon occurrence in the novel as a whole and reminds one of Lenehan, who likes to sprinkle his speech with corrupt French. If we select a few pages at random, we find "*Jupiter Pluvius*," "*fidus Achates*," "*en route*," "*re*" (614); "*genus homo*" (621); "*sangfroid*," "*hoi polloi*," "*protégé*," "*apropos*," "*tête-à-tête*" (622); even "*venue*" (627), a word that is an old part of English

law, is italicized, as is *"stiletto"* (629), a word with respectable standing in English.

The narrator is "nice" in the same way as is the narrator of
Nausikaa. He will not make a derogatory remark, at least not directly:

> To his taciturn, and, not to put too fine a point on it, not yet per-
> fectly sober companion. (614)

> And called him to Stephen a mean bloody swab with a sprinkling of
> other uncalled-for expressions. (617)

> Stephen's anything but immaculately attired interlocutor. (618)

The style is very funny in its circuitousness and the odd relations that
exist among its clauses and phrases. Consider the relation between the
first part of the sentence beginning "For the nonce" and its final clause,
"during which Stephen repeatedly yawned" (613), or the Germanicism
of "one man was reading by fits and starts a stained by coffee evening
journal" (629). Here is a sentenceful of such strained relations:

> Although unusual in the Dublin area, he knew that it was not by
> any means unknown for desperadoes who had next to nothing to
> live on to be about waylaying and generally terrorising peaceable
> pedestrians by placing a pistol at their head in some secluded spot
> outside the city proper, famished loiterers of the Thames embank-
> ment category they might be hanging about there or simply ma-
> rauders ready to decamp with whatever boodle they could in one
> fell swoop at a moment's notice, your money or your life, leaving
> you there to point a moral, gagged and garotted. (616)

Subsequent paragraphs show odd relations in their larger members.
First Corley's background is described, then his plight; in the middle
of the second subject, the narrator returns to the first, in the way that
a tedious storyteller does: "No, it was the daughter of the mother,"
and finally concludes: "Anyway, he was all in" (617). Sometimes the
syntax is so wrenched that it is difficult to make sense of a passage:

> Briefly, putting two and two together, six sixteen, which he point-
> edly turned a deaf ear to, Antonio and so forth, jockeys and
> esthetes and the tattoo which was all the go in the seventies or
> thereabouts, even in the House of Lords, because early in life the

occupant of the throne, then heir apparent, the other members of the upper ten and other high personages simply following in the footsteps of the head of the state, he reflected about the errors of notorieties and crowned heads running counter to morality such as the Cornwall case a number of years before under their veneer in a way scarcely intended by nature, a thing good Mrs Grundy as the law stands was terribly down on, though not for the reason they thought they were probably, whatever it was, except women chiefly, who were always fiddling more or less at one another, it being largely a matter of dress and all the rest of it. (646)

Finally, compare the style of this narrator with the style of Bloom's interior monologue on the same subject:

The face of a streetwalker, glazed and haggard under a black straw hat, peered askew round the door of the shelter, palpably reconnoitring on her own with the object of bringing more grist to her mill. Mr Bloom, scarcely knowing which way to look, turned away on the moment, flusterfied but outwardly calm, and picking up from the table the pink sheet of the Abbey street organ which the jarvey, if such he was, had laid aside, he picked it up and looked at the pink of the paper though why pink? His reason for so doing was he recognized on the moment round the door the same face he had caught a fleeting glimpse of that afternoon on Ormond Quay, the partially idiotic female, namely, of the lane, who knew the lady in the brown costume does be with you (Mrs B.), and begged the chance of his washing. Also why washing, which seemed rather vague than not? (632)

A frowzy whore with black straw sailor hat askew came glazily in the day along the quay towards Mr Bloom. When first he saw that form endearing. Yes, it is. I feel so lonely. Wet night in the lane . . . Off her beat here. What is she? Hope she. Psst! Any chance of your wash. Knew Molly. Had me decked. Stout lady does be with you in the brown costume. Put you off your stroke. That appointment we made. Knowing we'd never, well hardly ever. Too dear too near to home sweet home. Sees me, does she? Looks a fright in the day. Face like dip. Damn her! O, well, she has to live like the rest. Look in here. (290)

The effect of the style of Eumaeus is exactly what its characteristics suggest. The use of euphemisms and circumlocutions implies an avoidance, a concealment or obscurantism. The self-conscious, italicized use of phrases originally foreign but long since fully assimilated into English, like *apropos* or *en route*, or foreign phrases that are totally unnecessary—why *Jupiter Pluvius*, for instance?—is another falsifying and artificial element. The ungrammatical relations among members of a sentence, a paragraph, or several paragraphs symbolize wrenched, distorted, or inadequate relations among things. The wrenched syntax also acts to conceal when the distortion is a result of lacunae in the thought.[2] Just as the narrator of the first part of Nausikaa uses a demonstrative pronoun to contain what cannot be thought, this narrator uses sheer gaps in the sense. For instance, in the paragraph just quoted, beginning "Briefly," the subject is homosexuality in royalty and in women, but this is not easily apparent.

The indirectness and strained relations have relevance to the actual scene. There is some involved and purposeless walking around. Bloom is trying to sound intelligent, to talk to Stephen about things that he thinks might interest the younger man. Certainly the relations between the two men are strained. Bloom is discomfited by Stephen's curtness and withdrawal. Both are fatigued, and the meandering style, the sentences that keep losing their subjects, emphasize this fatigue as well as the loss of the reader's subject matter.

But on another level, the chapter itself is an obscurant: we have wanted to see what would happen when Bloom and Stephen finally came together, here they are, and nothing happens. If anything is happening, if Stephen is glancing occasionally at Bloom, or thinking about him, if he is noticing a kindness of eye or a gentle gesture of hand, the style obscures this, and we cannot see it. The syntactical strain, the tension between the characters, the tension between them and their surroundings, all are analogues to our strain at this point: we are tense, wrenched out of what we feel to be the proper and acceptable next step for the novel, and forced to follow this tedious, pointless peripateia.

R. M. Adams has pointed out that Joyce often deflates intellectualism by placing falsehoods and mistakes in the mouths of the educated, of Deasy, for instance, or Stephen himself, and then placing truths in the mouth of a Nosey Flynn. While Joyce "shows the pretenders to erudition (including himself) as consistently fake, he often shows the barroom philosopher and streetcorner sophist as unexpectedly right."[3] Adams concludes that Joyce's idea of wisdom was exemplified by common sense and the common man. Unquestionably Adams is correct about Joyce's game-playing with pieces of knowledge and about his delight in deflating intellectuals, but if Joyce makes a Nosey Flynn right, he does not make Stephen consistently wrong, and he does not idealize the common man. These two chapters, Eumaeus and Ithaca, represent the twentieth century, the democratic era of the common man in Eumaeus, and the era of objective research, science and technology in Ithaca. Many critics have seen *Ulysses* as an indictment of the modern world. To a degree it is, but most of the novel spends time and energy showing that the modern world is essentially much like any other time and place, that the human condition does not change. If there is an indictment primarily of the twentieth century, it is in Eumaeus and Ithaca, in the satire of the tasteless, rambling, carefully unoffending sentiments of the common man—the male equivalent of the Nausikaa narrator—and the impersonal categorizations of science.

Both these techniques are dehumanizing because they cannot deal with feelings—the subjects of Sirens, Cyclops, Nausikaa, and Circe. Reading the following, one finds it difficult to believe that Stephen has feelings, and impossible to imagine them getting the better of him: "Though this sort of thing went on every other night or very near it still Stephen's feelings got the better of him in a sense though he knew that Corley's brandnew rigmarole, on a par with the others, was hardly deserving of much credence" (617). Stephen's surly rebuke of Bloom hurts the older man; he is disconcerted and, after some musing, picks up a newspaper and idly reads it. These events occupy over two pages of the novel. But one needs to inject quite a quantity of blood into the dessicated paragraphs that follow the rebuke in order to apprehend Bloom's feelings:

At this pertinent suggestion, Mr Bloom, to change the subject, looked down, but in a quandary, as he couldn't tell exactly what construction to put on belongs to which sounded rather a far cry. The rebuke of some kind was clearer than the other part. Needless to say, the fumes of his recent orgy spoke then with some asperity in a curious bitter way, foreign to his sober state. Probably the home life, to which Mr Bloom attached the utmost importance, had not been all that was needful or he hadn't been familiarised with the right sort of people . . .

For which and further reasons he felt it was interest and duty even

to wait on and profit by the unlookedfor occasion, though why, he
could not exactly tell, being, as it was, already several shillings to
the bad, having, in fact, let himself in for it . . .
So to change the subject he read about Dignam, R.I.P., which, he
reflected, was anything but a gay sendoff. (645-647)

Because one wants to feel with the characters, one goes on pumping
in blood. The reader rebels against the veil, the nearly impenetrable
shroud of cobwebs with which the style drapes the scene. And
whether we are projecting emotions that are not delineated, or rebel-
ling against the technique that shrouds them, we are in the process
asserting the importance of human feeling; essentially, we are defining
humanness as emotion. Actually, Eumaeus is a very funny chapter. It
is no more tedious than the first part of Nausikaa. It *feels* tedious to
critics who have denigrated it because it is in the way, it seems to keep
us from what we want, it seems to slow the "action."

The primary subject of Eumaeus is language as deception, and the
episode is therefore the counterpart to Oxen of the Sun. As usual, the
subject is incorporated on every level. Just as the style obscures what
is "really" happening, conceals feeling, which has become equivalent
to significance, the vague and circumambulatory journey of Stephen
and Bloom obscures the actual outlines of the city. In addition, the
events of the chapter are a series of deceptions, false leads, false clues,
mistakes. Some of these are small mistakes, such as Corley thinking he
has seen Bloom "a few times in the Bleeding Horse in Camden street
with Boylan the billsticker" (618). On being apprised of this, Bloom
gazes "in the direction of a bucket dredger" (619). Bloom mistakes the
tenor of the Italian conversation going on outside the cabman's shelter
and has to be told by Stephen that "they were haggling over money"
(622). Bloom also misunderstands Stephen's comment "Sounds are
impostures . . . What's in a name?" (622) and replies that his family
name also was changed. The sailor mistakes Stephen's father and
comes up with a totally different Simon Dedalus. On a somewhat
wider plane, there is a question about whether the keeper is Skin-the-
Goat, and about the identity of W. B. Murphy, the sailor whose stories all smack of spuriousness. The theme of homosexuality is comically linked with the sailor and his Antonio, in a parallel to Bloom's
questions about Stephen's sexual adaptation. Bloom, who rarely takes
things personally, mistakes Stephen's curtness as a slight; Stephen is

unbearably priggish and supercilious during this chapter, but we know that his bitterness is directed largely at himself. Bloom misunderstands the motto he quotes to Stephen: "*Ubi patria, Alma Mater, vita bene*" he misquotes and mistranslates. Errors appear in the newspaper account of Dignam's funeral. Even Stephen seems to make a mistake: he claims the song he sings was written, rather than collected, by Johannes Jeep, a seventeenth century composer. There are more examples of such errors and falsehoods in the chapter.[4] In the end, however, we have about as much sense of what happens in this chapter as we have in Oxen of the Sun. We may have even more knowledge about details. The point made by these errors and deceptions is analogous to the point to be drawn from characters like Deasy and Nosey Flynn. The educated man is full of falsehood; the "no-brains" is full of accuracies. Oxen, in which language is the vehicle of truth, in fact offers no more truth about reality than Eumaeus, in which language is a vehicle of deception. Even without our conscious knowledge, we are aware of this by now: we do not trust the narrator, and we look to the characters, to their dialogue and to their interior monologue, to discover the facts. The reader is by now paranoid with distrust, and the novel does not help, since we hear little dialogue, and most of that is inconclusive, and we overhear no interior monologue at all. Can we trust the narrator when he tells us that Bloom slips his arm through Stephen's and Stephen feels "a strange kind of flesh of a different man approach him, sinewless and wobbly and all that" (660)? Does this indicate that Stephen has indeed met not-himself, met the other, encountered not-himself on his doorstep?

This narrator, as malicious as any other, will not tell us. He carries the question right to the conclusion of the chapter, which is very strange. In the concluding paragraphs apparently meaningless phrases from a song are interjected into an otherwise ordinary descriptive paragraph. The phrases—italicized in the original—do not even make sense in context:

The driver never said a word, good, bad or indifferent. He merely watched the two figures, as he sat on his lowbacked car, both black —one full, one lean—walk towards the railway bridge, *to be married by Father Maher*. As they walked, they at times stopped and walked again, continuing their *tête-à-tête* (which of course he was

utterly out of), about sirens, enemies of man's reason, mingled with
a number of other topics of the same category, usurpers, historical
cases of the kind while the man in the sweeper car or you might as
well call it in the sleeper car who in any case couldn't possibly hear
because they were too far simply sat in his seat near the end of lower
Gardiner street *and looked after their lowbacked car.* (665)

The phrases come from a ballad by Samuel Lover called "The Low-
Backed Car." They seem to have several functions. The first is to indicate again the way perception is influenced by the self. The man is sitting in a low-backed car; he looks out at figures walking past and sees
them in a low-backed car, projecting his own state sleepily upon the
rest of the world, like a comic Socrates or Judas meeting himself. [5] The
second function is more complex and subtle, having to do with sexuality and the relations between Bloom and Stephen. The love ballad
from which the lines come is a wishing ballad, for the marriage that
the narrator of the ballad desires and posits does not occur within the
poem. The last stanza reads:

> I'd rather own that car, sir,
> With Peggy by my side,
> Than a coach and four and gold galore
> And a lady for my bride.
> For the lady would sit forninst me,
> On a cushion made with taste,
> While Peggy would be beside me,
> With my arm around her waist,
>   As we drove in the low-backed car,
>   To be married by Father Maher,
> Oh my heart would beat high
> At her glance and her sigh
>   Though it beat in a low-backed car.

Sexuality in Eumaeus is obscured like everything else, but it is an
important theme. The number six sixteen, Antonio, and homosexuality are linked by Bloom in his long meditation. He briefly questions
Stephen's sexual adaptation:

With a touch of fear for the young man beside him, whom he fur-
tively scrutinized with an air of some consternation remembering he

had just come back from Paris, the eyes more especially reminding him forcibly of father and sister, failing to throw much light on the subject, however, he brought to mind instances of cultured fellows that promised so brilliantly, nipped in the bud of premature decay, and nobody to blame but themselves. For instance, there was the case of O'Callaghan, for one, the half crazy faddist . . . with his mad vagaries, among whose other gay doings . . . he was in the habit of ostentatiously sporting in public a suit of brown paper . . . he got landed into hot water and had to be spirited away by a few friends, after a strong hint to a blind horse from John Mallon of Lower Castle Yard, so as not to be made amenable under section two of the Criminal Law Amendment Act, certain names of those subpoenaed being handed in but not divulged, for reasons which will occur to anyone with a pick of brains. (645-646)

During the conversation in the shelter, the subject turns to that frequent male topic, woman as destroyer, Eve: "—That bitch, that English whore, did for him, the shebeen proprietor commented. She put the first nail in his coffin" (650). The conversation that follows, on the attractiveness of Kitty O'Shea and the impotence of her husband, leads Bloom to some personal musings on the subject: "Whereas the simple fact of the case was it was simply a case of the husband not being up to the scratch with nothing in common between them beyond the name and then a real man arriving on the scene, strong to the verge of weakness, falling a victim to her siren charms and forgetting home ties" (651). Although the last phrases relate this meditation to Bloom's encounter with Gerty, and sound more like her interpretation of it than his, the rest refers to the affair of Molly and Boylan. Nevertheless, immediately afterward, Bloom shows Molly's picture to Stephen. It is clear that he is pandering:

As for the face, it was a speaking likeness in expression but it did not do justice to her figure, which came in for a lot of notice usually and which did not come out to the best advantage in that getup. She could without difficulty, he said, have posed for the ensemble, not to dwell on certain opulent curves of the . . . He dwelt, being a bit of an artist in his spare time, on the female form in general. (653)

On the other hand what incensed him more inwardly was the blatant jokes of the cabmen and so on . . . it being a case for the two parties themselves . . . the upshot being that her affections centred on another, the cause of many *liaisons* between still attractive married women getting on for fair and forty and younger men . . . It was a thousand pities a young fellow blessed with an allowance of brains, as his neighbour obviously was, should waste his valuable time with profligate women, who might present him with a nice dose to last him his lifetime . . . To think of him house and homeless, rooked by some landlady worse than any stepmother, was really too bad at his age. (655-656)

It is also clear that Bloom is using Molly as bait because he himself wants Stephen's company: "The vicinity of the young man he certainly relished, educated, *distingué,* and impulsive into the bargain" (653).

Eumaeus is the last chapter, excluding Penelope, in which the theme of sexuality is important. What the chapter does with the theme is to pull together all the chaotic strands of sexuality revealed in Circe. There what is invisible is made visible. In Eumaeus, the secret and hidden is suppressed again, and we are shown the confused and deceptive surface of such emotions. Bloom panders to Stephen—why? Some critics claim that it is because he would prefer Stephen to Boylan as Molly's lover, but I suspect that most men, including Bloom, would prefer their wives not to have lovers at all. In Molly's monologue, she seizes on and questions the fact that Bloom has shown her picture to Stephen; indeed, she carries the implicit suggestion to completion in her imagination.

Bloom loves Stephen. He is not fully aware of this and does not know why he remains with him: "he felt it was interest and duty even to wait on and profit by the unlookedfor occasion, though why, he could not exactly tell, being, as it was, already several shillings to the bad" (646). He admires Stephen, he sees him in need, he wants to give him something. In fact, he wants to give Stephen exactly what Stephen needs—a Molly, a person he could love who would provide him with a center, some sense of a fixed star, even in the midst of the void. The male desire to share a woman is frequently characterized by psychologists as a homosexual impulse. Perhaps it is. But to characterize Bloom's love and *caritas* toward Stephen as homosexual is in our culture to disparage, even to annul it.[6] Bloom's love springs from innocence: it issues in an act or acts of kindness. What seems to be implied is that all affection is sexual at root. The sexual theme, which functions in *Ulysses* partly to point out the void underlying sexual conventions and morality, unquestionably functions so in this chapter.

The interjections from the ballad have an additional purpose. The statement is made that Bloom and Stephen are going *"to be married by Father Maher."* This encourages us to believe that Bloom and Stephen are moving toward a genuine at-onement. But within the ballad itself, the sentence is in the subjunctive mode, indicating a condition or a statement contrary to fact. The consummation that the ballad-narrator desires does not take place within the poem. And comically, the passage from *Hamlet* used in this episode is "that consummation devoutly to be or not to be wished for" (641). The degree of rapprochement achieved by the characters in *Ulysses* may be partly dependent on how much the reader sees, how much he is willing to settle for, and how much he affirms. But at no time does Joyce let us forget that between Stephen and Bloom, as between the word and the act, falls the shadow.

Ithaca

Stephen is a theologian of sorts, Bloom a scientist of sorts. Each tries to understand the universe primarily through his chosen discipline. From primitive times until the seventeenth century, theology was the major approach to explaining the workings of the universe; science has increasingly superseded it. In the episode that offers us our final view of Bloom and Stephen, the two major disciplines for investigating the universe, and the very disciplines the characters themselves espouse, are merged and directed in investigation of them. Bloom and Stephen are examined by a scientific catechist.[7]

The point of view is Archimedean: we can see the globe turning, partially lighted, and all space rumbles with vibrations of the solemn questions and answers. Comic appreciation of the catechismal form is sharpened if one has a recollection of the solemnity and mysteriousness—for what child could understand?—of the weekly catechism lesson to be memorized, those enormous questions and their simple answers:

Who made us?
God made us.
(a) Reason unaided by revelation can prove that God exists. It knows that this vast universe could not have come into being by its

own powers. The movement of creatures and their dependence upon one another, the various degrees of perfection found in them, the fact that they come into being and cease to be, and, finally, the marvellous order in the universe demand the existence of an almighty power and the wisdom of an eternal intelligent cause that we call God.

Who is God?

God is the Supreme Being, infinitely perfect, who made all things and keeps them in existence.[8]

However, the questions and answers in Ithaca are couched in the language of a newer theology, a newer metaphor for the operations of the universe, science. The two great approaches to the unknown, which contain between them most of our hypotheses as to our nature and origin, our significance and that of the universe, are merged into one great piece of nonsense.

The main device of the technique is burlesque: trivial matter contained in a solemn and pompous form. Trivial questions, such as those about water—"Did it flow?," "What in water did Bloom, waterlover, drawer of water, watercarrier returning to the range, admire?" (671-672)—receive gigantic technical answers. Pedantically phrased and seemingly serious questions receive ridiculously trivial answers:

Which domestic problem as much as, if not more than, any other frequently engaged his mind?

What to do with our wives. (685)

This set is especially funny because it occurs just after an extremely verbose and pedantic answer to a similar question.

A further level that may be categorized as burlesque is the nature of the questions asked in relation to the questions the reader would like to ask. At a time when we are asking for final significance, for the author's deeply felt commitment to provide an emotional and philosophical context that will let our hearts and minds rest, the narrator is asking things like, "What did Bloom see on the range?" (670).

Some of the sets of interrogation are serious indeed:

As in what ways?

From inexistence to existence he came to many and was as one received: existence with existence he was with any as any with any:

from existence to nonexistence gone he would be by all as none perceived. (667-668)

But these sets are presented in such abstract, technical, or pedantic
language that we get no sense of the humanity of the characters. If
Ithaca were the first chapter in the book, few would read further—yet
it is probably the greatest chapter in the novel. Another paradox
about it is that this "inhuman" chapter includes the smallest details of
human experience, even to Bloom picking his toenail and smelling it.
What is missing from the episode, as it is missing from Eumaeus, is
feeling—not in the characters, but in the style. After all the lively animus of the narrative voices from Sirens through Circe, the completely
unemotional tone of these two chapters feels indeed like the "cold of
interstellar space" (704). As usual, it is up to the reader to supply the
missing element, be it sympathy, contempt, or a sense of balance. In
this chapter, Frank Budgen suggests, "it is for the reader to assign the
human values"; he would be more precise to say "feel them."[9] Joyce
was clearly including the reader in his calculations when he discussed
this episode: "All events are resolved into their cosmic, physical, psychical etc. equivalents . . . so that not only will the reader know everything and know it in the baldest coldest way, but Bloom and Stephen
thereby become heavenly bodies, wanderers like the stars at which
they gaze."[10]

The subject matter of the episode is the subject matter of both religion and science: relationships among things. However, the moral and
spiritual relations examined by the scholastics give way here to the
quantitative and parallactic relations examined by science. On the
highest, most distant level are the stars, the macrocosm; on the terrestrial level is water; and on the microcosmic level are the relations
between two people (Bloom and Stephen), between man and his environment (Bloom alone in garden and house), and between man and
the other (Bloom and Molly). Although we, the readers, are taken by
the narrator further and further away from earth until all we can see is
a dot, the chapter itself conforms to the shape of an ellipse, beginning
on earth with two men and including a treatise on water, moving to a
treatise on the stars, and returning to earth, to Bloom and Stephen
separating and Bloom moving back into relation with his home, himself, and his listener.

Many chapters of *Ulysses* have dealt with the relations among things: Aeolus deals with relations among people and ideas; Wandering Rocks concerns incomplete relations among people; Oxen of the Sun deals with relations between reality and the mode of perception; Eumaeus with relations between reality and the faulty or deceitful expression of it; and many other chapters, such as Cyclops, have a subsidiary theme of relation of feeling to language (form). Ithaca is the final and biggest joke: at the point when the reader desires the human relations finally to interlock, to marry, he is presented with a series of irrelevant parallels, contrasts, quantitative relations, and intermeshings of totally inane crossing points.

The chapter opens with the two men walking a parallel course, discussing certain topics as a "duumvirate," and discovering "common factors of similarity between their respective like and unlike reactions to experience" (666). Comic as this is, it suggests what is suggested elsewhere in the novel, that beneath like and unlike there is similarity. Then there is a divergence: "Stephen dissented openly from Bloom's view on the importance of dietary and civic selfhelp while Bloom dissented tacitly from Stephen's views on the eternal affirmation of the spirit of man in literature," immediately followed by a convergence: "Bloom assented covertly to Stephen's rectification of the anachronism involved in assigning the date of the conversion of the Irish nation to christianity from druidism by Patrick son of Calpornus, son of Potitus, son of Odyssus, sent by pope Celestine I in the year 432 in the reign of Leary" (666-667), and by another divergence, which ends in a parallactic convergence: "The collapse which Bloom ascribed to gastric inanition . . . Stephen attributed to the reapparition of a matutinal cloud (perceived by both from two different points of observation, Sandycove and Dublin) at first no bigger than a woman's hand" (667). The entire figure—the cloud perceived by both, and its function in their disagreement—is emblematic. Since both saw the cloud, it is verified, that is, it is a reality; since both saw it differently, from different modes of perception, it is an example of parallax; and it is used differently—Bloom simply sees a cloud, Stephen makes it significant by echoing a phrase from the Elijah story, and even makes its second appearance responsible for his collapse in Nighttown. The cloud is emblematic of the method of the novel, although on a microcosmic and trivial level, and while its triviality makes it comic, its components make it serious. It suggests the identity of *a* reality, an actual and ultimate reality which is alike for all people and the differing interpretations made of it. This like/unlike communality is neutralized in the next question, the "point on which their views were equal and negative" (667).

Afterward there is a series of questions concerning Bloom alone, in his relations with the past and the future. Bald and abstract as these are, they point poignantly to the void that underlies all relations: isolation. The terrible aloneness of Bloom's life would be less moving if it were rendered movingly:

> Had Bloom discussed similar subjects during nocturnal perambulations in the past?
> In 1884 with Owen Goldberg and Cecil Turnbull at night on public thoroughfares between Longwood avenue and Leonard's corner and Leonard's corner and Synge street and Synge street and Bloomfield avenue. In 1885 with Percy Apjohn in the evenings, reclined against the wall between Gibraltar villa and Bloomfield house in Crumlin, barony of Uppercross. In 1886 occasionally with casual acquaintances and prospective purchasers on doorsteps, in front parlors, in third class railway carriages of suburban lines. In 1888 frequently with major Brian Tweedy and his daughter Miss Marion Tweedy, together and separately on the lounge in Matthew Dillon's house in Roundtown. Once in 1892 and once in 1893 with Julius Mastiansky, on both occasions in the parlour of his (Bloom's) house in Lombard street, west.
> What reflection concerning the irregular sequence of dates 1884, 1885, 1886, 1888, 1892, 1893, 1904 did Bloom make before their arrival at their destination?
> He reflected that the progressive extension of the field of individual development and experience was regressively accompanied by a restriction of the converse domain of interindividual relations. (667)

The section is funny because Bloom's (or the narrator's) memory of person, place, and date is so minutely precise, and because of the abstract pedantic language of the answers. But it is appalling that someone's intimate conversations could be so precisely and sparsely totted up, that as one gets older one gets lonelier, that one must recognize his own death will not stop the world. This is of course all true; but Bloom seems even more alone with his sorrow because of the unemotionality of the language in which it is described:

> From inexistence to existence he came to many and was as one received: existence with existence he was with any as any with any:

from existence to nonexistence gone he would be by all as none perceived. (667-668)

These questions also merge the trivial with the terrible by paying more
attention to the places and dates of meeting than to the emotional, or
human content. Space and time thus supersede feeling, as an object
does in the next set of questions, which deal with a key. Although
emotion is suggested—"Why was he doubly irritated?"—it is quenched
by the answer: "Because he had forgotten and because he remembered
that he had reminded himself twice not to forget" (668). The questions
about the key lead up to another intersection between Stephen and
Bloom: they are a premeditatedly and inadvertently "keyless couple"
(668). It has been suggested that keylessness indicates ineffectuality,
an admission that one has no authority over one's life.[11] This is true,
but what is important is how one interprets such a situation. If one
considers those characters who do possess keys—Mulligan, Deasy,
Crawford, O'Connell—and the contexts in which references to the
possession of keys occur, it is clear that Joyce sees authority of this
sort as a delusion. The keys to the kingdom equal certitude, which
only a fool or a liar claims to possess. That Stephen has willfully, premeditatedly repudiated the certitude he once claimed, that Bloom has
unknowingly made Molly his fixed star and thus inadvertently lost
certitude this day, reflects an intellectual and emotional difference
between them, but not a moral one: like their creator, both characters
are too honest to pretend. Keylessness is therefore a sign of weakness
only insofar as all people are weak or ineffectual, lacking full control
over their lives, and lacking certitude.

The convergence of Stephen and Bloom is immediately broken: in
comically quantitative and descriptive terms, Bloom's acts and
Stephen's perception—and his one act—are described, as Bloom
jumps into the areaway and enters the area door and Stephen watches.
Bloom continues to act—he lights the fire—and Stephen continues to
perceive, recalling others he had watched light fires. Stephen observes
the laundry line, Bloom the saucepan and kettle, then Bloom again
acts, turning on the tap and releasing the hymn to water. The little
treatise on water relates it to measurement; to the globe, earth and
sky; and to the moon: "the noxiousness of its effluvia in lacustrine
marshes, pestilential fens, faded flowerwater, stagnant pools in the

waning moon" (672). Many of the characteristics attributed to the moon contain human value judgments: universality or perseverance, for instance. Water is related also to human concerns. Bloom is a "waterlover, drawer of water, watercarrier" (671), Stephen a "hydrophobe" (673). Like the cloud, water is, but the two characters perceive it differently.

Stephen possesses an "equal and opposite power of abandonment and recuperation" (673), another image for the method of the novel. Fire and water, two other equal and opposite powers, now merge into "ebullition" and "water vapor" (673-674), which leads to a possible use for convergence, to wit, shaving. Bloom's androgyny is referred to again, positively: he has "surety of the sense of touch in his firm full masculine feminine passive active hand" (674). This picks up the earlier mocking references to his having a "soft hand under a hen," made in Cyclops and reinforced in Oxen and Circe, as well as the references to his feminacy. Although the tone of Ithaca is nearly emotionless, Bloom is made fun of in the chapter (consider his dream house), but this reference does not seem pejorative. Its implication seems to be wholeness. Bloom is the new hero, repudiating old "masculine" standards, like those found in Cyclops, and adopting the "feminine" ones of compassion and nutritiveness, found in medieval Christian literature. Despite his repudiation of violence, Bloom knows how to be both active and passive, contains within himself both yin and yang. This is emphasized by another question and answer:

What quality did it (his hand) possess but with what counteracting influence?
   The operative surgical quality but that he was reluctant to shed human blood even when the end justified the means, preferring in their natural order, heliotherapy, psychophysicotherapeutics, osteopathic surgery. (674-675)

A series of questions directly related to Bloom's androgyny follows. Lacking a key, lacking "home rule," abjuring violence, he is vulnerable to usurpation. Several questions contain visible clues to that usurpation, but Bloom is not yet ready to deal with the subject and moves instead to thoughts of the Gold Cup race, which in fact has relevance to his situation. He realizes that he might have won money on the race had he placed significance on the proper clues; in Barney

Kiernan's he suffers because of the race, and without cause. Nevertheless, he is serene: "he had not risked, he did not expect, he had not
been disappointed, he was satisfied . . . to have sustained no positive
loss. To have brought a positive gain to others. Light to the gentiles"
(676). A loser (because a nonbettor), he wins, like the dark horse; a
cuckold (because he has not tried to hinder Molly), he wins her respect
and affection despite Boylan's "manlier" performance.

The questions lead back to a connection between the two men as
Bloom prepares cocoa and "relinquishing his symposiarchal right to
the moustache cup" (677) drinks his from a cup identical to Stephen's.
William York Tindall explains that the botanical name of cocoa is
theobroma, "god food"; Joyce refers to it as a "massproduct" and a
"creature." Like the silence in which the two men drink it, the cocoa is
"jocoseriously" (677) a communion food. Their communion, jocose-
rious as it is, does not last long. Bloom moves into his own mind again,
but he is thinking about Stephen with charity and concern, although
his thoughts soon drift to other things and issue in a divergence
between them in "name, age, race, creed" (678). Two passages on his
"literary" past, directly inspired by Stephen's presence, interrupt this
subject, which is picked up again: "What relation existed between their
ages?" (679). The questions and answers that follow move swiftly in
and out of parallels, divergences, and intersections between the two
men. Their past acquaintance with each other and with Dante moves
to a comparison of Bloom's physical condition in the past and the present, and thence to their racial difference, which includes a kind of
similarity: "he thought that he thought that he was a jew whereas he
knew that he knew that he knew that he was not" (682). Comparison
and contrast continue with one important intersection, at which they
emerge as Stoom and Blephen! They uncouple, and Bloom moves off
again into thoughts about his ideas, scientific, inventive, and commercial, the last of which inspires Stephen's story idea, which creates
another intersecting, the mention of the Queen's Hotel. Stephen is
unconscious that his allusion touches Bloom's life; Bloom is aware
that Stephen is unaware of this. But in fact, most of the correspondences or intersections between them are made not by them but by the
narrator. It is the narrator speaking to us who works out the parallactic relations between their ages or who names them Stoom and
Blephen. Their points of connection are thus not only unconscious but

for the most part ludicrous: at this point the narrator is mocking the reader for his desire to find significances and convergences. For a number of chapters, the reader's emotions have been riddled with the same pellets used on the characters; in Ithaca, as in Eumaeus, the reader's desire for meaning, for a purposeful relationship, is mocked even as the narrator offers him hundreds of relationships.

The characters move apart again when Stephen recites his parable to Bloom's complete incomprehension. Bloom is momentarily self-absorbed in his own literary efforts and his funny devices with Molly. Molly, incidentally, is rarely referred to by name in this section, and when she is, her name is preceded by her relationship to someone: at one point she is the daughter of Major General Tweedy, at another she is "his wife Marion (Molly) Bloom" (702). The same thing is true of Milly. Persons are not people in this impersonal chapter; they are functions within a relationship.

Stephen's parable then leads to another parallel as he and Bloom discuss Jewish figures and compare the Irish and Hebrew languages. They converge, both having theoretical rather than practical knowledge of the languages under discussion. At the hundredth question, an important number for Joyce as well as for Pythagoras, the convergence between Bloom and Stephen is raised to another level, a convergence between the Irish and the Jews. A shaky alternation between divergence and convergence continues between them as Bloom attempts to sing a chant, as "their mutual reflections merge" in a "common study" (689), and as Stephen writes his name. Then they move both together and apart simultaneously as each does the same thing—studies the other:

What was Stephen's auditive sensation?
    He heard in a profound ancient male unfamiliar melody the accumulation of the past.

What was Bloom's visual sensation?
    He saw in a quick young male familiar form from the predestination of a future.

What were Stephen's and Bloom's quasisimultaneous volitional quasisensations of concealed identities?
    Visually, Stephen's: The traditional figure of hypostasis, depicted by Johannes Damascenus, Lentulus Romanus and Epiphanius Mon-

achus as leucodermic, sesquipedalian with winedark hair.
   Auditively, Bloom's: The traditional accent of the ecstasy of catastrophe. (689)

This is one of the closest points of their meeting. Each is fully conscious of the other; each sees significance in the other. Bloom sees a possible future, and Stephen sees Bloom as the "traditional figure of hypostasis," the figure depicting the two natures of Christ as God and man, or the unique essence of the godhead of the Christ. In other words, Stephen momentarily sees Bloom as sacred, but Bloom is only a kind and sometimes foolish man: Stephen sees suddenly the godhead of the human race. The two have drunk communion cocoa and have really looked at one another, each finding significance for himself, finding himself on his own doorstep: thus they are married, and if their rapprochement is not accompanied by choirs of angels, there *is* singing. Stephen sings his offensive parallel to Bloom's anthem and in exegesis of it unknowingly recapitulates Bloom's day: "One of all, the least of all, is the victim predestined. Once by inadvertence, twice by design he challenges his destiny. It comes when he is abandoned and challenges him reluctant and, as an apparition of hope and youth holds him unresisting. It leads him to a strange habitation, to a secret infidel apartment, and there, implacable, immolates him consenting" (692—the challenge "by inadvertence" is the tip on the Gold Cup; the challenges "by design" are the argument in Cyclops and the masturbation in Nausikaa, Bloom's two overt acts of defiance of convention; the "destiny" that comes as "an apparition of hope and youth" is Stephen; the "secret infidel apartment" is the brothel). Stephen unconsciously moves close to Bloom here, but Bloom at the same time moves further away, hurt by Stephen's song. The series of questions surrounding the song alternate regularly between a focus on Stephen and a focus on Bloom, but at its conclusion "the father of Millicent" (691) moves into a consideration of Milly and her relation to him: his "hallucination" (693) that she might not be his daughter, the similarity between their noses, his memories of her, separation from her, and her relation to the cat.
   At the end of this reflection, charitable Bloom returns to a relation with insensitive Stephen, offering him a bed for the night. They again move in and out of parallel and intersecting moments. Stephen's re-

jection of his offer leads Bloom, despite the "counterproposals" that are "alternately advanced, accepted, modified, declined, restated in other terms, reaccepted, ratified, reconfirmed" (696), to feel suddenly lonely. He does not anticipate that they will meet again: neither the clown nor Stephen is Bloom's son. Bloom's sorrow over his lack of a son is connected with his despair at ever perfecting, or even understanding human life. At this moment of isolation Bloom and Stephen come together again in the most important intersection they achieve. Unlike, they are like:

Did Stephen participate in his [Bloom's] dejection?
He affirmed his significance as a conscious rational animal proceeding syllogistically from the known to the unknown and a conscious rational reagent between a micro- and a macrocosm ineluctably constructed upon the incertitude of the void.

Was this affirmation apprehended by Bloom?
Not verbally. Substantially.

What comforted his misapprehension?
That as a competent keyless citizen he had proceeded energetically from the unknown to the known through the incertitude of the void. (697)

Just as the choruses of the saved and the damned in Circe repeat the same words in reverse order, Stephen and Bloom affirm their truths in reverse order. Stephen feels he is moving from the "known to the unknown": he is looking at his passage from birth (the known, the past) into an unknown future; on another level, he is moving from Martello Tower out into an unknown space; on still another, he is moving from the certitude he once possessed into full incertitude. Bloom, looking at his present life (significance unknown), is moving toward a foreknowable death; on another level, he is returning home after a chaotic day; on still another, he is moving from incertitude into certitude (death). Stephen, the artist, affirms his significance, his rationality, his logic. As an artist, he is also a reagent, capable of detecting or measuring the operations of life, of converting the void into edifice, significance. Bloom is merely man, a "citizen," and keyless to boot, but he is competent and he too survives. Both must travel, as we travel in this novel, "through the incertitude of the void."

Their departure from the house is a parallel movement with the intonation *"secreto"* of Psalm 113 (114 in the King James Version), which is sung when the dead are carried into the church, as well as at the entrance to Dante's Purgatorio, and signifies man's redemption, the conversion of the soul from sin to grace. Insofar as redemption is possible in this uncertain, ambiguous world, Stephen and Bloom have achieved it. Bloom has conquered—for today at least—his guilts, his fears and his possessiveness; Stephen has confronted—for today at least—his guilts, his fears of incertitude, and his solipsism. Stephen has come far enough out of himself to accept and to act and to encounter another, a not-self. The two emerge silently from the darkness to see "the heaventree of stars hung with humid nightblue fruit" (698). They move apart again as Bloom thinks about the macro- and microcosm and the possibility of redemption, social and moral. Implicit in this meditation is the smallness, the insignificance of mankind. At the same time, however, he sees his own star and Stephen's in the heavens, and Molly's star, the moon. Mankind may be minute, but its members have a significance or importance equal to that of the heavenly bodies in this universe built on analogy. As the moment of complete divergence between Stephen and Bloom approaches, Bloom's sense of isolation also approaches its zenith, the dominant key from which no movement is possible except a *ricorso* toward the fundamental. The heavens are the outer limit for mankind, and long as we may contemplate them, we can go no further but must return to earth. So Bloom moves from stars to moon to Molly, alluding to her "with indirect and direct verbal allusions or affirmations: with subdued affection and admiration: with description: with impediment: with suggestion." Though on a comic level he is again acting the pandar, on a symbolic level he is pointing to a "visible splendid sign" (702) which is also exactly what Stephen needs: a center to his concerns.

Finally, Bloom returns to Stephen, and the two reach the condition of separate but consubstantial unity. Each exists in the other's eyes: "each contemplating the other in both mirrors of the reciprocal flesh of theirhisnothis fellowfaces" (702). They perform parallel actions (urination), in comically different ways, and with comically different thoughts: Bloom concerned with the scientific aspects of his organ, Stephen concerned with the problem of "the sacerdotal integrity of Jesus circumcized" and the degree of worship owed to the "divine prepuce" (703). Here science and religion mingle again. The situation is even more comic in that it is triggered by Stephen's knowledge that Bloom is Jewish, but Bloom is in fact not circumcized.

They move in parallel as both watch "a star precipitated with great apparent velocity across the firmament from Vega in the Lyre above the zenith beyond the stargroup of the Tress of Berenice towards the zodiacal sign of Leo" (703). Tindall has uncovered this symbolism for us also: Vega is a falling, the Lyre is the lyrical or self-centered, Berenice is a mother killed by her son, and Leo is mankind as well as Bloom, the polled lion.[12] The two men then make their only physical contact: they shake hands, in what is surely the most mathematical description ever written of such an act. Their physical contact is totally emptied of sensory content. Both are still perceiving the same outer reality: the bells of St. George. But they have completely returned to their own modes of perception, into their own flesh, and Stephen hears:

> *Liliata rutilantium. Turma circumdet.*
> *Iubilantium te virginum. Chorus excipiat.*

Bloom hears:

> Heigho, heigho,
> Heigho, heigho. (704)

Most of the points on which the two men make contact are comically trivial; some, like the relation between their ages or educations, are ludicrous. Nevertheless, twice—once when each sees in the other glimmerings of meaning, and once when each feels a communion with the other's flesh—they are able to transcend the difference between their intellects, experience, and ages, and the similarity of their gender. The significance of these moments of rapport is not something we can estimate. We surely cannot say that meeting each other will change the life of either. However, these moments of communion between such different people, when seen in the context of all we know of Dublin, and the thick texture of correspondence and analogy that surrounds the events of this day, have a significance that transcends the personal. In Circe, Joyce demonstrates the underlying unity of mankind by showing us the hidden feelings that lie beneath the surface. In Wandering Rocks, he shows us the moral interrelations that exist, invisible to those participating in them, on the surface. In Ithaca, he shows us silly relations between people, but also two very different human beings warily and tentatively perceiving that unity and interrelatedness. The communion, incomplete as all human contact is doomed to be, and only obscurely perceived, symbolizes the fellow feeling of all mankind, a recognition, however tenuous, of the vulnerability and similarity of all people who suffer from the indifference of the stars and the impulses of the flesh, all caught in one universal pattern of experience, the human condition, made up of necessity, on the one hand, and incertitude, on the other.[13]

The universalization of the characters that occurs in this episode is accomplished through a number of methods. The long catalogue of facts about fire, water, and the stars; the analogies between Milly and the cat, Molly and the moon, Irish and Hebrew; and later, the merging of Bloom's face with the objects reflected in the mirror; as well as the similarities milked out of such different characters as Stephen and Bloom—all these set mankind in a universe inhabited by objects, animals, people, elements, and stars, all of which are shown to have common characteristics. Not only man but that which is not man travels the same course, suffers the same fate.

Richard Madtes claims Joyce "added much of his material simply because he wanted *more* . . . Catalogues and itemizations, substitution and multiplication, *things* and *things* and *things*—these are the life cells of Ithaca."[14] Things are important, but no more so than people: as in Circe, everything has equal importance. The two chapters represent Joyce's confrontation of nihilism, and his answer to it is our answer to it. If we, operating out of our modes of perception, continue to invest the characters with significance greater than that of things, then we affirm, whether we intend to or not, human value in the very midst of nihilism.

At the same time that people are lowered to the status of things, they are raised to the status of things. Some things, after all, are larger than lives: stars, water, rocks. Even a chamberpot might outlast a man. And some things and processes are immortal simply because they are not particularized: one imagines there will always be a cat or a fire. So too, it is suggested, there will always be a Bloom, a Stephen, a woman (Molly being relatively undifferentiated, function rather than person). Joyce's incredibly complex mind (the thought may be simple but its expression is not) has arranged things so that we confront nihilism and universalization at once, affirm human values to counter the first, and derive comfort from the second, yet remain largely unconscious of the mechanisms by which this is accomplished.

This process of universalization is emphasized in the second half of Ithaca, where Bloom is alone, in relation only with objects and his own mind. For a time he is suspended in isolation. Encompassed by two questions baldly presenting the sleeping world of Dublin and the sleeping world of the dead are two other questions that capture the essence of isolation seen as relationship with something that is absent:

Alone, what did Bloom hear?
The double reverberation of retreating feet on the heavenborn earth, the double vibration of a jew's harp in the resonant lane.

Alone, what did Bloom feel?
The cold of interstellar space, thousands of degrees below freezing point or the absolute zero of Fahrenheit, Centigrade or Réaumur: the incipient intimations of proximate dawn. (704)

Impersonal and objective as these paragraphs are, in context they are a poem about loneliness. Through them, the particular experience of one man touched with the chill of night and aloneness after saying goodbye to a guest is universalized into the loneliness of Pascal's man before the interminable silence of those terrible spaces. But again, lest we be tempted to idealize the lonely man, he is immediately made ridiculous as he returns into relationship with things, notably the sideboard. Yet there is a poignancy to Bloom's actions after he reenters the house. He no doubt feels something on seeing the position of the chairs in the front room:

What significances attached to these two chairs?
Significances of similitude, of posture, of symbolism, of circumstantial evidence, of testimonial supermanence. (706)

Yet these feelings are of no more consequence to the narrator than Bloom's feelings on seeing the betting tickets when he first enters the kitchen.

This section of the episode puts Bloom directly in relation with things. All things interact:

> What interchanges of looks took place between these three objects and Bloom?
>   In the mirror of the giltbordered pierglass the undecorated back of the dwarf tree regarded the upright back of the embalmed owl. Before the mirror the matrimonial gift of Alderman John Hooper with a clear melancholy wise bright motionless compassionate gaze regarded Bloom while Bloom with obscure tranquil profound motionless compassionated gaze regarded the matrimonial gift of Luke and Caroline Doyle. (707)

Bloom moves thence into relation with himself, ipso- and aliorelative, with his family line, his mind (reflected in the library), his body, his finances, and his ambitions, or rather daydreams. His reflections as he gazes in the mirror are described in a prose that emphasizes his aloneness simply by its abstraction from his feeling. The hopeless library and even more hopeless daydreams are comic but also pathetically familiar, as are the contents of the desk drawers with their incongruous bits and pieces of the past. The usually locked drawer, to which he adds Martha Clifford's letter, is like the Circe chapter of the novel, full of the ludicrous and pathetic objects people feel it necessary to hide. The desk and its contents represent Bloom's relation with the past, with some suggestions for a future:

> What possibility suggested itself?
>   The possibility of exercising virile power of fascination in the most immediate future after an expensive repast in a private apartment in the company of an elegant courtesan, of corporal beauty, moderately mercenary, variously instructed, a lady by origin. (722)

The real sadness behind Bloom's father's letter—both Bloom's and Rudolph's—is belittled by the jagged phrases quoted. The sadness of Rudolph's old age, which is also Bloom's future—and ours—is also comically but truthfully undercut:

> What object offered partial consolation for these reminiscences?
>   The endowment policy, the bank passbook, the certificate of the possession of scrip. (725)

After this summation of the remants which constitute the only consolation for the past, the future becomes ascendant.

> Reduce Bloom by cross multiplication of reverses of fortune, from
> which these supports protected him, and by elimination of all posi-
> tive values to a negligible negative irrational unreal quantity. (725)

Stripped of "all positive values," and crossed by fortune, Bloom ends
as an "aged impotent disfranchised ratesupported moribund lunatic
pauper" (725). So stripped and crossed, we would all suffer the same
fate: what Bloom is facing here are the fears underlying every human
existence. In a magnificent set of paragraphs, Bloom attempts to deal
with his fears about the future and the question he has been unable, all
this long day, to confront. Ludicrously, Bloom imagines a miserable
ending to life can be precluded "by decease (change of state), by departure (change of place)," and preferably "the latter, by the line of
least resistance" (726).

He then moves into direct relation with his feelings about Molly. He
considers the irritations, the cost, the boredom of marriage; he knows
that it is impossible "to form by reunion the original couple of uniting
parties" (726); he thinks that he would like to travel. But he realizes
that such a move would destroy his conscious identity:

> What universal binomial denominations would be his as entity and
> nonentity?
> Assumed by any or known to none. Everyman or Noman. (727)

This could be a liberation. He might receive tributes, "honours and
gifts of strangers, the friends of Everyman. A nymph immortal,
beauty, the bride of Noman" (727). He might also be reborn as a hero
in the old style: "an estranged avenger, a wreaker of justice on male-
factors, a dark crusader, a sleeper awakened, with financial resources
. . . surpassing those of Rothschild or of the silver king" (728). His
notion of leaving Molly is developed with the same exaggerated,
comic quality found in most of his plans for travel; but these passages,
though more comic than not, are tinged with the pathetic romantic
coloration of all false plans—the extravagant fantasies of a child plan-
ning to run away from home, the playboy bachelor apartment imagined by a husband who has no real intention of abandoning his wife.

And Bloom's reasons for remaining with Molly are so trivial and so profound that only impersonal itemization could communicate them: "The lateness of the hour, rendering procrastinatory: the obscurity of the night, rendering invisible: the uncertainty of thoroughfares, rendering perilous: the necessity for repose, obviating movement: the proximity of an occupied bed, obviating research: the anticipation of warmth (human) tempered with coolness (linen), obviating desire and rendering desirable: the statue of Narcissus, sound without echo, desired desire" (728).

Bloom's decision is made almost unconsciously. He rises to return to the bed of his unfaithful wife, recapitulating his day and its major enigma: "Who was M'Intosh?" (729). It should be evident by now that this question is not trivial at all; what it asks is what we ask about this book: who wrote it? Where does the author stand? Yet Bloom's relations to the day that constitutes this novel are summed up brusquely: he recapitulates the "past consecutive causes . . . of accumulated fatigue" (728); the enigma of M'Intosh; and the "imperfections in a perfect day" (729). As he moves toward Molly, he remembers her father, who is more important to Bloom than to Molly. He observes her discarded clothes "disposed irregularly" (730) on a trunk, a disposition complained about by the nymph in Circe. He perceives the other objects that belong to this world, removes his clothing, and arranges the bedclothes with the pillow at the foot. Finally, he enters Molly's bed.

The bed he enters partakes of the same ambiguous character as the front room, the kitchen, the house, the city, the world, and the cosmos in which he lives. He enters it with full awareness of its nature: "With circumspection, as invariably when entering an abode (his own or not his own): with solicitude, the snakespiral springs of the mattress being old, the brass quoits and pendent viper radii loose and tremulous under stress and strain: prudently, as entering a lair or ambush of lust or adder: lightly, the less to disturb: reverently, the bed of conception and of birth, of consummation of marriage and of breach of marriage, of sleep and of death" (731).

The snake of the creation myth is one with the sacred: sex remains the great mystery, the great threat, the great wonder. Bloom accepts his position in the bed as one of a series. In doing so, he expresses an understanding and acceptance of the principles of eternal recurrence and metempsychosis on a microcosmic level, his own personal life:

If he had smiled why would he have smiled?
    To reflect that each one who enters imagines himself to be the
first to enter whereas he is always the last term of a preceding series
even if the first term of a succeeding one, each imagining himself to
be first, last, only and alone, whereas he is neither first nor last nor
only nor alone in a series originating in and repeated to infinity.
(731)

Bloom's understanding of love and life stands here in contrast to
Stephen's, who wants a charm for *"Amor me solo."* Bloom is condemned by critics for being a hewer of wood and drawer of water for
Molly, and for dealing ineffectually with Boylan. But Bloom sees
Molly as the principle of life itself, nature, earth. (Even this is comic,
because Molly is, in the novel, an actual being. But if she were not, if
she were a saint or the Virgin Mary, Bloom's devotion would be
cheapened, for it is far easier to worship a disembodied ideal than to
accept a reality and worship the principle behind it. It is the latter that
Augustine denominated as "charity.") And to earth we are all hewers
of wood and drawers of water; for earth, warm, embracing, fickle,
indifferent, unjust, capricious, and cruel, we are all only one in a series. Stephen searches for certitude, a charm that will enchant someone
into loving him only; Bloom knows that there is no such thing, no
such charm, and no such love. Bloom ends with "envy, jealousy,
abnegation, equanimity" (732) about an act "as natural as any and
every natural act of a nature expressed or understood executed in
natured nature by natural creatures in accordance with his, her and
their natured natures." In a world where imperfection and incertitude
are the only certainties, adultery is "not as calamitous as a cataclysmic
annihilation of the planet . . . less reprehensible than theft, highway
robbery, cruelty to children and animals . . . felony, mutiny on the
high seas . . . criminal assault, manslaughter, wilful and premeditated
murder . . . not more abnormal than all other altered processes of
adaptation to altered conditions of existence . . . more than inevitable,
irreparable" (733).
    Bloom does not repress his feelings. It is through the largeness,
honesty, and humility of his feelings that he accomplishes the
slaughter of the suitors. And it is true that there are many suitors,
even if there is only one adultery. If betrayal occurs through any placement of love and desire, whether in thought, word, or deed, Bloom
and Molly have each betrayed the other many times. Bloom, that

"conscious reactor against the void incertitude," concludes by accepting "the futility of triumph or protest or vindication: the inanity of
extolled virtue: the lethargy of nescient matter: the apathy of the
stars" (734). On the final and simplest level of self, Bloom thinks what
Joyce wrote in his notes to this chapter: "how can her fuck fuck me."[15]
He accepts, and slides into pleasure at the proximity of Molly's body.
The sleeper, not mentioned by name, awakens, and the two talk, a
listener and a narrator. Molly is less or more than a person here: she is
a center to which he adjusts as he accepts his position in her realm—
the bed, the real earth—and takes his position in the bed in accordance
with hers. The flaws, incompleteness, and variableness of this relationship are both corporal and mental, but inconstancy and variableness are found also in the macrocosm, are found even in the reflection
of light hovering "visibly above the listener's and the narrator's invisible thoughts . . . an inconstant series of concentric circles of varying
gradations of light and shadow" (736).

Bloom lies upside down facing Molly as they move "at rest relatively to themselves and each other" in motion through space. His
relation to earth now defined, he moves into relation with the universe. Like Sinbad on a magic carpet, Bloom rests whirling through
"everchanging tracks of neverchanging space," a manchild in fetal
position, weary, "in the womb" (737)—there:

•

I cannot conceive of a technique that would more precisely delineate, define, chiaroscuro Bloom's particular state of mind than this
impersonal scientific itemization of the facts surrounding the being.
Graham Greene also uses a cold, objective, underkeyed style of expo-
sition to set in relief the emotions of his characters, but Greene does
not work on as many levels at once as Joyce does. The acceptance that
Bloom feels at the end of this day is basic to his personality; it pervades everything he does during the day, and it is rooted not just in
temperament, but in his intellectual and emotional conception of the
cosmos, of life, of himself. He chooses life: what is antilife he discards
in disgust (Cyclops), in insouciance (Nausikaa), in terror and contempt (Circe), in despair and a full acceptance of the rose's lamented
thorns (Ithaca).

The tone of the chapter, totally unemotional, sets human emotions down as unimportant before the larger facts of a universe of fire, water, stars, houses, keys, trees, and Plumtree's Potted Meat. The style implies the complete triumph of the Houyhnhnms: emotion has been successfully eradicated from the world. The message of the narrator of the chapters from Sirens through Circe has been received and acted upon. In the scientific, relativistic world of Ithaca, the impersonal narrator assumes that all phenomena except emotion are equally significant. But Joyce insists that man's essence consists in his being a conscious reactor against his uncertainty about having any significance. Joyce risks losing his reader, taking the chance that the reader is also a conscious reactor and will pump in the emotions that the narrator has extirpated, will affirm significance even in the face of the void.

If there were a way to move through the void without pain, if there were a way to do always the right thing . . . but there is not. This is what the greatest Christian thinkers meant by saying that all men are sinners. Aquinas saw sin as inevitable limitation, inadequacy, privation. So did Dante, with all his fierceness, and so did Joyce. But there is no way to escape privation.[16]

If, aware of the impossibility of perfection, and suffering all the anguish of the human condition, one gets through the day with decency, without maliciously or accidentally harming anyone else or oneself, without the "committal of homicide or suicide during sleep by an aberration of the light of reason, the incommensurable categorical intelligence situated in the cerebral convolutions," (720), one has endured as a human being. If, in addition, one is able to extend oneself to others in small ways—giving five shillings to the Dignams, attending the funeral of a man who was not an especially close friend, putting oneself out to help a blind boy, to visit a laboring woman, to attempt to rescue a young man one hardly knows, and granting *caritas*, which precludes resentment, to a wandering daughter and a wandered wife—one is indeed an unconquered hero. Bloom is insufficiently intelligent or educated to be intellectually admirable; he is insufficiently forceful to be impressive; and shown in his full emotional and bodily functioning, he is as ridiculous as we are. It is up to the reader to choose his hero, to ask which would be better, a world full of Blooms or a world full of Achilles.

Just as a number of statements are scattered throughout *Ulysses* that bear direct reference to the novel itself, there are in Ithaca many direct statements about the novel. But here they bear on the novel's significance and purpose rather than on its technique or its relation to the author. Stephen asserts at the opening of Ithaca the "eternal affirmation of the spirit of man in literature" (666). Joyce does not make things simple: he has Bloom tacitly disagree. Since from what we know of Bloom, it is unlikely that he has enough knowledge about literature to hold any opinion at all on this question, his disagreement seems more to indicate Joyce's unwillingness to allow any statement to stand unchallenged. Stephen's statement strikes a keynote for the chapter.

Ithaca is about relationships, and it discusses, among others, the relation of the book *Ulysses* to the actual world. There are 309 questions—surely a significant number—in the episode. Numbers were as important to Joyce as they were to Dante, and they are especially so in this quantitative chapter. The hundredth question in Ithaca broadens the relationship between Bloom and Stephen to include all the Jews and all the Irish: shortly afterward, the two men see traces of significance in each other. The three hundredth question, which occurs close to the end of the last chapter (excluding the coda), explains the reason for much of Bloom's conduct during this day: he has felt inhibited from having full sexual intercourse with Molly for "10 years, 5 months and 18 days" (736). And the three hundred and ninth question places Bloom among the stars.

It is possible to prescind any number of trinities from this novel. Triangular relations could be sketched among intellect, emotion, and morality, or earth (nature), world (human reality), and significance, which may be heavenly (certitude) or hellish (incertitude). Ithaca is sprinkled with analogies suggestive of the significance of the novel *Ulysses*, the significance of artistic creation, and the significance of life. The three are equated. All three are described when Bloom ponders the cosmos, the macrocosm with its "parallax or parallactic drift of socalled fixed stars, in reality evermoving from immeasurably remote eons to infinitely remote futures in comparison with which the years, threescore and ten, of allotted human life formed a parenthesis of infinitesimal brevity" (698), and its analogous microcosm, "the universe of human serum constellated with red and white bodies, themselves universes of void space constellated with other bodies, each, in continuity, its universe of divisible component bodies of which each was again divisible in divisions of redivisible component bodies, dividends and divisors ever diminishing without actual division till, if the progress were carried far enough, nought nowhere was never reached."[17] Parallactic drift in *Ulysses* places human life in increasingly distant perspective; yet despite this, despite the void, despite incertitude, within each character and within the novel, "nought nowhere . . . [is] never reached." An essence stands. The method of the novel works to raise "to the utmost kinetic elaboration of any power of any of its powers," the "nucleus of the nebula of every digit" or object, state, or emotion which contains "succinctly the potentiality of being raised" (699). It is the notion of epiphany that is here being described in different terms.

Bloom finds the notion of an earthly or cosmic paradise doubtful, because "an apogean humanity of beings created in varying forms with finite differences resulting similar to the whole and to one another would probably there as here remain inalterably and inalienably attached to vanities, to vanities of vanities and all that is vanity." The possibility of redemption by a savior is also dismissed: "the minor was proved by the major" (700).

The scientifically accurate discussion of the constellations concludes with an assignment of human values to the stars: Bloom, Stephen, and Rudy take their places with Shakespeare as cosmic occurrences.[18] Not only they but "other persons" are announced or lamented by the appearance or disappearance of a star, and solar and lunar phenomena are seen as affected by "abatement of wind, transit of shadow, taciturnity of winged creatures, emergence of nocturnal or crepuscular animals, persistence of infernal light, obscurity of terrestrial waters, pallor of human beings" (701).

Bloom concludes about the heavens "that it was a Utopia, there being no known method from the known to the unknown: an infinity, renderable equally finite by the suppositious probable apposition of one or more bodies equally of the same and of different magnitudes: a mobility of illusory forms immobilised in space, remobilised in air: a past which possibly had ceased to exist as a present before its future spectators had entered actual present existence" (701). This paragraph describes the macrocosm of the novel as well as the macrocosm at which Bloom is gazing. There is no dogma in *Ulysses*, no key, no right way, "no known method from the known to the unknown." *Ulysses* is a finitely rendered symbol of infinity; on its pages "a mobility of illusory forms" is "immobilised in space," held static for eternity, but "remobilised" in air as we read. The book contains the illusory story of a past that had ceased to exist as a present before many of us, its "future spectators," had entered "actual present existence." The entire universe is linked together: astrological influences affect the sublunary world as much as do "the lake of dreams, the sea of rain, the gulf of dews, the ocean of fecundity." Our apprehension of the universe is "as attributable to verifiable intuition as to fallacious analogy" (701).

S. L. Goldberg affirms that Ithaca places the characters in a "spatio-temporal setting far larger than they could hope to command, for we see them as a completed *action*, which is fulfilled both by the book itself to which it points as its goal and in the silent luminous *stasis* wherein all men appear as adventurers, all adventurers appear as one, and all adventure, all process, a simultaneous, static, eternal pattern."[19] The truth of *Ulysses*, what really happens in it, is that Stephen affirms "his significance as a conscious rational animal proceeding syllogistically from the known to the unknown and a conscious rational reagent between a micro- and a macrocosm ineluctably constructed upon the incertitude of the void" (697), and that Bloom affirms himself" a conscious reactor against the void incertitude" (734), "a competent keyless citizen" who nevertheless is able to proceed "energetically from the unknown to the known through the incertitude of the void" (697).

Affirmation of the self is an affirmation of the human. Bloom and Stephen, fictional categories for human thought and feeling, do survive, and their survival is an affirmation of the human race. Given the size, the complexity, and the ambiguity of the space traversed, survival alone is a triumph, entitling Bloom and Stephen, along with the generations of humankind, to the right to become immortal "wanderers like the stars at which they gaze."

[7] Coda: The Earth

Joyce described the last chapter of *Ulysses* as a "last word (human, all too human)," which would stand as the "indispensable countersign to Bloom's passport to eternity," and explained that he wanted to "depict the earth which is prehuman and presumably posthuman."[1] Penelope is a coda to the novel proper, for the action ends in Ithaca.[2] At the conclusion of that episode we stand out in the cold of interstellar space, gazing down at the dot that is Bloom whirling gently on the globe. In Penelope we make the "ultimate return," not to the world but to earth, Gea-Tellus, the womb of us all.[3]

Penelope

Despite Joyce's characterization of Molly as a "perfectly sane full amoral fertilisable untrustworthy engaging shrewd limited prudent indifferent *Weib. Ich bin der* [sic] *Fleisch der stets bejaht*," and despite the apparently simple surface of the chapter, interpretations of it have differed greatly.[4] Hugh Kenner argues:

> Molly in "Penelope" has no direction but that imposed by the vagaries of her appetites, and no audience but herself . . . Some readers have oversentimentalized the final pages of her monologue. They are in key with the animal level at which this comic inferno is conceived: and they are the epiphany of all that we have seen and heard during the day. The "Yes" of consent that kills the soul has darkened the intellect and blunted the moral sense of all Dublin. At the very rim of Dante's funnel-shaped Hell is the imperceptible "Yes" of Paola and Francesca; they are blown about by the winds, but Molly lies still at the warm dead womb-like centre of the labyrinth of paving stones. Her "Yes" is confident and exultant; it is the "Yes" of authority: authority over this animal kingdom of the dead.[5]

R. M. Adams, on the other hand, claims Molly is not simply a realistic creation but "woman as conceived by a man trained to think the
flesh naturally dirty":

> She is the principle of fleshly existence, foul, frank, and consciously
> obscene . . . She is a slut, a sloven, and a voracious sexual animal as
> conceived by one of those medieval minds to whom the female can
> never be anything but a *saccum stercoris;* she is a frightening ven-
> ture into the unconsciousness of evil, and certainly, deliberately
> obscene . . . But Molly Bloom is not only obscene, she is holy; she is
> life itself, profuse, repetitive, forever polluting and renewing itself
> . . . Molly, with her young eyes, is the freshness of an eternal recep-
> tivity, the vital responsiveness which contrasts magnificently with
> languid, pallid Stephen, and exhausted Bloom.[6]

Both critics, despite the differences in their interpretations, see
Molly in hyperbolic terms. The character of Molly seems to invite,
even demand, hyperbole, as only archetypes do. The way a reader
interprets this archetype depends on how he interprets the novel as a
whole.[7] But no one doubts that Penelope is indeed the cap or seal to
the rest. Nor do I. I do believe, however, that not only are most interpretations of Molly too extreme in whatever direction they take, but
they also ignore the many ambiguities and contradictions that exist in
the chapter itself. For the chapter is not as simple as it seems; it is a
mass of contradictions.

The style of the episode, direct interior monologue, symbolizes the
place we are in. Whereas a style that uses third person description of
action is positing the action as fact, as part of the real, direct interior
monologue clearly indicates that everything related about feelings *and*
action is filtered through the narrator's mind and is possibly unreliable.

The point of view in this section, which is entirely Molly's own,
contrasts with the divided narration of the rest of the book where,
either because of the use of third person description or because of
authorial intrusion, we are always conscious of more than one voice.
This single point of view, coming after the duet of Cyclops, the trio of
Sirens, the whole chorus of Oxen and Circe, and the reverberating
voice of Ithaca, emphasizes Molly's wholeness, oneness. The single
voice symbolizes an unawareness of ambiguity, an ability to think and

act simply. In fact, Molly's thoughts and actions are not simple, but her motivations are. The lack of punctuation symbolizes the lack in Molly's mind of the laws and rules of the "built" world, and the rhythms flow like water, which frequently in the novel is associated with sex, eternal recurrence, continuation.

Molly represents the opposite of the void. The void exists in the "built" world, the "masculine" world of reason and unreason; of morality and immorality; law and crime; and dogma and heresy. Molly is the "female" principle that exemplifies the state of humanity in Eden, at one with nature and natural processes. Her *telos*, like that of the animal, is survival and continuation, enduringness. She is whole because she is able to synthesize all opposites, obliterate contradictions by her innocent self-interest. No term adequately describes this aspect of Molly's character: "selfhood" implies more individuality than Molly possesses; "self-interest" carries connotations of the assertion of self over others, of selfishness and even greed. Molly's self-interest is like the self-interest of the cat, or of a puppy; it has about it the innocence of the infant or of the queen bee, whom no one can judge for fulfilling her biologically-given nature. If Molly is selfish or greedy—and there are elements of both qualities in her character, for she has at least a tendency to be grasping—it is not in order to stockpile diamonds toward her old age, but to get something from a man— where else can she get it?—that will make her more attractive to men, new clothes or a piece of jewelry. Her self-interest is essentially innocent, directed wholly toward beingness and not toward gain.

Whereas Stephen is paralyzed by equal and intolerable opposites, and Bloom hotfoots his way through a maze of ambivalences, Molly glides effortlessly in her own clear direction, without interest in or even apparent awareness of contradiction. She is concerned always and only with the needs of her self, which are essentially the inexorable movements of nature. She fills the void or presents its opposite aspect because she requires no "reason" for existence, no *raison d'être* beyond her own vital animal drive to stay alive and to be alive. Thus, she, or what she symbolizes, exists in most human beings. The principle she represents is what makes Stephen exclaim, "I say! Not yet awhile. A look around" (242), and what makes Bloom say, "I do not like that other world she wrote. No more do I. Plenty to see and hear and feel yet" (115). Molly is less realized as a character than are

Stephen and Bloom; she is more representative of the principle of life (as *bios*) blessedly joined to the actuality of life—not just an accepter of nature, but part of it.

Molly totally disregards the "built" world; she is not even aware of contradictions. But this quality of hers has no relation with Gerty MacDowell's or Father Conmee's avoidance of reality. They shrink from what they do not want to see; Molly sees everything, but only as it relates to her, and she adopts a momentary position toward things in accordance with her momentary needs.

Molly's complete disregard for contradictions shows up in her ideas on the fairly simple subject of keeping a servant, which crop up in her monologue:

> Not that I care two straws who he does it with or knew before that way though Id like to find out so long as I dont have the two of them under my nose all the time like that slut that Mary we had in Ontario terrace padding out her false bottom to excite him bad enough to get the smell of those painted women off him once or twice I had a suspicion by getting him to come near me when I found the long hair on his coat without that one when I went into the kitchen pretending he was drinking water 1 woman is not enough for them it was all his fault of course ruining servants then proposing that she could eat at our table on Christmas if you please O no thank you not in my house stealing my potatoes and the oysters 2/6 per doz going out to see her aunt if you please common robbery it was but I was sure he had something on with that one it takes me to find out a thing like that he said you have no proof it was her proof O yes her aunt was very fond of oysters but I told her what I thought of her suggesting me to go out to be alone with her I wouldnt lower myself to spy on them the garters I found in her room the Friday she was out that was enough for me a little bit too much I saw too that her face swelled up on her with temper when I gave her her weeks notice better do without them altogether do out the rooms myself quicker only for the damn cooking and throwing out the dirt I gave it to him anyhow either she or me leaves the house I couldnt even touch him if I thought he was with a dirty barefaced liar and sloven like that one denying it up to my face and singing about the place in the W C too because she knew she was too well off. (739-740)

> Its his fault of course having the two of us slaving here instead of getting in a woman long ago am I ever going to have a proper servant again of course then shed see him coming Id have to let her

know or shed revenge it arent they a nuisance that old Mrs Fleming
you have to be walking round after her putting the things into her
hands sneezing and farting into the pots well of course shes old she
cant help it. (768)

Most of the comedy of the chapter derives from this unwitting trait
of Molly's, for she herself has little sense of humor, humor being a
response to and way of handling the absurdities of the masculine, built
world. Molly can praise and belittle Bloom in one breath and for the
same set of actions (italics mine):

Yes because he never did a thing like that before as ask to get his
breakfast in bed with a couple of eggs since the *City Arms* hotel
when he used to be pretending to be laid up with a sick voice *doing
his highness to make himself interesting to that old faggot* Mrs Riordan that he thought he had a great leg of and she never left us a
farthing all for masses for herself and her soul greatest miser ever
was actually afraid to lay out 4d for her methylated spirit . . . her
dog smelling my fur and always edging to get up under my petticoats especially then *still I like that in him polite to old women like
that and waiters and beggars too hes not proud out of nothing.*
(738)

No its better hes going where he is besides something always happens with him the time going to the Mallow Concert at Marybor-
ough ordering boiling soup for the two of us then the bell rang out
he walks down the platform with the soup splashing about taking
spoonfuls of it *hadnt he the nerve* and the waiter after him making a
holy show of us screeching and confusion for the engine to start but
he wouldnt pay till he finished it the two gentlemen in the 3rd class
carriage said he was quite right *so he was too hes so pigheaded
sometimes* when he gets a thing into his head a good job he was able
to open the carriage door with his knife or theyd have taken us on
to Cork. (748)

Molly gets furious with Milly's behavior, then immediately turns
around to say she understands it, she acted the same way herself at
Milly's age, it is all Bloom's fault after all. She is mean-minded one
moment and generous-minded the next: after her excoriation of Mrs.
Riordan, she adds, "but she was a welleducated woman certainly,"
and her disgust at Mrs. Fleming is countered by "of course shes old she
cant help it." Molly is so unaware of contradictions that even after her

thoughts about the disconcerting Mrs. Fleming, she can imagine a picnic with Boylan and seizes on Mrs. Fleming as a partner for Bloom.

Molly is logically ridiculous. Consider her meanderings on the woman accused of poisoning her husband or her notions about religion. After hearing the thunder and feeling guilty, Molly continues: "and they come and tell you theres no God what could you do if it was running and rushing about nothing only make an act of contrition the candle I lit that evening in Whitefriars street chapel for the month of May see it brought its luck though" (741). The luck it brought, of course, is her affair with Boylan. That there is an inherent absurdity in lighting a candle in a church that condemns adultery and being grateful that it brought about that adultery is not something Molly could see even if it were pointed out. She lighted the candle to ask for something she needed; that was why she prayed, that was what she got, and she is grateful.

Molly's sexuality is riddled with ambiguities. She masturbates:

No satisfaction in it pretending to like it till he comes then finish it off myself anyway and it makes your lips pale. (740)

He was clever enough to spot that of course that was all thinking of him and his mad crazy letters my Precious one everything connected with your glorious Body everything underlined that comes from it is a thing of beauty and of joy forever something he got out of some nonsensical book that he had me always at myself 4 or 5 times a day sometimes. (771)

After I tried with the Banana but I was afraid it might break and get lost up in me somewhere yes because they once took something down out of a woman that was up there for years covered with limesalts. (760)

She puts up with Bloom's fetishes, his adoration of drawers, gloves, her bottom:

Its a wonder Im not an old shrivelled hag before my time living with him so cold never embracing me except sometimes when hes asleep the wrong end of me not knowing I suppose who he has any man thatd kiss a womans bottom Id throw my hat at him after that hed kiss anything unnatural where we havent 1 atom of any kind of expression in us all of us the same 2 lumps of lard before ever I do that to a man pfooh the dirty brutes the mere thought is enough I

kiss the feet of you señorita theres some sense in that didnt he kiss
our halldoor yes he did what a madman. (777)

Molly incorporates all sexual adaptations. Despite her complaints,
she goes on accepting Bloom's actions, and there is surely a hint of
double meaning in her "Id throw my hat at him," although she is
doubtless unaware of it. She is willing to try anything, enjoys everything. Although she is immensely drawn to men, she has narcissistic
and homosexual inclinations:

> The smoothest place is right there between this bit here how soft like
> a peach easy God I wouldnt mind being a man and get up on a
> lovely woman. (770)

> O well I suppose its because they were so plump and tempting in my
> short petticoat he couldnt resist they excite myself sometimes its
> well for men all the amount of pleasure they get off a womans body
> were so round and white for them always I wished I was one myself
> for a change just to try with that thing they have swelling upon you
> so hard. (776)

The relation with Hester Stanhope, "dog" to Molly's "Doggerina,"
with whom Molly slept with "her arms around" (755-756), may not
seem homosexual at first, but if two men were having the same sort of
relationship, the homosexual tinge would be immediately apparent.[8]
But "moral" implications do not exist for Molly.

In sum, Molly was "polymorphous perverse" long before Norman
O. Brown popularized the phrase.[9] She enjoys everything sexual, and
none of her attitudes bothers her. This is the difference between her
and the two men. She shows some sadism in her relation with Bloom;
she exhibits masochism in her willingness to be the object of his fetishes; and she has narcissistic, onanistic, homosexual and incestuous
inclinations—but unlike her husband and Stephen, she has no guilt.[10]
(There is only one sexual act she does feel somewhat guilty about, her
affair with Boylan.) It is difficult to tell whether the thing that most
shocks people about her and makes her seem "obscene" is the catholicism of her sexual tastes or the fact that she feels no guilt.

Molly's ability to resolve or vacate inner contradictions is profound, and next to her interest in sex, this is the characteristic Joyce
most emphasizes. Surely the author's point is clear: it is contradictions

that are destroying Stephen, while Bloom is spending all his time trying to resolve them, but they fall like rain from Molly's ample shoulders. One reason it may be possible for Molly to ignore them is that she has no intellectual life, as suggested in her remark that she hates politics or that she never knows the time. She disregards the built world where contradictions are rooted. But Joyce's point in Penelope as well as elsewhere in *Ulysses* is that the unremitting intellect is the cause of much human torment. Could Stephen and Bloom accept their sexuality as fully as Molly does hers—accept their bodies, their place in nature, as she does—the universe would fall into place for them as it does for her. But of course they cannot. No real human being could ever have Molly's absolute and blind ignorance of all events except sexual ones that occur in the world; no one on earth is that narrow. Molly is in fact extremely isolated: she has neither friends nor neighbors; the only people she sees are Mrs. Fleming, Milly, Bloom, and Boylan. But she is isolated as well within her own sexuality, because sexuality is the only thing she is aware of. This is surrealistic, or symbolic, not naturalistic characterization. There is no person like Molly: she is a principle, an archetype, and as such, lives in both characters and permits them to endure. Molly never thinks about immortality, about making a mark that will outlast her on the world. She thinks only about being, feeling like the person she is, and seeing what she is reflected in the world around her. Molly finally represents the nonrational sense of being which supports us all, which impels us to stay alive even when life seems a blight.

Molly's attitude, illogical on the surface, has total integrity with the needs of the self. There is no gap in her between self and not-self, because everything in the universe exists for her, the sun shines for her, she believes that. She is emotionally self-sufficient, a quality often ascribed to the Eternal Feminine.

Besides Molly's two dominant characteristics, her polymorphous sexuality and her unawareness of contradiction, the Penelope episode has other troublesome levels. It even has what appear to be inner contradictions. Not only is Molly less realized as a character than are Bloom or Stephen, but we do not reach her until the very end of the novel, and much of what we know about her is gathered from other characters. In other words, we begin Penelope with certain expectations; they seem to be realized, so we do not probe further. As David

Hayman points out, "we get to know her as Bloom knows her and as others think they know her." We know she is the person of supreme importance in Bloom's life; his thoughts revert to her repeatedly, and almost always with passion, affection, admiration, even awe, to the point where he considers making a collection of her sayings.[11] He views her limitations tolerantly and with amusement and is constantly thinking of ways to please her, ways that generally involve the purchase of clothes, especially underclothes (if it were not for Molly's interest in that item, one might wonder whom he wanted to please). As Hayman explains, "for Bloom she is all in all, the omphalos about which he turns, the womb to which he returns."[12]

Most of the remarks made about Molly in the course of the novel are consistent with Bloom's impressions of her. This in itself should make us suspicious, for nothing in this novel can be so sure and simple. The remarks made about Molly by Dublin's males follow:

—And *Madame*, Mr Power said smiling. Last but not least. (93)

—O, to be sure, John Henry Menton said. I haven't seen her for some time. She was a finelooking woman. I danced with her, wait, fifteen seventeen golden years ago, at Mat Dillon's, in Roundtown. And a good armful she was . . . In God's name, John Henry Menton said, what did she marry a coon like that for? She had plenty of game in her then.
—Has still, Ned Lambert said. (106)

—And Madame Bloom, Mr O'Madden Burke added. The vocal muse. Dublin's prime favourite.
Lenehan gave a loud cough.
—Ahem! he said very softly. O, for a fresh of breath air! I caught a cold in the park. The gate was open. (135)

—She's well nourished, I tell you. Plovers on toast. (177)

[Lenehan's story, 234-235.]

—Ay, ay, Mr Dedalus nodded. Mrs Marion Bloom has left off clothes of all descriptions. (269)

—The wife has a fine voice. Or had. What? Lidwell asked . . .
—Very, Mr Dedalus said, staring hard at a headless sardine . . .
—Very, he stared. The lower register, for choice. (288-289)

Hoho begob, says I to myself, says I. That explains the milk in the cocoanut and absence of hair on the animal's chest. Blazes doing the tootle on the flute . . . That's the bucko that'll organise her, take my tip. (319)

The only characters who mention Molly without putting her into a tacit or explicit sexual context are Mrs. Breen, who asks after an old friend; the "frowzy whore," who sees only "a stout lady . . . in the brown costume" (290); and the nameless one, who describes her as "crying her eyes out with her eight inches of fat all over her" (315). Yet fleshiness seems to be one of Molly's attractions, so remarks about her stoutness do not substantially counter the tone of other remarks. And it is the nameless one himself who quickly leaps to the assumption that Molly is having an affair with Boylan. All the other men who mention Molly obviously think of her in sexual terms. In other words, we come to feel that Molly has a reputation for promiscuity. Bloom's list in Ithaca seals the case, and a quick reading of Penelope does not dispel the impression. As Hayman indicates: "We fall readily into the trap prepared for us by the arranger who, playing on our prior hearsay knowledge, permits us to turn the neophyte adulteress into a whore."[13]

But the facts of Molly's attitudes and actions are very different.[14] During her monologue, Molly thinks about fourteen of the twenty-five men on Bloom's list, some of whom are patently ridiculous as lovers. These are characteristic of her thoughts on thirteen of them:

[On Mulvey] I wouldnt let him he was awfully put out first for fear you never know consumption or leave me with a child embarazada that old servant Ines told me that one drop even if it got into you at all [her feelings toward Mulvey are nevertheless highly sexual, far more so than appears here]. (760)

[On Penrose] that delicate looking student that stopped in No 28 with the Citrons Penrose nearly caught me washing through the window only for I snapped up the towel to my face that was his studenting. (754)

[On Professor Goodwin] the day old frostyface Goodwin called about the concert in Lombard street and I just after dinner all flushed and tossed with boiling old stew dont look at me professor I had to say Im a fright yes but he was a real old gent in his way it was impossible to be more respectful. (747)

[On Menton] that big babbyface I saw him and he not long married flirting with a young girl at Pooles Myriorama and turned my back on him when he slinked out looking quite conscious what harm but he had the impudence to make up to me one time well done to him mouth almighty and his boiled eyes of all the big stupoes I ever met and thats called a solicitor. (739)

[On Father Corrigan] I hate that confession when I used to go to Father Corrigan he touched me father and what harm if he did where and I said on the canal bank like a fool . . . what did he want to know for when I already confessed it to God he had a nice fat hand the palm moist always I wouldnt mind feeling it neither would he . . . Id like to be embraced by one in his vestments. (741)

[On Matt Dillon] was an awfully nice man he was near seventy always good humour well now Miss Tweedy or Miss Gillespie theres the pyannyer. (758)

[On Valentine Dillon] the lord Mayor looking at me with his dirty eyes Val Dillon that big heathen. (750)

[On Lenehan] that sponger he was making free with me after the Glencree dinner coming back that long joult over the featherbed mountain. (750)

[On the unknown gentleman] that gentleman of fashion staring down at me with his glasses. (769)

[On Ben Dollard] base barreltone the night he borrowed the swallowtail to sing out of in Holles street squeezed and squashed into them and grinning all over his big Dolly face like a well-whipped childs botty didnt he look a balmy ballocks sure enough that must have been a spectacle on the stage imagine paying 5/- in the preserved [sic] seats for that to see him. (774)

[On Simon Dedalus] such a criticiser with his glasses up with his tall hat on him at the cricket match and a great big hole in his sock one thing laughing at the other . . . he was always turning up half screwed singing the second verse first . . . he was always on for flirtyfying too when I sang Maritana with him . . . and he was married at the time to May Goulding but then hed say or do something to knock the good out of it. (768, 774)

[On Pisser Burke] that other beauty Burke out of the City Arms hotel was there spying around as usual on the slip always where he wasnt wanted if there was a row on you vomit a better face there was no love lost between us thats 1 consolation. (765)

[On Joseph Cuffe] he gave me a great mirada once or twice first
he was as stiff as the mischief . . . yes he was awfully stiff and no
wonder but he changed the second time he looked . . . but I could
see him looking very hard at my chest when he stood up to open the
door for me it was nice of him to show me out in any case Im
extremely sorry Mrs Bloom . . . I just half smiled I know my chest
was out that way at the door when he said Im extremely sorry and
Im sure you were. (752-753)

Molly considers other men during the course of her monologue,
some without names, some with names we have not heard before, like
Doyle. She thinks about Bartell d'Arcy, who is on Bloom's list, and
who may have been her lover: "Bartell dArcy too that he used to make
fun of when he commenced kissing me on the choir stairs after I sang
Gounods *Ave Maria* what are we waiting for O my heart kiss me
straight on the brow and part which is my brown part he was pretty
hot for all his tinny voice too my low notes he was always raving
about . . . then he said wasnt it terrible to do that there in a place like
that I dont see anything so terrible about it" (745). She also thinks
about Gardner, whom Bloom apparently knows nothing about. It is
possible that Gardner may have been Molly's lover before she married
Bloom, although all she thinks about with him, as with d'Arcy, is a
kiss, and given the explicit nature of her thoughts about Boylan, it
seems likely she would have others ways of remembering the other
two men had they in fact been lovers.

Molly's unhappiness with the word *adulteress* and her guilt about
the affair with Boylan—"I thought the heavens were coming down
about us to punish" (741)—combine to create a slightly different picture from what we anticipate. Her remark, "anyhow its done now
once and for all with all the talk of the world about it people make its
only the first time after that its just the ordinary do it and think no
more about it," (740) seems to indicate that this is the first time she has
been unfaithful to Bloom. (Though it is possible to interpret the "its"
as referring to the original sexual experience, the loss of virginity, the
word "now" seems inappropriate for such a meaning, and the position
of the passage, following a long series of questions Bloom has asked
Molly about whom she would or would not sleep with, suggests that
adultery is what she is referring to.) Bloom's great anguish about
Molly and Boylan would be inexplicable if he really believed that she

had done the same thing twenty-three times before: both Bloom and Molly would act, think, and feel in a different way if Molly were as amoral in fact as she is in thought.

In other ways, Molly is shown to be a middle-class woman with an eye to respectability. She is upset about Bloom's climbing over the railing: "if anybody saw him that knew us" (768), and at the possibility that there might have been underwear hanging on the line in the kitchen when Bloom brought Stephen in: "my old pair of drawers might have been hanging up too on the line on exhibition for all hed ever care with the ironmould mark the stupid old bundle burned on them he might think was something else" (768). She is shocked that Bloom wants her to put an ad in the paper for the gloves she lost in a ladies' lavatory; she is distressed about people coming to the front door when she is "all undressed or the door of the filthy sloppy kitchen blows open." The thought of the possibility of Bloom's becoming sexually active with her at Belfast disturbs her because "I couldnt tell him to stop and not bother me with him [Boylan] in the next room or perhaps some protestant clergyman with a cough knocking on the wall" (747). The jingling of the bed troubles her: "This damned old bed too jingling like the dickens I suppose they could hear us away over the other side of the park till I suggested to put the quilt on the floor with the pillow under my bottom" (769). She is offended by Rabelais' use of the word *bumgut*, because he is a priest, and defends Bloom because he wipes his feet before he enters the house. She dislikes names with *bottom* in them. She expresses a guilty confusion over which of them, Molly or Bloom, enjoys variations of sexual practice, continually switching the pronouns when she thinks about the subject. One's overall impression is that Bloom initiated such practices, Molly was reluctant, Bloom sulked, then she gave in and now enjoys them. But that is an ordinary progression and does not reflect the character of a whore-goddess. Molly has picked up Bloom's masochism and plays a complementary role, sadistically threatening the very things he desires.

A further remarkable fact is that she exaggerates the number of ejaculations Boylan is able to attain: she says first "3 or 4 times" (742), then "4 or 5 times" (763), finally "5 or 6 times" (780).[15] Although for the most part Molly calls a sexual spade a spade, she, like Gerty MacDowell, never mentions menstruation by name. For her too it is "that thing" or "then." She also avoids thinking in concrete terms about masturbation, though she is more direct about it than Gerty is. These facts hardly add up to a sexual sophisticate; they do add up to a woman who thinks somewhat frankly about sex: "I hate that pretending of all things" (751), but who is in all other respects an ordinary, middle-class woman and faithful wife—at least until today. She is very sexual; that is, she has not denied or repressed her sexual interests. But she is not the whore-goddess she has been thought. Hayman, the only other critic who has approached Molly as I do, claims that she is "almost as faithful as Penelope."[16]

There is a further set of contradictions. Molly, despite her ignorance, is not unintelligent. She has the kind of acuteness that is frequently called "intuition" when it appears in women. This intelligence is perfectly compatible with conventional notions of what women are —and Molly is built out of conventional notions. She knows that Bloom has had an orgasm; she knows that he is secretly writing to a woman; she is aware that Bloom knows about Boylan and suspects that this knowledge was what "set him off" (742). Despite her own near-illiteracy, she neither overestimates nor underestimates Bloom's knowledge: "He knows a lot of mixed up things" (743). She is aware that the men of Dublin mock Bloom, and has some idea of why: "because he has sense enough not to squander every penny piece he earns down their gullets and looks after his wife and family" (773-774). Her estimates of character are immediate and accurate: consider her judgments of Menton, Simon Dedalus, and Lenehan. She instantly perceived that Josie Breen's embracing her when Bloom was present was an indication that Josie was interested in Bloom. She is conscious of Boylan's coarseness and viciousness: she connects his bad temper at losing the bet on the race with his apparent prosperity and, without making an explicit judgment, lets the two facts stand staring at each other. She sees the flower in his lapel and immediately wonders what girl gave it to him (as do the barmaids at the Ormond); she knows he has been someplace drinking something sweet and syrupy.

But most of her sensitivity goes into sexual matters. She thinks about almost nothing but sex. She is gratified at being sexually attractive—as is Bloom, who thinks about "the possibility of exercising virile power of fascination . . . in the company of an elegant courtesan" (722). Molly is irritated with the denseness of men in the sexual area:

As bad as now with the hands hanging off me looking out of the window if there was a nice fellow even in the opposite house that medical in Holles street the nurse was after when I put on my gloves and hat at the window to show I was going out not a notion what I meant arent they thick never understand what you say even youd want to print it up on a big poster for them not even if you shake hands twice with the left he didnt recognize me either when I half frowned at him outside Westland row chapel where does their great intelligence come in Id like to know grey matter they have it all in their tail if you ask me. (757-758)

She knows in a natural, untaught, unintellectual way what Stephen discovers in Circe: her assumption in "when I put on my gloves and hat at the window to show I was going out . . . arent they thick never understand what you say" is "that gesture, not music, not odours, would be a universal language, the gift of tongues rendering visible not the lay sense but the first entelechy, the structural rhythm" (432).

If we have to deal with Molly as an actual character and not just a symbol, we are faced with a psychological contradiction. A person who is as easy with her own sexuality as Molly is, and as hungry for sexual relations as she describes herself to be, would not patiently wait chastely for ten years, five months, and eighteen days. She would complain to her husband or find a lover. But there is no indication in Bloom's monologues or in Molly's that she has done the former. Given the view of her held by Dublin males, it seems unlikely that it would take Molly all these years in sex-starved Dublin to find a lover.

There are, then, three levels of contradiction. The first is the inner contradiction of Molly's thinking, which is resolved, or rather canceled, by her lack of awareness of it, lack of interest in such things. The second is a contradiction of fact: throughout the novel, Joyce makes Molly out to be a sexual goddess, promiscuous, insatiable, eminently desirable, but the circumstances of her life as he presents them do not bear out this delineation. This contradiction is too carefully wrought to be accidental. The third contradiction is the corollary or opposite face of the second. Since Molly is confortable with her own sexuality, and has so engrossing an interest in sexual life, it is inconsistent that she for so long denied herself an active sexual life. This contradiction makes Molly a little unbelievable. Penelope is also a little unbelievable, and for the same reason. Joyce has built the parallel into his novel.

Molly, like Bloom, or Shakespeare, is "all in all." She is a perfectly
ordinary Dublin housewife (it is as a housewife rather than profes-
sional singer that she comes across); she is "the chaste spouse of Leopold . . . Marion of the bountiful bosoms" (319); she represents continuation, but has only one child; she is sexuality incarnate, yet for ten
years has lived without sexual intercourse; she is faithful Penelope,
weaving then unweaving a sexual tapestry; she is fickle Cressida,
giving Mulvey's ring to Gardner; she is seductive Helen, attracting all
of Dublin's males; she is, potentially at least, the virgin/mother-whore
/hag, the triple goddess, and her birth date is the same as the Virgin's.
Less realized as a character than are either Stephen or Bloom, she is all
women as function, woman in relation to men. She acts out all
"female" functions: she cooks and cleans, gives birth and buries, is an
object of desire, a creator of frustration, uncontrollable, unpposses-
sible, unable to be pinned down or fixed. Like the life presented
throughout the novel, she is ambiguous. Like nature—the eternal
recurrence that terrifies Stephen, horrifies and comforts Bloom—she is
enduring and elusive. It is in order to make her all these at once that
Joyce spends so much time building up one image, exaggerating it in
her monologue, then quietly inserting little facts that undercut or con-
tradict the image.

In her appearance in the world of Dublin, Molly is largely a product
of male imagination, male modes of vision. The characters of *Ulysses*
do not perceive her thoughts; rather, they constantly project their
own desires onto her. In the process, however, they are realizing a
truth. Whether they are picking up vibrations from Molly, or whether
the truth in their perception is intended as another of the many correspondences of this novel, does not matter. We, who are privileged
to stand above all of Dublin, yet are also able to hear her thoughts,
can see an interlocking significance between the symbol Molly and the
real world of men. As usual, that significance is dual: Molly is the
goddess-whore in reality, but she is neither goddess nor whore in
actuality. She partakes of the goddess through her feelings; in her
actions she is more respectable than her husband, who has never been
considered a Priapus symbol, despite his public masturbation.

The same problem that causes a critical distortion of or exaspera-
tion with the chapters from Sirens through Ithaca—the assumption

that the naturalistic level is primary, to the reader if not in the text—causes a distortion of the text of Penelope. Critics try to deal with her as if she were a realistic character, like Bloom and Stephen in the early chapters. But Molly never acts in the novel; even her thought patterns are impossibly obsessive. Her relation to actual women is only tangential. She is built of shreds of realistic but very conventional characteristics of "women." Many of her thoughts show her to be a prude, housewifely and bourgeois. The directness and lack of shame of other of her thoughts are either very natural or very sophisticated, and I assume Joyce intended us to think them the former, even though she is not so "natural" at other times, as in her disapproval of the Rabelaisian "bumgut." Her adultery with Boylan partakes of both categories: her guilt about it fits the bourgeois housewife, and the glee with which she thinks about intercourse with him fits her image as a child of nature. But realism ends there. Bloom and Stephen represent not only mankind, but humankind: Molly is the mythic, the archetypal other. Not only for Bloom but for the rest of Dublin, she is woman as the object of desire. She is nature, other, woman: contradictory, fickle, illogical, prudish or promiscuous, "untrustworthy engaging shrewd limited prudent" and "indifferent." The last adjective shows Joyce's standing place, which is Bloom's when he asks, "What do they love? Another themselves?" (379). What Molly is finally found indifferent to are men, the very men for whom she seems to exist, for whom she is expected to exist: "What else were they invented for?" (40). Her obsession with sex is symbolic of her relation to humankind: she can relate to it only housewifely or sexually. She is inhuman in the way Cordelia, Marina, Goneril, and Lady Macbeth are inhuman: she exists as a circumference bounding the human (male) world. To discuss her as if she were a discrete and autonomous character is to mistake her function in the novel. The contradictions that pervade her make-up cannot be resolved on the naturalistic level: she has a mysterious unity. She is a symbol for the feminine principle as it exists in the mind of a feminate (androgynous) male.[17]

Joyce wrote Frank Budgen that Penelope was the *clou* of the book, and paradoxically it is this chapter with its symbolic character that nails the book down to solid earth.[18] Molly has no inner contradictions because she totally accepts her own judgments and feelings, because she has no need for any other truth to serve as touchstone of right and wrong. She has no need for an outer truth because she has an inner one: the needs of her body. Hayman observes that "she perceives the world as relating to her."[19] She rarely requires justification because she rarely feels guilt, but when she does need justification, as when she has been unkind to Milly, she can always find it by claiming there was "a weed in the tea" (768). That she acts on her feelings so little makes her more like the weaving unweaving Penelope. Penelope's completed day-woven tapestry is the equivalent of a new lover: Molly Tweedy Bloom weaves sexual impulses but also does not act on them.

Molly's likeness to Penelope supplies an irony in this supposedly simple, down-to-earth finale. Even the earth is not simple and fixed. It may unexpectedly choose to remain chaste for ten years. Bloom has made Molly the fixed center of his universe. People do such things and never imagine that the fixed center may betray them, yet such betrayal is inevitable if one believes, as Joyce was taught to believe, that an act is an act whether committed in thought, word, or deed. And even here the void appears. Lady Belvedere may have committed adultery not fully. Molly, after all her sexual play with Mulvey, is still technically a virgin. So is Gerty after her flirtation with Bloom. Joyce, unlike his character Mrs. Mooney in "The Boarding House," cannot cut moral issues with a meat cleaver. Even electricity-eating nymphs cannot promise absolute fidelity. Bloom, as he is honest and intelligent, cannot choose but see Molly's sexuality whole. What makes him fine is that he is able to accept it, which is tantamount to accepting his limitations as a man, his participation in nature, his smallness before the universe, and his ignorance in the face of the void.

That in the end he is right to do so, even though throughout the book he is anguished by and mocked for Molly's adultery, is established by Molly's monologue. His acceptance is probably the only action or movement in the book that Joyce indicates as "right."[20] Molly is finally faithful to Bloom: fairly faithful physically and totally so emotionally.[21] That is, her emotional commitment is to him above any other man.

Her deepest commitment, of course, is to sexuality itself, to hearing the voice of her own body and merging it with the voices of nature. It is in this way that she is Bloom's "passport to eternity." She expresses the immortality of the human body as Bloom expresses the immortality of the human soul and as Stephen expresses the immortality of the human mind. Molly does not simply affirm life; she embodies the life force. She is the vehicle of the humanity of the race.

[8] *Conclusion*

The journey is complete. The *ricorso* has returned us not to the same place we started from, but to its octaval complement, to the place of first departure, the earth, the womb. That is where Odysseus ended, after all. The reader, Ulysses, has made the great circular journey through the macrocosm, while Stephen and Bloom, like Socrates and Judas, trace their own analogous, microcosmic circles.

Hugh Kenner claims that "Joyce's irony goes deep indeed. Not only does Bloom not know that he is Ulysses (the meaning of his own actions); he does not know he is an analogue of Christ inhabiting a sacramental universe (the meaning of his own thoughts). Stephen on the other hand is aware that he is Hamlet, but his awareness is put to the wrong uses. It provides him with no insight. It merely feeds his morbidity."[1] But Bloom does not know he is Ulysses or Christ, for in fact he is neither: he is Leopold Bloom. The author draws those analogies for the reader's benefit. Stephen is and is not Hamlet or Lucifer. Stephen does have insight into his dilemma, but that does not eradicate it. We stumble through life learning, if we do learn, by suffering through what we live. Insight about the nature of life, or about what one is, does not necessarily change what one is; it simply provides another level of being it.

That Bloom and Stephen be aware of their significance is neither possible nor important. Joyce insists they are mere mortals, human beings; as such, they cannot rise above their humanness, cannot see themselves in a distant perspective nor become more than men. The great tragic heroes achieve, at some crucial final moment, an illumination: they see human vulnerability, smallness, or insignificance, human inability to transcend the human condition, or the paradox of human life. Bloom and Stephen already have such knowledge; their problem is living with it, day by day. Joyce insists that mere humans cannot perfect their lives; all they can do is to live them out as decently as possible.

Stephen, in fact, does undergo some change in the novel. His statement in Circe that he was born "today" (562) has foundation. From his first appearance he meditates on birth—birth into a pre-existent culture in Telemachus, birth into adulthood set against the nightmare of history in Nestor, and birth into loathsome mortality or unbelievable immortality in Proteus. Afterward, he takes three steps: a tentative acceptance of his participation in the human condition in Proteus, a decision to focus as much as possible on the real ("Dubliners"), and a forcing of himself to "act speech" in the library scene as well as Aeolus. He produces, in the course of the novel, two fine pieces of fiction. What remains to him is the tumble in a cornfield, on both the real and symbolic levels. He must love sexually, engage his emotions with another; he must risk genuine intercourse with the real. It is not necessary to read Stephen as an autobiographical figure, to allude to the facts that June 16, 1904, was the date on which Joyce first walked out with Nora and that *Ulysses* was begun in ten years, in line with Stephen's prediction. Stephen leaves Bloom's house in full awareness of what he must do to survive. He has the awareness as early as Proteus, and he lives out the steps it involves by the end of the library scene.

There is no suggestion that Stephen will ever fully resolve his intellectual and emotional antinomies, or that Bloom will ever become more acceptable to cultural standards of maleness, or that either will ever be able to modify his loneliness. Bloom's future is death; Stephen's is maturity. This is predicted in Ithaca. The particular events that will occupy the years ahead for each will be similar in character to those that occupy this day. What is suggested is that each will survive as he is, and that this is enough. It is enough for them that they live out their lives; it is enough for us that as incarnations of moral and intellectual excellence, they are immortal. Their meeting has little "real" significance: each has a glimmering of what the other is; each is able to get beyond his own mode of perception enough to see another in his selfhood. Their meeting is an intercourse with external reality, even though each may end up finally with only himself on his own doorstep. Joyce suggests that one returns not to an identical place, but to the same place slightly changed by the experience one has undergone, an octave away, just as one returns as the same person, yet slightly changed by one's experience. An essence remains immutable. Surely this is an honest way of seeing reality.

Just as surely, Joyce intended the reader also to be slightly, if inessentially, changed by his encounter with the world of the book. The various stances and voices of the narrator mock and deride human actuality; at the same time, another voice plays a monotonous background music, droning out the constrictions inherent in the human condition. Between them, they constrain the human material like the grinding stones of a mill. If we have mind, sense of humor, or love of language, we recognize ourselves in the malicious voices; if we have feelings, we recognize ourselves in the matter being mercilessly pounded. Joyce carefully manipulates the reader's ambivalence, however. By making Stephen admirable and Bloom likable, by making the voices of Dublin vivid, he attaches us to the human characters. The bottom stone of the mill, those inescapable problems of the human condition, operates to constrict the characters but also provides ground for further sympathy with them. The triumphant malice of the narrational voice is so extreme that in time it repels us. And the last two chapters, Eumaeus and Ithaca, in which the narrational voice completely vanquishes the human material, eradicates it by eradicating emotion, are intended to assure our affirmation of what is lacking. Thus, the method of the book is tied to one of its themes: the Hebrew-Irish-Greek analogy, the theme of lost causes. The narrator's triumph is Pyrrhic; not only that, but the winner finally loses. The spirit triumphs over the worldly forces that seem to defeat it. The objective, malicious, and finally indifferent narrator wins: mankind is indeed a foolish, deluded, paltry, and rather smelly worm heap. The reader responds with a *but*. But—mankind is also long-suffering, enduring, intolerably constrained, noble, intelligent, and feeling.

Joyce could not offer the "gift of certitude" directly to his readers. What he was able, in his genius, to provide was a form through which the reader could work out the grounds of his own certainties. The reader is forced to fall back on what he knows and feels, and finds himself insisting that man is significant simply because he is, that the real is also the meaningful. The reader affirms, consciously or not, that actual human emotions and doubts, rather than superhuman ideals which lead to inhuman perversions, are the grounds from which we must begin to define the creature man. Man, for Joyce, is above all a feeling animal, but feeling, linked as it is to reason and to the social necessity for making moral distinctions, is a difficult thing, a burden. Joyce insists that it may not be laid down, resigned, or repressed without a concomitant loss in humanness. It must be felt, lived through, and acted on in a way as little harmful to others as possible. Joyce's morality is an insistence that man recognize his own limitations and his needs, which are sometimes called desires and made to appear illegitimate, and that he act on these despite his incertitude about higher significance, final purpose. Action should be guided by *caritas*, which is possible only if one can come out of one's own categories and preconceptions enough to see the other in its selfhood. This is a humane and earthbound morality. Although it denies the ideals of earlier eras, it is pervaded by the same generosity of spirit that characterizes Shakespeare, Homer, and even Dante as he weeps for the doomed. The worst perversion of Joyce is to be blind to this quality in him, to assume he is identical with his narrator.

Human life is built at the heart of the void, where the only certitude possible is biological necessity and urge, continuation, endurance, the side of things that Molly represents.[2] Any other "key" is necessarily false; those who claim to possess keys to a kingdom are liars or fools who mislead and betray those who believe them. Yet standards of decency, of intellectual and emotional excellence, remain and have remained over all the centuries, changed and yet the same.

Joyce's notions are not revolutionary. What makes *Ulysses* great is that it is so brilliantly and complexly devised, so vividly imagined and written, that it forces the reader to discover and affirm, that it presents a world as seemingly chaotic as the real one, so that the reader's discovery has the impact and intensity of a discovery in actual life. What Joyce wants is that the affirmation made in the course of reading the novel be an affirmation about life, not the more abstract, more narrowly relevant discovery of the governing principle of a work of literature.

Joyce insists that we make this affirmation against a dismal background. His characters are for the most part spongers, wastrels, idlers, drunks, or victims. His Dublin is a grim place, containing little that supports or comforts life. Even the main characters are never exalted: whatever in them touches the ideal is suggested by a narrational level of allusion rather than by outright idealization. Along with his fine mind and talent, Stephen drags a dirty body, shabby clothes, bad teeth, and a personality that is often priggish and supercilious. Bloom's moral excellence is sometimes difficult to perceive through his gooey sensuality, his comic misapprehensions, his ordinariness.

Samuel Beckett writes books and plays in which everything "good" in life is stripped away. There are no trees, flowers, rivers majestically flowing, delicious foods, beautiful rooms, paintings, lovely bodies to admire or love, lovely minds to encounter. Everything is gone—sometimes even the body itself of the protagonist—and only the isolated, bewildered, obsessive human mind remains, questioning, questioning. *Dubito ergo sum.*[3]

Joyce's technique is less extreme than Beckett's (who may well have learned this technique from Joyce), but it has the same tendency. Joyce presents us with a bleak city, a world full of violence, bigotry, hatred, deceit, hunger, hopeless desire, moral and physical deformity. He presents us with characters who are in many ways unworthy of respect or affection. If we affirm the feeling and significance of the characters, if we affirm their intelligence, moral stature, enduringness, we are affirming the characters in spite of everything. And if we do this, we are affirming our own human value and dignity despite our limitations. On the highest level we are affirming all of humankind, and doing so with everything in the book stacked against it.

Thus, the journey is ours and we Ulysses. Everything in the novel fits into the macrocosm, which is a microcosm of the real world. The narrative level, the correspondences, the allusions, as well as many pieces of the "plot," exist for us alone; we are the only people fully aware of them. The novel suggests that if we were gods in the actual universe, we could gaze down and discern interlocking patterns over the face of the earth, and would understand those patterns as mythic. Susanne Langer defines myth as "a recognition of natural conflicts, of human desire frustrated by non-human powers, hostile oppression or contrary desires; it is a story of the birth, passion, and defeat by death which is man's common fate. Its ultimate end is not wishful distortion of the world, but serious envisagement of its fundamental truths."[4] Thomas Mann asserts that "the myth is the foundation of life; it is the timeless schema, the pious formula into which life flows when it reproduces its traits out of the unconscious." He adds that the artist aware of the mythical, the typical in life, gains "an insight into the higher truth depicted in the actual; a smiling knowledge of the eternal, the everbeing and authentic; a knowledge of the schema in which and according to which the supposed individual lives, unaware in his naive belief in himself as unique in space and time, of the extent to which his life is but formula and repetition and his path marked out for him by those who trod it before."[5]

Without "distortion of the world," wishful or otherwise, Joyce shows us the lives of two unique beings who are also part of a larger pattern of human experience. That larger pattern is expressed by the changing points of view and by the parallax effected by time and space. Changes in space are symbolized by the changing distances between the narrator and events in the novel; changes in time are symbolized by the chronologically determined style changes and by the many allusions to and analogies with items from history, literature, and theology. The changes in the narrative points of view symbolize the varied modes of perception available to an observer.

Joyce, the arrogant seer, ate the apple of the tree of the knowledge of good and evil, read God's book, the world, with all its mysteries, coincidences, and ambiguities, and became himself a god. Then Joyce, the arrogant creator, made his world, the book, careful to reproduce symbolically what he had "found in the world without as actual."

To the extent that Joyce refuses us any final certitude about the world he has created, he is an indifferent god; to the extent that he dons a mask, a persona, and scorns the characters, he is a *dio boia*; to the extent that he puts his own book and his own beliefs into the book, his world, and inserts hints as to the method and purpose of his creation, he is submitting himself to his creation, making himself another character in it, a human, not a god. Whatever role he momentarily plays, Joyce, in *Ulysses*, is probably the most intrusive author ever to write a piece of fiction.

Critics complain that in *Ulysses* and *Finnegans Wake* Joyce was willing to use any detail at all, that it did not matter to him what his materials were, that he would include even the slamming of a door or a sneeze.[6] But this is precisely the point. If everything in the world is interrelated, if the patterns comprehend all of us and all that occurs, everything that exists, then any detail will serve; there is significance in everything if you know how to discover and reveal it.

The structure of the novel is a series of concentric circles in the shape of a cone, like the "upcast reflection of a lamp and shade, an inconstant series of concentric circles of varying gradations of light and shadow," which hovers above the invisible thoughts of Molly and Bloom in Ithaca. At the bottom of this Dantean shape are the characters Stephen and Bloom. Led by perverse guides, we move upward and outward through the series of circles. The variation of light and shadow depends on what the narrator knows and sees or what he does not know. Our vision gradually comprehends the city, the world, and the universe. The hub of all these circles is the void, incertitude, upon and around which all human life is built. Molly's monologue turns the cone upside down and shows us the underside of the void. It is a cap, a seal that nails the void firmly to certitude, the earth, continuation, beingness that endures, neverchanging everchanging under everchanging neverchanging forms.

Ulysses is a monument defining morality in a relativistic world. It does not sentimentalize or idealize that world, but neither does it sentimentalize or idealize any past time. While Eliot was seeing fear in a handful of dust, Joyce was seeing eternity in a grain of sand. Humankind endures, but Leopold Bloom endures decently: he is a moral hero rather than a heroic, tragic, or romantic one. *Ulysses* is the *Commedia* of the twentieth century, and a far more agreeable one than its predecessor.[7]

Joyce's technique varies greatly but falls into certain general categories. It presents the material in a naturalistic, symbolic style; it attacks the material through derisive narrators; and it bombards the material with the destructive missiles of a pair of impersonal, inhuman narrators. When the narrative style has threshed this poor wheat into the dust to which we all return, there remain the small, shining, stubborn seeds of human decency, human suffering, human aspiration— the nobility that is the other face of ignominy, the significance contained in a mass of trivia, the godliness shining in a handful of slime. If you can see that godliness, it is your own you are seeing.

Notes
Index

Notes

Introduction

1. Stuart Gilbert, *Joyce's "Ulysses"* (London, 1938), pp. 8-9.
2. Richard Ellmann, *Ulysses on the Liffey* (New York, 1972), p. 2.

1. The Reader and the Journey

1. C. J. Jung, *"Ulysses: A Monologue,"* trans. W. Stanley Dell for the Analytical Psychology Club of New York, Inc. (Spring 1949), p. 16, originally published as *"Ulysses"* in *Wirklichkeit der Seele*, Psychol. Abhandlungen, vol. 4 (Zurich, 1934).
2. Richard M. Kain, *Fabulous Voyager: James Joyce's "Ulysses"* (Chicago, 1947), p. 17.
3. Robert Scholes and Richard M. Kain, *The Workshop of Daedalus: James Joyce and the Raw Materials for "Portrait"* (Evanston, Ill., 1965).
4. Erich Kahler, *The Inward Turn of Narrative*, trans. Richard and Clara Winston (Princeton, 1973), pp. 110-111.
5. James Joyce, *Letters*, ed. Stuart Gilbert (New York, 1957), I, 129.
6. Ellmann, *Ulysses*, p. 62.
7. Ellmann, *Ulysses*, p. 92.
8. Frank Budgen, *James Joyce and the Making of "Ulysses"* (New York, 1934), p. 257.

2. The World as Book

1. See esp. William T. Noon, *Joyce and Aquinas* (New Haven, 1957); J. Mitchell Morse, *The Sympathetic Alien: James Joyce and Catholicism* (Washington Square, 1959); J. Mitchell Morse, "Augustine's Theodicy and Joyce's Aesthetics," *ELH* 24 (1957): 30-43.
2. The terms are those of Aquinas. See e.g. *Summa Theologica* I.iii.119.1. But Augustine also sees the world as full of signs. See e.g. Augustine, *On Christian Doctrine* I.II.
3. Hugh of St. Victor, *The Didascalicon* I.9, trans. Jerome Taylor (New York and London, 1961). Hugh is turning to his own purposes a distinction made by Chalcidus in commenting on the Timaeus. Cf. *Platonis Timaeus*

interprete Chalcidio cum eiusdem commentario, ed. Johannes Wrobel (Leipzig, 1876), p. 88.

4. Erich Auerbach, "Figura," *Scenes from the Drama of European Literature* (New York, 1959), p. 62. Augustine portrays God as an artist in *De Musica.*

5. R. M. Adams, *Surface and Symbol: The Consistency of James Joyce's "Ulysses"* (New York, 1962), pp. 239, 244-245.

6. Richard Ellmann, *James Joyce* (New York, 1959), p. 377.

7. That this was Joyce's intention is testified to by an entry in the Notesheets to Circe 1:83-84: "SD drunk remember somethg smby told, not know what reader also not." See Phillip F. Herring, ed., *Joyce's "Ulysses" Notesheets in the British Museum* (Charlottesville, 1972), p. 268.

8. Richard Kain, "James Joyce and the Game of Language," *Studies in the Literary Imagination,* special issue, *James Joyce in the Seventies: The Expanding Dimensions of His Art,* 3, no. 2 (October 1970): 25.

9. Joyce, *Letters,* I, 55; James Joyce, *Letters,* ed. Richard Ellmann (New York, 1966), II, 166.

10. James Joyce, *Stephen Hero* (New York, 1944), p. 202.

11. Hugh Kenner, *Dublin's Joyce* (Bloomington, 1956), p. 243.

12. See e.g. Joseph Warren Beach, *The Twentieth Century Novel: Studies in Technique* (New York, 1932), p. 420: "The point . . . is obviously the ironic exposure of contemporary Irish futilities"; Harry Levin, *James Joyce: A Critical Introduction* (Norfolk, Conn., 1941), p. 133: "Joyce's work commemorates the long-standing quarrel between the bourgeois and the bohemian. The art of a society which has little use for art, it expresses that society by way of protest"; Kenner, *Dublin's Joyce,* passim.

13. Mary T. Reynolds points to numerous allusions to Dante in *Ulysses* and suggests that Joyce modeled himself on the Italian poet. Reynolds, "Joyce's Planetary Music: His Debt to Dante," *Sewanee Review* 76, no. 3 (July-September 1968): 450-477.

14. Robert Scholes and Robert Kellogg, *The Nature of Narrative* (New York, 1966), p. 265.

15. Joyce's concern for the real as opposed to the ideal is actually a moral position. Although he occasionally enjoyed posturing as having "Lost . . . [his] diadem" (*The Holy Office*), his insistence that "life we must accept as we see it before our eyes, men and women as we meet them in the real world," endorses a moral idea. See James Joyce, *The Critical Writings,* ed. Ellsworth Mason and Richard Ellmann (New York, 1964), pp. 45, 128. See also Joyce's comments to Alfred Kerr (Ellmann, *Joyce,* p. 701): "It's a mark of morality not only to say what one thinks is true—but to create a work of art with the utmost sacrifice: that's moral too." No doubt the remark made by Stephen in *Portrait* refers to the Irish by the word "race"; however, as Dublin came increasingly to represent all of Western civilization, the Irish came to represent humankind itself.

16. Joyce, *Letters,* II, 311.

17. Wilbur Sanders, *The Dramatist and the Received Idea: Studies in the*

Plays of Marlowe and Shakespeare (Cambridge, 1968), p. 320.

18. L. C. Knights, "The University Teaching of English and History: A Plea for Correlation," *Explorations* (London, 1958), p. 193.

19. Helen Gardner, *The Art of T. S. Eliot* (New York, 1959), p. 85.

20. Morse, "Augustine's Theodicy," p. 34.

21. Fritz Senn, "Nausicaa," in *James Joyce's "Ulysses": Critical Essays*, ed. Clive Hart and David Hayman (Berkeley, 1974), p. 310.

22. *Macbeth* I.iii.10, *The Riverside Shakespeare*, ed. G. B. Evans (Boston, 1974).

23. A reference to action occurs on Notesheet 1:10-12 for Nausikaa:
onanism: Sterne, Swift, Wilde
        (pruriency: misanthropy—satire
        ? prolongation—cloacism—hatred of action)

Herring (*Notesheets*, p. 27) comments that Oscar Wilde's distaste for action led to his trial and that Stephen (573) also hates action. It is clear in Joyce's note, however, that he believed onanism to be tied to hatred of action; thus, Bloom's masturbation is a form of sexual paralysis shared with some of the aesthetes in the library. Again in a note for Circe 11:76, Joyce remarks: "SD hates action." But perhaps the most interesting note is that to Oxen 10:1-4:

I hate (≃)   I hold (course)
ago = push   remit = 1. s. d.
itus   act   ?   wind

The Latin *ago* can mean "to steal" as well as "to drive," "do," or "act"; *itus* is a "departure" or "going away." It is perhaps presumptuous to interpret so opaque a note, but it does seem to suggest that hatred is ≃ (roughly equivalent to) action, which is here a departure, and that half of the note refers to Stephen. It could then be deduced that the other half refers to Bloom, who holds his course against the wind. In a note to Cyclops 4:110, Joyce writes, "commit his ideas to paper," and in *Finnegans Wake* the writer is seen as a criminal. Action is tied to writing as well as to sexuality and departure. Finally, the phrase in *Ulysses* spat out by Farrell on a streetcorner, "*Coactus volui*" (250), is repeated by Virag (520) in a specifically sexual context. The phrase, "I wanted to be constrained," suggests sexual masochism, although it is uttered both times by aggressive and virulent characters. It would seem that the ability to act stands as a kind of salvation for Joyce, despite the risk that action may lead to horror. Stephen perceives this dilemma. Speaking of Hamlet, he says, "A deathsman of the soul . . . Not for nothing was he a butcher's son wielding the sledded poleaxe and spitting in his palm. Nine lives are taken off for his father's one, Our Father who art in purgatory. Khaki Hamlets don't hesitate to shoot. The bloodboltered shambles in act five is a forecast of the concentration camp sung by Mr Swinburne." Stephen, who hates action, is caught "Between the Saxon smile and yankee yawp. The devil and the deep sea" (187).

24. Augustine, *On Christian Doctrine* II.X.15, trans. D. W. Robertson, Jr. (Indianapolis, 1958).

25. Augustine, *On Christian Doctrine* II.X.16.

26. Ellmann, *Joyce*, pp. 567-568. See also S. L. Goldberg, *The Classical Temper: A Study of James Joyce's "Ulysses"* (New York, 1961), p. 112: "He [Richard] will accept nothing less than an allegiance fully and freely given, nor will he accept beliefs and assurances to disguise the void in which such acts of choice must be made. The course of the play is in effect the purification and justification of his resolve to accept the void, and Joyce permits himself a certain irony about the masochistic pleasure his hero takes in contemplating the void, and even about the unconscious motives of his personal ruthlessness."

27. There are tens of phrases dealing with sexuality in the Notesheets. Herring (*Notesheets*, p. 29) comments that many of them "reveal the humorous contradictions of man as sexual animal," then cites from the Nausikaa notes:

2:74	love marriage is a sacrilege
4:80-81	Love? excuses all: Coition without love in & out of wedlock not desired
5:18	N. puts key in door with LB
6:82	Friggers live by themselves
6:84	Frigging, girls little paps
6:107	Martha gives virility to man
8:49	false lover: daddy

28. Joyce to Stanislaus Joyce, *Letters*, II, 191-192.

29. Quoted in Ellmann, *Joyce*, p. 551.

30. Ellmann (*Joyce*, p. 477) discusses Joyce's notion of Jews as effeminate and describes him as being in agreement with the racist and sexist views of Otto Weininger. It seems certain that Joyce had contempt for women, but less so that he had contempt for Bloom as the "new womanly man." If he did, he must have had contempt for Stephen as well, because both share this characteristic. Herring lists phrases in the *Notesheets*: Oxen 14:51 "ladylike man" (p. 232); Circe 16:52 "womanly man" (p. 344); Ithaca 10:70 "LB's sure womanhand showing" (p. 460); Ithaca 14:20 "Leopold Paula Bloom" (p. 477). The theme of androgyny is also connected with Stephen, as shown by Ralph Jenkins, who lists a number of "sexual perversities" to be found in the chapter and comments, "Artistic creation is compared in the chapter to the phenomenon of birth, and birth by the androgynous, the womanly man." Jenkins, "Theosophy in 'Scylla and Charybdis,' " *Modern Fiction Studies* 15, no. 1 (Spring 1969): 35-48. Stephen is also said to have a "woman's hand" (561). The little cloud seen by both Stephen and Bloom is described as "no bigger than a woman's hand" (667), in alteration of its original appearance in 1 Kings 18:44. Other references to androgyny appear in the Notesheets:

Oxen 9:25-26	ovocita hermaphrodite
	globes = elimination of male=monosexual

Circe 16:43   waters of Salmacis make hermaphrodite
      16:68   Sa père son mère

Herring (*Notesheets*, p. 346), remarks: "Joyce first wrote *la père, le mère*. The reversal in genders is probably connected with the hermaphrodite theme in line 43." Norman Silverstein asserts that the "sinister" and "lefthanded" references in Circe are associated with the black arts, falseness of modern culture, the false arts, mystery, magic, and evil, all of which he ties to the feminine principle. Silverstein, "Magic on the Notesheets of the Circe Episode," *JJQ* 1, no. 4 (Summer 1964): 19-26. And one of Joyce's notes to Ithaca 3:10 is "gynecocracy coming" (*Notesheets*, p. 423). The notion appears in Penelope (778), and Herring (*Notesheets*, p. 426n) mentions Joyce owning Jacques Desroix, *La Gynecocracie ou la domination de la femme . . . précède d'une étude sur le masochisme dans l'histoire et les traditions par Laurent Tailhade* (Paris, 1902), a book in which such an event is predicted. All told, allusions to feminacy in men are rife throughout *Ulysses* and the Notesheets: that it is a major theme is not debatable. What is at question is Joyce's point of view toward feminacy in men. To judge from his treatment of traditional manliness in Cyclops, and from the fact that both heroes of *Ulysses* have "feminine" traits (Bloom's compassion and nutritiveness; Stephen's dislike of action; the distaste of both for oppression and violence; Stephen's notion of the artist as pregnant, creating the work out of his own innards, a kind of "androgynous angel" [213], and of God as "He who Himself begot" [197]), Joyce saw feminacy in men somewhat positively, despite the narrator's scorn. This is not to say, however, that he saw manliness in women equally positively, although he does give Molly some "masculine" traits—her name Marion, dominance, some independence. Joyce's standard of humanness, like that of most Western culture, was male: what he does is to redefine maleness.

    31. Senn, "Nausicaa," in *James Joyce's "Ulysses,"* p. 279.

    32. Stanley Sultan, *The Argument of "Ulysses"* (1964), p. 320; Darcy O'Brien, *The Conscience of James Joyce* (Princeton, 1968). This is a continued assertion. D. S. Savage claims that "Bloom is the cuckold who acquiesces phlegmatically and even with a perverse satisfaction in his wife's successive infidelities. It does not in the least disturb him to think of her as a whore." Savage, *The Withered Branch* (London, 1950), p. 188. However, since Molly's infidelity is a source of anguish to Bloom throughout the novel, this remark seems to indicate a somewhat superficial reading of the book. Nor is it clear that Molly has had "successive infidelities." For Kenner (*Dublin's Joyce,* p. 186), the words "feminized" and "decadent" are synonymous; his assertion of Bloom's "unprotesting effeminacy" is therefore pejorative. Kenner explains that the "masculine culture in *Ulysses* is in a process of relapse from ethos into pathos: the feminization toward habit and toward matter of the world of purposefulness, eloquence and factive energies" (p. 25), and he claims that Bloom is "drowned in a metaphorical sea . . . of matter" (pp. 211-212). More recent criticism is even more damning. Sultan, (*Argument*, p. 317) argues that Bloom exhibits a "classic development of male perversion from passivity to

masochism and feminization." He suggests, however, that Bloom triumphs over his sickness. In Circe, Sultan explains, Bloom conquers all his perverse tendencies and rejects "shabby prurience, unmanly submissiveness, masochistic pandering" and dispels all his guilt (p. 328), a strange conclusion given Bloom's behavior in Eumaeus and Ithaca. O'Brien (*Conscience*, p. 177) goes even further. He finds no saving grace in Bloom, whom he describes as "a weak little man, driven by his uncontrolled lust to degrade himself in a most comical fashion." O'Brien believes Joyce to have seen Bloom as only an object of mockery, a "sensualist, masochist, narcissist, and perhaps, homosexual" (p. 197), which qualities presumably eradicate Bloom from the roster of humanity. Sultan claims not only that "*Ulysses* asserts Bloom's only salvation is in becoming a proper husband and father again" but also that the novel provides "personal and social but also explicitly religious grounds for the assertion" (p. 455).

33. Kenner, *Dublin's Joyce*, p. 25; see also p. 339n14.

34. Morse (*Sympathetic Alien*, p. 38) claims that "the narcissistic and homosexual impulses of Joyce's characters are more than accidental and more than merely perverse; they are inevitable expressions of man's nature as Erigena conceives it and a motive force of history as Joyce conceives it."

35. David Hayman, *"Ulysses": The Mechanics of Meaning* (New Jersey, 1970), p. 49.

36. Jenkins, "Theosophy," p. 47.

3. The Rock of Ithaca

1. Joyce, *Letters*, I, 129.

2. Ellmann, *Joyce*, p. 534n.

3. James Joyce, "The Boarding House," *Dubliners* (New York, 1916), p. 63.

4. Joyce, *Stephen Hero*, p. 174.

5. Melvin Friedman attempts to equate a particular technique to a level of human consciousness, such as interior monologue in the style of the character thinking, or "sensory impression" as rubric for an effort to render pure sensation, used to describe the technique of Sirens. Friedman, *Stream of Consciousness* (New Haven, 1955). Robert Humphrey distinguishes "speech" and "prespeech" levels of consciousness. Humphrey, *Stream of Consciousness in the Modern Novel* (Berkeley, 1959). Frederick Hoffmann uses psychological terms such as "preconscious," "subconscious," and "unconscious" to describe narrative styles. Hoffmann, *Freudianism and the Literary Mind* (Baton Rouge, 1967). The assumptions which lie beneath all these studies are that the author's primary subject matter is human consciousness itself, that the aim of the author is to render or reproduce levels of consciousness, and that there is a classifiable correlation between particular literary devices and particular mental states.

6. Kahler, *Inward Turn*, pp. 173-174.

7. Lady Wortley Montagu, *Letters* (London and New York, 1934), p. 466.

8. Adams (*Surface*, pp. 143-151) discusses Joyce's method of working incrementally, adding allusions and erudition afterward to rather simple manuscripts. He also (p. 125) shows that Joyce visited Marsh's library only twice, although he depicts Stephen as very familiar with it. W. T. Noon demonstrates Joyce's (or Stephen's) inadequate knowledge or understanding of the great scholastic Aquinas. Noon, *Joyce and Aquinas*. Noon also shows that all of Joyce's quotations from Newman are drawn from one book, *Characteristics from the Writings of J. H. Newman*, ed. W. S. Lilly (London, 1875). Noon, "A Portrait of the Artist as a Young Man: After Fifty Years," in *James Joyce Today: Essays on the Major Works*, ed. Thomas F. Staley (Bloomington, 1966), pp. 54-82. Simple sources have recently been discovered for the progression of styles in Oxen of the Sun. Joyce's notion of the writer as criminal is no doubt partly rooted in his sense of the writer as stealing what he needs from wherever he needs it. For Joyce's method, see also A. Walton Litz's many articles and his *The Art of James Joyce: Method and Design in "Ulysses" and "Finnegans Wake"* (London, 1961).

9. Adams, *Surface*, pp. 20-22.

10. Joyce, *Letters*, II, 300.

11. Kenner (*Dublin's Joyce*, p. 107) argues that "the principle perspective comes from Homer's characterization of Proteus as a source of universal information: hence 'signatures of all things I am here to read,' and the philological art of reading the Book of Nature in search of clues to the intelligible order abolished after Eden (. . . the missing father, Ulysses, is at one level God, at another the rational principle of social, aesthetic, and philosophical order)." This seems fine, except that it makes Stephen's search appear to be wholly intellectual and spiritual, which it is not. It engages his entire being, down to the most practical and mundane level. The spirit cannot endure unless the body does.

12. The question of how Christ could be present bodily in multiple masses celebrated at the same time in different places and without precise synchronization is one that Joyce set out to answer metaphorically in *Ulysses*, where the entire universe is seen as sacramental—and profane—at every moment.

13. Arnold Goldman, *The Joyce Paradox* (London, 1966), pp. 131-136.

14. The line comes from Thomas Moore's "Let Erin Remember the Days of Old" in *Irish Melodies*. J. V. Kelleher points out that "the collar—*Fail Tomhair*, Tomrar's torque, or more likely arm ring—was taken *from* the Dublin Norse by Malachi in 995, along with another treasure, the sword of Carlus. Both had belonged to Norse chieftains slain in the 9th century. See John O'Donovan's edition of the Annals of the Four Masters, i, 505; ii, 733.

"Malachi = Máel Seachlainn Mór of Midhe, high-king of Ireland from 980 to 1003 and again from 1014 to 1022. On the basis of the name it would be tempting to associate him with Malachy Mulligan who will usurp the tower from Stephen. However, Máel Seachlainn was himself the subject of usurpation. The high-kingship was taken from him by Brian Boru who had previously usurped the kingship of Munster and then the kingship of the southern half of Ireland. Brian's reign as high-king was, on the other hand, so successful that afterwards he was not commonly regarded as a usurper. He was killed by a Viking named Brodar in the Battle of Clontarf, in 1014, which according to tradition resulted in the expulsion of the Danes from Ireland, and at which Máel Seachlainn, Lynchlike, with a considerable army, was reported to have stood neutral, observing from the sidelines.

"Actually the battle was between the Munstermen and the Leinstermen, the latter having Viking allies. It did not bring about any expulsion of the Norse nor was Norse Dublin captured. In later years, however, so great was Brian's fame, a great deal of saga developed about the battle and its consequences were exaggerated.

"How much of this history Joyce knew or thought he knew and how much Irish history we are to assume that Stephen knows are moot questions. In Finnegans Wake considerable play is made with Clontarf and 1014, but again, apparently, more in terms of popular legend than actual history." Kelleher, letter to the author, Mar. 21, 1975.

15. For the riddle, see P. W. Joyce, English As We Speak It in Ireland (London, 1910), p. 187. The correct answer to the riddle contains the word mother rather than grandmother; thus on one level, it is connected with Stephen's guilt about his mother's death. Stephen's nervous recitation of it identifies him with the fox. William Hull informs me that The Golden Bough has the fox as the creature whose name is tabooed and who is guardian spirit and emblem of the corn spirit, the grandmother as the title of the Mother of Ghosts, and holly as an instrument for expelling ghosts. The ceremony of burial is designed to purge ghosts in order to preserve the spirit of fertility and creativity. Hull adds that "the Quaker founder, George Fox, said that Christ as inner light was a fox, subtle; he once eluded pursuit of a mob, a hueandcry, by hiding in a blighted tree." Hull, letter to the author, June 20, 1976. Stephen does associate the fox with Christ and also with Shakespeare: "Christfox in leather trews, hiding, a runaway in blighted treeforks from hue and cry" (193). Stephen has been thinking about the legend that Shakespeare was accused of poaching; the lines that follow conflate Shakespeare with Christ. Joyce merges Shakespeare with deity in Finnegans Wake also: "Shapesphere" (p. 295). The motif is thus another analogy between God and the artist.

16. The panther is, by a mistaken etymology, all beasts: pan (all) + ther (beast). It became both all beasts and an ideal single beast, godless as well as Pandera, the actual father of Christ, according to an ancient legend. The Pandera tradition dates back to the fourth century A.D. and may be found in the Babylonian Talmud, the Toledoth Jeshua, and the Strassburg MS. It has various forms. See Elwood Worcester, Studies in the Birth of the Lord (1932), pp. 231-249; Thomas Boslooper, The Virgin Birth (Philadelphia, n.d.), pp. 39-40. In the Huldreich Vindabona MS, Joseph Pandera was the husband of Mary and Jochanan was the adulterer who seduced her without her knowledge. In the Adler of Jemen MS of Toledoth Jeshua, Jochanan was Mary's husband and

the seducer was Joseph, son of Pandera. In the Talmud and according to Celsus, Pandera was the seducer. The panther theme in *Ulysses* is therefore linked to the Taxil theme: "c'est le pigeon, Joseph," and to the controversy over Molly's promiscuity.

17. For the definition of "morose delectation," see Aquinas, *Summa Theologica* II.74.6.

18. *Oomb* probably refers to "Oom," an old spelling of the sacred Hindu word, usually these days spelled "Aum." The connection of womb and tomb, and the tone of the poem itself, are thus linked to the Oriental mysticism of A. E. and Eglinton in the library chapter.

19. For an explanation of the relations between Berkeley's thought and Stephen's, see J. Mitchell Morse, "Proteus" in *James Joyce's "Ulysses,"* pp. 35-37.

20. O'Brien (*Conscience*, p. 166) finds Bloom's compassion for Mrs. Purefoy ludicrous and sentimental. He says that Bloom's "sentimentalism must be recognized as largely self-indulgent and as an act singled out for our scrutiny by Joyce's conscience, which no longer rails at human weaknesses but which continues to probe and to satirize them."

21. At the same time, Stephen is the person Bloom would like to be. The Notesheets to Ithaca contain two notes to this effect: 1:32 "SD will win else LB wouldn't"; 1:49 "SD what LB like to be." Herring, *Notesheets*, p. 416.

22. See R. M. Adams, *James Joyce: Common Sense and Beyond* (New York, 1966), p. 152.

23. Joyce described his use of Vico in *Finnegans Wake:* "I use his cycles as a trellis." Quoted in Mary and Padraic Colum, *Our Friend James Joyce* (New York, 1958), p. 122.

24. Rudolph Von Abele insists that many of the parallels, analogies, and identifications are comic, many are made by the characters rather than the narrator, and many operate to diminish the characters. Von Abele, *"Ulysses:* The Myth of Myth," *PMLA* 69, no. 3 (June 1954): 358-364. All this is true; but it is also true that some are serious. It is not important whether the parallels exist seriously or for comic effect; what is important is that they are *there*—for the characters sometimes, for the reader always. They are part of the macrocosm of the novel: they provide the mythic, historical, or eternal framework in which the events of the novel take place and find their larger pattern. Just as a member of a primitive tribe may eat his meal or walk a path in exactly the way that a god is said to have done, Bloom and Stephen, whether knowingly or not, comically or not, recapitulate archetypal actions of mythic, historical, or literary figures.

25. R. M. Adams lists many figures of speech containing clue words to the subject of this chapter. Adams, "Hades," in *James Joyce's "Ulysses,"* p. 102.

4. The City

1. There are 63 headlined sections in this episode. Humphrey (*Stream of Consciousness*, p. 60), claims that Aeolus presents "another of the glimpses

. . . into Bloom's consciousness, unified and made to seem logical by the device" of the headlines. This is patent nonsense. Bloom is generally present in only 25 of the 63 sections; in the twenty-second section he is in an inner office; in the thirty-sixth he telephones in from outside the office; and in the twenty-fifth he is outside on the sidewalk, being observed from within. In only 16 of these sections is there interior monologue in his style; in 9 sections he either speaks or overhears. Stephen is generally present in 33 of the 63 sections; in the fourteenth there is interior monologue in his style. In the opening two sections, as well as in the twenty-fifth, twenty-sixth, and fifty-ninth, neither Bloom nor Stephen is present.

2. J. V. Kelleher writes: "Any Irishman of Joyce's generation would be familiar from childhood with the general outlines of the pseudohistorical origin legend that prefaces early Irish history. In Irish it is called *Lebor Gabála hÉrenn,* literally the Book of the Taking of Ireland but commonly translated Book of Invasions. It most likely dates back to the 7th century and, as has been speculated, was perhaps originally a short Latin text, *Liber Occupationis Hiberniae,* which sought to account only for the coming of the Gaels. By the 11th or 12th centuries the story had become immensely complicated and full of contradictions. The long texts dating from that time describe a series of occupations of the island, the earliest being by a group led by Noah's niece Cesair, which arrives shortly before the Flood and is of course drowned. One man, through a series of shape-changes into various long-lived creatures— salmon, eagle, stag, etc.—survives long enough to tell the story to St. Patrick.

"Several other invasions also fail to take hold. At last the Firbolgs come from Greece, hold Ireland for three centuries, and are then conquered by the Tuatha Dé Danann, the peoples of the goddess Danu, who are presented as greatly skilled in magic and are really the old Celtic gods.

"Meanwhile the Gaels or Scots have originated in Scythia (compare *Scotti*) and come from thence to Egypt where their leader marries Scotta, daughter of Pharoah. They are on very good terms with the Hebrews, with Moses in particular, and in one version are invited to accompany the Hebrews in the Exodus. After Pharoah and his hosts have been drowned in the Red Sea, the remaining Egyptians, fearing the growing power of the Gaels, drive them out. In the later texts they endure vast voyages and wanderings before they arrive in Spain which they conquer. It would seem clear, however, from Nennius, writing *circa* 800, that the original story depicted them as wandering for an appropriate forty years across the deserts of North Africa before they crossed to Spain.

"On the north coast of Spain one of their chiefs, Bregon, builds a great tower from which one clear winter evening his son Ith sees Ireland. Ith then goes to Ireland where he is treacherously killed by the Tuatha Dé Danann. His kin, led by Eber and Éremón, sons of Mil Espáine (whence the Gaels are also known as Milesians), invade Ireland and conquer it.

"Henceforth the Gaels are the ruling people. The Tuatha Dé Danann, defeated but still mighty, retire into the fairy hills or underground. The Firbolg, twice conquered, remain as the subject race.

"The original tract was clearly based on a rather hazy knowledge of the Bible and on the account of world geography given by Orosius in *Historiarum Contra Paganos Libri Septem* (419), Bk. I, ch. 2. Its major purpose, clearly implied though never directly expressed, is to affirm that the Gaels were the second Chosen People and Ireland the second Promised Land.

"In *A Portrait of the Artist*, Davin, who is Stephen's mirror-image as an Irishman, is described as a Firbolg—dark, a serf, one who knows the secret ways of Irish life. It is to be understood that Stephen is thus a Milesian—fair, free, bravely open. In *Ulysses* aspects of the *Lebor Gabála* theme appear throughout the book. Naturally the most important of these are the mutual amity of the Hebrews and the Gaels and their departure, though for different reasons, from Egypt. Needless to say, the parallels with *Lebor Gabála* are not logically or extensively worked out. However they do underlie, along with much else, the John F. Taylor speech in Aeolus, Stephen's relationship with Bloom, the Moses theme, and so on.

"It would be as pointless to try to determine where Joyce got his knowledge of *Lebor Gabála*, or how much of it he knew or in what detail, as it would be to attempt to ascertain how an American writer learned about the first Thanksgiving, Pocohantas, and George Washington's cherry tree. One likely source, however, would be P. W. Joyce's *A Child's History of Ireland* [New York, 1901], Chapter VII, "The Legends," from which he could have got most of what he uses. It would be surprising if he were not given that book to read during the couple of years between Clongowes and Belvedere, when he went to a Christian Brothers school." Kelleher, letter to author, Mar. 21, 1975.

3. Joyce, *Stephen Hero*, p. 76.

4. David Worcester defines types of burlesque. High burlesque is satire that "treats a trivial subject in an elevated manner"; low burlesque treats an elevated subject in a trivial manner. Worcester describes the movement from invective to subtler forms of satire (like burlesque) as requiring greater reader participation: "As the process of communication approaches the universal, the part played by the reader or auditor also changes. A curse . . . is driven down the throat . . . there is no room for qualification or criticism. The greater the time-lag, the more he [the reader] is called on to participate in the game . . . He shares the work of authorship with the writer; his labor is necessary to complete the meaning; and he presses on, flattered and interested. Reading has become a game of wits. The reader's creative participation is essential to the writer's design, and this principle of participation, though only rudimentary in invective, rises to great importance in burlesque and irony." Worcester, *The Art of Satire* (New York, 1960), pp. 31, 49.

5. Many critics have commented that the effect of the analogies and juxtapositions in Cyclops is a leveling one. For instance, David Daiches writes:

"The interpolations of heroic and fantastic—and sometimes purely ridiculous—description seem to serve two purposes. The first is simply to emphasize the fact that in *Ulysses* distinctions such as that between the heroic and the fantastic do not exist; the monstrous, the mythical, the normal, fade into each other, periodically, and that is part of the general tendency." Daiches, *The Novel and the Modern World,* rev. ed. (Chicago, 1960), p. 116; see also pp. 113, 115.

6. Augustine, in *De Immortalitate Animae,* says, "the intention to act is of the present, through which the future flows into the past." *Patrologia Latina,* ed. J. P. Migne (Paris, 1877), XXXII, 1023A. This sentence is echoed in Stephen's "Hold to the now, the here, through which all future plunges to the past" (186) in the library chapter, when he exhorts himself to act. Aquinas develops Aristotle's notion: "Form is the principle of action . . . we observe that man sometimes is only a potential knower, both as to sense and as to intellect. And he is reduced from such potentiality to act . . . the mode of action in every agent follows from its mode of existence." Aquinas, *Summa Theologica* I.III.84.3, 89.1. The passage from Augustine's *Confessions* quoted in *Ulysses* (142) involves an acceptance of the real as opposed to the ideal or the perversion. Thus, all the foundations of Joyce's moral vision—acceptance of the real, ability to act, and *caritas*—may be found in scholastic philosophy.

7. The importance of *parallax* to Joyce is suggested by his inclusion of the term as one of the characters in this chapter. Circe 20:(8)45, Herring, *Notesheets,* p. 455.

8. Adams, *Surface,* p. 160.

9. Northrop Frye, *Anatomy of Criticism* (Princeton, 1957), p. 271.

10. Joyce made this comment to Frank Budgen. Ellmann, *Joyce,* p. 490.

11. Frank Budgen, *James Joyce and the Making of "Ulysses"* (New York, 1934), p. 107.

12. Kenner, *Dublin's Joyce,* p. 253. Many critics agree that there is no unifying principle except time and space in the chapter.

13. Life does not flood in against Joyce's wishes, as Daiches holds (*Novel,* p. 130). Joyce could be mechanical enough when he chose to, as in Eumaeus and Ithaca. But these sketches are small masterpieces of vividness and vitality despite the overall theme. This should disprove the belief of some critics that Joyce intended to demonstrate the sterility and barrenness of the modern world. If that had been his intention, he would not have had to go beyond the technique of this chapter, which is perfectly adequate to such a task. The style of Wandering Rocks is able to convey the sterility and inadequacy of Dublin without itself being sterile, dull, or mechanical.

14. This image is also used in Clive Hart, "Wandering Rocks" in *James Joyce's "Ulysses,"* p. 194.

15. The names of these students contain another of Joyce's private jokes uncovered by R. M. Adams. Adams, *Surface and Symbol,* p. 15. Sohan, in real life, became a pawnbroker, Lynam a bookie, and Ger. Gallaher was the

younger brother of the real Ignatius. Although one does not have to know this to perceive the benevolent condescension of the priest, knowing it makes the scene even more comic and the absurdity and perverseness of the rector's values even more pointed.

5. The World

1. Joyce, *Letters,* I, 149. Ellmann (*Joyce,* p. 456n) reproduces Joyce's notation at the end of the Scylla and Charybdis chapter on the MS sold to John Quinn: "End of first part of *Ulysses,* New Year's Eve, 1918."

2. To quote all the disparaging criticism of this chapter would be tedious. S. L. Goldberg, Richard Kain, and Edmund Wilson, *Axel's Castle* (New York, 1931), among others, censure the episode. The complaints may be summarized as charging the formal elements with either weakness or its seeming opposite—over-rigidity. In either case, it is held, they hinder the plot or dissociate themselves from the content. Objections to the prelude are as rife as those to the chapter. L. A. G. Strong calls the opening of Sirens an "interesting but unsuccessful experiment doomed to failure because words and phrases cannot stand by themselves, apart from their meaning." Strong, *The Sacred River* (London, 1949), p. 37. Gilbert (*Ulysses,* p. 14) cites Curtius' objections to the same effect. See also Levin, *James Joyce,* pp. 98-99; Friedman, *Stream of Consciousness,* p. 131.

3. Frye, *Anatomy,* p. 275.

4. Ezra Pound, *Pound/Joyce: The Letters of Ezra Pound to James Joyce,* ed. Forrest Read (New York, 1965), p. 157.

5. Kenner, *Dublin's Joyce,* p. 254.

6. Herring (*Notesheets,* p. 50) comments: "Of the twenty-odd classical references in the 'Cyclops' notesheets, it is significant that none point to the corresponding episode in the *Odyssey.* Most are concerned with the *Iliad,* Herodotus, and Greek history generally."

7. David Hayman ("Cyclops," in *James Joyce's "Ulysses,"* p. 262) notes that Kiernan's hobby was collecting and exhibiting items connected with crime. Joyce chose the scene with his usual care.

8. Wayne Booth, *The Rhetoric of Fiction* (Chicago, 1961), p. 367.

9. Some interesting references to violence appear in the Notesheets. One links the violence implicit in legal transactions with that of birth: Cyclops 4:98-101 "Contracts invalidated by violence done to 1 party . · . social contract no validity for individual constraint by violence of birth to enter the society of the living on their terms." Another may suggest Joyce's political ideal: Cyclops 1:72 "Neither with violence suppressed nor achieved (Anarchy)." Herring, *Notesheets,* pp. 97, 83.

10. See Ch. 2, n.32.

11. The passage has been thought to imitate the work of Standish James O'Grady, but J. V. Kelleher (note to author, November 1971) finds more simi-

larity to the poems of T. W. Rolleston, "The Dead at Clonmacnoise," and "The Grave of Rury."

12. Daiches, *Novel*, p. 116. But Goldberg (*Classical Temper*, p. 198) in discussing Joyce's use of the Homeric myth, claims the differences between the myth and "the world of present fact . . . sharpen the edge of his action as a critical definition of a particular society at a particular time, but in turn the action also subjects the high and 'poetic' Homeric ideals to the scrutiny of commonplace reality."

13. J. V. Kelleher informs me that this is parody of typical Dublin journalism on the subject of Celtic poetry and criticism, especially by Douglas Hyde.

14. Kenner, *Dublin's Joyce*, pp. 255-256.

15. Henry James, *The Art of the Novel* (New York and London, 1934), pp. 33-34.

16. Senn, "Nausicaa," in *James Joyce's "Ulysses,"* pp. 279-81.

17. Kenner, *Dublin's Joyce*, p. 258.

18. Philip Toynbee writes: "The infinite elaboration of . . . ox imagery in the hospital . . . section presents us with an obstacle which is very nearly as gratuitous as some purely physical feat would have been. Yet it is an obstacle which we cannot circumvent, for Joyce's villainous adroitness has often made the corn quite inextricable from the chaff." Toynbee, "A Study of James Joyce's *Ulysses*," in *James Joyce: Two Decades of Criticism*, ed. Seon Givens (New York, 1948), p. 245. Friedman (*Stream of Consciousness*, p. 237) adds: "One is struck by the inappropriateness of this episode to the rest of the book." And Edmund Wilson agrees: "The worst example of this too synthetic, too systematic method seems to me the scene in the maternity hospital." Wilson, *Axel's Castle*, p. 214. See also Kain, *Voyager*, pp. 30, 44; Goldberg, *Classical Temper*, p. 284.

19. Anthony Burgess, *Re Joyce* (New York, 1965), p. 156.

20. Herring, *Notesheets*, pp. 169, 172n.

21. Joyce to Frank Budgen, *Letters*, I, 139; Goldberg, *Classical Temper*, p. 284.

22. See A. M. Klein, "The Oxen of the Sun," *Here and Now* 1, no. 3 (January 1949): 28-48.

23. James, *Novel*, p. 46.

24. In support of this, Arnold Goldman claims that the style of Oxen of the Sun "points up the arbitrariness of any particular presentation by showing that the individual interpretations of the action are part of the historical ethos of the writer—as the *courtesy* of Bloom . . . is the Malorian interpretation while to emphasize the ethical plight of Stephen is to bring a Bunyanesque allegorical presentation to bear on the subject." Goldman, *The Joyce Paradox* (London, 1966), p. 95. Wilson (*Axel's Castle*, p. 208) suggests a similar interpretation: "Joyce has achieved here, by different methods, a relativism like that of Proust: he is reproducing in literature the different aspects, the different proportions and textures which things and people take on at different times and under different circumstances."

25. Critics like O'Brien (*Conscience*, pp. 197-199), who use Joyce's actual

jealousy in judging Bloom's toleration of adultery, should consider that, despite his "assertions" in Oxen of the Sun, Joyce and Nora had only two children and he impregnated her only three times.

26. Joyce wrote to Harriet Weaver: "Do you mean that the Oxen of the Sun episode resembles Hades because the nine circles of development (enclosed between the headpiece and tailpiece of opposite chaos) seem to you to be peopled by extinct beings?" Joyce, Letters, ed. Richard Ellmann (New York, 1966), III, 16.

27. See e.g. Levin, James Joyce, p. 109; Goldberg, Classical Temper, p. 185; Goldman, Paradox, pp. 97-99; Sultan, Argument, pp. 335-361.

28. Clive Hart, James Joyce's "Ulysses" (Adelaide, 1968), pp. 70-71. Hart suggests that some of the hallucinations are conscious visions of the characters, some are dramatizations of their unconscious thought, and some are the "author's expressionistic commentary. . . .There is a great deal here [in Circe] that depends on modern concepts of the unconscious, but Joyce is not attempting to create an accurate naturalistic rendering of what might have been in the minds of his characters in these particular circumstances. This is included, but it is only a part of a greater whole. Stephen and Bloom play roles in a stylized and symbolic reality . . . Many readers seem to expect Joyce to follow accurate psychological truth and are consequently worried when they discover that the characters say and think things of which they could have no knowledge. In reading Ulysses one must often remove oneself from the standpoint of simple psychological realism."

29. Hugh Kenner comes to similar conclusions: "No one is hallucinated but ourselves . . . The whole episode is phantasmagoric; the dramatic surface, with its objectivity, its naturalism, is a rhetoric throughout." Kenner sees the hallucinations as expressing the characters' sense of guilt, as transient wisps of feeling "given the corporeality of Dante's journey." Kenner, "Circe," in James Joyce's "Ulysses," pp. 346, 351, 354-355.

30. See 1 Kings 18:44; 2 Kings 2:23.

31. A strained identification of Bloom and the Christ occurs in Lestrygonians when Bloom is handed a throwaway and thinks "Bloo . . . Me? No. Blood of the Lamb" (151).

32. Levin, James Joyce, p. 109.

33. The word "Tarnkappe" appears in the notes to Hades. Phillip F. Herring, "Ulysses Notebook VIII.A5 at Buffalo," Studies in Bibliography 22 (1969): 287-310. Some critics disapprove of drawing one of Joyce's works into the interpretation of another. But the fact is that he worked with the same feelings, the same ideas, and the same material in all his books. Although change and growth are evident, so is similarity. What is more, Joyce insists on this identification by his own references and allusions.

34. See Ch. 2, n. 23.

35. Goldman, Paradox, p. 98.

36. See Hart, "Ulysses," pp. 70-71; Kenner, "Circe," James Joyce's "Ulysses," p. 351.

37. "In the Circe episode gestures reveal the secret intentions that Joyce's

characters fear to make public." Silverstein, "Magic," p. 23. See also Kenner, "Circe," in *James Joyce's "Ulysses,"* pp. 354-355.

38. Sultan, *Argument*, p. 355.

39. An entry in the Notesheets to Circe 8:92 reads: "whores not persons." Herring, *Notesheets*, p. 310.

40. See also Joyce's note 6:81 to Nausikaa: "Molly lustful only when well dressed." Herring, *Notesheets*, p. 68.

41. Joyce quoted Blake's phrase in his essay on the poet. Joyce, *Critical Writings*, p. 215.

42. The notes for Circe include a chapter-by-chapter listing of the major characters in each episode. Herring, *Notesheets*, p. 362-367.

43. The identification of Virag with the man in the mackintosh seems justified by Joyce's presentation of Virag in a brown mackintosh. Joyce is never careless about such details. Because of information offered about this mystery man in Oxen (427), he has been associated with Mr. Duffy of "A Painful Case." Duffy is known to be partly modeled on Stanislaus Joyce. See his *My Brother's Keeper* (New York, 1958). Stanislaus Joyce also contributed to the character of Shaun in *Finnegans Wake*, where he is the antagonist but also the alter ego of his brother Shem. The rebellious yet intractable and rigid nature of Joyce's brother, with his undying hatreds and his aversion to irrational behavior, is part of the personality of the various narrators of *Ulysses*.

44. See Eugene Jolas, "My Friend James Joyce," Givens, *Two Decades*, p. 9.

45. Norman Silverstein, "Evolutions of the Nighttown Setting," in *The Celtic Master: Contributions to the first James Joyce Symposium Held in Dublin, 1967* ed. Maurice Harmon (Dublin, 1969), p. 30.

6. The Universe

1. Wilson (*Axel's Castle*, p. 216) describes the "interminable letdown of the cabman's shelter," and Toynbee ("James Joyce's *Ulysses*," in *James Joyce*, p. 278) quotes with agreement Wilson's judgment that Eumaeus and Ithaca are "artistically indefensible." Goldman (*Paradox*, p. 104) claims that Eumaeus reduces the action "to a superficial account and the manner of it only exposes its own inability to encompass the matter." But Kenner (*Dublin's Joyce*, p. 260) suggests that Eumaeus "has incurred the displeasure of those who don't read closely."

2. Gerald L. Bruns discusses the special kind of irony found in this episode, and describes it as a "discontinuity between narrator and reader." Bruns, "Eumaeus," in *James Joyce's "Ulysses,"* p. 367.

3. Adams, *Surface*, p. 160.

4. That Joyce intended everyone, including Bloom and Stephen, to be involved in the general falseness, is indicated by his note to the chapter (6:7): "SD & LB both lie." Herring, *Notesheets*, p. 400.

5. Joyce also wrote a letter to Curran (*Letters*, I, 379) in which he used the figure "that battered cabman's face, the world."

6. The characterization of Bloom as a superficial *parvenu* that is deduced by Bruns ("Eumaeus," in *James Joyce's "Ulysses,"* p. 382) is also a distortion. The style of each chapter reflects a human truth that is yet not the whole truth about the characters, and reflects also the attitude of the narrator. It is not reasonable to blame the narrator's excesses on Bloom's nature.

7. R. A. Copland and G. W. Turner show the indebtedness of Joyce's technique in Ithaca to Richmal Mangnall's *Questions,* actually *Historical and Miscellaneous Questions for the Use of Young People, with a Selection of British and General Biography* (1862). The technique of *Questions* is catechistical, though its subject matter is neither religious nor scientific but historical. The authors comment, "The final impression given by the technique is of anonymity, or of a book talking to itself." Copland and Turner, "The Nature of James Joyce's Parody in 'Ithaca,' " *MLR* 64, no. 4 (October 1969): 759-763.

8. *The New Confraternity Edition Revised Baltimore Catechism,* p. 5.

9. Budgen, *Making of "Ulysses,"* p. 257.

10. Joyce, *Letters,* I, 159-160.

11. Patrick White offers a careful study of the key motif as it appears in the novel and as critics have dealt with it. White, "The Key in *Ulysses,"* *JJQ* 9, no. 1 (Fall 1971): 10-25.

12. William York Tindall, *James Joyce* (New York, 1950), p. 30.

13. Joyce clearly intended to show incertitude as operating in the cosmos as well as the world. Consider the following notes to Ithaca: 9:52-53 "No fixed stars/variable suns"; 9:78 "parallax aberration of light"; 9:83 "deal logically with the unknown." Herring, *Notesheets,* pp. 454-455.

14. Richard Madtes, "Joyce and the Building of Ithaca,"*ELH* 31 (1964): 453.

15. Ithaca 6:84, Herring, *Notesheets,* p. 439.

16. "Although privation is an accidental principle, it does not follow that it is unnecessary for generation. For matter is never lacking privation: inasmuch as it is under one form, it is deprived of another." Aquinas, *The Principles of Nature* II.9, *Selected Writings,* trans. Robert P. Goodwin (New York, 1965), p. 10.

17. Cf. Stephen's "heresy" in *P,* 79.

18. Mark E. Littmann and Charles A. Schweighauser confirm that Joyce's astronomy is accurate, and that it is a fact that "every state of being in the spectrum resembles man—a solitary wanderer subject to perturbation, attraction, repulsion, cycles, and change." Littmann and Schweighauser, "Astronomical Allusions, Their Meaning and Purpose in *Ulysses,"* *JJQ* 2, no. 4 (Summer 1965): 238-246.

19. Goldberg, *Classical Temper,* p. 196.

7. Coda: The Earth

1. Joyce, *Letters,* I, 159-160; 180.

2. "The Ithaca episode . . . is in reality the end as *Penelope* has no beginning, middle or end," Joyce, *Letters,* I, 172.

3. Penelope 7:41: "MB= spinning Earth." Herring, *Notesheets*, p. 515.

4. Joyce, *Letters*, I, 169-170.

5. Kenner, *Dublin's Joyce*, pp. 243-244, 262.

6. Adams, *Joyce*, pp. 166-167.

7. Critical contention has recently surrounded David Hayman, who is free enough from preconceptions to see that the Molly presented in the text is somewhat different from most critics' image of her. See Letters to the Editor, *JJQ* 9, no. 4 (Summer 1972): 490-494.

8. Herring (*Notesheets*, p. 524) records that the Notesheets for *Exiles* describe the feelings of a young girl about the departure of a dear friend, and the lesbian attraction between the two women. The Emily Lyons of these notes (which were apparently based on an incident in Nora's life) became the Hester Stanhope of *Ulysses*.

9. Norman O. Brown, *Life Against Death: The Psychoanalytical Meaning of History* (New York, 1959).

10. Penelope 4:92: "incestuous MB." Herring, *Notesheets*, p. 504.

11. This is one of several points of mutual admiration between the two, for Molly also considers making a collection of Bloom's sayings. It also parallels Haines' collecting Stephen's witticisms.

12. Hayman, *Ulysses*, p. 35.

13. Hayman, *Ulysses*, p. 99.

14. The delusion that the list of Molly's lovers in Ithaca is accurate remains, although a few critics suggest that it is false. See e.g. Adaline Glasheen, "Calypso," in *James Joyce's "Ulysses,"* p. 55.

15. This was pointed out to me by Monroe Engel.

16. Hayman, *Ulysses*, p. 100.

17. See also Phillip Herring, "The Bedsteadfastness of Molly Bloom," *Modern Fiction Studies* 15, no. 1 (Spring 1969): 60-61.

18. Joyce, *Letters*, I, 169-170.

19. Hayman, *Ulysses*, p. 35.

20. That Nature, or Penelope, has the legitimacy, the rightness, denied to mere mortals is intimated by a note in the Notesheets, Ithaca 1:48: "Laertes and Ul. only kings by marriage, Penelope right." Herring, *Notesheets*, p. 416.

21. Budgen (*Making of "Ulysses,"* p. 264) explains: "Both Bloom and Marion have this in common that they bring out of inconstancy tributes to fidelity." And Jane Vogel comments: "Once we accept the premise of *Ulysses* that betrayal and compromise come with life, it comes to seem mildly inspiring that Molly and Leopold Bloom are unfaithful to lovers for the sake of something apparently alive between them." Vogel, "The Consubstantial Family of Stephen Dedalus," *JJQ* 2, no. 2 (Winter 1965); 109.

8. Conclusion

1. Kenner, *Dublin's Joyce*, p. 209.

2. Budgen (*Making of "Ulysses,"* p. 265) claims that Molly "dwells in a

region where there are no incertitudes to trouble the mind." He adds that Joyce's pervasive use of the body emphasizes that that is where all begins.

3. Actually Descartes' original formulation was "Je doute, donc je suis, ou bien ce qui est la même chose: je pense, donc je suis." Thus, Descartes indentified doubt with thought. See Hannah Arendt, *The Human Condition* (Chicago, Cambridge, and Toronto, 1958), p. 279.

4. Susanne Langer, *Philosophy in a New Key* (New York, 1948), p. 153.

5. Thomas Mann, "Freud and the Future," *Essays of Three Decades* (New York, 1948), pp. 422-423.

6. See Adams, *Surface,* p. 246. Samuel Beckett had a story about Joyce allowing an accidental "come in" to remain in the MS of *Finnegans Wake.* Ellmann, *Joyce,* p. 662.

7. Anthony Cronin notes: "More than any other book, *Ulysses* marks the end of heroic literature." Cronin, *A Question of Modernity* (London, 1966), p. 96. And Joyce in *Stephen Hero* (174), discussing the necessity for irony in modern love poetry, comments: "This suggestion of relativity . . . mingling itself with so immune a passion is a modern note: we cannot swear or expect eternal fealty because we recognize too accurately the limits of every human energy. It is not possible for the modern lover to think the universe an assistant at his love-affair and modern love, losing something of its fierceness, gains also somewhat in amiableness."

Index

Abbas, Joachim, 71, 75, 77
Action motif: moral dimensions of, 40-42, 74, 117; connection with Shakespeare motif, 41, 115; necessity of, 73, 115-117; connections with history, 115; difficulty of, 182-183; Notesheet reference to, 193, 273n23; *"Coactus volui,"* 198-199, 273n23; Aquinas and Augustine on, 282n6; mentioned, 23, 183. *See also* "Fetter" motif; Paralysis motif
Adams, R. M.: ambiguity of *U*, 26; Joyce's erudition, 71; facts revealed by, 72, 279n25; on Joyce's treatment of intellectuals, 212-213; on Molly, 244; mentioned, 282n8, 289n6
Addison, Joseph, 175
Aeolus episode: analysis, 94-103; position in structure of *U*, 6, 9, 93; theme of, 8-9; narrational stance in, 14-15, 271-272n1; Stephen's development in, 23, 24, 73, 115, 202, 263; technique of, 54, 104-105, 127; relation to Oxen, 169, 170, 172; relation to Ithaca, 222; mentioned, 92, 189
Androgyny: in Stephen, 47, 191; in Bloom, 47-48, 123-124, 139, 143, 147-148, 191, 198, 225; relation to creativity, 51, 191; in Virag, 204; in Joyce, 259; Joyce's notion of, 274-275n30; mentioned, 50
Aquinas: view of sin, 239; on action, 282n6; on privation, 287n16; *Summa Theologica*, 25, 271n2; mentioned, 25, 71, 79, 277n8
Arendt, Hannah, 289n3
Aristotle: part of dichotomy in *U*, 26, 33, 115; connected with world of matter, 70; connected with action, 115; mentioned, 71
Arius, 69, 71

Auerbach, Erich, 25
Augustine: view of God, 39, 272n4; on charity, 42; on action, 282n6; mentioned, 271nn1-2

Beach, Joseph Warren, 272n12
Beckett, Samuel, 65, 266, 289n6
Berkeley, Bishop: *esse est percipi*, 27, 79; mentioned, 26, 279n16
Betrayal motif: adultery, 17, 36, 47, 165, 248-261 *passim*, 275n32; as theme in *U*, 43, 113; connection with incertitude, 113; in Virgin Mary, 113, 181, 197, 278n16
Bible: Moses in, 97-98; style of, 143; Elijah in, 148, 222; ideals of, 154, 178-179; *Amos*, 155; *Genesis*, 33; *Jeremiah*, 155; *Kings*, 274n30, 285n30; *Psalms*, 77, 230; mentioned, 2, 37, 52, 90
Blake, William, 44, 72, 115, 181, 286n41
Booth, Wayne, 140
Boslooper, Thomas, 278n16
Brown, Norman O., 249
Browne, Sir Thomas: style of, 91, 170; *Hydriotaphia*, 92
Bruno, Giordano: notion of, 117; mentioned, 84
Bruns, Gerald L., 286n2, 287n6
Budgen, Frank, 22, 221, 259, 282nn10-11, 288-289n2
Bunyan: style of, 177; mentioned, 175
Burgess, Anthony, 168
Burton, Robert, style of, 91

Calypso episode: analysis, 82-92 *passim*; position in structure of *U*, 6; theme of, 8, 9, 13; outhouse scene in, 159; mentioned, 23